Plays from Romania

Plays from Romania

DRAMATURGIES OF SUBVERSION

Lowlands
The Spectator Sentenced to Death
The Passport
The Man Who Had His Inner Evil Removed
Stories of the Body: Artemisia, Teresa, Eva, Lina
Sexodrom

Edited and translated by
JOZEFINA KOMPORALY

methuen | drama
LONDON · NEW YORK · OXFORD · NEW DELHI · SYDNEY

METHUEN DRAMA
Bloomsbury Publishing Plc
50 Bedford Square, London, WC1B 3DP, UK
1385 Broadway, New York, NY 10018, USA
29 Earlsfort Terrace, Dublin 2, Ireland

BLOOMSBURY, METHUEN DRAMA and the Methuen Drama logo are trademarks of
Bloomsbury Publishing Plc

First published in Great Britain 2022

Introduction copyright © Jozefina Komporaly, 2022
Foreword copyright © Faynia Williams, 2022
Lowlands copyright © Herta Müller, adapted for the stage by Mihaela Panainte (original title in German: *Niederungen*), 2022
The Spectator Sentenced to Death copyright © Matéi Visniec (original title in Romanian: *Spectatorul condamnat la moarte*), 2022
The Passport copyright © György Dragomán (original title in Hungarian: *Kalucsni*), 2022
The Man Who Had His Inner Evil Removed copyright © Matéi Visniec (original title in Romanian: *Omul din care a fost extras răul*), 2021
Stories of the Body: Artemisia, Teresa, Eva, Lina copyright © András Visky (original title in Hungarian: *A test történetei: Artemisia, Teréz, Éva, Lina*), 2022
Sexodrom copyright © Giuvlipen Theatre Company, 2022
Afterword copyright © Melissa Lorraine, 2022

Jozefina Komporaly has asserted her right under the Copyright, Designs and Patents Act, 1988, to be identified as editor of this work.

For legal purposes the Acknowledgements on p. ix constitute an extension of this copyright page.

Cover design: Rebecca Heselton
Cover image: *The Passport* by György Dragomán (directed by András Visky)
taken by István Bíró © Hungarian Theatre

All rights reserved. No part of this publication may be reproduced or transmitted in any form or by any means, electronic or mechanical, including photocopying, recording, or any information storage or retrieval system, without prior permission in writing from the publishers.

Bloomsbury Publishing Plc does not have any control over, or responsibility for, any third-party websites referred to or in this book. All internet addresses given in this book were correct at the time of going to press. The author and publisher regret any inconvenience caused if addresses have changed or sites have ceased to exist, but can accept no responsibility for any such changes.

No rights in incidental music or songs contained in the work are hereby granted and performance rights for any performance/presentation whatsoever must be obtained from the respective copyright owners.

A catalogue record for this book is available from the British Library.

A catalog record for this book is available from the Library of Congress.

ISBN: HB: 978-1-3502-1429-3
PB: 978-1-3502-1428-6
ePDF: 978-1-3502-1430-9
eBook: 978-1-3502-1431-6

Typeset by RefineCatch Limited, Bungay, Suffolk
Printed and bound in Great Britain

To find out more about our authors and books visit www.bloomsbury.com
and sign up for our newsletters.

Contents

List of Illustrations vi

Notes on Contributors vii

Acknowledgements ix

Foreword *Faynia Williams* x

Introduction: Playwriting, Transnational Dramaturgies and the Contemporary Romanian Theatre Landscape *Jozefina Komporaly* 1

Play Synopses and Production Histories *Jozefina Komporaly* 11

Lowlands Herta Müller 19

The Spectator Sentenced to Death Matéi Visniec 37

The Passport György Dragomán 97

The Man Who Had His Inner Evil Removed Matéi Visniec 149

Stories of the Body: Artemisia, Teresa, Eva, Lina András Visky 221

Sexodrom Giuvlipen Theatre Company. 315

Afterword *Melissa Lorraine* 339

Illustrations

1. Herta Müller/Mihaela Panainte: *Lowlands* – Vasile Alecsandri National Theatre of Iași, Romania (directed by Mihaela Panainte). Premiere: 13 October 2018. Poster design: Mihaela Panainte.   21

2. Matéi Visniec: *The Spectator Sentenced to Death* – Le Théâtre de ... Nantes (directed by Claude Kagan). Premiere: 8 June 2009.   39

3. György Dragomán: *The Passport* – Hungarian Theatre of Cluj, Romania (directed by András Visky). Premiere: 16 November 2016. Poster design: Dénes Miklósi.   99

4. Matéi Visniec: *The Man Who Had His Inner Evil Removed* – book cover design by Andra Badulesco Visniec for Cartea Românească, 2014.   151

5. András Visky: *Stories of the Body: Artemisia* – Theatre Y, Chicago (directed by Melissa Lorraine and Andrej Visky). Premiere: 25 May 2018. Poster design by Péter Szabó.   225

6. András Visky: *Stories of the Body: Teresa* – Theatre Y, Chicago (directed by Melissa Lorraine and Andrej Visky). Premiere: 25 May 2018. Poster design by Péter Szabó.   254

7. András Visky: *Stories of the Body: Eva* – Theatre Y, Chicago (directed by Melissa Lorraine and Andrej Visky). Premiere: 25 May 2018. Poster design by Péter Szabó.   274

8. András Visky: *Stories of the Body: Lina* – Theatre Y, Chicago (directed by Melissa Lorraine and Andrej Visky). Premiere: 25 May 2018. Poster design by Péter Szabó.   292

9. Giuvlipen Theatre Company: *Sexodrom* – National Centre of Dance, Bucharest, Romania (directed by Bogdan Georgescu, produced by Giuvlipen). Premiere: 7 May 2019. Poster design: Andrei Ionita.   317

Notes on Contributors

György Dragomán (born 1973) is an award-winning Hungarian author and literary translator, originally from Transylvania (Romania). A lot of his work deals with the legacy of growing up under totalitarianism, and often features young protagonists whose narrative perspective he adopts. His best-known work, *The White King* (2005), has been translated into over thirty languages and was adapted for film. His most recent publication in English is *The Bone Fire*, translated by Ottilie Mulzet (2021). He has received numerous literary awards, including the Sándor Bródy Prize (2003), the Tibor Déry Prize (2006), the Sándor Márai Prize (2006), the Attila József Prize (2007) and the Jan Michalski Prize for Literature (2011). In translation, Dragomán's fiction has been published in *The Paris Review*, *The New York Times*, *Le Monde*, *Die Zeit* and *Neue Zürcher Zeitung*. Dragomán's website can be accessed at: http://gyorgydragoman.com/?lang=en.

Giuvlipen Theatre Company (Giuvlipen means 'feminism' in the Romani language) is the first independent Roma feminist theatre company in Romania, established in 2014 by actresses Mihaela Drăgan and Zita Moldovan. Giuvlipen's work is challenging, experimental and highly performative, and openly discusses topics that history, mentality and social or political constraints have often silenced. In each show, the company seeks to reclaim the art, history and cultural identity of the Roma community, through stories told by Roma artists. Giuvlipen's founder Mihaela Drăgan has developed a strong international reputation in her own right, being invited to numerous residencies and receiving prestigious acknowledgements of her work, such as nominations for the LPTW Gilder/Coigney International Theatre Awards. Giuvlipen's website can be accessed at: https://giuvlipen.com/en/.

Jozefina Komporaly (editor and translator) lectures at the University of the Arts London, and translates from Romanian and Hungarian into English. Komporaly is editor and co-translator of the anthologies *Matéi Visniec: How to Explain the History of Communism to Mental Patients and Other Plays* (2015) and *András Visky's Barrack Dramaturgy: Memories of the Body* (2017), and author of numerous publications on translation and adaptation, including the monograph *Radical Revival as Adaptation* (2017) and the essay 'András Visky & Matéi Visniec: Challenging boundaries of cultural specificity' (in *Contemporary European Playwrights*, 2020). Her translations have appeared in *Asymptote*, *Index on Censorship*, *Words without Borders* and *World Literature Today*, and have been produced by Foreign Affairs in London and Trap Door and Theatre Y in Chicago. Recent translations include two volumes on theatre by Mihai Măniuțiu (co-translated with Nicoleta Cinpoeș) and the novel *Mr K Released* by Matéi Visniec.

Herta Müller (born 1953) is a Romanian-born and Berlin-based German novelist, poet, essayist and recipient of the 2009 Nobel Prize in Literature. Her writing has been translated into more than twenty languages. Müller is well known for a body of work depicting the effects of violence, cruelty and terror, set against the backdrop of the Socialist Republic of Romania under Nicolae Ceaușescu's dictatorial regime. Many of her works are told from the viewpoint of the German ethnic minority in Romania, and present the history of the Swabian German community in the Banat Region and Transylvania. Her much acclaimed 2009 novel *The Hunger Angel* (*Atemschaukel*) depicts the deportation of Romania's German minority to Soviet gulags in the aftermath of the Second World War. *Niederungen* was Müller's first book, initially published in a censored version in Romania in 1982, followed by an uncensored edition in Germany (1984) and an English translation by Sieglinde Lund as *Nadirs* (1999). *Lowlands*, Panainte's version included in this anthology, is an original stage adaptation of Müller's fiction.

Mihaela Panainte (born 1982) is a Romanian theatre and opera director. Panainte has worked with an impressive array of creatives both in Romanian and abroad, and is the author of numerous radical stage adaptations, including *The Chairs* by Eugène Ionesco (Antares Chair Factory Cluj), *The Trial* by Franz Kafka (National Theatre of Cluj), *Lowlands* by Herta Müller (Vasile Alecsandri Theatre of Iași), *The Book of the Elderly* by Szilágyi Domokos (Hungarian Theatre of Cluj), *Gianni Schicchi* by Puccini (State Opera Ruse, Bulgaria), *Cavalleria Rusticana* by Pietro Mascagni (Hungarian Opera of Cluj), *The Human Voice* by Francis Poulenc (Transit House Cluj), *Jonah* by Marin Sorescu (Turda Salt Mines) and *Medio Monte* (Baia Mare Artists' Colony). Panainte's experimental work often takes place in non-traditional spaces, and fuses an interest in visual arts with corporeality and forms of movement-based performance. Panainte often works with emerging artists and community performance groups, and is currently pursuing a doctoral project in performance at the University of Timișoara.

András Visky (born 1957) is an award-winning playwright, poet and essayist and the resident dramaturg at the Hungarian Theatre of Cluj, Romania, where he is also associate artistic director. He lectures in performance at the Babeș-Bolyai University in Cluj and the Károli University in Budapest, and is a member of the Széchenyi Academy of Literature and Arts. Visky writes in Hungarian about issues stemming from Romanian realities. In parallel with his playwriting, Visky has developed the concept of 'barrack dramaturgy', inspired by his experience of growing up in an Eastern European gulag, through which he explores what it means to be a prisoner and the significance of being set free. Visky's plays have been staged in Romania, Hungary, France, Italy, Poland, Slovenia, England, Scotland and the United States. Visky's work is available in English in the critical anthology *András Visky's Barrack Dramaturgy: Memories of the Body* (edited by Jozefina Komporaly, 2017). Visky's official Facebook page can be accessed via: https://www.facebook.com/andrasvisky/.

Matéi Visniec (born 1956, aka Matei Vişniec) is a Romanian-born playwright, poet, novelist and journalist based in Paris. Visniec's plays are among the most frequently performed works at the Avignon OFF festival, and he has a solid international profile, with productions taking place regularly across four continents. In his native Romania, Visniec has achieved quasi-canonical status since the fall of communism (his work was banned prior to 1989), and the recently founded Suceava Theatre was named in his honour. In addition to the anthology *Matéi Visniec: How to Explain the History of Communism to Mental Patients and Other Plays* (edited by Jozefina Komporaly, 2015), Visniec's drama appeared in English translation in the collection *Balkan Plots* (edited by Cheryl Robson, 2002), and his Kafkaesque novel *Mr K Released* was published in 2020. Visniec's website can be accessed at: https://www.visniec.com/home.html.

Acknowledgements

This volume, resulting from my translation practice over the last few years, was inspired by my ambition to champion lesser-known dramatic traditions. Emboldened by the interest of practitioners and theatre companies who had explored this work in performance, I hope to contribute to translation flows between literatures on the perceived periphery and the hyper-centre that is the medium of English. Heartfelt thanks to artistic directors Trine Garrett and Camila França and the ensemble at Foreign Affairs London, who nurtured several of my translations included in this book, and also to William Gregory, Paul Garrett and Roland Glasser for their advice in the course of my translation process. Warmest thanks to Melissa Lorraine, who commissioned *Stories of the Body* for Theatre Y, Chicago and who has been encouraging my work for years, and to Faynia Williams for her endorsement and ongoing support to Romanian theatre. I am grateful to Mihaela Panainte for inviting me to Iași to see her innovative production of *Lowlands*, which has led to the English translation of her adaptation of Herta Müller's novel and to thinking more inclusively about the structure of this book. As a supporter of Giuvlipen's extraordinary campaign for state theatre status, I am thankful to the first Romanian Roma theatre company for their bold and much-needed contribution towards decolonizing public discourse, and to Mihaela Drăgan and Bogdan Georgescu for their help with finetuning the translation of *Sexodrom*. Many thanks to András Visky and Ildikó Ungvári Zrínyi for their constructive comments on my introduction to the volume, and to Eleonora Ringler-Pascu for her advice on the bibliography. Last but not least, I am grateful to Matéi Visniec, whose works were the first drama texts I translated, and to György Dragomán, whose play *The Passport* continues to remain more topical than ever.

Foreword

FAYNIA WILLIAMS, ARTISTIC DIRECTOR, BRIGHTON THEATRE

In 1989, while Ceausescu was still in power, I had the great good fortune to be sent by the British Council to look at Romanian theatre, about which we in Britain knew so little at that time. I found a thriving, colourful, intellectually demanding cultural phenomenon that fired me to return with a determination to spread the word about, what has been called, 'the tragic comic condition' of this dynamic theatre scene. Romanian theatre showed the power of the arts, not only to draw audiences in their overcoats in the freezing winter, but also to play a frontline role in the events that were to overthrow the dictator. Their leading actor, Ion Caramitru, whose Hamlet I saw then, became the vice president of the new regime.

On my return to England, I began by directing Marin Sorescu's *The Third Stake* as *Vlad the Impaler* for BBC Radio 3, starring John Hurt, and on the stage in Glasgow and at the Brighton Festival. I then directed Matéi Visniec's *Body of a Woman as a Battlefield in the Bosnian War* at the Brighton Festival, which went on to be produced at the Young Vic in London. I also chaired a panel on the work of Visniec and Romanian theatre.

And I returned to Romania in 1990 and 1991, when I directed *The Brothers Karamazov* with Romanian actors at the National Theatres of Craiova and Bucharest, while thousands were demonstrating in the square outside.

Yet still so little of Romanian theatre is known or produced in the UK. So, I welcome this volume of exciting works for theatre. The very title that describes the plays as 'Dramaturgies of Subversion' should arouse the interest of those working in British theatre, and those who long to see that theatre remain central to European cultural thought and deed.

The only area missing in detail in this comprehensive volume is that of the Romanian Yiddish Theatre. It was here in 1989 that Romanian theatre-makers used to find inspiration for bringing music and dance into their work, and it is now run by the brilliant Maia Morgenstern, whom we discovered on our first visit to the country.

What is important about this volume, aside from the variety and quality of the works it contains, is the international nature of the contributors and the many languages they represent as Romanians both in Romania and abroad.

The year of my discovery of Romanian theatre is the year the country emerged from totalitarian rule, allowing it to share theatrical riches of which most of us in the West were unaware.

Reader, you have a real treat to explore and pass on to the theatre-going public.

Introduction

PLAYWRITING, TRANSNATIONAL DRAMATURGIES AND THE CONTEMPORARY ROMANIAN THEATRE LANDSCAPE

Aiming to reflect on the diversity of dramatic writing that explores the past and present of Romania, this collection takes stock thirty years after the collapse of communism, celebrates the vitality and variety of writing for the stage after 1990, and endeavours to place Romanian theatre in a forward-looking transnational context. To this end, in addition to plays originally written in Romanian, the anthology includes work by German, Hungarian and Roma authors born and/or working in Romania, and brings together plays written during the communist period and its aftermath. Hoping to complement the game-changing contribution of the volume *Romanian Literature as World Literature*, edited by Mircea Martin, Christian Moraru and Andrei Terian for Bloomsbury, this volume wishes to engage with the geopolitics of both writing and reading dramatic works, in addition to examining the reception of stage productions and the broader context of theatre-making. For this reason, my priority as editor has been to foreground key aspects of the Romanian theatre system alongside the discussion of landmark dramatic authors. Historically, Romanian theatre has privileged text-based theatre and some influential plays continue to get published as literary texts, independent from potential tie-in productions by major companies, even though contemporary playwriting is not necessarily widely popular or lucrative, and not many theatres programme new writing. As a recent Fabulamundi survey concluded, 'contemporary playwriting activity by state-funded theatres very much depends on individual artistic directors', whereas independent theatres 'tend to programme more new writing because they are able to take more risks, and they also tend to cater for younger audiences' (Lacra 2020). In parallel with this, recent years have seen an upsurge in experimental performance and collaborative creative processes that no longer depart from textual prompts. Whether text-centred or rooted in devising principles, however, the majority of Romanian theatre outputs references urgent concerns of the moment, reflects directly or indirectly on a unique history, and eloquently argues for the continued political and cultural relevance of theatre.

As I suggest elsewhere, it is still difficult to conduct a conversation about Romanian theatre without addressing the country's emergence from totalitarian rule in December 1989,[1] even though theatre and performance artists have been intensely preoccupied in the last thirty-odd years with embracing current European and global trends and with finding a space in a diverse cultural climate. The impact of the Romanian Revolution continues to loom large, not only because of the extended period of time needed to emerge from under the influence of communism, but also because, on a practical level, we are dealing with a different relationship with censorship. During the communist era, all performances were subject to political screening – and, if necessary, purging – carried out by a specialist team within the Communist Party, and a range of topics were forbidden to write about outright. After the change of regime, this scrutiny was lifted and any topic could become the subject of stage representation, as long as there was a theatre to put it on and an audience to watch it. Following a notable gap in theatre attendance in the early 1990s, spectators returned to live theatre, this time, however, having an opportunity to take their pick from a much more stratified offer. Important expat theatre-makers were invited back to Romania to take over the management of most public theatre institutions, while younger practitioners, uninvolved in this overhaul, focused on setting up alternative platforms, thus giving rise to an independent theatre scene, hitherto absent from Romanian culture.[2] As Iulia Popovici points out (2015), alternative theatre movements did not exist because Romania did not have a samizdat culture, hence independent theatre could only appear after the 1989 Revolution.

As opposed to a centralized system of subsidised theatres with permanent companies, post-1990 the number of theatre and performance organizations has multiplied, and many existing ones have changed status and focus. To this day, the mainstream is affiliated with dominant power structures and the independent sector is in ongoing opposition.[3] This dual structure, replicated at funding level, is common to many countries, but in Romania it has led to the co-existence of radically opposed cultures: state-funded theatres benefitting from financial security yet often steering clear of risk-taking approaches, while independent theatres battling an ongoing lack of financial means but passionate about fresh topics and innovative means of expression. Despite this, Romanian theatre demonstrates extraordinary vitality and capacity for reinvention. Theatres put on performances in multiple forms, genres and languages – in addition to Romanian, in Hungarian, German, Serbian and Yiddish, and there is a consolidating movement to represent the experience of the Roma community. In fact, Romania has the largest network of minority theatres in the European Union. From a funding point of view, the fact that most theatres staging work in languages other than Romanian have a 'state theatre' status is crucial, as this implies the maintenance of a regular company and the possibility of producing a guaranteed number of shows a year. It is in this context that Roma company Giuvlipen is currently campaigning for state theatre status: company member Mihaela Drăgan draws attention to the fact that Giuvlipen's demand for state theatre status is nothing more than being in line with other institutions catering for ethnic minorities, and this claim is widely supported by a large number of prominent cultural figures.[4]

Giuvlipen was founded in 2014 with the aim to enhance cultural integration and the visibility of Roma performers, to counterbalance negative or incorrect stereotypes and to bring taboo subjects to public attention.[5] Seeking to reclaim the history and cultural identity of the Roma community, the company has strong ties with global theatre organizations, is a regular participant in the Roma Heroes Festival, and is frequently involved in public debates on identity and gender. Company founder Mihaela Drăgan's play *Del Duma*, translated by Diana Manole, has been anthologized in *Roma Heroes: Five European Monodramas* (2019),[6] and she was a nominee of the LPTW Gilder/Coigney International Theatre Award in 2017 and 2020, and beneficiary of an International Residency at the Royal Court in London in 2019, where she developed the playtext *Romacen*. She is the initiator of Roma Futurism – an art movement that lies at the intersection of Roma culture with technology and witchcraft, and in her invited manifesto for the prestigious collection *Why Theatre?* – edited by Kaatje De Geest, Carmen Hornbostel and Milo Rau for the National Theatre of Ghent – Drăgan talks about 'making theatre a safe place for everyone' and about having transformed their collective into a 'sacred space': 'I feel like a witch on the stage and my words are my wand. For me the words I deliver on the stage have the same power as the words in an incantation or magical ritual'. This much needed confidence and call for action against erasure from public memory and theatre history will no doubt continue to cement the artist's role as an influential voice in a European context, and is likely to energize marginal groups in championing their agendas.

German-speaking theatre in Romania dates back to 1788, when one of the bastions protecting the city of Sibiu was transformed into a performance space. Radu-Alexandru Nica (2013) meticulously documents the unique history of the longest-running institutional form of theatre-making in Romania from its beginnings to the fall of communism in 1989, and excavates key stages in the trajectory of a performance tradition representative for an influential ethnic minority. As Nica rightly argues, German-speaking theatre in today's Romania only makes sense as long as it simultaneously celebrates its unique origins and stays connected to ongoing trends in the German cultural sphere, and refrains from reverting to provincial self-sufficiency or wallowing in self-pity.[7] Currently, there are two state-subsidised theatres founded in the post-war period, offering productions in German: the German company (Deutsche Abteilung) at the Radu Stanca National Theatre of Sibiu and the German State Theatre of Timișoara. Both have a permanent ensemble and regularly collaborate with creative partners from Romania and the international theatre scene (cf. Ringler-Pascu, Mazilu et al.). In terms of repertoire, both theatres programme a selection of landmark plays from the canon, as well as important contemporary works. Neither of these theatres has the remit to exclusively stage works originally written in German; however, the language of performance continues to be German even when the collaborative team is from other backgrounds. In addition to these professional companies with strong ties with specialist platforms in the German-speaking world, there are also a number of amateur theatre initiatives conducted in German, thus establishing an important connection with the local alternative performance scene, as well (cf. Puchianu). The most notable contemporary Romanian playwright of German extraction is Elise Wilk (born 1981), whose work circulates in Romanian, German and Hungarian versions (as well as in translations into other languages), and is published by Schauspiel Henschel. Her recent play *Disappearing* (*Dispariții/Werschwinden*) is crystallized local history par excellence, telling a story of migration and disappearance via the lives of three consecutive generations in the Transylvanian-German community.

Theatre performances in Hungarian are also concentrated in the Transylvanian region of Romania, and include subsidized companies and independent organizations, the majority founded in the post-war period. (See Kántor and Kötő for details on theatre history until the early 1990s, and Jákfalvi, Kékesi and Ungvári Zrínyi for more contemporary cultural contexts.) Internationally most significant is the Hungarian Theatre of Cluj, which is also the longest-running Hungarian professional theatre company looking back on a history of over two hundred years. Led by artistic director Gábor Tompa and affiliated to numerous organizations including the UTE (Union des Théâtres de l'Europe), the theatre is the organizer of the biannual Interferences Festival and has a firm presence on the European festival circuit, alongside regular collaborations with major international practitioners. As a result, the theatre has pioneered the use of simultaneous translation and surtitling for its Hungarian-language productions in

Romanian, and frequently in English, thus transcending its original remit as a community theatre and catering for a national and indeed global spectatorship. Similar openness towards a larger transnational audience can be witnessed in the case of the Tamási Áron Theatre of Sfântu Gheorghe, which also hosts the Reflex international festival, and of the Csíky Gergely Hungarian State Theatre of Timişoara, which organizes the Euroregional Theatre Festival (TESZT). Cutting-edge intercultural work is carried out by the Tompa Miklós Company of the National Theatre of Târgu-Mureş and the Yorick Studio in Târgu Mureş, pioneering multilingual theatre projects and collaborations with especially the younger generation of creatives representing the different ethnic and cultural backgrounds in Romania. The Figura Studio in Gheorgheni is an important incubator for experimental talent, alongside independent platforms such as the Váróterem (Waiting Room) project. Collaborative creations such as *Parallel, (In)Visible, (In)Correct* and *Homemade* have carved out a new path in the landscape of Hungarian theatre and performance in Romania, in the shape of highly sensitive socially committed work that braids devising with urgent concerns of the here and now, and reaches out to a non-traditional demographic in alternative performance venues. Writing for the stage in Hungarian looks back on an extensive tradition, and has achieved an identity of its own as a facet of Transylvanian-Hungarian literature. Some of the most important authors have tried their hand at writing drama, such as Áron Tamási (1897–1966) and Károly Kós (1883–1977) in the interwar period, and János Székely (1929–1992), András Sütő (1927–2006), Géza Páskándi (1933–1995), László Csíki (1944–2008) and István Kocsis (born 1940) after 1945. Major names in contemporary playwriting include András Visky (born 1957, also known for his dramaturgical concept 'barrack dramaturgy'),[8] Csaba Székely (born 1981), András Hatházi (born 1967). György Dragomán (born 1973), whose play *The Passport* is included in this volume, is one of the most prominent novelists writing in Hungarian today, with most of his fiction available in English translation.[9]

A regrettable absence from this collection is Romanian Jewish drama. A dedicated theatre institution continues to exist, the State Jewish Theatre Bucharest, which is the oldest Yiddish-language theatre with uninterrupted activity in the world. Its repertoire includes plays by Jewish authors and/or on Jewish topics, and some productions are performed in Yiddish (with simultaneous translation into Romanian). This theatre, currently led by internationally acclaimed actress Maia Morgenstern, is one of the most prominent remaining secular Jewish institutions in Romania, continuing what Israil Bercovici called 'a tradition of humanist theatre'. The number of available contemporary texts, however, is increasingly limited. In a collection spanning a broader historical range, the plays of Ludovic Bruckstein (1929–1988) would have certainly been included, notable as he is for the first Holocaust play in Romanian culture (*The Night-Shift*, 1947).[10] The work of Mihail Sebastian (1907–1945) would have also warranted attention; however, in the context of the ongoing revival of interest in his fiction, the celebrated play *The Star with No Name* (1944) was also recently published in English.[11] With these developments in mind, an up-to-date history of Romanian Jewish theatre that addresses the present as well as the past in addition to questions of reception would be more than welcome, in order to continue the investigations initiated by the theatre's former literary secretary, Israil Bercovici, in the landmark study *One Hundred Years of Jewish Theatre in Romania* (1998).[12]

While the presence of dedicated theatre institutions creating work in the languages of ethnic minorities is an essential contribution to the democratization of Romanian cultural life, it is important to stress that these organizations do not operate in isolation and there are intense collaborations across the board. Most high-profile Romanian theatre directors, for example, have worked at the theatres mentioned above. A number of important companies are in the enviable position where they can work as a collective, under the guidance of a stable creative team and thus form long-lasting creative partnerships. Silviu Purcărete's work with the Radu Stanca National Theatre of Sibiu is the ultimate example for this trend, culminating in their landmark *Faust* production (2008), which epitomizes Purcărete's penchant for monumental productions of total theatre that offer an overwhelming immersive experience. Andrei Șerban, Mihai Măniuțiu, Gábor Tompa, Alexandru Dabija, Victor Ioan Frunză and Radu Afrim also work with ensembles at a regular basis, and there is a strong cluster of younger directors, who integrate devising and work collaboratively, in a wide range of venues, responding to topical social concerns. Bogdan Georgescu, Gianina Cărbunariu and Eugen Jebeleanu are heavily engaged with civil agendas and identity politics, alongside a group of artists who draw on the tradition of performance art in order to forge a feminist politics in a predominantly patriarchal culture (Ioana Păun, Mihaela Drăgan). Devised principles are gradually becoming prevalent, and there is an emerging movement that champions improvisation and collective creation (e.g. *Don't Cry, Baby*; *Familia Offline/Offline Family*).[13]

Frequently staged Romanian playwrights of the communist era include Marin Sorescu (1936–1996), Paul Everac (1924–2011), Aurel Baranga (1913–1979) and D. R. Popescu (born 1935), alongside oppositional figures Iosif Naghiu (1932–2003), Teodor Mazilu (1930–1980), Horia Lovinescu (1917–1983) and Ion Băieșu (1933–1992) – writing for the stage nearly coming to a halt, due to severe censorship, towards the end of the 1980s.[14] After a brief hiatus, the noughties ushered in an upsurge in playwriting, and in parallel with dramatists who started their careers in the eighties, such as the internationally renowned Matéi Visniec (born 1956),[15] Horea Gârbea (born 1962) and Vlad Zografi (born 1960), a host of diverse voices came to prominence introducing variety in terms of form and content. The first platform dedicated to new dramatic texts was Dramafest (1997), launching Andrea Vălean's *When I Want to Whistle, I Whistle* – a play influential to this day for its direct, up-to-date language – followed by the platform for new writing dramAcum (dramaNow) initiated by Gianiana Cărbunariu. The plays of Saviana Stănescu (born 1967), Ștefan Peca (born 1982), Gianina Cărbunariu (born 1977), Alina Nelega (born 1960), Alexandra Pâzgu (born 1985), Alexandra Badea (born 1980) and Mihaela Michailov (born 1977) have been instrumental in addressing burning social and political concerns, and foregrounding an approach whereby theatre actively intervenes in public life.[16] Equally noteworthy is the fact that several Romanian playwrights have embraced a transnational perspective and write in both Romanian and their adopted language(s), such as English (Saviana Stănescu), French (Alexandra Badea, Matéi Visniec) and German (Alexandra Pâzgu).

Although such an anthology can by no means act as an exhaustive sample of a given playwriting or theatre tradition, it is predicated both on the inventiveness of younger practitioners, who have taken theatre and performance into hitherto unexplored environments and contexts, and on the ability of (some) established figures to continuously re-invent themselves. Within the multi-tiered structure of Romanian theatre, there is space for conformity alongside risk-taking, and radical interventions are situated side by side with more traditional takes on drama. As this selection will hopefully demonstrate, Romanian drama is not simply a form of microliterature or a platform for cultivating a national mythology, but an area of intersections and geo-cultural connections that re-evaluates the local and the global. In a situation where some of the most prolific authors of Romanian drama are also emigrant writers, who systematically express themselves in both their native and acquired languages and lay claims to both their Romanian and chosen nationalities, the notion of exile gains new interpretations and invites a fresh investigation of the territorial deployment of cultural outputs. When selecting plays for this book, my editorial concern has been to offer insights into the variety of playwriting practices dealing with Romania as a subject matter, and to highlight the diversity of theatre-making within theatre institutions and broader cultural platforms that nurture creative arts for the stage. A major consideration has been to address theatre as transnational and de-territorialized art form, and in this respect, I have been guided by relevance in terms of content rather than the current geographical location of playwrights and/or practitioners.

The plays included in the anthology, fully published for the first time in English, deliberately run the gamut of form- and content-based diversity – ranging from family dramas to allegories, and absurdist experiments to modular texts rooted in open dramaturgy. In terms of genealogy, they are either the work of individual playwrights, adaptations of pre-existing literary texts, commissions from theatre companies or the results of collective creation. Irrespective of their origin, these works share a preoccupation with critically reflecting burning concerns rooted in Romanian realities and are notable dramaturgical experiments that push the boundaries of the genre. In addition, these plays also seek novel ways to examine universal experiences of the human condition, such as love, loss, abuse, betrayal, grief, violence, manipulation and despair.

Notes

1 Cf. Komporaly's essay on Romanian theatre in the *Routledge Companion to Theatre and Performance*, eds Aneta Mancewicz and Ralf Remshardt (forthcoming). In parallel with continuing to haunt personal and cultural memory, the experience of communism has a long-standing presence in dramatic representation. Note the emblematic works reflecting on the excesses of the communist era: such as *How to Explain the History of Communism to Mental Patients* by Matéi Visniec or *Porn* by András Visky, the re-enactment of events from the December 1989 Revolution (e.g. *Waxing West* by Saviana Stanescu), or the representation of the dictatorial couple (*A Day in the Life of Nicolae Ceaușescu* by Denis Dinulescu) – the latter two discussed 'as post-communist revenge parodies' (cf. Manole 2013). In the early 2000s, Alexandru Tocilescu staged a number of innovative productions at the Bulandra Theatre, in addition to Dinulescu's play, including *Red Comedy* by Ion Turturica and *Elisaveta Bam* by Daniil Kharms, with the aim of scrutinizing the workings of the communist regime and shedding light on the traumas it had caused. For a comparative study on pre- and post-communist Romanian theatre (alongside the situation in Hungary and Bulgaria), see Orlich (2017).

2 For a more nuanced discussion of contemporary Romanian theatre culture, see Cristina Modreanu's study *A History of Romanian Theatre from Communism to Capitalism:*

Children of a Restless Time (Routledge, 2020). For an account of the early years of the post-communist period, cf. Marian Popescu, *The Stage and the Carnival* (2000), available at http://marianpopescu.arts.ro/the-stage-and-the-carnival-romanian-theatre-after-censorship/#cartea (accessed 22 October 2020). An excellent online resource is the multimedia dictionary of Romanian theatre, available at https://www.dmtr.ro/. A rare discussion in English, looking back on the period before 1989, can be found in 'Retrieved from oblivion' by Dragan Klaic, prefacing Daniel Gerould (ed.) *Playwrights before the Fall: Eastern European Drama in Times of Revolution*. Also see a recent survey, conducted as part of a broader European project, by Margherita Laera, 'Romania', *Critical Stages*, December 2020. http://www.critical-stages.org/22/romania/.

3 Cf. Runcan (2018).
4 Cf. https://cronicaromana.net/2020/10/20/peste-50-de-personalitati-si-institutii-de-cultura-sustin-infiintarea-unui-teatru-rom-de-stat/?fbclid=IwAR2CQttyAMAcMejS8OGbpyzls_7EUP3sUszyx9dBCKsTkw5qvkROxJnfv8g (accessed 20 October 2020).
5 Company website: https://giuvlipen.com/en/; @giuvlipen (Facebook, Instagram)
6 The play *Who Killed Szomna Grancsa?* by Mihai Lukacs and Giuvlipen Theatre Company and translated by Diana Manole is included in the second *Roma Heroes* anthology (Budapest: Independent Theater Hungary/Women for the Future Association, forthcoming).
7 Monica Andronescu, 'Cronicarul Radu Alexandru Nica și Teatrul German din Sibiu' (Chronicler Radu Alexandru Nica and the German Theatre of Sibiu), *Yorick.Ro*, no. 456, 25 June 2013. https://yorick.ro/cronicarul-radu-alexandru-nica-si-teatrul-german-din-sibiu/?fbclid=IwAR1wuznGTtZiGo_tNKgtmpClNONnlGGLJqKeJOtL5YZgZJrxcX7bSoEgS8A accessed 5 February 2021).
8 Cf. András Visky, 'Barrack-Dramaturgy and the Captive Audience', in Magda Romanska (ed.) *The Routledge Companion to Dramaturgy* (Abingdon: Routledge, 2015), 466–471 and the critical anthology Jozefina Komporaly (ed.) *András Visky's Barrack Dramaturgy: Memories of the Body* (Bristol: Intellect, 2017). Visky's official Facebook page can be accessed at https://www.facebook.com/andrasvisky/.
9 A companion text of sorts to *The Passport* has recently been translated into English by Ottlie Mulzet as *The Bone Fire* (Boston: Houghton Mifflin Harcourt, 2021). Dragomán's website can be accessed at http://gyorgydragoman.com/?lang=en
10 Two volumes of Bruckstein's fiction, *The Trap* and *With an Unopened Umbrella in the Rain*, both translated by Alistair Iain Blythe, were published by Istros Books in 2019 and 2021.
11 Mihail Sebastian, *For Two Thousand Years*, trans. Philip Ó Ceallaigh (London: Penguin Modern Classics, 2016); *The Star with No Name*, trans. Gabi Reigh (Aurora Metro Press, 2020).
12 Israil Bercovici, *O sută de ani de teatru evreiesc în România* (*One Hundred Years of Jewish Theater in Romania*), 2nd edition (Bucharest: Integral, 1998) – revised edition of the original Yiddish-language volume *Hundert ior idis teater in Rumenie* (Bucharest: Kriterion Publishing House, 1976). An important contribution specifically focusing on staging the Shoah is the article: Corina L. Petrescu, '"The People of Israel Lives!" Performing the Shoah on Post-War Bucharest's Yiddish Stages', in Valentina Glajar and Jeanine Teodorescu (eds) *Local History: Transnational Memory in the Romanian Holocaust* (New York: Palgrave Macmillan, 2011): 209–223.
13 Cf. I. Popovici (ed.) *Sfârșitul regiei, începutul creației colective în teatrul european/The End of Directing, The Beginning of Theatre-Making and Devising in European Theatre* (Cluj: Tact, 2015).
14 On Romanian playwriting culture, see Mircea Ghițulescu, *Istoria dramaturgiei române contemporane* (*The History of Contemporary Romanian Playwriting*). (Bucharest:

Albatros, 2000). Also noteworthy is the multi-volume reassessment of theatre under communism by Miruna Runcan, *Teatru în diorame* (*Theatre in Dioramas*) (Bucharest: Tracus Arte, 2019 and 2020).
15 Matéi Visniec's work has been staged on four continents, most notably in English by Trap Door Theatre, Chicago and UK-based directors Faynia Williams and Vasile Nedelcu. His work was anthologized in the volumes *Balkan Plots*, ed. Cheryl Robson (Aurora Metro Books, 2002); *Playwrights before the Fall: Eastern European Drama in Times of Revolution*, ed. Daniel Gerould (New York: Martin E. Segal Centre Publications, 2009); and *Matéi Visniec: How to Explain the History of Communism to Mental Patients and Other Plays*, ed. Jozefina Komporaly (Seagull Books, 2015).The playwright's website can be accessed at https://www.visniec.com/home.html.
16 A more detailed discussion of Cărbunariu's work can be found in Cristina Modreanu's contribution to *The Routledge Companion to Theatre and Performance*, eds Aneta Mancewicz and Ralf Remshardt (forthcoming). Also see Andrea Tompa, 'The Rest is Copy-paste from Reality: On Gianina Cărbunariu's Performances', *Theater Heute* (October 2014). Cărbunariu's play *Kebab* was staged at the Schaubühne and the Royal Court in 2007, and *Artists Talk* was included in the 2019 Brexit Stage Left Festival at the Yard Theatre in London. Saviana Stanescu's work written in English is widely staged in the US and available in print, while Alexandra Badea's *The Pulverised*, translated by Lucy Phelps, was staged at the Arcola Theatre in London in 2017. Alina Nelega's *Nascendo* was published in the collection *Eastern Promise* (Aurora Metro Books, 1999).

Bibliography

Asociaţia Română pentru Promovarea Artelor Spectacolului, Universitatea Babeş-Bolyai and Universitatea de Arte Târgu-Mureş (2020) *Dicţionarul multimedia al teatrului românesc* (*Multimedia Dictionary of Romanian Theatre*). Available at https://www.dmtr.ro/ (accessed 8 October 2020).
Bercovici, Israil (1976) *Hundert ior idis teater in Rumenie* (*One Hundred Years of Jewish Theater in Romania*). Bucharest: Kriterion.
Bercovici, Israil (1998) *O sută de ani de teatru evreiesc în România* (*One Hundred Years of Jewish Theater in Romania*). 2nd edition. Bucharest: Integral.
Cadariu, Anda (2018) 'The Emergence of Independent Theatre in Romanian Postcommunist Society', *Symbolon*, Vol. XIX/2 (35): 5–16.
Dávid, Gyula (ed.) (2003) *Erdélyi magyar drámairók* (*Hungarian Playwrights from Transylvania*). Cluj: Kalota.
De Geest, Katje, Carmen Hornbostel and Milo Rau (eds) (2020) *Why Theatre?* National Theatre, Ghent.
Ghiţulescu, Mircea (2000) *Istoria dramaturgiei romăne contemporane* (*The History of Contemporary Romanian Playwriting*). Bucharest: Albatros.
Independent Theater Hungary/Richard O'Neill/Michael Collins/Mihaela Drăgan/Dijana Pavlovic/Franciska Farkas (2019) *Roma Heroes: Five European Monodramas*. Budapest: Women for the Future Association/Independent Theater Hungary. http://independenttheater.blogspot.com/p/buy-now-roma-heroes-five-european.html
Jákfalvi, Magdolna, Kékesi Kun, Árpád and Ungvári Zrínyi, Ildikó (eds) (2019) *Erdélyi magyar színháztörténet – Philther-elemzések* (*Hungarian Theatre History in Transylvania – Philther Analyses*). Bucharest-Târgu Mureş: Eikon–UartPress.
Kántor, Lajos and Kötő, József (1998) *Magyar színház Erdélyben, 1919–1992* (*Hungarian Theatre in Transylvania, 1919–1992*). Bucharest: Integral (first edition Bucharest: Kriterion, 1994).

Klaić, Dragan (2009) 'Preface: Retrieved from Oblivion', in Daniel Gerould (ed.) *Playwrights before the Fall: Eastern European Drama in Times of Revolution*. New York: Martin E. Segal Centre Publications, pp. xi–xxi.
Komporaly, Jozefina (ed.) (2015) *Matéi Visniec: How to Explain the History of Communism to Mental Patients and Other Plays*. Seagull Books.
Komporaly, Jozefina (ed.) (2017) *András Visky's Barrack Dramaturgy: Memories of the Body*. Bristol: Intellect.
Komporaly, Jozefina (2020) 'András Visky and Matéi Visniec: Challenging Boundaries of Cultural Specificity', in M. Delgado, B. Lease and D. Rebellato (eds) *Contemporary European Playwrights*. London: Routledge. DOI: 10.4324/9781315111940
Komporaly, Jozefina (forthcoming) 'Romania', in Aneta Mancewicz and Ralf Remshardt (eds) *The Routledge Companion to Theatre and Performance*. Abingdon: Routledge.
Laera, Margherita (2020) 'Romania', *Critical Stages*, December 2020. http://www.critical-stages.org/22/romania/ (accessed 4 January 2021).
Manole, Diana (2013) 'The Post-Communist Revenge Parody: Embodying Nicolae Ceaușescu on Stage after 1989', *New England Theatre Journal*, 24: 95–117.
Martin, Mircea, Moraru, Christian and Terian, Andrei (eds) (2018) *Romanian Literature as World Literature*. London: Bloomsbury.
Mazilu, Alina, Weident, Medana and Wolf, Irina (eds) (2011) *Das rumänische Theater nach 1989: Seine Beziehungen zum deutschsprachigen Raum* (*Romanian Theatre after 1989 and Its Connections with the German-Speaking World*). Berlin: Frank & Timme.
Modreanu, Cristina (2020) *A History of Romanian Theatre from Communism to Capitalism: Children of a Restless Time*. Abingdon: Routledge. DOI: 10.4324/9780429281372
Nica, Radu-Alexandru (2013) *Nostalgia Mitteleuropei: o istorie a teatrului german din Sibiu* (*Nostalgia for Mitteleuropa: A History of the German Theatre of Sibiu*). Bucharest: Eikon.
Orlich, Ileana Alexandra (2017) *Subversive Stages: Theatre in Pre- and Post-communist Hungary, Romania and Bulgaria*. Budapest: Central European University Press.
Petrescu, Corina L. (2011). '"The People of Israel Lives!" Performing the Shoah on Post-War Bucharest's Yiddish Stages', in Valentina Glajar and Jeanine Teodorescu (eds) *Local History, Transnational Memory in the Romanian Holocaust*. New York: Palgrave Macmillan, pp. 209–223.
Popescu, Marian (2000) *The Stage and the Carnival: Romanian Theatre after Censorship*. Pitești: Paralela 45. DOI:10.13140/RG.2.1.3149.4169. http://marianpopescu.arts.ro/the-stage-and-the-carnival-romanian-theatre-after-censorship/#cartea (accessed 22 October 2020).
Popovici, Iulia (2015) 'Theatre-Makers, Directors, and the Independent Theatre: The Founding Narrative', in Iulia Popovici (ed.) *Sfârșitul regiei, începutul creației colective în teatrul european/The End of Directing, the Beginning of Theatre-Making and Devising in European Theatre*. Cluj: Tact.
Puchianu, Carmen Elisabeth (2017) 'Deutschsprachiges Theater der Alternativszene in Rumänien aus der Sicht einer Theatermacherin' (German Theatre on the Romanian Alternative Stage from the Perspective of a Theatre Maker), *DramArt*, 6: 129–143.
Ringler-Pascu, Eleonora (2013) 'Das Deutsche Staatstheater Temeswar – deutschsprachiger Kulturträger im südosteuropäischen Raum' (The German State Theatre of Timișoara – A German-speaking Cultural Platform in South-East Europe), in Harald Haslmayr and Andrei Corbea-Hoișie (eds), *Pluralität als kulturelle Lebensform: Österreich und die Nationalkulturen Südosteuropas* (*Local History, Transnational Memory in the Romanian Holocaust Plurality as a Cultural Way of Life: Austria and South-East European National Cultures*). Kolloquienreise-Band. Wien–Berlin: LIT Verlag, pp.153–162.

Runcan, Miruna (2018) 'Romanian Theatre as Public Service. A Critical Perspective of the Last Decades', *STUDIA UBB DRAMATICA*, LXIII/1: 227–240.
Runcan, Miruna (2019) *Teatru în diorame: Discursul criticii de teatru în comunism*. Vol. I *Fluctuantul dezgheț* (*Theatre in Dioramas: The Discourse of Theatre Criticism under Communism*. Vol. I *The Fluctuating Thaw*), Bucharest: Tracus Arte.
Runcan, Miruna (2020) *Teatru în diorame. Discursul criticii teatrale în comunism*. Vol. II *Amăgitoarea primăvară 1965–1977* (*Theatre in Dioramas: The Discourse of Theatre Criticism under Communism*. Vol. II *The Deceptive Spring, 1965–1977*), Bucharest: Tracus Arte.
Visky, András (2015) 'Barrack-Dramaturgy and the Captive Audience', in Magda Romanska (ed.) *The Routledge Companion to Dramaturgy*. Abingdon: Routledge, pp. 466–471; reprinted in Komporaly, Jozefina (ed.) (2017) *András Visky's Barrack Dramaturgy: Memories of the Body*. Bristol: Intellect. pp. 25–30.

Play Synopses and Production Histories

Lowlands **by Herta Müller, adapted for the stage by Mihaela Panainte (original title in German:** *Niederungen***)**

This innovative stage adaptation is based on a volume of short stories by Herta Müller written in German in 1982 and published in Romania in censored form; the full text appearing in Germany in 1984 and in Romania only after 1989. *Lowlands* focuses on the perspective of a child narrator, by way of a series of episodes that centre on mundane aspects of daily life in a remote village against the backdrop of the oppressive atmosphere of mid-twentieth-century Romania. As a German-speaking author writing in 1980s Romania, Müller conjures up the world of her childhood in the Swabian community of the Banat region, situated in the western part of the country. This is a frank and penetrating view of an isolated population, on the verge of dissolution due to accelerated migration to Germany, perceived with reticence by some Banat-Swabians who found Müller's portrayal unsympathetic. Indeed, Müller makes no attempt at idealizing this childhood, drawing instead on internal tensions and generational conflict in a close-knit and impoverished community. Her aim is a declared exercise of free speech that she also practiced on an overt political level as member of Aktionsgruppe Banat, a group of German-speaking writers in Romania who spoke up against censorship under Nicolae Ceaușescu's dictatorial regime. Müller has kept returning, time and time again, to this subject matter, most famously in the novel *The Land of Green Plums*, and received the 2009 Nobel Prize for depicting the 'landscape of the dispossessed' with 'the concentration of poetry and the frankness of prose'. Panainte's stage adaptation, created for a studio production that explores corporality in a mesmerizing installation, is an excellent vehicle for testing the boundaries of autobiographical writing in and for performance. By turning to an initially censored piece of fiction that is rather economical with words, Panainte's production celebrates the precision of carefully chosen words and theatrical images, and highlights the universality of the source material. This production has also successfully enticed new audiences to contemporary experimental theatre-making that intersects the tradition of text-based drama with visual arts and forms of movement-based performance.

Number of characters and gender split: flexible – Panainte's production had ten (three female, seven male).

Production history

- Vasile Alecsandri National Theatre of Iași, Romania (directed by Mihaela Panainte) – premiere 13 October 2018 (https://www.teatrulnationaliasi.ro/stagiunea/tinuturile-joase--179.html)
- Rehearsed reading by Foreign Affairs, London, UK (directed by Trine Garret and Camila França) – 25 November 2020

The Spectator Sentenced to Death by Matéi Visniec (original title in Romanian: *Spectatorul condamnat la moarte*)

This play, written in Matéi Visniec's trademark absurdist style, is a bitter parody of the Stalinist justice system, which totally disregards the fundamental question whether the accused is actually guilty or not. In this system, anybody can find themselves charged with crime – be it genuine or fictitious – and, consequently, end up declared guilty and sentenced accordingly. Examining what it means to be a victim, the play posits that any criminal investigation is in fact a trial of sorts for the audience, seeing that spectators can remain impassive when it comes to the artistic propositions of directors, performers and playwrights. In this context, reminiscent of reverse psychology, the play is pitting most participants in the theatre-making process against one another, until even the defence counsel steps up as a virulent prosecutor, accusing the spectator of having no personal opinions of their own and arguing that they should have been killed straightaway upon their arrival at the performance venue. This play, written in the early 1980s but only published later, was one of Visniec's first forays into drama and was used as a key argument for the playwright's blacklisting by the communist regime. In this sense, *The Spectator Sentenced to Death* is one of the few truly anti-totalitarian plays written in Romania during the communist regime.

Number of characters and gender split: Fourteen (two female, twelve male) – with some possibilities for doubling.

Production history

- Le Théâtre de... Nantes, France (directed by Claude Kagan) – premiere 8 June 2009
- Atelier théâtral Saint Remacle, France (directed by Colette Régibeau) – premiere 13 May 2010
- Théâtre À Petit Feu, Quebec, Canada (directed by Michel-Maxime Legault) – premiere 15 March 2012
- National Theatre of Cluj, Romania (directed by Răzvan Mureşan) – premiere 21 December 2013 (https://www.teatrulnationalcluj.ro/piesa-646/spectatorul-condamnat-la-moarte/)
- Caliband Théâtre Rouen, France (directed by Matthieu Létuvé) – premiere 2014
- Charsoo Theatre Company, Australia, titled *The Spectator* – premiere 14 September 2018
- Théâtre Alizé, France (directed by Karine Boutillon) – premiere 18 May 2019

The Passport **by György Dragomán (original title in Hungarian: *Kalucsni*)**

Translation developed at Cove Park Translation Residency, 2019
Translation longlisted for the Theatre503 Playwriting Awards, 2020

The Passport is set pre-1989 in a small, close-knit Transylvanian town, in which the lives of the various social classes and the fate of the persecuted and that of those who persecute are closely intertwined. The premise is an *Iphigenia*-story of a kind: a sixteen-year-old girl is offered up to the head of the secret police in exchange for passports with which the family could leave the country for a better world. The play is an introduction of sorts to the 1980s through the life of a middle-class family, where everything is shown, *cinema verité*-style, from an unflattering close-up. The father's love affair with a young actress, incidentally the daughter of the secret police chief, conjures up the sinister reality of back street abortions, together with punishment with prison for anyone caught in the act of carrying them out. Ultimately, the play foregrounds surveillance and emotional blackmail as the sole currency in operation in this society, second only to betrayal, which eradicates everyone's escape routes and institutes a new secret police chief at the service of the same old totalitarian regime. As yet another house search is about to start, the play blacks out with a full circle return to its beginning. There is no such thing as private life, and the double act of the removal men, this time destroying rather than packing boxes, conjures up a disturbing authenticity that can impact on anyone, including those without previous immediate experience of this traumatising time and place.

Number of characters and gender split: Eleven (four female, seven male – with some possibilities for doubling).

Production history

- Hungarian Theatre of Cluj, Romania (directed by András Visky) – premiere 16 November 2016 (https://www.huntheater.ro/eloadas/420/kalucsni/)
- Móricz Zsigmond Theatre, Debrecen, Hungary (directed by Rémusz Szikszai) – premiere 2 March 2019
- Radio adaptation (directed by Gábor Rusznyák), MR1 Kossuth Rádió – 25 September 2011
- Rehearsed reading by Foreign Affairs, London, UK (directed by Trine Garrett and Camila França) – 29 April 2020

The Man Who Had His Inner Evil Removed **by Matéi Visniec (original title in Romanian:** ***Omul din care a fost extras răul)***

Translation shortlisted for the 2017 Eurodram competition

This topical and complex play on the existence of inner evil is a fierce critique of increasingly dominant tendencies to abandon moral criteria in public life, and a sharp reflection on the voluntary servitude in which we place ourselves, often unawares, in conditions of our contemporary consumer culture. By juxtaposing popular news anchors with politicians in the context of international summits, the play considers our obsession with celebrity, vanity and fame. Intertwining tragi-comedy with philosophical fable, Visniec satirizes the ruthlessness and sensationalism of media outlets, and addresses the impact of globalization on our society. Visniec points out the totalitarian strand inherent in both socialist regimes and Western conspicuous consumption, claiming that whilst brainwashing was centrally imposed under the former, it has become self-inflicted in conditions of the latter: 'Disinfecting language will open up the way towards true essence'. As a practising journalist (for Radio France Internationale), Visniec has first-hand insight into the workings of mass media; the drive for sensationalism at the expense of accuracy has reconfigured the ways in which people are exposed to facts, which has an impact not only on understanding the past but also on shaping the present and on charting the future. The metaphor of rats offering a helping hand to humankind has also appeared in Visniec's plays *La mémoire des serpillières* (The Memory of Rags, 2015) and *Le roi, le rat et le fou du roi* (The King, the Rat and the King's Fool, 2002) as well as the novel *Dezordinea preventivă* (Pre-emptive Disorder, 2010).

Number of characters and gender split: Twenty (ten female, ten male – with possibilities for a lot of doubling).

Production history

- Compania D'Arte, Timișoara, Romania (directed by Mariana Luca) – premiere 17 June 2016

Stories of the Body (Artemisia, Teresa, Eva, Lina) **by András Visky (original title in Hungarian:** *A test történetei: Artemisia, Teréz, Éva, Lina*)

Stories of the Body comprises four plays based on real life stories as experienced by remarkable women (including Mother Teresa and Italian Renaissance painter Artemisia Gentileschi), and are connected to various cities including Budapest, Cluj/Kolozsvár, Kolkata and Rome, from the seventeenth to the twenty-first century. All four plays deal with the exploration of the self in various configurations, often in conditions of serious conflict or tension and at times of significant societal opposition to women's sense of personal fulfilment. Dealing with such denial, which is often synonymous with exploitation, is central to these protagonists' lives, and is foundational to their ultimate decision to defy the rules and mores of their times. Despite clear historical references and accuracies, the plays themselves are works of fiction, and are rooted in the technique of open dramaturgy. As Visky recommends in his stage directions, theatres might wish to put on various combinations of the plays, and as a result, spectators could watch different productions each time, perhaps in a different order. In this way, the plays – and their approximately fifty-minute stage versions – would gain new meanings in each other's light and context: illuminating the stories of the body in the most varied refractions, as a variation of a single theatrical space and set design. The plays also have the potential to be staged in their own right, as full-length performances.

Artemisia dramatizes the life of seventeenth-century artist Artemisia Gentileschi, the first professional female painter in the Western world. She painted violent and subversive masterpieces against the backdrop of her father's public trial against Agostino Tassi, her art tutor and rapist. Over the last century, her life and work have become emblematic of women's defiance of a society that still considers them second-class citizens, subservient to the authority of men.

Eva is based on documentary interviews with a Hungarian sex worker. Born Roma, unwanted, abused and sold off at a young age, Eva struggles to assert her claim to a life of her own based on at least a modicum of dignity and trust. The play explores the traumatised psyche of a true innocent, who strives to seek agency and is adamant to redefine happiness against all odds.

Lina, written in response to the music of Pēteris Vasks, conjures up the trauma of a friend and the perception of the world from the perspective of the mutilated body. It centres on the moment when a beautiful and highly flexible body suddenly loses its mobility. As a former dancer explores what is available beyond movement, they discover the still dance of the dragonfly and, in the process, experience the love and forgiveness that is still available within reach. The play comprises visions and fairy tale elements, thus bending fantasy with life writing.

Teresa draws on the early life of Mother Teresa of Kolkata and, presenting her as a modern-day Antigone, addresses urgent moral duties in times of major crisis. Sharing an inner commitment to attend to the unburied, Antigone and Teresa blur the boundaries between the living and the dead, and explore the self-imposed renunciation of mundane life in the name of a higher calling.

Number of characters and gender split: flexible

Artemisia: one (female) or three (one female, two male)

Teresa: one (female), three (two female, one male) or four (two female, two male)

Eva: one (female), three (one female, two male) or four (two female, two male)

Lina: six (three female, three male – interchangeable)

Production history

All four plays premiered at Theatre Y Chicago, USA (directed by Melissa Lorraine and Andrej Visky) on 25 May 2018 (http://www.theatre-y.com)

- *Teresa*, then titled *The Unburied: The Saint of Darkness* (directed by Camila França and Trine Garrett for Foreign Affairs, London, UK) – premiere 20 November 2017

Sexodrom by Giuvlipen Theatre Company (original title in Romanian: *Sexodrom*)

Texts by Mihaela Drăgan, Bety Pisică, Nicoleta Ghiță, Oana Rusu, Zita Moldovan, Antonella Lerca Duda, Raj A. The project was developed as part of the Active Art workshop 'Politici în privat' (Private Politics), coordinated by playwright-director Bogdan Georgescu

Sexodrom is a work of collective creation by members of the Roma Theatre Company Giuvlipen, aiming to bring to public attention taboo subjects, to enhance the visibility of Roma performers and to experiment with new forms of theatre-making in a Romanian and indeed international context. Resulting from the active art workshop 'Private Politics' coordinated by Bogdan Georgescu, in which young Roma artists explore taboo subjects in the Romanian public space, the play is a bold interrogation of the ways in which social and political structures impact on private life, and is a firm challenge to mainstream attempts at silencing alternative and minority voices. By way of braiding the exploration of ethnic and sexual identities, the play juxtaposes queer politics and Roma emancipation, and acts as a symbolic rebellion and a political declaration of love at the same time. Integrating musical elements and replicating the format of an interactive children's game, *Sexodrom* is participatory theatre par excellence. It is also an open invitation to expose hidden truths, collating a number of Romanian #MeToo stories and articulating in a novel context that the personal is political.

Number of characters and gender split flexible (approximately six female, one male).

Production history

Premiere: Centrul Național al Dansului București/National Centre of Dance Bucharest, Romania (directed by Bogdan Georgescu, produced by Giuvlipen) – 7–8 May 2019 (https://giuvlipen.com/en/sexodrom/)

Tours:

- Teatrul Rom nu e nomad/Roma Theatre Is Not Nomadic, National Centre of Dance Bucharest – 29 October 2019, 7 March 2020
- Caleido Festival, Unteatru Bucharest – 1 December 2019
- 'Kollokvium' Festival of Minority Theatres, Figura Studio Gheorgheni – 17 October 2019
- Festival for Young Audiences, FIX Theatre Iași – 4 October 2019
- 11+1 Independent Contemporary Festival, 'Marin Sorescu' National Theatre of Craiova – 1 October 2019
- Roma Theatre Is Not Nomadic/'Zilele Clujului', Hungarian Theatre of Cluj, Romania – 28 September 2019
- Bucharest Pride 2019, National Centre of Dance Bucharest – 24 June 2019

Lowlands

Herta Müller

Stage adaptation by Mihaela Panainte
Translated into English by Jozefina Komporaly
(Original title in German: *Niederungen*)

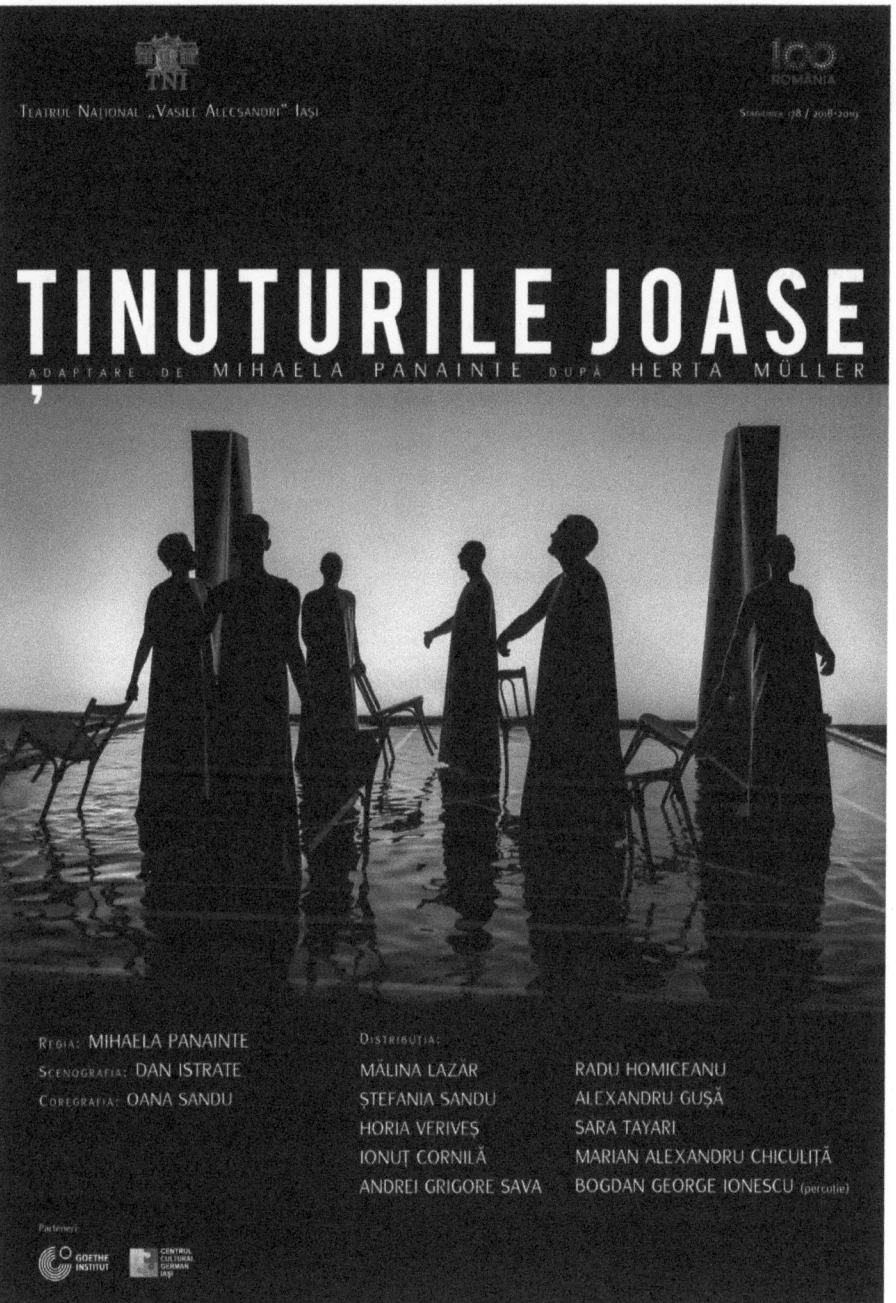

1 Herta Müller/Mihaela Panainte: *Lowlands* – Vasile Alecsandri National Theatre of Iași, Romania (directed by Mihaela Panainte). Premiere: 13 October 2018. Poster design: Mihaela Panainte.

Characters

Narrator
Child Narrator
Chorus
Mother
Father
Grandmother
Grandfather
Aunt
Tony
Blonde Girl
Man with Matchsticks
Scarecrow

Scene One: Workday (I)

Chorus   20, 21, 22, 23, 24, 25, 26, 27, 28, 29 . . . driiiiin . . .

Narrator + Child Narrator   Five thirty.

Chorus   The alarm rings.

Narrator + Child Narrator   I get up, slip out of my dress, place it on the pillow, put my pyjamas on, go to the kitchen, get into the bathtub, take the towel, wash my face with it, take the comb, dry myself with it, take the toothbrush, comb my hair with it, take the sponge, clean my teeth with it. I go to the bathroom, eat a slice of tea and drink a cup of bread . . .

I remove my wristwatch and my rings.

I take my shoes off.

I go to the stairwell and open the front door.

I take the elevator from the fifth to the first floor, walk up nine flights of stairs and find myself in the street.

I buy a newspaper, walk to the nearest stop to pick up some buns, and get on the tram.

Three stops before boarding the tram, I get off.

I respond to the porter's greeting, he says hello and points out that it's Monday again, yet another week is over.

I go to my office, and say

Chorus   Goodbye!

Narrator + Child Narrator   I hang my jacket on the desk, take a seat at the coat rack and start working. I work for

Chorus   1, 2, 3, 4, 5, 6, 7, eight hours.

Scene Two: Obituary (I)

Narrator   Coffin . . . Father was lying in a coffin . . .

Mother   in the middle of the room.

Narrator   There were so many pictures hanging everywhere . . .

Mother   one could just about see the wall.

Narrator   In one of the pictures, Father was half as tall as the chair . . .

Mother   he was holding on to.

Narrator   He was wearing a dress, with rolls of fat on his bow legs.

Mother   In another picture, Father was the bridegroom.

Narrator   One could only see half of his chest. The other half was a bunch of wilted white flowers you were holding in your hand.

Mother   Our heads were held so close together that our earlobes kept touching.

Narrator   In another picture, Father was standing upright by a fence. In the picture next to this, Father had a hoe resting on his shoulder. In the following picture, Father was behind the steering wheel of a truck. In all these pictures, Father was captured frozen in mid-gesture. In all these pictures, Father looked as if he had no idea what to do next.

Mother   But Father always knew what to do.

Narrator   That's why all these pictures were false.

Child Narrator   I wanted to get off the chair, but my dress got frozen to the wooden seat. My dress was see-through and black. It crackled as I moved. I got up and touched Father's face.

All   The coffin was swinging. Their arms and ropes got longer and longer. Despite the drought, the grave was filled with water.

Scene Three: Village Chronicle (School)

Narrator   The church?

Tony   Right in the centre of the village.

Narrator   The cooperative store?

Tony   Next to the barbershop.

Man with Matchsticks   The villagers call it . . .

All   'the shop.'

Man with Matchsticks   It's five square metres and stocks pots and pans,

Tony   scarves,

Blonde Girl   marmalade,

Tony   salt, fustian cloth, slippers . . .

Man with Matchsticks   and a stack of books from the early sixties.

Tony   Ever since only eleven pupils and four teachers have been left in the village, they were known together as . . .

All   the primary school . . .

Blonde Girl   In our village, women are called Magdalena,

All   Leni,

Blonde Girl   or Theresia,

Scene Three: Village Chronicle (School)

All   Resi.

Blonde Girl   The men in our village have names like Matthias,

All   Matz,

Blonde Girl   or Johann,

All   Hans.

Aunt   How about family names in our village?

All   Shoemaker, Taylor, Wheeler, Woolf, Bear, Fox.

Tony   There are also two additional names . . . Shudder and Bungler. Aside from these, there are a few nicknames, such as . . .

All   Troublemaker, Shifty, Pennypincher.

Tony   Next to the cooperative store is the Cultural Centre.

Child Narrator   The Cultural Centre is where the village festival, the *Kerwei*, is held when it's raining.

Man with Matchsticks   And weddings, too, in case it's raining, hailing, snowing or the weather is nice.

Tony   Next to the marketplace is the People's Council.

All   'The Community Hall'.

Tony   Among those in attendance, there are . . .

Man with Matchsticks   some smokers who are smoking with their heads in the clouds,

Tony   non-smokers who aren't smoking but sleeping, alcoholics,

Aunt   you mean 'drunkards',

Child Narrator   who keep their bottles under their seats,

Man with Matchsticks   as well as non-alcoholics and non-smokers

Aunt   who are plain stupid.

Tony   People display ornamental trinkets on their furniture, in our village these are called

All   'figurines',

Tony   that represent all sorts of living beings, from beetles to butterflies and horses. Very popular are

Mother   lions,

Man with Matchsticks   giraffes,

Tony   elephants and polar bears.

26   Lowlands

Tony   The dead in our village have eaten and drunk themselves to death,

All   worked themselves to death.

Tony   With the exception of the heroes,

All   'the fallen',

Tony   about whom everybody assumes that

All   they fought themselves to death.

Tony   The heroes,

All   'the fallen',

Aunt   are given two burials in the same cemetery: first in their family grave, and then under the Memorial Cross. In actual fact, these heroes lie elsewhere, in some unknown mass grave, which in the village is called

All   'remaining in the war'.

Narrator   I close the black cemetery gate behind me. I climb a tree on the edge of the meadow, even though it could just as well be in the village centre, and perhaps it is actually there. I hold on to a branch with both hands and can see as far as the church in the next village, where, on the third step, a ladybird is cleaning its right wing.

Scene Four: *Kerwei*

Narrator   Ever since the village had shrunk in size, because people migrated either to Germany or to the nearby towns, church and village festivals, such as the *Kerwei*, had grown bigger and bigger. We'd laugh till late into the night, by which point the lights would come on in the village. Music would be playing. The pairs would follow the one leading the dance.

Scene Five: My Family

Narrator   My mother . . .

Scarecrow   is a woman in disguise.

Narrator   My grandmother . . .

Scarecrow   is blind from cataracts. In one eye, she has a grey cataract, in the other, she has a green cataract.

Narrator   My grandfather . . .

Scarecrow   has a hernia.

Narrator   My father . . .

Scarecrow   has another child by another woman.

Narrator   The other child is older than me . . .

Scarecrow   that's because he was fathered by another man.

Narrator   My father gives Christmas presents to this other child . . .

Scarecrow   and tells my mother that the other child was fathered by another man.

Narrator   My mother says that I'm not the child of another man though. Grandmother married Grandfather because he owned a field, despite being in love with another man. She says that it would have been better to marry the other man . . .

Scarecrow   because she is closely related to my grandfather, and this is plain incest.

Narrator   Other people say that my mother is the child of another man and so is my uncle, though not the same man but another one. That's why another child's grandfather is my grandfather, and people say that my grandfather is the grandfather of someone else . . .

Scarecrow   though not of the same child, but another one.

Narrator   And my great-grandmother? She died at a very young age of a supposed flu, but that was in fact something quite different, not natural death but suicide. Other people say that it was actually something other than both illness and suicide, namely murder. Year in, year out, my great-grandfather would go to a small spa town.

Scarecrow   He was even seen in public holding the hand of another child, with whom he spoke in a different language.

Narrator   That is worse than pure incest, that's an outright disgrace!

Scene Six: Cursed Woman

Grandfather   Once upon a time, a man died in the open field. He was struck by lightning. He was the first husband of this woman, who then married her brother-in-law that later died of lung disease; she carried on living on her own because nobody would marry her, but when her son had grown up, the one that looked like the ragman and had a tuft of grey hair under his temple, unlike anyone in the village, she married a man from a nearby village; he's still alive and had to carry his own child to baptism, seeing that nobody wanted to be the godfather in fear that they'd also be taken by death if they got anywhere near this woman's child.

Scene Seven: You'll End Up a Blockhead . . .

Grandfather   You mustn't eat corkscrew grass, it turns you into a blockhead. You don't want to end up a blockhead.

Narrator A beetle crawled into my ear. Grandfather poured some alcohol in my ear, to make sure the beetle didn't get into my head. I cried.

Grandfather We have to do this, otherwise the beetle creeps into your head, and you'll end up a blockhead. You don't want to end up a blockhead. You mustn't eat acacia blossoms, they contain black midges and if these get into your throat, you'll end up dumb. You don't want to end up a blockhead.

Narrator Caterpillars have once been butterflies, they emerge from their cocoons. They leave a gooey cottonwool behind them, sticking to the vine branches.

Child Narrator Grandpa, where did the first butterfly come from?

Grandfather Give me a break with these silly questions! Nobody knows, just go play!

Grandfather If a bee flies into your mouth, you die. It stings you on the palate and the roof of your mouth swells up, so you suffocate.

Child Narrator While picking flowers, I kept thinking that I wasn't allowed to open my mouth.

Yet I really felt like singing every now and then. So I clenched my teeth, crushing my song.

Narrator My well-behaved child, who's dumb and has no neck, arms, legs, hands or face.

Scene Eight: Scarecrow

Scarecrow The sun goes down at the end of the street. A sack plunges down the village, bringing the night sewn into it. Next thing, the lights are being put out in the dark rooms. At night, dreams sneak into people's beds, having made their way from the backyard.

Narrator At times, I'm just lying in bed still, but even so, I can hear the sound of rustling.

Scarecrow Fear descends!

Narrator I fear that the tall man was in the room,

Scarecrow that bony one,

Narrator about whom everybody knew that he didn't need to work . . .

Scarecrow because he had sold that huge skeleton to the museum.

Narrator This man was in my room for nights on end. I keep seeing him behind the curtain and under the bed . . .

Scarecrow This isn't fear as such, but fear of fear, fear of forgetting to be afraid, fear of the fear of being afraid.

Scene Nine: The Man with Matchsticks

Man with Matchsticks   The village burns down night after night. The clouds are the first to burn. Dusk tumbles through the streets. That's when there's a smouldering somewhere down below, in the haystacks and the weeds.

Narrator   And there's only one person in the know, the man with matchsticks . . .

Man with Matchsticks   who carries his hatred through the potato plants, all the way to the back of the cornfield. As a frail child, he had to lug sacks across the rocky field and hoe carrots. At this house, he was meant to sleep in the barn.

Narrator   At this house, a girl his age, who had her blonde hair in braids and would eat oranges in winter, called him a servant.

Man with Matchsticks   The flames flare up at once, writhing in their fiery red skirts and climbing onto the roof tiles. On the sky above the village, the embers are ablaze.

Child Narrator   I am the one who started the fire.

Scene Ten: The Woman Next Door

Narrator   We're sharing a meal and having all sorts of things on our minds. I'm thinking about something else while eating. I don't see with their eyes, and don't hear with their ears. I don't have their hands, either.

Aunt   I'd only been married for three days. It was a wartime marriage that took place during my husband's short leave from the front. He had to go back straightaway. Then it was time for Russia, together with its harsh winters, and I hadn't received any sign of life from him or any notice of his death ever since. Night after night, I carried on waiting for him to knock on my window.

Mother   Her face remains unchanged. She looks exactly the same when she talks about the weather.

Scene Eleven: Peaceful and Quiet Evening

Narrator + Child Narrator   Then there were those few quiet evenings. Night would fall in all the quarters, leaning against the fences with its back. My shoes were trodding carefully across the yard. There wasn't a slightest breeze in the trees. Wherever I went, a glass barrier was formed between myself and the things of the world. One could make out several cats in their reflection. My face, however, was barefoot. I was wearing a dress in humid air. I found a pair of large shoes by the door. They belonged to my father. Grandmother and Grandfather were already in their bedroom. One could hear the radio through the wall. Mother and Father were barely talking to one another, and this little was mainly about money and about the cow. There were nights, when I was allowed to comb Father's hair. He had thick hair. I was looking out for bits of grey. I was allowed to create a parting, tie up his hair with a ribbon, cover his head with a handkerchief, or hang a scarf or a necklace or two around his neck.

Father Take your hands off there!

Narrator The only place I wasn't allowed to touch was Father's face.

Child Narrator That moment I knew that I had no parents, these two didn't mean anything to me,

Narrator and I wondered what I was doing with them in this house and kitchen, being familiar with their pots, pans and habits, and why didn't I leave home, go to another village, to be among strangers, and stay in each house for just a moment and then head off, before people could get the chance to turn evil.

Child Narrator May a hand grow out of your nose or your cheeks that you'd always have to carry on your face and couldn't make go away.

Mother He would have liked to play with you, but you had to ruin everything, why don't you just stop whining once and for all.

Narrator + Child Narrator Mother has a broom.

Scene Twelve: Scene with Brooms

Mother Mother has a broom . . .

Aunt that she uses for sweeping the bedrooms . . .

Tony another for the kitchen . . .

Aunt another for the front garden . . .

Tony another for the back yard . . .

Aunt a broom for the cow stable . . .

Tony another for the pigsty and the henhouse . . .

Aunt one for the woodshed and one for the barn . . .

Tony one for the house, another for the pavement, and yet another for the lawn.

Narrator Mother buys a new broom every single month. With her new broom, Mother first cleans the walls.

Mother Mother has several brooms for the summer . . .

Narrator to gather the fallen leaves.

Mother Mother has several brooms for the winter, too . . .

Narrator to sweep the snow that covers the yard and the streets.

Mother Mother sweeps the dust off the pendulum.

Narrator   She opens its tiny door and sweeps the clockface.

Mother   With her smallest broom, mother sweeps . . .

Narrator   the water jug, the candlesticks, the lampshade, the glasses case and the medicine boxes.

Mother   Mother sweeps . . .

Narrator   the radio knobs, the cover of the prayerbook and of the family photo album. She yanks off the spiderwebs. The spiders seek refuge underneath the furniture.

Mother   Mother finds them even there . . .

Narrator   she lies down on her belly and squashes them with her thumb.

Mother   In the table drawer, Mother keeps a special broom

Narrator   for breadcrumbs . . .

Father   With all these brooms, Mother keeps the entire house nice and tidy.

Scene Thirteen: Bells Ringing for Morning Mass

Child Narrator   Grandma!

Grandmother   The bells are ringing for morning mass!

Narrator   Every time I took a seat in the front pew, where children were meant to sit, the Virgin Mary would raise her index finger. Her face was friendly though, so I wasn't afraid of her. She'd always wear a long, pale blue dress, and she had pretty lips. The sky was in fact a wall in the church. It was sky-blue and dotted with stars.

Child Narrator   Grandma, which one is the evening star?

Grandmother   You fool!

Child Narrator   I tell myself that this Mary isn't the real Mary but a woman made of plaster, the angel isn't a real angel, either, or the sheep real sheep, and that this blood is nothing but oil paint.

Scene Fourteen: Geraniums in Soup Bowls

Grandmother   Grandfather's pockets are all full of nails.

Grandfather   Grandmother can't imagine anything more beautiful than some geraniums in a soup bowl.

Grandmother   Even the pockets of his Sunday best are full of nails.

Mother   Your father didn't touch me on our wedding night. He threw up in the toilet, and then slept on the floor.

Father   We're a happy family, for fuck's sake!

Aunt   It was May, and the cherries had already ripened. Spring had arrived very early that year. Your father and I went to pick cherries on our own.

Mother   We didn't exchange a single word on our way back. Your father didn't come near me even when we were all alone in that huge, deserted orchard.

Father   For fuck's sake, happiness goes out of the window as soon as the broth begins to boil . . .

Grandfather   She has a shelf of geraniums in the hallway, a shelf of geraniums near the door leading to the staircase, and a shelf of geraniums by the garden door.

Grandmother   One can hear two sounds at once when he's hammering, one coming from the hammer and the other from the village.

Aunt   Straight as a pole, he was standing at some distance from me, spitting out wet slithery pits.

Mother   I knew at once that he'd often beat me in the course of our life together.

Father   For fuck's sake, anger grabs hold of us in a wink, happiness grabs hold of us in a wink, for fuck's sake, happiness swallows our lives right up.

Grandfather   She has geraniums planted in soup bowls, both in the living room and kitchen window. The sandpile by the pigsty is also covered in geranium seedlings, and there are dozens of soup bowls hanging from the beams, too.

Grandmother   Grandfather never said a word about them. In his eyes, the geraniums were neither ugly, nor pretty. It would be pointless to expect him to do that even now. Grandfather hadn't said a word about them to this day.

Narrator   Mother is crying and talking, Mother is talking and crying. Mother is talking while crying, and crying while talking. When Grandfather died, she took all the geraniums to his room. Grandfather was lying in state amidst a forest of geraniums planted in soup bowls.

Grandmother   This morning, they've got up to cry, then they've had breakfast and lunch in order to cry some more. In the afternoon, they've loosened the tie cords on their aprons and smocks, letting them drop to the floor, and have taken their black garments out of the wardrobe. As they make their way to the wardrobe, they look up to the ceiling so they don't see themselves naked, after all there's nowhere in the house where acts known as shameful or lewd couldn't take place. Wearing clothes, one is human, without clothes, one is not. Such a huge surface of skin! They put on their clothes in order to cry, get dressed in black from the tip of their toes to the fringes of their angular headscarves, and keep swaying their creases back and forth. Their large cold eyes are transfixed and they get the chills in the candle-lit room laden with fake flowers and the stench of death, where the devil has paralysed behind the door in fear of the mirror covered in black Swabian aprons, so that the prayers of the living and the soul of the deceased can make it to heaven.

Narrator + Child Narrator   Gaunt and cold, such were the hands of the old people I'd see resting in their canopy beds, in front of whom everybody would just sit in silence and pray. Grandma used to call such beds coffins, and the people lying in them, dead. She imagined that I didn't understand what she meant by this word. But I did, without ever having heard it before. I couldn't understand why everything connected with death had to be always locked up behind four walls, so we could never see it except when everything had already come to an end, despite having lived side by side for a lifetime.

Scene Fifteen: Beautiful Women on the Train

Narrator   A lovely train used to pass by the river. Seeing it, I'd jump with joy and wave. Sometimes, there were women in beautiful summer dresses in the windows. I knew that these women would never get off at our small station, precisely because it was far too small. The train was taking these beautiful women to town, while I'd end my days next to a pile of horse dung surrounded by a swarm of buzzing flies. I was looking forward to my death. I imagined that my family would wonder how I could possibly die so unexpectedly. My mother would cry a lot for me, and the entire village would be able to see how much she had loved me. But death still failed to come and get me.

Scene Sixteen: The Town

Narrator   Later, when I came to town, I did see dying in the streets even before it came to a proper end.

People would collapse on the pavement, twitching and whimpering, and they didn't belong to anyone. Once, I ended up on my own with a dead stranger. I scuttled off and kept looking up, as if from the bottom of an abyss, at the blocks of flats, saying that from where I'd come from, people didn't just lie in the streets but in canopy beds, in front of which people would sit in silence and pray. And that they, the dead, were being preserved for quite some time in the house. Only when their ears started to turn green and their bodies began to decompose did people stop crying and take them out of the village.

Grandmother   Suicides don't take place in beds, because village folk are wise enough not to lose their common sense at an advanced age. The biggest cross is the Memorial Cross.

Scene Seventeen: The Swabian Bath

Narrator   The Swabian bath.

Mother   It's Saturday night.

Grandmother The bath stove has a glowing belly.

Grandfather The trickle vent is shut tight.

Mother The water is still boiling hot!

Child Narrator The soap is making bubbles.

Mother Mother is rubbing grey rolls off her neck. Mother's rolls are floating on the surface of the water.

Narrator The bathtub has a yellow ring.

Mother The water is still hot!

Father The water is warm.

Child Narrator The soap is making bubbles.

Father Father is rubbing grey rolls off his chest.

All Father's rolls, together with Mother's rolls, are floating on the surface of the water.

Narrator The bathtub has a brown ring.

Father The water is still hot!

Grandmother The water is lukewarm.

Child Narrator The soap is making bubbles.

Grandmother Grandmother is rubbing grey rolls off her shoulders.

All Grandmother's rolls are floating together with Mother's and Father's rolls on the surface of the water.

Narrator The bathtub has a black ring.

Grandmother The water is still hot.

Grandfather The water is ice cold.

Child Narrator The soap is making bubbles.

Grandfather Grandfather is rubbing grey rolls off his elbows.

All Grandfather's rolls are floating together with Mother's, Father's and Grandmother's rolls on the surface of the water.

Narrator Grandfather lets the water out of the bathtub. Mother's, Father's, Grandmother's and Grandfather's rolls are whirling together above the drain.

Scene Eighteen: Obituary (II)

Narrator The mourners gathered on the opposite side of the grave. I took a quick look at myself and got scared because one could see my breasts. I was cold.

Everybody was staring at me. Their eyes looked empty, with pupils stabbing from under the eyelids. The men had guns on their shoulders, while the women were rattling their rosaries. A man tugged at a rose. He tore off a blood-red petal and started to eat it. The speaker waved at me with their hand. I knew that it was my turn to make a speech. Everybody was looking at me. A man rested his walking stick against a rock. He positioned the gun and aimed at one of my sleeves. When it dropped to the ground in front of me, it was covered in blood. The mourners clapped. My arm was bare. I could feel it petrify in the air. The speaker beckoned the mourners. The applause came to an end at once.

Scene Nineteen: Winter

Tony   It was snowing in the valley. Heaps of snow had fallen, and the county had vanished overnight without a trace. Cars coming from the village had lost their way. Huge shiny crows kept scratching around the snow to find their nests. See-through and barren, and climbing to the sky, the trees were trembling from the cold. The clouds huddled together due to the frost. The wild geese were deafening themselves with the piercing noise of their own honking. Meanwhile the postman, getting to the village only in the afternoon, got practically blinded because the road was entirely hidden under the snow. His face was shimmering. When I opened the newspaper, snow fell out from between the pages, and I could see that it was actually made up of stars, larger and whiter than the ones falling on the village. I got dressed. My hands were shaking as I buttoned my clothes. My sleeves and my trouserlegs felt like a sack. All my clothes felt like a sack. The whole room felt like a sack. I myself felt like a sack.

The icicles, suddenly branching out, would carry with them large mirrors. In every icicle, one could see a frozen image – the village.

It looked as though it had never been built from scratch but rather tossed down, ready-made, after having been dragged here from some distant place or other.

Scene Twenty: Night

Scarecrow   The night is no monster, all it contains is a touch of wind and sleep. The mothers are asleep. The fathers are asleep, the grandmothers are asleep, the grandfathers are asleep, the children are asleep, the pets are asleep. The village stands there in the landscape like a chest. Mother doesn't cry, Father doesn't drink, Grandfather doesn't work with the hammer, Grandmother doesn't have her poppy, Wendel doesn't stammer. They're all resting to be fit tomorrow, and tomorrow they'll be exactly the same as they were today. An endless number of feet are lying on the field, one next to the other.

Narrator   I had seen Mother lying naked and frozen in Russia, with her feet covered in wounds and her cheeks turned green from fodder beet. I had seen Mother translucent from hunger, drained and worn-out like an exhausted little girl, having lost all her sensations. Mother had fallen asleep. I could never hear her breathe when she was awake. But when she was asleep, she'd snore as if she still had the Siberian wind in her throat, with me lying frozen by her side, haunted by terrible nightmares.

Scene Twenty-One: The Window

Narrator   I lay down in the tall grass, dripping into the ground right away. I was waiting for the big willows to come to me from the other side of the river, and to root their branches and spread their leaves in me. I was hoping for them to say that I was the most beautiful swamp in the world. We shall all come to you. We shall also bring our tall slender waterbirds with us, but note that they will flap their wings and scream in you. And you won't be able to weep, because swamps have to be brave, and you'll have to put up with everything once you've decided to join us . . . 20, 21, 22, 23, 24, 25, 26, 27, 28, 29. . . . It's Saturday, half past five in the morning.

The End.

The Spectator Sentenced to Death

Matéi Visniec

Translated from the Romanian by Jozefina Komporaly
(Original title in Romanian: *Spectatorul condamnat la moarte*)

Play in two acts

2 Matéi Visniec: *The Spectator Sentenced to Death* – Le Théâtre de . . . Nantes (directed by Claude Kagan). Premiere 8 June 2009.

Characters

Judge
Prosecutor
Defence Counsel
Court Clerk
Witness 1 – *the man who checks tickets*
Witness 2 – *the young girl from the cloakroom*
Witness 3 – *the fat woman from the bar*
Witness 4 – *the theatre photographer*
Witness 5 – *a spectator*
Witness 6 – *the director*
Witness 7 – *the author*
Witness 8 – *a man waiting in front of the theatre*
Witness 9 – *the blind man playing the harmonica at the street corner*
Sergeant
Soldiers, citizens, heads

Act One

The performance space is laid out like a courtoom. Right at the front of the stage, on a pedestal, there is the mask of the **Judge**. *Slightly lower, there are the desks of the two counsels, for the* **Prosecution** *and* **Defence**. *Some of the spectators will be randomly selected to sit on the jury. A spectator will take a seat on the chair reserved for the* **Defendant**.

The entire court, with the exception of the **Defence Counsel**, *is waiting, looking sombre and cadaverous, for the auditorium to settle. The* **Prosecutor** *takes a few steps, stares at the* **Defendant**, *then adresses the audience in a serious voice.*

Prosecutor Ladies and gentlemen, there's a criminal among us.

Judge (*calmly*) My learned friend, may I draw your attention to procedure. Nobody can be classed as a criminal until a crime is actually proven.

Prosecutor (*tenaciously, to the audience*) Ladies and gentlemen, there is no need to prove anything. The crime is written on his face.

Judge (*hitting the gavel*) I have to remind you once more that there is a mandatory procedure in place.

Prosecutor (*ignoring the* **Judge**, *and addressing the audience*) Our criminal is right here! (*Points at the* **Defendant**.)

Judge (*furiously*) This is no way to go about it!

Prosecutor (*furiously*) Nothing and nobody will hinder us from making things right! This man has to be executed right here, right now!

Judge (*keeps hitting the gavel louder and louder*) My learned friend! I forbid you to address the court in such a . . .

Prosecutor (*demented*) Get hold of him! Tear him to pieces! This man has to die, look at his face, just look at him! This man has to die right here, this very evening, crushed to death under the soles of our feet! Ladies and gentlemen, don't let yourselves be deceived!

Judge (*fuming*) Order!

Prosecutor (*with paroxysm*) It's pointless to waste any more time! Let's kill him and go home!

Judge (*howling*) This man must stand trial!

Prosecutor (*also yelling, to the audience*) I beg you, kill him! It makes no sense to prolong all this. This way, we'll gain time, time, time! (*To the* **Defendant**.) Stand up you beast!

Judge (*to the* **Court Clerk**) What's with this commotion?

Court Clerk (*scared*) No idea. He's insane.

Prosecutor (*twitching*) Right here, right now! I'll kill him with my very own hands. Who's for it? (*Running up and down the auditorium.*) Who's for it?

Judge (*to the* **Court Clerk**) Make him shut up!

Prosecutor (*among the spectators*) Who's for it? Let's have a show of hands! Come on, up with your hands! Hey you, why don't you raise your hand? Cowards! Raise those hands once and for all!

Court Clerk (*grabs hold of the* **Prosecutor** *and drags him towards the raised platform*) Shut your trap!

Prosecutor Get off me!

Court Clerk (*furiously, to the* **Judge**) Your Honour, I'll beat him up!

Prosecutor (*to the audience*) You cowards! Make a move, do something! (*To the* **Court Clerk**, *while trying to slip away.*) Leave me alone!

Judge Order, or I shall evacuate the room!

Court Clerk (*to the* **Judge**) No way, people have paid good money!

Prosecutor We don't need their money! (*Produces some banknotes and coins and throws them around the auditorium.*) Take your money back! Take it and clear out of here!

Court Clerk (*drags the* **Prosecutor** *all the way up the* **Judge**) What shall I do with him?

Judge Give him a drink of water.

Court Clerk (*throws a glass of water in the* **Prosecutor's** *face*) Shall I give him some more?

Judge Ask him.

Court Clerk Would you like some more water, sir?

Prosecutor (*slowly coming back to normal, gasping*) I . . . (*Shakes his head.*) I'm sorry if I . . . (*Blows his nose.*) All I wanted was to . . .

Court Clerk Shall I light your cigarette?

Prosecutor All I wanted . . . (*Dries himself on the forehead and face with a tissue.*) It would have been better for everyone if . . .

Judge (*grabs the* **Prosecutor** *by the collar*) Can you see me?

Prosecutor (*almost his usual self*) Yes.

Judge Can you hear me?

Prosecutor Perfectly.

Judge It's no fun if we don't observe the law.

Prosecutor I have witnesses, Your Honour! He's a detestable criminal, rotten to the core. I can produce witnesses!

Judge Do it then. (*Takes a sip of water, rinses his mouth and swallows.*) Quickly.

Prosecutor (*arranges his attire and takes a seat at the table reserved for him*) Bring in the first witness!

Witness 1 (*enters, looking fairly self-assured, bows in front of the court and begins to rattle on*) Ladies and gentlemen, the man you see here . . .

Prosecutor Your name and profession!

Witness 1 My name is Bruno. I'm the usher.

Judge Phua! (*To the* **Prosecutor**.) Continue!

Prosecutor Tell me, Bruno, for how long have you been checking tickets here?

Witness 1 Ten years.

Prosecutor Every night?

Witness 1 Every single night.

Prosecutor Tonight included?

Witness 1 Yes.

Prosecutor Please take a look in the auditorium. Can you see any well-known figures?

Witness 1 (*takes a look*) Yes, I can.

Prosecutor Who?

Witness 1 Everyone. I know them all. He's the only person I don't know. (*Points at a spectator in the first row.*) Maybe he got in through the stage door.

Prosecutor Take a look at the man in front of you.

Witness 1 (*takes a look*) I just have.

Prosecutor What can you say about him?

Witness 1 You want me to say what I think about him?

Prosecutor Tell us everything that happened.

Witness 1 I don't dare, sir.

Prosecutor It's in the interest of the law, Bruno.

Witness 1 I can't say, I can't possibly say . . . (*Agitated.*)

Judge (*banging the gavel*) Shut it! You'll tell us all! Raise your hand! Swear that you'll only tell the truth, the whole truth and nothing but the truth!

Prosecutor (*urging the intimidated* **Witness**) Raise it!

Court Clerk (*whispering*)   Raise it!

Judge   Higher!

Prosecutor   Like so! Repeat after me! I swear that I will tell the truth, the whole truth and nothing but the truth!

Court Clerk (*whispering*)   Say it!

Witness 1 (*with tears in his eyes*)   You're wrecking me, sir . . .

Judge   Say it!

Witness 1 (*swallowing hard*)   I swear that I will tell the truth, the whole truth and nothing but the truth.

Judge   Leave him alone!

Witness 1 (*takes a few steps towards the* **Defendant**)   Sir, please know that I mean no harm . . .

Prosecutor   Bruno! (**Witness 1** *returns to his place*.) Sit down, Bruno. (*Stands up and takes a few steps around him*.) Try to recall: when have you first seen this man?

Witness 1   Fifteen minutes ago.

Prosecutor   In what circumstaces?

Witness 1   It was a dead end . . .

Prosecutor   Meaning?

Witness 1   I was at my usual place.

Prosecutor   Tell us where that is.

Witness 1   By the door. I was waiting for the clock to strike half past.

Prosecutor   Perfect.

Witness 1   At half past, on the dot, I opened the theatre doors.

Prosecutor   Did you see anybody in the foyer?

Witness 1   The foyer was almost full.

Prosecutor   Can you point out a few people who were in the foyer?

Witness 1 (*looks around*)   I think so.

Prosecutor   Please do then.

Witness 1   Well, I think this gentleman was there . . . (*Points at a spectator*.) And they, too . . . And that gentleman with the double chin . . .

Prosecutor   The acccused, was he also in the foyer?

Witness 1   No, I don't think so.

Prosecutor   Think about this very carefully.

Witness 1   No, I'm sure he wasn't.

Prosecutor   Perhaps he was in front of the box office. Can you see the box office from where you are usually standing to check tickets?

Witness 1   Yes, perfectly.

Prosecutor   Were there many people by the box office?

Witness 1   Yes, some people were waiting there.

Prosecutor   Can you affirm under oath that the accused wasn't waiting by the box office?

Witness 1   Most definitely, he wasn't.

Prosecutor   Very well, continue. What happened after you opened the doors?

Witness 1   The spectators started to arive.

Prosecutor   Could you indicate the first person to arrive?

Witness 1 (*looks around*)   Yes, I think so.

Prosecutor   How about the second to arrive?

Witness 1 (*looks around the auditorium again*)   Yes, I think so.

Prosecutor   And the third?

Witness 1 (*takes his time looking*)   Perhaps, not quite sure . . . But I could point out the fourth!

Prosecutor   Take a good look at the accused. Could you tell me approximately at which point he arrived?

Witness 1   No, I don't think I could.

Prosecutor   Still, do try to remember. Do you think the accused got in with the first or the second half of the audience?

Witness 1   I think he must have got in with the second half.

Prosecutor   How do you know?

Witness 1   I feel it.

Prosecutor   How can you feel such a thing?

Witness 1   Based on their appearance.

Judge (*banging on his desk with his palm*)   Liar!

Witness 1   I'm not lying, Your Honour. I learned to distinguish between people's appearances after ten years.

Judge   What appearances?

Witness 1 There are different kinds. Some are meant to get in with the first half, and others with the second. I can estimate with an error margin of one per cent who is meant to get in with the first and who with the second half.

Judge And it seems to you that this man is meant for the second half?

Witness 1 Absolutely. I'm convinced that he was one of the last people to get in, but not late enough to stand out.

Prosecutor Let's get down to business. You're saying that everybody who is in the auditorium went past you.

Witness 1 Yes, with a few exceptions. (*Makes an attempt at charging at the spectator who came in through the stage door.*)

Prosecutor Do you normally look the people walking past you in the eye?

Witness 1 No, I have no time for this. I only look at their hands.

Prosecutor Why their hands? And not the eyes, too?

Witness 1 Because I have to pay attention to the tickets. It's natural that I should look at their hands.

Prosecutor Please come closer and take a look at the hands of the defendant. Do you recognize these hands?

Witness 1 (*awkwardly*) Sir, the defendant is hiding his hands . . .

Prosecutor What?!

Witness 1 I mean he's keeping them too close to his body. I can't see them.

Prosecutor (*furiously*) Your Honour, the defendant doesn't want to show his hands.

Judge Shame on you! What a disgrace! Don't you imagine that in this way you can hinder the course of this hearing. We know all there is to know about you! Your hands are right here, multiplied in thousands of copies! (*From a drawer, he produces a pile of photographs showing hands from all possible angles, and throws these around the auditorium.*) Look at your hands! We know everything, we know about each and every wart and crease! Don't be so naïve to think that you can hide your hands! (*Pulls on a lever and suddenly the lights fade and two interconnected hands are projected onto a huge screen.*) There you go! (*To* **Witness 1**.) Do you recognize this?

Witness 1 Yes! These are his hands!

Prosecutor Are you sure?

Witness 1 They are definitely his! It was with these very hands that he held my ticket and returned the part I was supposed to keep!

Judge What?!

Court Clerk Are you sure, Bruno?

Prosecutor (*triumphant, calming the spirits*)   Just a moment! (*To the* **Witness**.) Repeat word by word.

Judge (*shaken*)   Are you suggesting that this man walked up to you and held out his ticket so you could tear it off?

Witness 1 (*troubled*)   Yes . . .

Judge   I'll kill him!

Prosecutor   I've told you! He should have been killed with the first shot.

Judge   I've had enough! This makes me sick!

Prosecutor (*to* **Witness 1**)   Tell us everyhing! Absolutely everything!

Witness 1   Well, after I checked his ticket he entered the auditorium . . .

Court Clerk   With these very hands?

Judge   Sergeant! (*Twitching and rattling at the doors.*) Sergeant! Take him away! Take him! (*Enter the* **Sergeant**.) Out! Everybody out! Security! Evacuate the room! Out with this criminal . . . (*Starts punching* **Witness 1**.) Why did you let him in? Why? Why did you let him?

Prosecutor   Your Honour, please . . . there's no point in this!

Judge   Shut it, you little snot! Shut it! (*To the soldiers who are approaching, stomping their feet with a hellish noise.*) Security! Everybody out on the street! (*The soldiers enter the stage from two sides and surround the spectators, menacingly raising their rubber batons in the air.*)

Judge   Go home! Everybody, go home! (*Produces a gun.*) Where is he? (*Charging after the* **Defendant** *in a frenzy, while the* **Court Clerk** *and the* **Prosecutor** *are trying to calm him down.*) I'll shoot him! I'll shoot him with my own hands!

Defence Counsel (*dashes in through the door where the spectators have also entered*)   Idiots! (*Challenging the* **Judge**.) Why did you let him drink?

Judge   I'll smash him to smithereens!

Defence Counsel (*harshly*)   Shut up, you old codger! (*To the* **Sergeant**.) Sergeant! Get out of here!

Sergeant   But, sir, I . . .

Defence Counsel   Shut it! Take your troops with you and clear out!

Sergeant *blows his whistle and the soldiers withdraw at once.*

Defence Counsel (*shaking the* **Judge**)   You've started without me? Are you out of your mind? (*To the* **Prosecutor**.) How could you take the liberty to start in the absence of the defence counsel?

Prosecutor   You know, your father-in-law saw fit that . . .

Defence Counsel (*about to crush him, screeching*)   What father-in-law? (*Dragging the* **Judge** *back to his place.*) Enough, enough with all this bullshit! Nobody says another word! (*To* **Witness 1**.) Who the hell are you?

Witness 1   I'm Witness . . . (*Standing up.*)

Defence Counsel   Stay right there! (*To the* **Judge**.) Are you in pain?

Judge (*gasping for air*)   I'm dead . . .

Defence Counsel   Did you get mad?

Judge (*gasping*)   I did, big time. My throat hurts.

Defence Counsel   Water! Bring him some water!

The **Court Clerk** *pulls a lever: two palms are being shown on the screen as they are being washed.*

Defence Counsel   I said water!

Court Clerk   In a moment! (*He gives it a few goes on the lever and finally the lights come on.*) It's on your desk.

Defence Counsel (*gives some water to the* **Judge**)   Stop howling, okay?

Judge   I won't howl.

Defence Counsel   And don't you start without me again.

Judge   We won't.

Defence Counsel   Don't you move from here.

Judge   How's Grete?

Defence Counsel   Shut up and stay here! Got it? (*To the* **Prosecutor**.) What's all this about?

Prosecutor   Crime.

Defence Counsel (*pointing at* **Witness 1**)   And him?

Prosecutor   He knows the criminal.

Defence Counsel   And who is the criminal?

Witness 1 (*pointing at the* **Defendant**)   Him.

Defence Counsel   And why have you been quibbling over this for so long?

Prosecutor   He doesn't want to admit anything.

Defence Counsel   We don't need a criminal to admit anything!

Prosecutor   My thoughts exactly.

Defence Counsel (*to* **Witness 1**)   Do you know this man well?

Witness 1   Yes. I tore off his ticket at the entrance.

Defence Counsel Are you sure that he had a ticket?

Witness 1 Yes, he had.

Defence Counsel Look at his appearance. Doesn't he come across as a dubious person?

Witness 1 He does.

Prosecutor Precisely.

Defence Counsel (*to* **Witness 1**) And yet, despite his dubious appearance, don't you think that there is a serene and honest light in his eyes? Take a good look at his eyes.

Witness 1 Quite, his eyes are radiant.

Defence Counsel Still, there's a lot of evil concentrated in an area at the bottom of these eyes.

Witness 1 Sure, one can clearly see that.

Defence Counsel He clearly has the appearance of a criminal.

Witness 1 I swear that he looks like a criminal!

Defence Counsel His eyes, though, can't be that of a criminal. Take a look for yourself. His eyes are more like the eyes of a victim than those of a criminal.

Witness 1 (*confused*) Of course.

Defence Counsel The hand that killed couldn't be guided by such eyes.

Witness 1 (*knocked out*) Yes.

Defence Counsel So you admit that I speak the truth?

Witness 1 Indeed. You've spoken nothing but the truth.

Defence Counsel Repeat what I said.

Witness 1 (*on the verge of crying*) All you said was right.

Defence Counsel Repeat!

Witness 1 The man carries light, can't be a criminal!

Defence Counsel You're lying, I didn't say this.

Witness 1 You're right, I'm always lying.

Defence Counsel You swore an oath that you'd tell the truth. Tell it then!

Witness 1 It's me who's a criminal, sir!

Defence Counsel Who did you kill, you beast?

Witness 1 I killed my mother.

Defence Counsel   How could you do such a thing? How could a man with such a kind face as yours do such a thing?

Witness 1 (*confused*)   What do you mean?

Defence Counsel (*to the* **Prosecutor**)   What kind of witness is this? Are you trying to undermine justice?

Prosecutor   I have other witnesses.

Defence Counsel (*to* **Witness 1**)   Get out of here! Leave!

Judge (*wakes up*)   Boo!

Court Clerk   Get lost!

Defence Counsel (*slams himself down on his chair and lights a cigarette*) I'll wait.

Prosecutor   This is what I wanted to know. (*To the* **Court Clerk**.) Bring in the cloakroom attendant.

Witness 2 (*shy and cute*)   I'm right here.

Prosecutor   Name and profession.

Witness 2   My name is Hilda. I work at the theatre.

Prosecutor   Meaning?

Witness 2   I'm the cloakroom attendant.

Prosecutor   Please take a look in the auditorium. Do you recognize anybody?

Witness 2   I do.

Prosecutor   Who?

Witness 2   Everybody.

Prosecutor   Can you tell us a bit more about what your job entails?

Witness 2   Yes.

Prosecutor   Please.

Witness 2   My job is to handle coats and hats.

Prosecutor   And what else?

Witness 2   Sometimes scarves and gloves, too.

Prosecutor   And? And? Tell us all, miss. Would you want us to make you swear an oath?

Witness 2   I think that would be best. Otherwise, I might forget something . . .

Prosecutor   Raise your hand and repeat after me: I swear to tell the truth, the whole truth and nothing but the truth.

Act One   51

Witness 2   I swear to tell the truth, the whole truth and nothing but the truth. Oh! At times, I'm also asked to look after some batons.

Prosecutor   Anything else? Bags, handbags?

Witness 2   Less often.

Prosecutor   Miss Hilda, please focus. Take a look at this man. Do you recognize him?

Witness 2   I do.

Prosecutor   How exactly?

Witness 2   By his umbrella and overcoat.

Prosecutor   He had an umbrella and an overcoat?

Witness 2   Yes indeed.

Prosecutor   Would you like to tell us how exactly this happened?

Witness 2   I'm embarrassed, sir.

Prosecutor   We must find out about all the details. Tell us please.

Witness 2   This man . . . (*Hesitates.*) He . . . (*Starts sobbing.*) I can't, I can't . . .

Prosecutor (*helps her sit back on her chair*)   Calm down, please. Look into his eyes. Are you sure it's him?

Witness 2   I can't look into his eyes! Don't ask me to do such a thing!

Prosecutor   How do you know it's him?

Witness 2   I feel it. I can tell from a glance what overcoat suits him and what umbrella he can get away with.

Prosecutor   Try to recall everything, second by second!

Witness 2 (*wiping her eyes*)   I don't want to, I can't!

Prosecutor   Was it that unpleasant?

Witness 2   It was horrible!

Prosecutor   I'm really sorry to stir up such memories, I'm really sorry. (*Agitated.*) I don't know how I could . . .

Witness 2   No, do what you have to do . . .

Prosecutor (*to the* **Judge**)   Your Honour, there are certain things that, if stirred up without the necessary tact, can endanger the lives of witnesses . . .

Judge   Let her drink some water.

Prosecutor   Do you think a sip of water might . . .

Court Clerk (*to the young woman*)   Hold out!

Witness 2 (*wipes her tears*) Ready. It's over. I'm ready to face anything.

Prosecutor So, this man is known to you.

Witness 2 Yes.

Prosecutor You met him this very evening.

Witness 2 Yes.

Prosecutor When exactly?

Witness 2 Shortly before the start of the show.

Prosecutor Can you be more precise?

Witness 2 About seven or eight minutes before.

Prosecutor Try to recall the exact moment.

Witness 2 I was standing behind the counter. He came up to me . . .

Judge (*with trepidation*) Slower! Take it slow!

Prosecutor Excuse me?

Judge Talk slower!

Prosecutor (*to the young woman*) And?

Witness 2 (*mortified*) He came closer . . . and closer . . . . and closer . . .

Defence Counsel Until?

Witness 2 He came so close that . . .

Defence Counsel Were there any other spectators nearby?

Witness 2 A few, maybe five or six.

Defence Counsel And he just came up to you without any embarrassment?

Witness 2 Without any reservations.

Defence Counsel Did he say anything?

Witness 2 Nothing.

Judge Nothing? Nothing at all? Not even utter a sound of some sort?

Witness 2 Nothing. He simply handed me his overcoat and umbrella.

Judge (*jumping up*) He had such temerity?

Defence Counsel (*to the* **Judge**) Shush!

Judge (*harshly*) Give me a break! (*Steps down from his raised desk to be nearer to the young woman.*) What was the overcoat like?

Witness 2 Navy blue.

Judge (*to the* **Court Clerk**)   Make a note of this!

Court Clerk   I am.

Judge   What was the umbrella like?

Witness 2   Black.

Judge (*to the* **Court Clerk**)   Hear that? Black! Write it down!

Court Clerk   Black . . .

Judge   So we are dealing with an overcoat and an umbrella!

Witness 2   Yes, a thousand times yes!

Judge (*breathing fire*)   He's lost! (*To the* **Defendant**.) Sir, you're lost.

Defence Counsel (*to the* **Judge**)   Don't raise your voice. You know it's bad for you.

Judge (*entrenched*)   So? (*To the young woman.*) And then?

Witness 2   He placed them on the counter.

Judge   Impossible!

Witness 2 (*standing up, in hysterics*)   Oh, yes! He put them right in front of me on the counter. In other words, he simply handed them to me.

Judge   The scum!

Witness 2   Your Honour, please keep in mind my situation. I'm a simple soul, without any protection . . .

Judge   Are you sure that he handed them over to you?

Witness 2   He did, to me indeed. I was standing right in front of him and he placed the items on the counter.

Judge   And you?

Witness 2   Me?

Judge (*grabs her by the collar*)   What did you do?

Witness 2   I gave him a number.

Judge   You gave him a number!

Witness 2   Yes . . .

Judge   What number?

Witness 2   What number?

Judge (*howling*)   What number? What number?

Prosecutor (*whispering*)   Was it an even number?

Witness 2   Can't recall . . .

Judge Bad, very bad! What kind of witness are you?

Witness 2 (*lost*) Can't remember, can't remember all the numbers. I don't like numbers, I wanted to be an actress . . .

Judge Clerk!

Court Clerk Yes?

Judge Produce the evidence!

Court Clerk They are already here, Your Honour.

Judge Where? When?

Court Clerk I brought them here myself, Your Honour. They are in the left-hand drawer.

Judge (*furious, opens the drawer*) Aha! (*Victorious, produces the umbrella.*) Is this it?

Witness 2 *nods*.

Judge So ugly!

Prosecutor Yuck!

Judge (*produces the overcoat*) Do you recognize this?

Witness 2 This is it.

Court Clerk May I draw some conclusions, Your Honour?

Judge Please go ahead.

Court Clerk It's a bit mangy.

Defence Counsel (*checks the drawer*) Because it has been in the drawer.

Judge And this? (*picks up a number*) Is this the number?

Court Clerk The ticket number.

Judge Read it!

Court Clerk 98!

Judge I knew it! An even number.

Prosecutor This is not all, Your Honour!

Judge Of course not! (*Starts going through the pockets of the overcoat.*)

Prosecutor Can I make a small demonstration? (*To the* **Court Clerk**.) Can you please check the number of the defendant's seat?

Court Clerk (*goes behind the* **Defendant**, *checks the number on the seat and shouts*) 102.

Prosecutor Take a good look!

Court Clerk 102. I'm positive.

Prosecutor Thank you. Watch this, Your Honour. If we add the cloakroom number and the seat number . . .

Judge Why?

Prosecutor Why not? It's impossible for this figure not to have a significance.

Judge Clerk! Add them up!

Prosecutor 98 and 102!

Judge (*nervously*) Add them, clerk, add them up!

Court Clerk I'm adding, Your Honour!

Judge Do it then! Ready?

Defence Counsel 200!

Court Clerk Extraordinary!

Prosecutor See? Didn't I tell you?

Judge Impossible! Add them again!

Court Clerk 200. It's crystal clear.

Judge What is this supposed to mean? (*To the* **Prosecutor**.) Tell us!

Prosecutor Well, can't you see?

Judge Oh, yes, I can.

Prosecutor This is one of the most even numbers.

Judge Miss Hilda, how could you give this man such a number?

Witness 2 I was in a rush.

Prosecutor This man is outright hellish!

Judge (*hands him the overcoat*) Here, check it yourself.

Prosecutor There's nothing . . .

Court Clerk Me, too! Me, too! (*Going through the pockets*.) Nothing. Would you like to have a go, miss?

Witness 2 (*putting on airs*) I don't know if should . . .

Court Clerk (*to the* **Judge**) Can she take a look?

Judge Sure.

Court Clerk Please have a go, miss. You've been given permission.

Witness 2 (*coyly, but with excitement*) Just a moment . . . a single pocket . . . You know, due to my profession, I refrain from checking pockets. Not even as a joke.

Court Clerk (*to the* **Defence Counsel**) Would you like to have a go, sir?

Defence Counsel No, no, I don't. But I'd like to open the umbrella if I may.

Court Clerk Please.

Witness 2 *screams.*

Judge Did you find anything?

Witness 2 (*transfigured, panting*) I think so.

Prosecutor (*losing his temper, to the young woman*) Slowly please, don't lose your composure!

Court Clerk Where, in which area?

Witness 2 (*slowly recovering from her shock*) Here . . .

All leaning over the coat.

Prosecutor Careful, please, for the love of God!

Judge Is it something hard?

Witness 2 Can't tell. I think my fingers are sweaty.

Defence Counsel Is it something cold? If it is, I can take it out.

Witness 2 It's something tiny.

Prosecutor Perhaps we should call the head of security.

Witness 2 No, no, this object is between my fingers . . .

Judge Go for it! Now! Pull it out, miss, before it's too late!

Witness 2 *produces a toothpick.*

Beat; everybody seems fascinated, while the young woman keeps her eyes closed.

Witness 2 May I open my eyes? Is this anything obscene?

Judge (*stunned, aetherial*) A toothpick!

Witness 2 A toothpick?

Defence Counsel It's so black!

Court Clerk It's not black, it's dirty!

Prosecutor See, miss, what has been handed in at the cloakroom?

Judge (*vibrating*) What a beast! Devil's ape! (*Spitting.*)

Prosecutor Hellish! Absolutely hellish!

Judge (*rips the overcoat apart*) There! See what I'm doing with your coat?! Behold! (*Puts it on the floor and starts pulling, ensuring that one of the heads is under his feet.*) Look what I'm doing with your overcoat!

Prosecutor Me, too! (*Pulls it and rips off a chunk.*)

Defence Counsel (*whacking the floor with the umbrella*) Wretched criminal!

Court Clerk This is excellent.

Judge Leave me a piece of the umbrella!

All descend upon the two objects and rip them apart; they ambush one another, snatching the best bits from other people's hands; the coat, torn to shreds, is being thrown around the auditorium.

Judge Assassin! This is the word! Assassin! We have to clear things up. Everything has to be torn apart, until the very last shred!

Court Clerk Going back to the ancient Greeks!

Defence Counsel Everything! (*Rips with his teeth.*) Go on and tear away, ladies and gentlemen! (*Asks one of the spectators.*) Hold this please, sir!

Prosecutor (*to the* **Judge**, *who is struggling to destroy the umbrella*) Did you manage?

Judge It's hard. Swiss-made.

Witness 2 Give it to him, so he can distroy it himself!

Judge (*howling savagely*) I want some more! (*He rushes to grab a large piece of fabric, and in the kerfuffle someone rips one of the* **Judge**'s *sleeves off; nobody seems to notice the provenance of this new prey and they are all cramming together over it.*) Enough, enough!

Prosecutor No! No! We have to carry on until the bitter end!

Judge No! Enough! Tell him to shut up!

Defence Counsel (*excited by the distruction, he picks up the drawer and smashes it on the ground*) Nevermore!

Judge Enough, boys, enough!

Witness 2 (*screaming hysterically*) He should help out, as well! Why doesn't he?

Judge Come on, boys, we are turning into a laughing stock . . .

Court Clerk (*hurries to rescue the pages of notes from the hands of the* **Defence Counsel**) No! Not these notes!

Witness 2 Oh, yes! Your Honour! We have to destroy any memory of this man, any trace of his presence, here, in this universe. So that nothing can ever be known about him, only the wind should blow . . . (*He starts blowing on the bits of paper lying about.*)

Judge (*produces a hip flask and takes a few deep gulps before handing it over to the* **Defence Counsel**) Drink! Let it go!

Defence Counsel (*drinks*) She's right. We haven't achieved anything if we don't root him out altogether.

Court Clerk We have to forget that we've ever seen him. We must simply lose our memory.

Defence Counsel (*takes another sip and hands the flask to the* **Prosecutor**) It would be best for all of us to lose our memory at the same time, in public, if possible. It's very important that we lose our memory in an organized fashion and beyond hope! All of us, looking one another in the eye. It would be awful if some of us were to abscond . . .

Court Clerk (*taking the flask*) I swear that I won't have peace until I kill the brain of this man, one brain cell at a time! The brain of this man, who's keeping silent.

Prosecutor Now, please, let's do this right now! There's plenty of time to head home later.

Judge What home? I have no home! My home is law and justice!

Prosecutor But it's clear that this man is a criminal! I've demonstrated to you that he's a criminal!

Judge I know, yeah, I know. But look at him, please take a good look at him! (*The* **Prosecutor** *leans towards the* **Defendant** *and stares at him.*) Can you see him?

Prosecutor I can see him perfectly.

Judge He doesn't think so!

Prosecutor He doesn't?

Witness 2 Why not? Why doesn't he think so? He should!

Judge Shush! (*To the* **Court Clerk**.) Get rid of her! (*To the* **Prosecutor**.) He doesn't think he's a criminal.

Prosecutor Impossible!

Judge Take a good look at him. This isn't the face of a criminal convinced that he's a criminal.

Court Clerk And yet, judged by the wrinkles around his lips . . . (*He is carefully examining the* **Defendant**.)

Prosecutor Definitely not. He doesn't think so.

Judge Didn't I tell you? He doesn't think so. We must make him think so.

Prosecutor But it's obvious, and clear as day. Everybody thinks so. Why doesn't he? (*To the audience.*) Ladies and gentlemen, say something! Make him think so! (*To the* **Defendant**.) Sir, say something, stand up, do something. You know full well who you are, what your thoughts are – you also know that we know everything.

Court Clerk Admit it!

Judge I know him. He'll never open his mouth.

Defence Counsel There's no point in stretching this any further. Tell us everything. I'm your defence counsel. It's pointless to hide anything from me. I know you're a criminal and I want to defend you. Yes, I want to defend and protect you. Not from your guilt, because you are wearing that on your face. I want to protect you from your own person!

Court Clerk (*fascinated by the* **Defence Counsel's** *words*) Bravo!

Witness 2 What a man!

Judge (*to the* **Court Clerk**, *whispering*) Throw her out!

Defence Counsel Dear spectator! I'm asking you again. It's so important to call a spade a spade at least once in a lifetime. This is a unique opportunity for you. A chance that very many people would like to have. You have the chance to admit everything, in public, in front of everyone, in front of the civilized world. This is likely to bring about a major relief, so don't miss out on this opportunity! Admit that you are a criminal. Admit that you are guilty. Everybody is keeping an eye on you. Everybody is prepared to listen to you and to believe you. Stand up! Tell us what's weighing on your mind. You were given the rare chance to occupy this position. One in a hundred, a thousand, ten thousand! Think about it! How much time would need to pass until fate threw you again on seat number 102! Come, tell us, once and for all!

Prosecutor Say it!

Judge Rubbish!

Court Clerk Be brave!

Defence Counsel Sir, I can't defend you if you are just standing there without saying a word and smiling. I wanted to protect you from lies, from the lies that are sprawling about in your brain. I wanted to protect you from this lie by making you admit everything. I wanted to protect you from this lie because the lie in your mind and soul was killing us all, ripping us apart and leaving us in tatters, splashing us with the darkest and slimiest mud possible. Even your silence is a lie because you actually have things to say. Take a load off your mind, allow yourself to ease up, and I can guarantee that you'll feel light as a feather.

Judge That's it, my learned friend, leave it. He doesn't want to, that much is clear. Let's carry on with the other witnesses.

Defence Counsel (*to the* **Defendant**) Why do you want me to call all these scruffy, good-for-nothing witnesses? Be a man!

Witness 2 Be like him! (*Pointing at the* **Defence Counsel**.)

Judge (*to the* **Court Clerk**) Throw her out at once!

Court Clerk (*to the* **Witness**) Come on, back to work, some of the spectators want to leave at the intermission.

Witness 2 No, I'll stay. Your Honour, I want to stay.

Court Clerk Miss, please go back to the cloakroom! Can't you hear that some people want to leave at the intermission?

Witness 2 Who wants to leave at the intermission? Nobody wants to do that. I'm not going anywhere.

Court Clerk There's always someone who wants to leave at the intermission. Look, I bet he wants to make himself scarce, for instance. (*Points at the* **Defendant**.)

Witness 2 Do you want to clear out at the intermission? (*Cosying up to the* **Defendant**.) A man like yourself?

Court Clerk Enough, back to the cloakroom! (*To the audience.*) Time for intermisssion, ladies and gents! Take a break! Be careful what you decide to do though! There's paper here and some pens, plenty of pens. All those who want to issue statements can do so. We also have various documents, ladies and gentlemen, that we can let you consult. We have photographs with the defendant, all of his photos in fact. We have thousands of photos dating back to the time when the defendant was just a kid. Please examine them. (*He opens the folding display boards around the stage to reveal the relevant evidence: tens of filing cabinets and shelves with various recordings, etc.*) We have all his clothes here, in these huge wardrobes – please take a look at them. We have his books, his napkins, his plates, his forks and knives, his glasses, his used train and tram tickets, all the newspapers he's ever read and crumpled, all the flowerpots he's ever broken – everything, absolutely everything. Please take a look and scrutinize them – truth is hovering above all these items like a drop of fat in a cauldron of water. Do come closer, ladies and gentlemen! You can read at these tables, have a coffee and look the defendant in the eye. Please, ladies and gentlemen, leave anonymity behind!

Intermission. The court retires and bar staff appear with trays carrying cups of coffee that they place on the desks belonging to the counsels and the judge. For the duration of the intermission, the stage turns into a foyer where spectators can drink coffee and smoke.

Act Two

Act Two kicks off among the dirty coffee cups and random objects scattered around the stage by the audience. The desks are covered in unwashed saucers and cups. The court resumes its activty unperturbed by the presence of these objects.

Prosecutor (*standing, holds up a cup with a tiny bit of coffee at the bottom, takes a sip, makes a face and puts it down*)   Bring in the third witness!

Court Clerk (*shouting backstage*)   The third witness, please!

Witness 3 (*enters very timidly – she's one of the fat women who have been serving coffee during the intermission*)   I'm here, sir.

Prosecutor   Name and profession.

Witness 3   My name is Gudrun. I work at the theatre bar.

Prosecutor   Meaning? What are you actually doing there?

Witness 3   Coffee, macaroons . . .

Judge (*furiously*)   But today you didn't have any macaroons!

Witness 3   We've run out of nuts, Your Honour.

Prosecutor   At last! When are you preparing all this anyway?

Witness 3   During the show.

Prosecutor   How about the intermissions?

Witness 3   Then I normally serve customers.

Prosecutor   Have you been serving this evening, too?

Witness 3   Of course.

Prosecutor   Be specific, give me details!

Witness 3   I brought in the trays with coffee and lemonade.

Prosecutor   How many trays?

Witness 3   Five with coffee and three with lemonade.

Prosecutor   How long did it take you to bring all these trays?

Witness 3   Not long, I don't think. I've had them prepared in advance.

Prosecutor   Did it take you longer than three minutes?

Witness 3   No, definitely not.

Prosecutor   Roughly how many cups were on a tray?

Witness 3   About fifty.

Prosecutor   So you brought in around 250 cups of coffee.

Witness 3   Yes, something like that.

Prosecutor   And how many glasses of lemonade?

Witness 3   About 25 glasses of lemonade per tray. So, about 75 glasses of lemonade in total.

Prosecutor   Why so few?

Witness 3   This is the ratio, sir.

Prosecutor   Explain what you mean by this ratio.

Witness 3   Not everybody who has coffee wants a lemonade, as well. So it makes sense to have fewer servings of lemonade than of coffee. On the other hand, some people don't drink coffee, but they are in a minority. There are also people who drink neither coffee nor lemondade, but there's so few of these that it's hardly worth mentioning them.

Prosecutor   Start from the beginning. So, most people drink both coffee and lemonade.

Witness 3   It's one way of putting it, sir. What happens, in fact, is that they drink all or nearly all of their coffee, and then they take a few sips of lemonade, only to keep their throat moistened. But this is enough to require a glass.

Prosecutor   Fine. A second category only drinks lemonade, but this is a smaller group.

Witness 3   Exactly. They drink either half a glass or a whole glass of lemonade. Some drink it in one go, others have the habit of playing with their glass, gargling a little . . .

Prosecutor   Finally, there are peole who only drink coffee.

Witness 3   Yes.

Prosecutor   And others who don't drink anything.

Witness 3   Yes.

Prosecutor   So we have four categories of people in total.

Witness 3   Four, indeed.

Prosecutor   Tell me, do you normally stay with the spectators during the intermission?

Witness 3   Yes, I'm there with them during the entire intermission.

Prosecutor   Did you stay today, too?

Witness 3   Yes, as always.

Prosecutor   Please take a good look around. Could you tell me who had coffee and who had lemonade?

Witness 3   Sure. (*Goes up to a spectator.*) He had coffee.

Prosecutor (*to the* **Judge**)   Your Honour, I'd like to bring unquestionable evidence to prove that our witness has a perfect memory and an exceptional spirit of observation. Look, Your Honour! (*Lights fade; an image of the spectator mentioned by the bar attendant is projected on the screen; it is a picture taken during the intermission, when the spectator is indeed drinking coffee.*) The witness was right! This gentleman did indeed have a coffee! (*To the bar attendant.*) Carry on!

Witness 3   This lady had both coffee and lemonade.

Prosecutor   In what order?

Witness 3   In the order I mentioned earlier. First coffee, then lemonade.

Prosecutor   Attention, ladies and gentlemen! Behold our distinguished spectator sipping her coffee among a group of friends! (*Projection.*) And here . . . (*Projection continues, showing other spectators.*) . . . we can see the moment when she is reaching for her glass of lemonade! *Voilà*!

Court Clerk (*in admiration*)   You're terrific!

Prosecutor (*to the* **Witness**)   Carry on, please, carry on. We want the audience to gain absolute trust in you. We want to get them to a point where they stop doubting our witnesses and accept witness statements as law. Continue!

Witness 3 (*from the auditorium, where she is scrutinizing the spectators' faces*) I could draw your attention to a gentleman who kept smoking throughout the intermission and didn't drink anything.

Prosecutor   Neither coffee, nor lemonade!

Witness 3   Neither coffee, nor lemonade!

Prosecutor   Let's see him!

Witness 3   Here he is!

The face of this spectator appears on the screen.

Prosecutor   Ladies and gentlemen, we have here an impressive array of slides with which we can indeed demonstrate that this gentleman didn't drink anthing. Take a good look, this is slide number 1. (*Moves on to the next slide.*) Here you can see him as he's getting off his chair to enjoy the forthcoming intermission. (*Next slide.*) Same image, seen from the back. The spectator is standing. You can see him with his hands in his pockets as he is probably searching for his cigarettes. In the backround, you can spot our witness, Gudrun, as she is bringing in the first tray with coffee. If you wanted to verify this claim, please note that his seat number was 46. (*Next slide.*) Observe the moment when spectator number 46 is lighting his first cigarette, with people crowding around the tables laden with coffee cups at the very back. (*Next slide.*) Here we have the half-smoked cigarette. Observe that spectator number 46 came alone to the show. (*Next slide.*) Note the moment when he's stubbing his cigarette out in the ashtray. Also observe that by this point smaller groups have also been formed, people chatting away and drinking coffee. (*Next slide.*) Spectator number 46 continues to stand by himself, though he has taken a few steps towards a table. (*Next slide.*) This image is rather unclear. Spectator number 46 stares at one of the cups full of coffee. He must be debating whether he should or shouldn't reach for the cup. (*Next slide.*) Victory! Spectator number 46 didn't grab the cup. He lit another cigarette instead and moved a few steps away from the table. (*Next slide.*) Here's the second half-smoked cigarette. (*Next slide.*) And now the second cigarette having reached its last third . . . (*Next slide.*) Here's the stub of the second cigarette, put out right next to the first one, in a very careful and orderly manner. Clap for spectator number 46! (*Lights focus on the spectator; the loudspeakers play thunderous applause.*) Your Honour, is it really still necessary for me to demonstrate that this witness has exceptional observation skills and that she embodies credibility itself?

Judge No, mate, you've been very eloquent!

Prosecutor Put your hands together for our Judge! (*Lights focus on the **Judge**, bowing; loudspeakers play thunderous applause.*) Madam Gudrun, please return to the witness stand!

Witness 3 I've spotted them all, sir, I really have. They have mingled a bit but I can immediately separate them into various categories.

Prosecutor This is no longer necessary. We are all convinced that truth is on your side.

Witness 3 (*returns*) As you see fit . . .

Prosecutor Now we'd like you to take a look at this person standing right in front of us.

Witness 3 Which one?

Prosecutor This one! (*Points at the **Defendant**.*)

Witness 3 I can't see anything . . .

Prosecutor (*gets closer to the **Defendant***) Him.

Witness 3 I'm sorry, I can't see him . . .

Prosecutor (*standing right next to the **Defendant**; places his hand above the latter's head*) Look at my hand.

Witness 3 I'm looking.

Prosecutor Can you see my hand?

Witness 3 Yes, I can.

Prosecutor Can you see my fingers?

Witness 3 I can.

Prosecutor What am I doing now?

Witness 3 You're shaking your fingers.

Prosecutor Excellent. You have sharp eyesight.

Witness 3 I have excellent eyesight.

Prosecutor Focus your attention on my palm. Now lower your gaze ever so slightly. What can you see under my palm?

Witness 3 Nothing!

Prosecutor Impossible.

Witness 3 I swear! I can't see anything.

Judge (*jumps up*) I beg you to concentrate, you must be able to see something.

Witness 3 Your Honour, I'm trying to look with all my might, but can't see anything.

Court Clerk Shall I switch on another light?

Judge Yes, go ahead!

Prosecutor Now? Can you see anything?

Witness 3 Sir, I have a headache . . .

Prosecutor Clerk, switch on all possible sources of light!

Judge Come forward a little.

Witness 3 (*steps forward*) Still nothing.

Judge Take another step, and another . . .

Court Clerk Perhaps there's still not enough light . . .

Prosecutor (*to the lighting engineer*) Switch on all the lights!

Court Clerk This is all we have.

Prosecutor Well, then, how about lighting some matches?

Prosecutor (*lights a match above the head of the* **Defendant**) Can you see anything now?

Witness 3 Well, I seem to be seeing something . . .

Prosecutor (*fascinated*) What can you see?

Witness 3 I can see an eye.

Judge (*takes a look himself*) Impossible, impossible!

Court Clerk (*confused, to the* **Judge**) Perhaps we got it wrong . . .

Judge (*to the witness*) Can't you see the whole person?

Witness 3 I think there's too much light actually. There's so much light that all I can see is light.

Prosecutor   Well, then, switch some off, so the witness can see properly.

A single spotlight is left on, focusing on the **Defendant**.

Judge   Well?

Court Clerk   Well?

Prosecutor   Say something! Impossible not to see anyhing!

Witness 3   I think I can see something now . . .

Judge (*sigh of relief, to the* **Court Clerk**)   So he exists!

Prosecutor   What can you see?

Witness 3   I can see . . .

Court Clerk   What? What?

Witness 3   I can see . . . a chair!

Prosecutor   A chair? That's all?

Witness 3 (*convinced*)   Yes.

Prosecutor (*going mad*)   Madam, please! We are relying on your exceptional observation skills. We want to know everything, we want you to see everything in our stead!

Judge   Open your eyes, madam!

Prosecutor   On the chair itself, can't you see anything on the chair?

Witness 3   Nothing. However, I can see something under the chair.

Judge   What?

Witness 3   A small coin.

Judge   Remove that stupid coin! Clerk! Why didn't you pick up all the coins from under the chairs? The witness is unable to see because of them!

Court Clerk   It must have gone astray, Your Honour. How was I meant to squeeze under the chair of the defendant? (*Bends down and crawls under the chair to pick the coin up. Victoriously.*) Here you go!

Prosecutor   Now, madam, now! There are no more obstacles in your way!

Witness 3   Yes, I think I can see something. Something black.

Judge   And! And! Tell us what it is!

Witness 3   I can see two black feet!

Prosecutor (*triumphantly*)   This is it! Two black feet! Ladies and gentlemen, we can certify at once that our witness saw correctly. (*Projection.*) Here we have the defendant's feet . . . from the front . . . (*New slide.*) and the back. Carry on, Madam Gudrun, what else can you see?

Witness 3   I can see a pair of shoes.

Prosecutor   Behold! (*Projection.*) The left shoe and the right shoe!

Witness 3   I think I can also see a neck. From the front and back!

Prosecutor (*projection*)   Here's the defendant's neck!

Witness 3   I can see a nose, sir!

Prosecutor   The defendant's nose! (*Monstrous projection.*)

Witness 3   A mouth!

Prosecutor   A mouth, a mouth! Of course! (*Projection.*)

Witness 3   An eye!

Prosecutor   Behold the left eye! (*Projection.*)

Witness 3   And another eye!

Prosecutor   Perfect, the right eye. (*Projection.*) This is going very well, we are making great progress!

Witness 3   I can also see a stain on the trousers.

Prosecutor   A stain? (*Confused.*)

Witness 3   Yes, a tiny grease stain.

Prosecutor   Give me a moment, just a moment. (*Looking for the right slide as he's quickly sifting through a range – each and every part of the defendant's body is recorded, including close-ups of his fingers, nails, wrinkles, hairs, etc.*) I can't find the stain, I'm afraid.

Witness 3   There is a stain, I'm sure of it.

Prosecutor   Could you tell me where?

Witness 3   On the cuffs of the right trouser leg.

Prosecutor (*projection of the left trouser leg*)   Here? No. (*The right trouser leg.*) Here?

Witness 3   Yes.

Prosecutor   And yet I can't see a thing. (*Zooming in on the image.*) Clerk! Why can't we see the stain?

It must be a drop of coffee that landed there during the intermission.

(*Projection of the defendant's trousers.*) Would you like to go up to the screen and point at the stain?

Witness 3   Sure, no problem. (*Goes to the screen and circles the stain with a piece of chalk.*) Here.

Prosecutor   Perfect. Can you add anything to what we have just seen?

Witness 3   No, this is it.

Prosecutor   What I mean to say is whether you can put all these elements together, in some sort of a coherent whole?

Witness 3   Which elements?

Prosecutor   These diverse elements: the mouth, the nose, the throat, the eye, the stain. All these belong to a whole. Can't you sense that there is a whole somewhere?

Witness 3   No, not really.

Prosecutor   You can't possibly leave us right now. What you've seen is quite correct, but it needs interpretation. Everything's connected. Can't you see the links?

Witness 3   I'm sick of links and connections!

Judge   Madam Gudrun, please give thinking through them a go! These elements can't possibly wander about the room freely . . . they belong together. You really can't see the body, the person?

Witness 3   No.

Court Clerk   Shall I put the lights back on?

Judge   Madam, there's a human being in front of you!

Witness 3 (*fascinated*)   A being! (*Transfixed.*) Astonishing! I overlooked this.

Prosecutor   Now you can see?

Witness 3   Hell, yes!

Court Clerk   The penny dropped?

Witness 3   Yes, a thousand times, yes! He's one of those who only drank coffee.

Prosecutor   Take a look at his face. Do you recognize him?

Witness 3   Yes, he has the face of a criminal. (*Everybody relieved.*)

Prosecutor (*lets out a sigh of relief*)   At long last.

Judge   Bravo!

Court Clerk   Spot on.

Prosecutor   How did you realize this is the face of a criminal?

Witness 3   One can see with the naked eye. It's a matter of common sense.

Prosecutor   What are your thoughts on his mouth? Isn't it an evil mouth, tight as a purse?

Witness 3   It's a narrow black mouth, I could see when he was sipping his coffee. A nightmare mouth, yuck! I wouldn't like to hear a single word uttered by this mouth.

Prosecutor   And his eyes, take a look at the eyes, what do you think about them?

Act Two   69

Witness 3   I'd say that his eyes really betray him.

Court Clerk   They are far too deep-set, no?

Witness 3   This isn't what I meant. They are immobile, cold and glassy, hinting at a state of anticipation, as if a jet of blood was about to spurt from them any minute.

Court Clerk   What can I say, he's a brute!

Witness 3   I could tell just from the way he was drinking his coffee. He was taking very slow and steady sips, like an animal devouring its victim and drinking its blood in ecstasy. I was observing him really carefully, I remember my fright when he took a glance at the glasses with lemonade.

Judge   Did he touch the lemonade?!

Witness 3   This is the point, he didn't. But he was looking at it with a contempt from which one could easily draw conclusions about the hellish mechanism in his mind.

Court Clerk   This is terrible, quite terrible.

Witness 3   He's a brute and a scabby toad, who should be thrown out on the streets as soon as possible.

Prosecutor   Your Honour, I think we've seen more than enough conclusive evidence. We can move on to the verdict.

Judge   Perhaps the defence counsel has something to add.

Defence Counsel   Gentlemen, I only have one word to add! Death! I can't soil my hands defending a man on whose face crime is written all over like a wound. As you can see, gentlemen, this face is transparent like a glass case. (*Projection of the face.*) Through it, one can see quite far, all the way to the brain. (*Draws with the chalk.*) This brain is rotten and steeped in doubt, fear and cowardice. This brain is the repository of all human vices and defects. Think about it! Remember the hearings! This man was declared a criminal and he didn't react. This man was insulted and he didn't react. This man had his clothes torn apart and his umbrella dismantled yet he didn't react. This man had photographs of him scattered around the auditorium yet he said nothing. He was told to his face that he was an obscene scum, a coward and a perjurer, and yet he just smiled. Every fibre of his being was dissected, photographed, analysed and publicly exposed on the walls of this court and yet he stayed silent, merely observing proceedings and without lifting a finger in protest. This man has never expressed an opinion, banknotes were thrown at him and he didn't jump off his chair, he was excluded from the human species and yet he didn't move a single muscle on his face. I can't possibly defend such a felon, there's no way I can defend a man who kills within his own self, against the teachings and norms of humankind. I can't defend him, Gentlemen, I can't defend someone who perverts his own brain until complete and utter self-immolation. There's no way I can defend him, I'm simply disarmed in the face of this case. Gentlemen, this man shouldn't have even made it to trial. It's outrageous that this trial took place, that it could even get scheduled. This man should have been killed at the entrance, crushed at the door or in his seat. Gentlemen, we shouldn't expect the legal system to reach a verdict in this horrible case of crime. A crime towards the humanity within us, because there are no laws that could possibly sanction this crime. What's more, we mustn't wait for a law that has no way to emerge, that simply can't come to the fore! Let's kill this man right here, right now, and just go home!

Prosecutor I'll do it! I'll kill him! I've told you a hundred times to kill him and just go home! (*He blows a kiss to the* **Defence Counsel**.) You're amazing!

Judge (*also blowing a kiss to the* **Defence Counsel**) Bravo!

Court Clerk (*shaking the hand of the* **Defence Counsel**) This was extraordinary! You've been amazing!

Witness 3 (*nearly crying*) I'm glad, sir, I'm glad! Should you ever need me again . . .

Judge Gentlemen, put your hands together! (*To the audience.*) This is a great day! (*The* **Prosecutor** *switches on the loudspeakers; applause.*) The criminal has been exposed!

Court Clerk Shall I fetch the gun?

Judge Yes! At once!

Prosecutor (*looking at his watch*) There might still be some hot water when we get home . . .[1]

Court Clerk (*bringing a dismantled gun*) Here it is . . .

Judge Very well! Go ahead!

Defence Counsel Please. You said you wanted to pull the trigger!

Judge No, no, I haven't fired a gun in a very long time. It makes no sense to miss our target.

Prosecutor Neither have I, and I have a stomach ache . . .

Defence Counsel Court clerk, would you like to . . .

Court Clerk No, I'm suffering with hernia, and can't stand the sight of blood.

Defence Counsel What, we're drawing a blank now?

Judge (*to the* **Defence Counsel**) You do it, close your eyes and shoot!

Defence Counsel I'm the defence counsel, it doesn't make any sense for me to shoot, it's not the done thing.

Judge Madam Gudrun, would you like to do us a small favour?

Witness 3 No, sir, I have to count cups and prepare coffee for the intermission.

Judge Ladies and gentlemen, would anyone like to fire the gun?

Defence Councel (*addresing the audience, too*)   Can anyone handle a gun? Please, the gun is loaded . . .

Prosecutor   We're off, we're going home an hour earlier than planned.

Judge   We are looking for a man – are there any men here?

Defence Counsel   Sir, would you like to have a go?

Judge   It's no big deal, you'll see. The next intermission is coming up, during which time the criminal will abscond.

Court Clerk   Kill him, please, don't let him flee!

Prosecutor   Ladies and gentlemen, the criminal is laughing at us! Shoot, please!

Witness 3 (*banging with the cups*)   Fire!

Judge   Can we please have a volunteer? We can't do everything, you must trust us and lend us a helping hand!

Defence Counsel (*facing the* **Defendant**)   Sir, be a man, just this once! Take the gun, go to the foyer and fire it in your temple.

Judge   Please, sir, you have a last chance, fire a gun in your mouth!

Prosecutor   A single bullet will do. It won't hurt, you won't have time to feel anything. People will clap, it will be a beautiful finale, and then we'll be off home. You doing this will mean that everything is not yet lost, your brain has still produced a spark, there was one last flash of enlightenment insofar that you realized the magnitude of your crime at the very last minute.

Court Clerk   Come on, take heart!

Judge   Doesn't want to . . .

Court Clerk   I have a feeling that he'll live for a long time . . .

Judge   It's not right though, it just isn't!

Defence Counsel   He'll live, you'll see, he'll live until the day of his death!

Court Clerk   We went to all this trouble for nothing.

Defence Counsel   What shall we do, Your Honour? I can tell that we won't be able to kill him.

Judge   Well, if we can't kill him, we should at least carry on with the trial!

Court Clerk   Sure, let's continue until he drops dead.

Prosecutor (*to the audience*)   Ladies and gentlemen, we'll have to confine ourselves here for the night, as if we were in a temple, and to tell everything . . . all of us to show our share of guilt.

Judge   We'll have to acknowledge our collective guilt!

Prosecutor I want to acknowledge my guilt! (*To the* **Defendant**.) Sir, please forgive me for swearing at you and for reprimanding you. I branded you a criminal, but I swear that this is what I believe you really are. (*He kneels in front of the* **Defendant**.) Have I ever called you a moron? Yes or no? Anyway, I do think you are a moron . . . in the same way, I also am a moron . . . Because I could just as well be in your shoes. And anybody in this auditorium for that matter. We are all mixed up in this and because we all know what pains us and from where this pain comes from and why it persists and keeps gnawing at us. Can you see how awful this is? I call you a fatheaded beast and you smile, thinking that this is what my part requires me to say. How do you know that I don't think the way my part requires me to think, how do you know that I'm not improving, how do you know that the part itself isn't an improvisation that tells the truth, fooling everybody who cares to listen?

Judge Have you quite finished?

Prosecutor (*enlightened*) Your Honour, please cross-examine me!

Judge I can't do that, you are the prosecutor, how could I cross-examine you?

Prosecutor Your Honour, if you cross-examine me, we'll be able to put the defendant down even more.

Judge Okay, your name and profession please.

Prosecutor I'm a filthy pig and a killer, a nasty bedbug!

Judge Klaus, it's not nice to . . .

Prosecutor Continue! Please continue. I'll explode if I can't answer these questions. I have a burning need to answer them. I want to confess all I know, everything I gathered in my brain. I have a soft and mushy brain. Take a look at my head, I'm rotten from the inside, I could collapse any minute. Ask me, Your Honour.

Judge What do you do for a living?

Prosecutor All sorts of scams, sir.

Judge Explain!

Prosecutor My hands are dirty. I couldn't be any clearer.

Judge Clerk!

Court Clerk Yes, Your Honour!

Judge Bring me the file of the defendant!

Court Clerk It's already on your desk.

Judge (*leafing though it*) You seem to be an actor.

Prosecutor That's correct. The dirtiest job there is. The dirtiest and the most thankless. I'm lying and pretending all the time.

Judge Where exactly are you an actor?

Prosecutor   Everywhere. In life, too.

Judge   What do you mean in life?

Prosecutor   In my personal life, I'm an actor, too. I can't get away from this disease. Not even when I'm sleeping. I'm sleeping in such a way that if someboody found me they should be able to say: this man is sleeping really beautifully!

Judge   This must be very uncomfortable.

Prosecutor   It's terrible. In restaurants, I'm always tempted to find a seat where I can be seen by most people. As I'm talking to the waiters, I look them in the eye and utter the words really slowly, in an almost singing voice. I keep going, hoping that they'd remember me, from TV or somewhere . . .

Judge   Bad, very bad.

Prosecutor   I commit incredible acts, absolutely incredible ones. I suffer from prostate, I have a very low libido. Still, there are many women whose feelings I sustain . . .

Judge   How?

Prosecutor   I simulate the tiredness of life, meditative states, anxiety . . . I talk to them about the cosmos, about metaphysics. They listen to me with fascination and drop the odd tear. Then I explain to them that my role in this world is much more elevated than making love to them.

Judge   Clerk! Make a note of the addresses of all these women!

Prosecutor   We are moving away from our topic, frightfully far away. I can't stand distances, Your Honour, I'm an easy-going man.

Judge   What are you hinting at?

Prosecutor   I want clear and simple questions that are subtle yet accusing.

Judge   How old are you?

Prosecutor   Thirty-three. The age of Jesus. I'm at an age where I want to start a new life.

Judge   Why do you want to start a new life? Why do you need a new life? What is it that you don't like? How do you want to start a new life?

Prosecutor   I'll show you. First and foremost, I want to totally immerse myself.

Judge   Where?

Prosecutor   In the swamp.

Judge   Why?

Prosecutor   I want to immerse so deep into the swamp that I get to its very bottom, to its very core. I want to drown in it for good, to submerge into it until I feel that there isn't any lower to go.

Judge   It's always possible to go lower than we imagined.

Prosecutor Nooo! Don't take away my last hope! I hope, want, believe that I can get as low as possible. This is because, once I'm at the lowest level of cowardice and shame, I have no other option than to rise up again.

Judge This is the way you'd like to elevate yourself?

Prosecutor It's one way of doing it, isn't it? You must admit that it's an option. Good or bad, it's my solution. Once I'm there, at the lowest level, at the very bottom of the swamp, all I'll have to do is start my flight in the reverse, towards light and humanity.

Judge Whatever, we aren't interested in your flights. You're an actor, and your flight seems muddled and uncertain. Where did you say you were an actor?

Prosecutor Didn't I tell you? In life.

Judge I meant, which theatre.

Prosecutor This one.

Judge Hm. And are you on stage a lot?

Prosecutor Almost every night.

Judge In which plays are you appearing?

Prosecutor I have a part in this very play.

Judge What's it called?

Prosecutor *The Spectator Sentenced to Death.*

Judge Court clerk! Make a note of the play.

Court Clerk Could he please repeat it again.

Judge Please repeat the title of the play.

Prosecutor *The Spectator Sentenced to Death.*

Judge And what's your role in this play?

Prosecutor I'm playing the role of the prosecutor.

Judge Aha. And what are you actually doing?

Prosecutor My job is to bring down the spectator.

Judge Not bad. And who's playing the role of the spectator?

Prosecutor The spectator is real.

Judge Seriously?

Prosecutor Hundred per cent. The spectator is a flesh and blood spectator.

Judge Isn't he played by a stuntman?

Prosecutor No. But you can check this out for yourself.

Judge No. I'm not interested if he's real. Who wrote this play?

Prosecutor The play was found in a rubbish bin, Your Honour.

Judge Okay, but isn't this embarrasing? We're simply putting on any old rubbish that's thrown out of random kitchens?

Prosecutor The play was found in the theatre bin, so to speak.

Judge Very well, I get that. But who took it out from there? Who's rummaging in the bins? Who's dirtying their hands with such filth?

Prosecutor There was no need to rummage. The bin was full to the rim and the rubbish spilled over. These sheets of paper simply slipped out.

Court Clerk How nice! Your Honour, I'd like to be cross-examined, too.

Judge What's with this bullshit? Gentlemen, come to your senses! We mustn't lose sight of the aim of this process. We have to produce evidence. The more, the better! We have to issue a death sentence, concerning this spectator we are dealing with right here. I'm not prepared to continue with cross-examinations if it doesn't serve our cause.

Prosecutor We are heading in that direction, I can assure you.

Judge Well, how much longer will it take?

Prosecutor Not much. Soon it will come to an end anyway.

Judge Were you on stage tonight?

Prosecutor Of course.

Judge I didn't really see you. Where were you in the first act?

Prosecutor I was on stage, right next to you.

Judge (*to the* **Court Clerk**) Was he?

Court Clerk I can't remember, Your Honour.

Judge How can you prove that you were actually on stage?

Prosecutor How can I prove? Well, everybody saw me.

Judge Who saw you? Show me someone who saw you.

Prosecutor Your Honour, this is an absurd question.

Judge Questions are never absurd. They have their purpose. You have to provide evidence showing that you were on stage during Act One.

Prosecutor You are driving me up the wall, Your Honour.

Judge It seems to me that you have the habit of playing truant. Were you on stage during Act Two?

Prosecutor Well, Act Two is happening right now.

Judge So you're under the impression that Act Two is being performed right now?

Prosecutor Well, that's clear as day.

Judge Nothing is clear until proven so. What evidence can you provide to the effect that Act Two is happening right now?

Prosecutor You're completely nuts, I swear!

Judge I advise you not to insult the justice system, because it can easily give you hell. Your sole preoccupation should be to produce evidence. I repeat, what evidence do you have that we are halfway through Act Two?

Prosecutor Myself, you, us all, we are here. This is Act Two.

Judge How can you prove that you are here?

Prosecutor I am, I exist, I can be seen! Lay a hand on me.

Judge No way I'll touch you. I'm not soiling my hands with anything. Your job is to provide evidence, got it?

Prosecutor I exist and that's that. I can't prove it in any other way. My existence is a certainty.

Judge I have to say that you have a mighty cheek and you're totally full of yourself.

Prosecutor Seeing that you are insulting me, I must exist.

Judge Let's say you do exist. Let's say you are in this very space. Let's say you are even answering my questions. So what?

Prosecutor Come on!

Judge You think we are playing roles here?

Prosecutor Maybe we are, maybe we aren't . . .

Judge How come?

Prosecutor During Act One, while I was accusing the defendant, I had a revelation.

Judge Why didn't you say this in Act One?

Prosecutor I realized that we were pretending to be mad in order to survive.

Judge Well said. Sir, can you do me a favour?

Prosecutor Sure.

Judge Cross-examine me, please.

Court Clerk Me first! I was here before you.

Prosecutor That's right, he was the first to ask.

Defence Counsel I think I'd also have something to share if . . .

Prosecutor One at a time, gentlemen.

Judge What was your revelation about?

Prosecutor I saw an image. My brain trespasssed into the future.

Judge And?

Prosecutor I saw the victim.

Judge What victim?

Prosecutor The dead.

Judge What dead?

Prosecutor The dead, killed by the defendant in cold blood and with a hellish grin on his face.

Judge (*shaken*) He had already done the killing?

Prosecutor He's very sneaky, just like an insect.

Judge Has the body been identified?

Prosecutor Yes.

Judge Where is it? Bring it here.

Prosecutor I'm the dead body.

Judge Is it you he's killed?

Prosecutor Yes! (*Heroically.*) I'm the victim. Well and truly hacked down.

Judge Absolutely disgusting.

Prosecutor He hacked me down and threw me into the water.

Judge Have you got evidence?

Prosecutor Yes, sir. There are few drops of water at the bottom of the glass.

Judge Do you think there is anything that could be done for you?

Prosecutor No, not for me. But I must warn you that the assassin won't stop here.

Judge Where will he stop?

Prosecutor He could choose another victim any minute now.

Court Clerk (*timidly*) Perhaps we should call . . .

Judge What do you think is drawing him to crime?

Court Clerk . . . a taxi . . .

Prosecutor Silence, sir.

Judge Are you sure?

Prosecutor His calm appearance, suggesting he is settled in his ways. His silence, his unassuming forehead and his sleepy eyes. Him looking like a head of a family, paired with this aura of a respectable citizen. All these push him towards crime.

Judge (*wiping the sweat from his face*) I must confess that there is something squeezing me at the back.

Prosecutor Why?

Judge Well, take a look in the auditorium.

Prosecutor I'm looking.

Judge Can't you see anything? They are all respectable.

Prosecutor How come?!

Judge They all have the faces of honest people, set in their ways.

Prosecutor That's right.

Court Clerk (*uptight*) Let's not anger them, Your Honour.

Judge They all seem to be calm, looking like heads of families. Watch out . . . Wherever you look, you see kind and sleepy eyes, there's nothing but silence, calm and silence . . .

Prosecutor I can't follow your point.

Defence Counsel They are a criminal gang!

Court Clerk Let's clear out of here.

Judge No, let's put them on trial.

Defence Counsel We can't possibly put them all on trial. We'd better get on with our busines.

Judge This is our business. To put them on trial.

Court Clerk They could jump on us any minute.

Prosecutor You're quite right about that. They are thirsty for blood. They could barge in here and crush us under their feet.

Defence Counsel It's much better if we just go now. Any man keeping silent the way they do amounts to concealing a criminal within.

Judge (*to the* **Defence Counsel**) Listen, step back a little.

Defence Counsel No, no, I don't dare to turn my back.

Judge Stay there! Stay right there! (*He focuses the light on him.*) Klaus, come here for a moment. Don't you think that he has a calm, almost jovial appearance?

Prosecutor Yes, and very kind eyes.

Defence Counsel Me, kind eyes?

Court Clerk Absolutely! There's a calm and casual feel to him.

Judge He looks like the head of a family, too.

Defence Counsel There's no such feel to me. I'm no father, and don't have a family. I'm alone all day, never invited to go anywhere.

Court Clerk Plus he has an unassuming forehead.

Prosecutor He looks very much like him. (*Pointing at the* **Defendant**.)

Court Clerk Spitting image.

Defence Counsel I don't look like anybody. I can't possibly look like anybody. I'm unique and indivisible.

Judge You look like everyone else in the auditorium, and that's that. You shouldn't have concealed this from us.

Prosecutor You were a pig, a filthy pig.

Defence Counsel Your Honour, you look a bit casual, too. And you also have a calm, almost jovial appearance.

Court Clerk That's about right. I guess he has.

Judge What are you trying to insinuate?

Defence Counsel You're always fresh and radiant. You have a dignified appearance, of utter respectability. You look just like me!

Judge I forbid you to compare me with you!

Defence Counsel (*takes a seat next to the* **Judge**) Can you really say that we don't look alike?

Prosecutor To be honest, there is a slight resemblance.

Court Clerk (*taking a seat next to the* **Prosecutor**) Like two drops.

Defence Counsel (*pointing at the* **Prosecutor** *and the* **Court Clerk**) In fact, they two look alike, as well.

Judge That's correct, how could I not notice?

Court Clerk (*indignantly*) Us?

Defence Counsel Yes, you. As if you had the same head.

Court Clerk (*to the* **Prosecutor**.) How can he permit . . .

Judge That's it. We are all alike.

Prosecutor I refuse to be included in the crowd!

Defence Counsel (*jovially*) You're one of us! (*Hands on his shoulder.*)

Court Clerk (*astonished, to the* **Prosecutor**) Are you suggesting that we are all criminals?

Prosecutor It would seem so.

Court Clerk Phew, what a relief!

Defence Counsel Were you afraid?

Court Clerk You could say that again. But now it's fine, it's clear. If we are all criminals, this means that we are among us.

Prosecutor You really think we are like them?

Judge Hundred per cent. We are just like them.

Defence Counsel Cowards, capable of treachery. We don't give a damn about anything.

Court Clerk Your Honour, am I allowed to show an image on the screen?

Judge What for?

Court Clerk To endorse what has just been said.

Judge What's this? (*He's stupefied at the sight of the image.*)

Court Clerk (*amused; the projection shows the* **Judge**, *looking bored and picking his teeth with his fingernails*) You.

Judge Me? How could this be me?

Court Clerk This is you during Act One. While Mr Klaus was delivering his submission, you were picking at your teeth.

Judge (*furiously, moves on to another image*) And how about this? You were stuffing your face with toffee!

Court Clerk Me, toffee?

Judge (*projects another image*) And he, too! (*Pointing at the* **Defendant**.) He has been lying low, like a mother hen, without saying a single word. (*The image captures the* **Defendant** *letting out a light, discreet yawn.*)

Defence Counsel I admit that I got bored. So what?

Prosecutor I also got bored while you were talking. Look what I was doing while you were screaming your lungs out. (*New projection: the* **Prosecutor** *cleaning his nails with the toothpick found in the* **Defendant**'s *jacket.*)

Judge Terrible. Could it be that we've been actually bored to death for two hours without having a clue?

Court Clerk The defendant got bored, too. Especially during Act Two, he got bored to death. (*Projection.*)

Judge Buah!

Court Clerk (*pointing towards the first few rows*) And him, look at him! (*Another image, of a spectator caught absent-minded.*) And so on, I could show you thousands of images. (*Keeps changing the slides; zooming in on other spectators caught in moments of unattention.*) Everybody is bored to death.

Judge   That's normal. Boredom leads to crime.

Court Clerk (*distressed*)   I didn't know we were so bad.

Defence Counsel   We are even worse than them.

Judge   We should be put on trial.

Defence Counsel   By whom?

Judge   By them. (*Pointing at the auditorium.*)

They all come closer to the audience, moving forward, step by step, with sad and wry faces, as if they were waiting to be put on trial. After a few long seconds, there is the sinister sound of an alarm bell, as if a fire has broken out.

Judge   What's this, what's going on? To hell with this, what's happening here?

Court Clerk (*stops the alarm that is fitted right under his desk*)   This is our kettledrum beat.

Judge   Are you insane? What kettledrum beat? You want to pack up shop here?

Court Clerk   Well, we have fifteen minutes left. We are approaching the end, Your Honour. Have you never listened to Verdi?

Judge   Ladies and gentlemen, history goes on. The trial continues. We are sorry about the awkward moments that occurred. Let's forget about the past. It was an unfortunate confusion, a bizarre state of irritation, uncertainty and stupid doubt. Order, however, has been restored. Everything is well. The court can promise you a swift and categorical ending that will be straightforward and reassuring for us all. No extra questions or withheld answers! We have exactly fifteen minutes. We must finish on time, history can only be assailed from within, by fitting into the allocated timeframe. We want an optimistic and fortifying finale. We need this closure. Thank you, ladies and gentlemen! (*He bows sneakily in front of the court and withdraws to one side, remaining a central figure in this act and continuing to keep watch on everything that takes place.*)

Court Clerk (*as if he were a changed man; self-assured, somewhat ashamed of his past decline*)   Next witness, please.

Witness 4 *enters.*

Prosecutor   Name and profession.

Witness 4   Rudolf. Photographer.

Prosecutor   What sort of photographs do you normally take?

Witness 4   People, birds . . .

Prosecutor   Birds? Why are you photographing birds?

Witness 4 I like them. You know, ever since my chidhood, I . . .

Prosecutor Where did you spend your childhood?

Witness 4 In a lagoon. You know what it's like in a lagoon. There are birds all the time, the wind is blowing, it's all very nice there. Have you ever been to a lagoon?

Prosecutor You'd better stick to answering my questions. Hear me? And stop photographing birds. Understood?

Witness 4 Yes.

Prosecutor Just stick to people.

Witness 4 That's what I'll do.

Prosecutor Where have you been this evening?

Witness 4 Around here, pottering about all the time.

Prosecutor For what reason?

Witness 4 I'm the theatre photographer.

Prosecutor Since when?

Witness 4 For the last ten years.

Prosecutor Have you been hiding?

Witness 4 I had to.

Prosecutor Who did you photograph?

Witness 4 Everybody.

Prosecutor Did you have difficulties with anyone among the spectators?

Witness 4 No.

Prosecutor What do you think about the defendant?

Witness 4 He blinks a bit much.

Prosecutor Repeat!

Witness 4 He blinks a lot.

Prosecutor When did you realize this?

Witness 4 While I was photographing him. I had to wait a few times for his blinking to stop.

Prosecutor With which eye does he blink?

Witness 4 Both.

Court Clerk How common!

Judge Shush!

Prosecutor Do you find it normal for someone to blink when they are being photographed?

Witness 4 No. It's a nightmare for a photographer.

Prosecutor And don't you think that a man who blinks when he is about to be photographed is ill-meaning?

Witness 4 I do.

Prosecutor And don't you think that a man who blinks is capable in fact of everything?

Witness 4 Possibly.

Prosecutor How do you feel when someone blinks?

Witness 4 I get annoyed.

Prosecutor Did you get annoyed tonight?

Witness 4 Yes. I felt like screaming.

Prosecutor How often did he blink?

Witness 4 He'd blink really quickly for a few seconds. Then, he'd stop for a few seconds, and then start again.

Prosecutor Maddening, absolutely maddening.

Witness 4 I ruined several good shots because of this.

Prosecutor Do you think that there are other people in the auditorium who blink so often?

Witness 4 No. All others blink in a normal way.

Prosecutor Do you think the defendant had particular reasons to blink?

Witness 4 On the whole, the lights were focusing on him too much.

Prosecutor Anyway, could you show us, really quickly and suggestively, how he blinked?

Witness 4 Something like this . . . (*Blinks to the audience.*)

Prosecutor Take a look, gentlemen. (*To the* **Judge**.) To me, all is very clear. I have no more questions.

Judge Defence counsel, have you got any questions?

Defence Counsel I don't think there is any point, Your Honour. Yet, I'd like to clarify something.

Judge Please do! The witness is at your disposal.

Defence Counsel (*to the* **Witness**) Don't you think that this tendency of the defendant has a deeper subtext?

Witness 4 Sure, it has.

Defence Counsel Don't you think that, in fact, this blinking is just a code for a deeper and more perfidious desire, namely to keep his eyes closed? Don't you think that his real intention was to close his eyes and this blinking was a sort of ritual to deceive us?

Witness 4 Absolutely correct.

Defence Counsel Have you ever spotted the defendant with his eyes closed?

Witness 4 No.

Defence Counsel But you acknowledge the fact that you could have done so.

Witness 4 Yes.

Defence Counsel Has the defendant wiped his eyes with a tissue?

Witness 4 No.

Defence Counsel But you acknowledge the fact that he could have done so.

Witness 4 Yes.

Defence Counsel This is what I wanted to know. And now, do tell us how often the defendant blinked this evening.

Witness 4 15,437 times.

Prosecutor Have you done the maths properly? Are you sure?

Judge Incredible, incredible!

Witness 4 (*chastizing them*) Gentlemen! How can you possibly doubt this?

Defence Counsel Please repeat the figure.

Witness 4 15,437 times. Having said that, he blinked another two times since I first uttered this figure, so we have a grand total of 15,439 blinks.

Defence Counsel Can you state this, assuming full responsibility for your claim?

Witness 4 Of course. I have a slide for every single blink.

Defence Counsel Perfect. Your Honour, may we proceed to watching these slides?

Judge Next! (*Pointing at the clock.*)

Witness 4 *exits; nobody enters.*

Prosecutor Clerk! Who's the next witness?

Court Clerk (*checks his notes*) A spectator.

Prosecutor Which one?

Court Clerk Whichever.

Prosecutor Clerk! Please attend to your job properly.

Court Clerk (*proceeds to setting in motion a lottery machine*)   The next witness is spectator number 147. (*This spectator is snatched by soldiers and brought into the witness box.*)

Prosecutor   What's your name?

Witness 5   My name is Manase.

Prosecutor   Mr Manase, what made you come to this play?

Witness 5   Nothing. I accompanied my wife.

Prosecutor   Was it difficult for you to get tickets?

Witness 5   No, my wife got them through work.

Prosecutor   Can you see the stage well from your seat, number 147?

Witness 5   No, it's rather far back.

Prosecutor   Did you get the chance to spot the criminal?

Witness 5   Yes. I caught a glimpse of him during the intermission as he was having coffee.

Prosecutor   What impression did he make on you?

Witness 5   Don't really know what to say. My wife laughed.

Prosecutor   Does she tend to laugh a lot?

Witness 5   She does . . .

Prosecutor   Do you think we are having a laugh here?

Witness 5 (*embarrased, intimidated, idiotic laughter*)   Well . . .

Prosecutor   Have you ever been under investigation for anything?

Witness 5   Yes, I had a car accident.

Judge   Did you come here in your car?

Defence Counsel   Shush!

Prosecutor   What do think about him (*pointing at the* **Defendant**), is he an actor or a real spectator?

Witness 5   My wife says he's an actor.

Prosecutor   Had you been in his shoes, would you have left?

Witness 5   Not sure.

Prosecutor   You wouldn't have taken all this rough and tumble, right?

Witness 5   It's not all that pleasant, you know.

Prosecutor   So you would have left.

Witness 5 Not sure . . .

Prosecutor Whoever leaves like that must feel guilty. Am I right?

Witness 5 *huffing and puffing, unable to find his place.*

Prosecutor Yet whoever stays is also guilty in a way. Such people are tortured by their own conscience, and this is the reason why they stay.

Witness 5 Sir, I'm not interested in . . .

Prosecutor In a way, you are an accomplice of the criminal. You neither want to defend him, nor to take his place. Can't get any worse than that.

Witness 5 I came here to have fun, I . . .

Prosecutor Are you saying that the evening wasn't entertaining enough for you?

Witness 5 No, I'm not . . .

Prosecutor So you did have fun.

Witness 5 Yes, I did.

Prosecutor What the hell did you find amusing here?

Witness 5 My wife . . .

Prosecutor You are mistaken, this wasn't meant to be a fun night out! Do you regret coming here?

Witness 5 Oh no, it isn't quite so bad . . .

Prosecutor Would you consider coming to this play again? To ascertain whether the defendant is an actor or a spectator?

Witness 5 Not sure, not sure . . . (*Starting to panic.*)

Prosecutor Would anybody else like to ask this witness some questions?

The spectator runs back to his seat.

Court Clerk Next!

Judge As fast as possible! Only strictly necessary questions please!

Enter the next witness.

Prosecutor Name and profession. Quickly!

Witness 6 I . . . directed this play.

Prosecutor Which play?

Witness 6 This one.

Prosecutor The one in which I'm performing right now?

Witness 6 Yes. I'm the director.

Prosecutor   Have you directed other plays, as well?

Witness 6   Yes, I have. All sorts of plays.

Prosecutor   What made you choose this play?

Witness 6   It seemed to me rather lively and topical.

Prosecutor   Are you pleased with the way the production has come out?

Witness 6   Yes, in general, yes.

Prosecutor   Do you think you've managed to come up with something new?

Witness 6   Something new . . . Well, it's hard to actually do that. I can't talk of something really new. But in any case I did come up with something.

Prosecutor   Have you understood the message of the play?

Witness 6   Sure. Although . . . See, there are several layers of understanding, each has another rhythm, another nuance. But little by little . . .

Prosecutor   Do you think that the spectators in the audience tonight have been affected at the level of their conscience?

Witness 6   I don't know. Hope so. There are plenty of aspects that give food for thought. When people leave the theatre, the play in fact continues in the mind of each and every spectator. Proper resolution only takes place later, at home, the next day.

Prosecutor   Are you pleased with the performance of the actors?

Witness 6   Yes, the actors were absolute darlings and very receptive.

Prosecutor   Could you tell me what made you choose me for this role?

Witness 6   You?!

Prosecutor   Yes, me.

Witness 6   Well, we know each other.

Prosecutor   Do you think this role suits me?

Witness 6   Come now!

Prosecutor   What solution have you chosen as far as the defendant is concerned? Actor or spectator?

Witness 6   I can't possibly reveal this . . .

Prosecutor   Weren't you concerned that by casting a spectator you've run the risk of them simply getting up and leaving? Or throwing something at your head?

Witness 6   Sure, there is a certain risk.

Prosecutor   Conversely, aren't you afraid that by placing an actor in this situation everything is basically no fun?

Witness 6   Actor or spectator, the idea is the same.

Judge   Explain, quick!

Witness 6   I mean to say that there is a tension that leads to an essential relationship between . . .

Prosecutor   Thank you. You're free to leave.

Witness 6   No, considering that I've made a start at addressing these issues, I think I should . . .

All (*screaming*)   Out with you!

Witness 6 (*confused, red in the face*)   I . . . think . . . there's no point in getting out of line . . .

Judge   Out! Out! (*Furiously.*) Next!

The soldiers bring in a man tied up, with a cloth hood over his head. This character is placed, as if it were an ordinary package, at the **Prosecutor**'s *feet. The man keeps fighting and, judged by the noises he's making, he has been gagged.*

Prosecutor   What's this?

Court Clerk (*timidly*)   The author, sir.

Judge   The author? This one here?

Defence Counsel   The author of what?

Court Clerk   The author of this play.

Judge   What? This piece of junk has an author?

Court Clerk   For all intents and purposes, yes.

Witness 7 *tries his best to stand up.*

Eventually, he manages to kneel.

Prosecutor   Strange. Are you claiming that this man has previously written down everything we are saying here?

Court Clerk   It would seem so.

Defence Counsel   Word by word?

Court Clerk (*edges towards* **Witness 7** *and pushes him to the ground*)   Yes.

Judge   You mean that everything we've said so far was already in the text?

Court Clerk (*casting a glance at the text*)   Basically, yes.

Prosecutor   Without skipping anything?

Defence Counsel   Or adding?

Judge   What if we feel like saying something that's not in the text?

Court Clerk   Well, he might get annoyed.

Act Two   89

Prosecutor   Why doesn't he talk?

Court Clerk   No idea. This is what these authors are like, kind of quiet and strange.

Prosecutor (*to* **Witness 7**)   Excuse me, sir, would you mind answering a few questions?

Defence Counsel (*to* **Witness 7**)   Or perhaps you'd like me to say a few words you have never written and could have never even imagined.

Prosecutor   It's obvious, he doesn't want to answer.

Court Clerk (*pushing* **Witness 7** *to the ground again*)   Come on, talk to us, why don't you say something? Just say something, to help justice, seriously . . .

Judge   What's he saying?

Court Clerk   Nothing.

Judge   Goodness gracious, what the hell is wrong with him?

Court Clerk   I think he's ignorig us, Your Honour.

Prosecutor (*to* **Witness 7**, *who's struggling in the sack*)   Answer please, sir. The prosecutor is asking you. We need your witness statement to shed light on the truth.

Defence Counsel   It's clear as day that he doesn't give a damn about the truth.

Prosecutor (*irritated*)   Oh dear! Incredible, seeing and not believing!

Defence Counsel (*to* **Witness 7**, *who carries on bellowing and fussing*)   Why this silence, sir? You really think we know nothing and have no idea about literature?

Court Clerk (*constantly looking for an opportunity to pin the author to the ground as soon as the latter has managed to get back on his knees*)   It's obvious that the witness is defying this court, Your Honour. We should really change our methods.

Prosecutor   Unbelievable, absolutely unbelievable! This man is the only person in a position to tell the truth and, alas, he refuses to speak!

Defence Counsel (*to* **Witness 7**, *with parental kindness*)   Come on, tell us the truth!

Prosecutor   At least two or three words.

Court Clerk (*to* **Witness 7**)   Please, sir, say YES three times.

Judge   He should at least raise his hand a little, the right palm, as high as possible.

Court Clerk (*to* **Witness 7**)   Listen, sir, we'll be satisfied if you raise your right palm a little.

Judge   Doesn't want to?

Defence Counsel   No.

Prosecutor   He doesn't want to.

Judge   What a brute! See where culture has taken us?

Defence Counsel What if we made an opening around his mouth?

Judge (*produces a pair of scissors*) There. Gently, please. There's nothing more sensitive in a writer than their mouth.

Defence Counsel, *assisted by the others, cuts a small hole into the cloth sack that covers the head of* **Witness 7**. *He keeps struggling and lets out a range of muffled sounds.*

Defence Counsel (*to* **Witness 7**) We are listening, sir.

Prosecutor Your play is nothing but a long waffle, just so you know. By the way, this line with the waffle is written down there, right?

Defence Counsel You really think that you can have us in your pocket? That you can simply wring the neck of your characters as you please, as and when you want to?

Prosecutor You really think that we are only capable of saying stuff that is already scripted? That all we are capable of thinking has to be already written down? That you can oblige us to say and do whatever you want? That all we can ever do and think until the end of our days is already scripted?

Defence Counsel What if I decide to keep silent?

Prosecutor What if I won't say a thing?

Defence Counsel Is this aspect also stipulated in the text?

Prosecutor Perhaps you've also stipulated that I, as your character, may not want to utter this text?

Defence Counsel What a megalomaniac!

Court Clerk It's all in vain, gentlemen. The witness refuses to speak.

Judge Goddamit, make that hole around his mouth bigger!

Court Clerk (*cutting another hole*) Same thing all over. The witness has an additional sackcloth under each hole cut into the top layer.

Defence Counsel (*also cutting a hole in the sack that covers the head of* **Witness 7**) Come on, tell us the truth.

Defence Counsel (*cutting another hole*) We're listening. What exactly did you want to convey with these rubbish plays of yours?

Court Clerk (*screaming hysterically*) The message, man! What is your message?

Prosecutor What shall we do, Your Honour? The author doesn't seem to have anything to say.

Judge (*sadly*) What a shame! A real shame.

Prosecutor Authors! That's what you get with these authors. They think they are the salt of the earth, but at the moment of truth, they just curl up in a ball, without saying a single word.

Defence Counsel Please talk to us, sir! You are our last hope! The very last one. The last hope for humanity, no less! The last hope for truth! Thousands and millions are waiting to hear your voice. To hear your words! Everybody has been waiting for you, as if you were the Messiah. Talk! Show us what's rotten and where! Show us where the evil is hiding, in each and every one of us, put your finger on rottenness and decay! Save us! We beg you, Sir, save us!

Prosecutor My ass! He's stubborn like a donkey.

Court Clerk (*to* **Witness 7**, *moved by the* **Defence Counsel**'s *speech*) Don't abandon us!

Judge (*wiping off a tear in the corner of his eye.*) In this way we'll end up all alone, until the end of times . . .

Prosecutor (*red with anger*) Here, take your text back! Take it! (*Tears out a page, rolls it up and sticks it into one of the holes cut into the sack.*) We refuse to take part in your masquerade!

Court Clerk (*same thing, another page torn out, rolled up and stuck back into the author's 'head'*) It's over!

Defence Counsel (*same game*) Enough! We've had enough!

Witness 7 *starts looking like an extraterrestrial, at the verge of desperation, as if wanting to shout, 'Water! Water! Water!'*

Judge Next witness!

Witness 7 (*screaming louder and louder as the soldiers drag him out of the courtroom*) Water! Water!! Water!!!

The soldiers return with the next **Witness**, *a terrified man who's nevertheless all smiles.*

Prosecutor Who are you?

Witness 8 I . . . I happened to be in front of the theatre . . .

Prosecutor What were you doing in front of the theatre?

Witness 8 Waiting for someone.

Prosecutor Who?

Witness 8 I was waiting for the performance to end.

Prosecutor Oh, you've lost your patience, haven't you? You don't want to see anything or hear anything, you just want to pull your head in.

Witness 8 No, not at all. Someone I know is in the auditorium. I was simply waiting here.

Prosecutor Who's in the auditorium?

Witness 8 My wife and daughter. It's late, you know, the show finishes fairly late.

Judge   Did you come here by car?

Witness 8 (*cheerfully*)   Yes, I did!

Judge   Which way are you going?

Witness 8   Anywhere.

Prosecutor   Next! Shut it! Next! We've got three more minutes!

Witness 8 *leaves in a hurry, feeling relieved.*

Court Clerk (*returns looking really frightend after having accompanied* **Witness 8** *on his way out*)   Gentlemen, there are crowds on the street, hundreds of people seem to have gathered outside.

One can hear the roar of the crowd, first on the street, then closer and closer, as if coming from backstage.

Judge   Why did they come here?

Court Clerk   To bear witness. There are hundreds and hundreds of witnesses.

Judge   Who told them to come here? We don't need so many witnesses.

Court Clerk   They came out of their own initiative. They started to show up just like that.

Defence Counsel   It would appear that people want to help us, Your Honour.

Prosecutor   But who asked them to help? Why do they want to help us anyway?

Court Clerk   People want to observe the law, sir. People want to take the side of the law.

Suddenly a head punctures through the screen onto which the images were projected earlier.

Head 1   Me, too! Me, too!

Judge   What's with this debacle, clerk?!

Court Clerk   How could I know? Have no idea.

A few other **Heads** *push through the screen.*

Head 2   We, too! We, too!

Head 3   We know everything! Everything!

Head 4   I know the defendant personally. Yes, I do! We did our army service together!

Head 5   Justice must be done! Justice!

Head 1, Head 2, Head 3, Head 4, Head 5   Justice! Justice!

Commotion, screams, agitation is building up behind the scenes.

Court Clerk (*toing and froing between the stage and the wings*)   They have started the hearing backstage, too!

Prosecutor   What?!

Judge   What hearing?

Court Clerk (*dashing from one place to the other*)   The cross-examinations have started, both on the street and in the foyer!

Prosecutor   What are you talking about? Who's cross-examining in my place?

Court Clerk (*going mental after all this running*)   There are hordes of people, sir. They are cross-examining one another.

One can hear the sprawling ripple of thousands of voices.

The rule of law triumphs!

Defence Counsel   What do you mean triumphs? Who has the temerity to cross-examine people on the street?

Court Clerk (*exhausted, but continuing his hectic toing and froing*)   The witnesses, Sir! They want to help you. There are thousands of witnesses, millions . . .

Further heads pierce the screen, and start clamouring and cross-examining one another in a stupefiantly cacophonic glee.

Defence Counsel   They are insane! Have to be dispersed.

Court Clerk   They are on our side, they came of their own initative. It makes no sense to disperse them.

Defence Counsel   They are breaking the law.

Court Clerk   No they aren't, they are defending it.

Defence Counsel   Your Honour, why don't you just come up with the verdict?! These people are stealing our defendant!

Prosecutor   The verdict! Yes!

Drum beat by the entrance to the auditorium. It seems to be getting nearer and nearer, and more and more solemn. The **Author** *enters, leading an almost imperial yet bizarre procession, looking as if they were spectres from another world that had invaded the space.*

The **Author**'s *head is still covered by the sack and the paper rolls are still sticking out of the holes. This time, however, he is behaving like a genuine master of ceremonies and will conduct the entire final sequence. In his right hand, he is holding a ceremonial baton with which he is punctuating the gradual approach of the procession.*

Behind the **Author**, *there are seven* **Witnesses**: **The Man who is Checking Tickets, The Young Woman from the Cloakroom, The Fat Woman from the Bar, The**

Theatre Photographer, The Spectator from the Auditorium, The Director, The Man Waiting in Front of the Theatre.

Three of them have drumkits hanging around their necks, and the other four are carrying a litter box. The witnesses are easy to recognize, even though their gestures recall those of marionettes and their faces are rather pale. Their new personalities and current state of hypnosis could be conveyed by subtle changes to their make-up.

They are easing forward in a majestically relentless fashion, as if they were about to attend the Last Judgement. Every now and then, the character in the litter box, concealed behind a curtain, is having a go at badly playing the harmonica. Drumrolls are alternating with the sound of harmonica.

Judge (*intrigued*)   What's this?

Author (*in a calm yet powerful voice*)   The last witness, Your Honour.

Judge   What? Which witness?

Autorul   The last one, Your Honour.

Judge   Out of the question!

Prosecutor   Enough! Please vacate the auditorium, understood?

Author (*unperturbed*)   The last witness, Your Honour!

Defence Counsel (*to the* **Judge**)   The verdict! Pass sentence, quick!

Author (*leading the procession, mounts the stage*)   Ladies and gentlemen, behold the last witness! The final witness!

The procession comes to a halt and the litter box is placed at the very centre of the stage.

The Blind Man who Plays the Harmonica at the Street Corner *draws the curtains and sticks his head out. Every time he speaks, he accompanies his words with a tune played on the harmonica.*

Judge (*scared*)   What's with this guy here?

Author   This man plays the harmonica at the street corner, Your Honour.

The Blind Man who Plays the Harmonica at the Street Corner (*comes out of the litter box, using his hands to feel his surroundings; he trips over, gets up, feels the air, the people and the objects; a grotesque and tragic hide and seek*)   Ladies and gentlemen, I went to war, I fought at the front line . . . (*Plays his harmonica.*) I was decorated, I have crosses, medals, long live the king! Long live the republic! (*Plays his harmonica.*) Yes, ladies and gentlemen, I was one of the heroes!

Court Clerk (*to the* **Judge**)   Lunatics, bloody psychos! We must call security!

Prosecutor   The sentence, in the name of God, come on, pass a quick sentence!

Judge (*howling, trying to outscream the* **Blind Man** *and his harmonica*)   Ladies and gentlemen! Following the hearing of witnesses and taking into account the severity of their statements . . .

The Blind Man who Plays the Harmonica at the Street Corner (*feeling the head of the* **Judge**)   Gentlemen, I don't know anybody, I'm blind, totally blind . . . (*plays his harmonica*) . . . because I had fought and spilled my blood on the battlefront . . .

As soon as **The Blind Man** *touches the* **Judge**, *the latter is paralysed, and left with his mouth open and with an arm up in the air. His pale face makes him look like the other characters in the procession.*

Prosecutor (*trying to re-enact the* **Judge**'*s speech in order to pass sentence*)   Following extended cross-examination and the severity of witness statements, not to mention the severity of statements that were not put forward by our witnesses . . .

The Blind Man who Plays the Harmonica at the Street Corner (*slips on the floor, edges forward to the* **Prosecutor**, *falls down in front of him and starts feeling the body from the legs up until he makes it to the face*)   Gentlemen, have pity on this former fighter! (*Plays the harmonica.*) I was no coward, I fought, I swear, I have been awarded crosses, decorations. Long live the king! Long live the republic!

The Prosecutor, *frozen mid-submission. The four* **Witnesses** *who carried the litter box form a magic quad around* **The Blind Man**, *whom they accompany from a respectful distance as if he were a king.*

The Blind Man who Plays the Harmonica at the Street Corner   Do believe me, folks! These aren't tall tales, everything I'm telling you is the truth, (*plays the harmonica*) the whole truth and nothing but the truth.

Defence Counsel (*terrorized by the proximity of* **The Blind Man**, *but unable to run away*)   I . . . I solemnly declare that . . . I declare here that . . . declare that . . .

The Blind Man who Plays the Harmonica at the Street Corner (*paralyses the* **Defence Counsel** *by way of a simple touch*)   Do believe me, gentlemen, it's true! (*Plays the harmonica.*) I got wounded for my coutry, long live the king, long live the republic!

Court Clerk (*left alone, already paralysed by fear and as if crying for help*)   Your Honour! (**The Blind Man** *is approaching, feeling the air with his hands.*) Prosecutor, please! (**The Blind Man's** *hands are conducting a bizarre ritual in the air.*) Defence counsel, please!

The Blind Man who Plays the Harmonica at the Street Corner   Gentlemen, I don't know anyone, I swear. (*Plays the harmonica.*) Anybody, anybody. (*Touches the* **Court Clerk**.) Anybody at all. Anybody and anything, please believe me! I'm all alone in the world! (*Touches the* **Heads** *that remain silent.*)

Meanwhile, the procession has circled the stage and, led by the **Author**, *is now heading towards the exit, traversing the auditorium one last time.* **The Blind Man who Plays the Harmonica at the Street Corner** *continues to feel the air and to play his harmonica. Every now and then, he may touch the shoulder of the odd spectator.*

Behind the **Author**, *there are the three* **Witnesses** *with drums and the other four* **Witnesses** *who form a magic square around* **The Blind Man**. *The* **Judge**, *the* **Court**

Clerk, *the* **Prosecutor** *and the* **Defense Councel** *all appear to be in a trance, and line up behind the others, following them on their way towards the exit.*

The procession leaves the auditorium. For a while, one can still hear the drumbeat and **The Blind Man** *play his harmonica. His cavernous voice bellows a few more 'Long live the king!' and 'Long live the republic!' slogans.*

The litter box is left behind in the middle of the empty stage, as if it were a magic and mysterious object, a sort of abandoned 'Trojan Horse'.

Lights fade until complete blackout.

The End.

Note

1   This is a reference to the severe shortages in 1980s Romania, when hot water was only supplied for a few hours in the course of the day.

The Passport

György Dragomán

Translated from the Hungarian by Jozefina Komporaly
(Original title in Hungarian: *Kalucsni*)

3 György Dragomán: *The Passport* – Hungarian Theatre of Cluj, Romania (directed by András Visky). Premiere: 16 November 2016. Poster design: Dénes Miklósi.

Characters

Gyuri – *husband*
Márta – *wife*
Annamari – *their daughter*
Grandma (Anna) – *Gyuri's mother*

Krisztina – *Gyuri's lover (an actress)*
Comrade Veress – *Krisztina's father*
Lieutenant Balla, Captain Bajko – *immediate subalterns of comrade Veress, plain-clothes secret police officers*
Barta – *secret police agent*
Two uniformed officers

Jánoska and Lajoska – *removal men*

The action takes place in one of the larger Transylvanian towns in the second half of the 1980s.

Scene One

*Kitchen, mid-afternoon. The walls are decorated with ceramic folk art and modern prints, indicative of a middle-class lifestyle in 1980s Transylvania. On the kitchen table, there is a huge bouquet of tulips still wrapped in paper, the flowers peeking through an opening on the wrapper. A middle-aged man (***Gyuri***) is sipping soup from a bowl. Enter* **Annamari***, his teenage daughter.*

Annamari Come on, Dad, why didn't you put these flowers in water? The poor things are wilting away.

Gyuri Sorry.

Annamari Never mind, I'll take care of this now.

She fetches a glass vase from the cupboard, fills it with water, takes it to the table, unwraps the flowers and puts them in the vase.

Gyuri Wow, you've grown into a fine young woman! I remember it well when you were a tiny baby, you were as tall as the table was wide.

Annamari Not this one again, please! You told me a thousand times how you'd just place me in the middle of the table in my baby bouncer and keep an eye on me while having lunch. Yuck.

Gyuri We were so happy that you'd finally arrived. It wasn't easy, you know, we thought we'd never have children, your poor mother was quite devastated.

Annamari You wanted a son. (*Keeps arranging the flowers.*)

Gyuri Everybody wants a son. People don't realize that a daughter is a much greater gift. When I look at you and see how tall and beautiful you've grown, I find it hard to believe that you were once such a fragile thing.

Annamari Enough of this, there's no need to remind me all the time what a hideous baby I used to be.

Gyuri Still, your head was covered in purple bruises, your legs looked like matchsticks, and we were worried sick because you wouldn't breastfeed. (*Notices the vase.*) Why this vase and not the blue one?

Annamari That one got broken.

Gyuri When?

Annamari Last week. When they searched our house. (*Beat.*) Dad, can you look at me, please?

Gyuri Yes?

Annamari Try looking at me as if I wasn't your daughter, but some stranger, and tell me the truth – do I look cross-eyed? Even a little bit?

Gyuri (*looks at her*) Absolutely not. Not at all. Your eyes are really beautiful. I swear. (*Stands up.*) Did you give Grandma her lunch?

Annamari She didn't want it. Could you talk to her? She may be asleep though.

Gyuri Not now, I'm already running late, have to go back to the office.

Annamari Dad, I need to ask you something else.

Gyuri Go on.

Annamari If I wasn't your daughter, just say a total stranger, and you'd see me on the street, what would you think of me?

Gyuri What is this supposed to mean?

Annamari Would you take me for a child or a young girl? You wouldn't, would you?

Gyuri Annamari, what's going on? Did anybody hurt you? Is there a problem?

Annamari No, nothing. (*Starts arranging stuff.*) Mum will be late today – she asked me to tidy up a bit.

Gyuri Give me your hand, dear. (*The two of them hold hands.*) When I was fifteen, I was madly in love with an actress. I saw her photo in an old Italian magazine, which I nicked from my father's desk drawer.

Annamari Why are you telling me this now?

Gyuri It felt like looking down from very, very high, it made me dizzy and also terrified, yet it was beautiful all the same. I can still remember that feeling quite clearly.

Annamari Dad, I'm not in love.

Gyuri First love is something one never forgets. You should try and pick someone worthy though. And you should know that you can always count on me. You can talk to me whenever you like. Just let me know if I can help you in any way.

Annamari Sure. Thanks, Dad.

Gyuri Is there anything I can do for you?

Annamari No, not really.

Gyuri Fine. But keep in mind what I told you. Soon enough lots of people will want lots of things from you. Trust me. And I'm not just talking about romantic stuff. You should never forget that you can always say no. To anything and anyone.

Annamari Come on, dad, don't get started with this again.

Gyuri Okay, okay, I have to go now. I won't be very late. (*Goodbye peck on the cheek.*)

Blackout.

Scene Two

Same day, an hour later. Well-appointed living room, plenty of books and paintings. One can also catch a glimpse of the entrance hall and the front door. Someone is knocking on the door, then the bell rings. **Annamari** *opens the door to a young woman (***Krisztina***).*

Krisztina Hello, you must be Annamari, you're the spitting image of your father. (*Enters the flat.*) You don't know me, but I've heard a lot about you. I've imagined you just the way you are. I'm Krisztina by the way.

Annamari Good afternoon, madam.

Krisztina Feel free to call me by my first name. (*Kiss, kiss.*)

Annamari Please come in. (*Looks puzzled.*)

Krisztina Thanks. I'm here to see your father.

Annamari He's not at home. Neither he, nor Mum. Only Grandma, but she's asleep. Shall I wake her up?

Krisztina No need, thanks. You're a darling. Do you happen to know where your father might be?

Annamari He went back to work. To the editorial office.

Krisztina No, he didn't. I've just been there.

Annamari Why are you looking for him, madam?

Krisztina I told you, we are on first-name terms. I have something to tell him. A miracle has just happened, you know?

Grandma's voice Annamari? Who's there? Has Mártika come home?

Krisztina Hush! (*Signals to* **Annamari** *not to tell about her.*)

Annamari No one, I've just been rehearsing this poem I have to recite.

Grandma's voice Excellent, good girl. (*Silence.*)

Krisztina Are you sure he isn't home?

Annamari Told you he wasn't.

Krisztina Can I wait for him here? It's absolutely essential that I speak to him.

Annamari Don't know . . .

Krisztina How cute. (*Looks round.*) Nice cosy place you have here. Would you mind getting me a glass of water? (*Slips her coat off and throws it to* **Annamari**.) You can also hang this up on your way out. (*Makes herself comfortable in the armchair.*). Is that really true that you recite poems?

Annamari Yes, it is.

Krisztina And what sort of stuff?

Annamari Right now it's Hungarian classics like Endre Ady's 'Hawk mating on the fallen leaves'.

Krisztina That's a difficult love poem. You can't possibly get such a thing at your age, but I can help you with it if you want. Mind you, I don't really like this poem. But it's simply too famous, so I had to include it in one of my solo shows. Allegedly, I wasn't too bad at reciting it.

Annamari So you're an actress?

Krisztina You can say that again.

Annamari (*recognizes her*) Goodness, you are . . .

Krisztina Yes, I'm Krisztina Veress.

Bewildered, **Annamari** *just stands there for a while, coat in hand, then leaves.*

Footsteps, key in door lock. Enter **Márta***,* **Annamari***'s mother,* **Grandma***'s daughter-in-law.*

Márta (*shouts back from the door*) Easy does it, no need to rush, I know that these four floors are no mean feat. (*Notices* **Krisztina**.) What are you doing here?

Krisztina I came to see Gyuri.

Márta Is that so? In what matter?

Krisztina In a matter I'll discuss with him in person.

Márta I see.

Two men, **Jánoska** *and* **Lajoska***, come in, carrying flatpack cardboard boxes. They come to a halt in the middle of the room.*

Jánoska Where should we take these, madam doctor?

Annamari *returns with a glass of water.*

Márta (*to the men carrying the boxes*) Doesn't matter, put them wherever you like. (*To* **Annamari**.) Annamari, what's this woman doing here?

Annamari Mum, she's . . .

Márta I know who she is.

Annamari She came to see father.

Márta Is that so? Why did you let her in, I told you not to let anybody in! Haven't all these house searches managed to put you off?

Annamari What are these boxes doing here?

Márta They're just boxes.

Jánoska *and* **Lajoska** *put the boxes down.*

Jánoska We'll get the rest. (*They're off.*)

Annamari Why do we need so many boxes?

Grandma's voice Mártika, is that you?

Márta (*shouts back*) Yes, Grandma, please hold on for a moment, I'll be with you in a second. (*To* **Annamari**.) Go get the coat of this missy. She can't stay any longer.

Krisztina I didn't come to see you. I came to see Gyuri.

Márta He's not in, as you can see!

Krisztina I'll wait. Do you want to throw me out?

Annamari Mum, can you please tell me what these boxes are for?!

Grandma's voice Mártika, please come to me. And bring me my lunch.

Márta (*to* **Annamari**) I'll tell you, just fetch that fucking coat! (*Shouts.*) Grandma dear, I told you I'll be with you in a second. (*To* **Annamari**.) Didn't you offer her some lunch?

Annamari I did. But she didn't want it.

Márta Bloody hell, I had enough. (*To* **Krisztina**.) Yes, darling, I'll throw you out if need be. You think you're the first little slut that had the courage to show up here?

Krisztina I'm not a slut.

Márta No? Then why did you come here to make a scene in front of my daughter and mother-in-law? If Gyuri wanted to find you, he'd obviously do just that, as he must have found you when he wanted to. Could it be that this thing between the two of you is now over? Could it be that he dumped you?

Krisztina Now I see why he left this place. I'd leave such a woman, too. He was happy with me. Really happy.

Márta Enough of this. Gyuri told me that you'd come here sooner or later, I didn't believe him, but he was quite right. He said I should kick you out. Send you away. Back to your fucking *Securitate* agent of a father.[1]

Krisztina Not true. Gyuri couldn't have said such a thing. And this has nothing to do with my father. This has only to do with Gyuri, Gyuri and me.

Annamari *returns with the coat.* **Márta** *takes it and sniffs it.*

Márta Oh, yes, the classic. Chanel Number 5. Very French. Most suited to a young talent. The question is whether you'd still have such a key position in the theatre company if you weren't your father's daughter.

Krisztina You'd know the answer to this if you had ever seen me on stage. My father has done an awful lot for this town. Everybody knows that.

Márta Sure, an awful lot. (*Beat.*) I must say I imagined you to be more mature when I occasionally smelled you on Gyuri. But he's getting on a bit, so needs some fresh blood. Still, I haven't smelled this scent for at least three weeks. That's when your love story must have ended. (*Throws the coat to* **Krisztina**.) Piss off!

Krisztina You think I came here just to buzz off like that? You think you can kick me out?

Márta Didn't I make it clear? Bugger off!

Krisztina If you really love Gyuri, then you must feel the same as I do and must understand me. Stop acting like a cunt! Trust me, it wasn't exactly easy for me to come here.

Márta Who cares, at least it will be easier for you to leave. Get out of here!

Krisztina . . . I have something very important to tell Gyuri.

Márta Out!

Krisztina (*to* **Annamari**) Annamari, I'm sorry to have dragged you into this business – one day you'll fall in love and then you'll understand these things. Don't be mad at your mother, she can't help it. I'd be jealous if I were her, too, but I must ask you a favour. Please pass a message on to your father. Tell him that I was here, I came here after all that happened because . . .

Márta Annamari, go to your room at once! I'll explain everything later.

Reluctantly, **Annamari** *makes a move. Meanwhile,* **Jánoska** *and* **Lajoska** *return with new boxes.*

Krisztina Annamari, listen to me, please listen to me, at least you, it's very important that your father finds out that . . .

Jánoska *and* **Lajoska** *throw all the boxes on the floor.*

Jánoska Here they are, all of them. Brought everything up.

Márta Thank you very much. You can start tomorrow. In the meantime, I shall think of a strategy.

Lajoska Madam doctor, this isn't what we agreed.

Jánoska You said you'd pay half of our money when we get here.

Márta As you can see, my husband isn't at home and he has the cash. You'll get it tomorrow, stop messing about.

Lajoska Excuse me, madam doctor, but these are top-quality boxes, one can't just nick these from any old place. They were meant for exportation and I'm unable to leave them here on trust.

Krisztina Shall I lend you some cash?

Márta (*to* **Krisztina**) Get the fuck out of here! (*To the removal men.*) Okay, okay, we'll sort this out in a moment.

Grandma's Voice Mártika, what's all this screaming and shouting? What's going on? Yet another house search?

Márta (*shouting*) Nothing, Grandma, the removal men are here, no house search whatsoever, please rest assured that everything will be just fine.

Grandma's Voice What removal men?

Annamari (*comes back*) What removal men?

Lajoska Madam doctor, you didn't even tell your daughter that you are moving away?

Jánoska At least your husband knows, I hope.

Lajoska Madam doctor, this won't work like this, one has to prepare for emigration – haven't you heard the joke about Kohn? He wants to emigrate . . .

Márta Don't you dare to tell me jokes, okay?

Lajoska *falls silent.*

Krisztina Annamari, listen up, tell your father that Krisztina was here and . . .

Annamari (*to* **Krisztina**) Leave me alone! (*To* **Márta**.) What do you mean we are moving away, how come?

Enter **Grandma**, *leaning on a walking stick. She's struggling to move.*

Grandma (*to the removal men*) Go away, we won't have another house search! Do you have any idea who my husband was? You think you can just keep putting us to the test forever? Get out of here at once!

Márta Calm down, Grandma, they aren't secret police agents, there's no house search.

Grandma You don't say, I know it full well, last time they came into my room and took all my pills away. Don't you tell me what's what, I can see for myself.

Jánoska Please calm down, we aren't from the police, and even less so from the secret services. My name is Jánoska and this is my son-in-law, Lajoska – we are moonlighting as removal men helping people about to emigrate with their packing, so everything is according to regulations and can get past customs.

Lajoska We're simply the best, we've been packaging furniture for exportation for years – there's no one better skilled at handling cardboard than Jánoska.

Annamari What emigration, Mum? We aren't emigrants. (*Beat.*) Why don't you ever tell me anything? We agreed you'd treat me like an adult!

Márta Come on, give me a break, Annamari! You're fifteen, we would have told you all about this when the time was right.

Annamari And when exactly would that have happened – after we'd done the packing?

Márta Enough! Stop it!

Annamari But I don't want to leave!

Márta Annamari, this is done and dusted! I don't want to hear a single word on this anymore!

Krisztina You really want to leave – this can't be! I know that Gyuri only started talking about leaving because of the break-up. Gyuri would never leave this town and this country, he'd never leave me. He always used to say that he'd never ever leave, he'd be the last man standing and the one to put out the lights.

Grandma Mártika? What's this? You must be joking. We aren't going anywhere – I won't leave the grave of my beloved behind. (*To the removal men.*) You are here by mistake – leave at once. And take all this rubbish with you. At once, understood, at once!

Márta Enough. Grandma, please calm down and go back to your room.

Grandma (*to* **Krisztina**) Who are you? Are you from the removal company, too?

Márta No, Grandma. She's Gyuri's lover. The latest.

Grandma Mártika, I didn't ask you! (*To* **Krisztina**.) What's your name?

Krisztina Krisztina. Krisztina Veress.

Grandma The daughter of that Veress?

Krisztina Yes indeed.

Grandma I've known your father ever since he was a teenager. I used to be his teacher. He thought he could learn to play the piano. He was already an idiot back then.

Krisztina Not much has changed.

Grandma Thought so. What do you want from my son?

Márta I told you she was his lover!

Grandma I didn't ask you.

Krisztina (*to* **Márta**) Yes, I am, so what? He was happy with me and loved me because I understood him and could relate to his problems, and didn't pester him all the time. I didn't turn his life into hell.

Márta What? What are you talking about?

Krisztina You know very well what I mean. I didn't want to tie him down, he could be free by my side. I loved him exactly the way he was, without forcing him to change or to earn more, I simply let him be!

Márta Stop it, or I'll slap you. Shame on you!

Krisztina I want to call a spade a spade. I want you to understand!

Márta Not interested! Get it? I don't give a damn about any of this!

Grandma Enough is enough!

Jánoska Sorry but we have to leave now, and if we don't get the cash you promised then we'll have to take the boxes away.

Lajoska As it happens, the family of doctor Huszár next door have also filed their emigration papers, and we'll just take everything over to theirs.

Jánoska And please sort your argument out later, you can't do this to us, we're honest working people.

Márta For God's sake, stop it! I'll take care of this. (*To* **Grandma**.) Grandma, I must borrow your secret stash.

Grandma No, Mártika. Out of the question. That's set aside for my funeral.

Márta Please don't make a scene, Grandma! Gyuri will be back soon and he'll give it back to you!

Grandma No.

Márta Annamari! Go to Grandma's room, and bring the footstool you'll find next to the armchair.

Grandma Annamari, you aren't going anywhere!

Annamari *makes a move.*

Grandma Annamari, stay right here!

Márta Grandma, please stop it! I told you that Gyuri will give the money back.

Grandma No!

Annamari *brings the footstool.*

Grandma Annamari! Take it back at once! Shame on you!

Márta Give it to me! (*Grabs the footstool from* **Annamari**.)

Annamari There won't be any problems, Grandma.

Grandma Give it back at once!

Krisztina Come on, stop it!

Márta Stay out of this!

Grandma Márta! What are you doing?

Márta You think I don't know that you keep your cash hidden in the lining?

Grandma Don't you dare touch it!

Márta You'll get it back. (*Reaches under the lining and pulls out an envelope.*) Here it is! (*Hands it over to* **Jánoska**.) There, this will do.

Jánoska (*takes it*)   We'll just count it if you don't mind.

Grandma (*gets hold of the envelope*)   I won't let you. I want a funeral just as grand as that of my poor darling. (*Tug of war.*)

Jánoska   Please let us have it! We've worked for it!

Grandma   Bloody secret police agents, get the hell out of here!

She yanks the envelope, and as it rips apart, bits of paper cut to the size of real banknotes fly into the air. Meanwhile, the door opens and **Gyuri** *enters.*

Jánoska   What the fuck! This isn't real money!

Lajoska   Bloody hell, madam doctor, this is just paper!

Annamari (*grabs one*)   Cut-up pages from a notebook! My old maths one!

Grandma   Where's my money? Where is it? Who took it?

Gyuri   I took it, Mum. I had to. But I'll give it back. Don't worry.

Grandma   But why, Gyurika? You know this was set aside for my funeral.

Gyuri   As far as I can see, you haven't died yet, have you? (*Notices that* **Krisztina** *is also there.*) What have you lost here?

Krisztina   I brought the money back. I know where you got it from.

Gyuri   What do you mean you brought it back?

Krisztina   I don't need it. Won't get rid of the baby.

Gyuri   What?

Krisztina   Can't you hear me, are you deaf? I won't get rid of it! I'll keep it!

Gyuri   No! We agreed that you wouldn't! It's best for everyone, can't you see?

Márta   Gyuri! What have you done?

Grandma   Gyurika? Is this true?

Krisztina   Yes, it is. (*Produces an envelope.*) Here. There you go. I brought it back. (*Heading towards* **Gyuri**.)

Grandma   Give it to me!

Lajoska   No, give it to us!

Jánoska   This is ours!

Gyuri   I have no idea who you are, but just shut it, will you? If not, I'll kick you in the arse, so you'll fly like two bloody birds in the sky! (*Makes his way over to* **Krisztina**.)

Jánoska   What have you just said? Lajoska, did you hear what he said?

Lajoska   You can't speak to us like this. We're out of here. Come, Jánoska. (*They start collecting the boxes.*)

Márta Ignore him, he always talks like this, he can't help it – you shouldn't take him seriously.

Grandma My funeral money! Have you got any idea what sacrifices I had to make, how could you just take it, how could you?

Gyuri (*to the packers*) Off you go, fuck you! (*To* **Grandma**.) Stop throwing a tantrum, Mum! I had no choice, do understand.

Grandma Shame on you! I would have given it to you if you had only asked. You know I'd do everything for you. But to steal in such a backhanded way, your father is turning in his grave!

Gyuri Okay, okay, Mum, just keep going on about your bleeding heart!

Grandma How dare you, shame on you. (*To* **Annamari**.) Annamari, help me! I want to sit down. Please help.

Annamari Of course, Grandma. (*Helps her.*)

Krisztina (*hands the envelope to* **Gyuri**) I wanted to do it, trust me, I really did. I started off as we agreed. But then, I could feel it move inside me, it moved its tiny hand, and I felt and knew that it wanted to live, and in that instant I also knew it was a boy. Get it? I know it's going to be a boy, and I understood everything, the whole thing, and . . .

Gyuri (*takes the envelope*) Good God. I should have gone with you. I should have accompanied you.

Krisztina I understood that inside me there was a tiny human, and I knew that it would turn out just like you, it will look like you, it will have your eyes, mouth . . .

Márta (*to the removal men*) You're going nowhere!

Jánoska Yes, we are!

Lajoska What do you mean we're going nowhere – we wouldn't stay here even if you paid us money. Come, Jánoska.

They get hold of a batch of boxes and head out.

Márta Stay!

They refuse.

Márta Why the fuck am I doing this – dammit, where will I find other packers? It's easy for you to scream but you have no idea how hard it was to persuade these people to take this job on. Do you think we're the only ones wanting to leave this bloody town?

Gyuri Calm down, dear, please, calm down.

Krisztina (*hugs* **Gyuri**, *and continues talking*) I wanted to hate you but I couldn't, and I understood everything, I understood that you did all this for my sake, you wanted what's best for me, you wanted me to get rid of it because you didn't want this to . . .

Gyuri (*tries to shake her off*) Okay, okay, no problem, calm down for God's sake, I should have accompanied you, I really should have!

Krisztina . . . as soon as this tiny human being started to move inside me, and I could feel that it wanted to live, I knew that all this didn't matter at all, only my baby mattered and that we loved each other. I know that you want what's best for me, but a man can't possibly understand this, I really don't want anything, I don't want success or leading roles, I want nothing except for this little boy to be born.

Gyuri Jesus!

Márta What week are you?

Krisztina Fourteen.

Márta It couldn't have moved then yet.

Krisztina Yes, it could. I felt it.

Márta You imagined it.

Krisztina And if I did, so what? It's inside me, and that's that. I carry it under my heart! It's mine. More important than anything else. And I'll keep it. And give birth to it.

Gyuri Okay, okay. Calm down, take a seat and have a glass of water, we'll talk this over and find a solution together.

Krisztina There's nothing to talk over, this is my child and my decision. This is nobody else's business. I didn't come here to tell you that.

Márta Are you sure, darling? It looked as if you did.

Krisztina No, I came to return your money, and to apologize.

Márta You think I care? You think the fact that you have a bun in the oven makes a difference? You're just a cheap little slut in my eyes.

Krisztina Apologize to Gyuri, not to you!

Márta Sure. Who else.

Gyuri Fine, apologies accepted, no harm done. But let's talk this over one last time.

Meanwhile, **Jánoska** *and* **Lajoska** *return and remove another batch of boxes.*

Jánoska The time will come, when they're going to regret this.

Lajoska I'll tell everyone, they'll never find other packers.

Jánoska None of their stuff will get past customs. Right, Lajoska?

Gyuri Shut it! If I see you here again, I'll punch you in the face!

Jánoska Really? I'll smash you to pieces!

Márta Ignore him, all he does is jabber.

Gyuri Stay out of this, dear!

Jánoska Leave it. Let's go. (*They are off.*)

Krisztina (*overlapping*) You can't get this, you don't know what I did. I hated you, please understand. When you said it was all over, I hated you more than I'd ever hated anyone. I was overwhelmed with dark, black rage, and I wished for your death, no, something worse still . . .

Márta (*cuts in*) This, I can relate to. What it's like when you think that they should just drop dead wherever they happen to be, and that you wouldn't mind if you never saw them again in your life.

Gyuri Very funny, dear. (*To* **Krisztina**.) Cut it, okay? We agreed we'd stay friends, we won't throw tantrums, and won't engage in emotional warfare.

Krisztina No, we didn't agree on anything, it was only you who kept talking.

Gyuri For a change.

Krisztina Get it, I hated you. (*Beat.*) I wanted something very bad to happen to you. (*Beat.*) I went to see my father.

Gyuri You did what?!

Krisztina Sorry, really sorry. I went to see him, yes. After five years. I haven't spoken to him since Mum's funeral. But then I went to see him, I hated you that much.

Gyuri When was this?

Krisztina Two weeks ago. After that massive argument we had. After you told me that you wanted to leave, after you dumped me, after you squeezed this wretched envelope into my hand and said that I should just deal with it on my own, that I should leave you alone, because I'm just a commie horse-face bitch and that you wouldn't hear of me from then on.

Gyuri Jeeesus.

Márta (*laughs*) He didn't try to chat you up like this, did he? I imagine he wrote poems to you, about you being the only one, the one and only who can understand his soul. Commie horse-face bitch. Not bad, not bad at all.

Gyuri I shouldn't have said that. It was far too over the top, sorry. What did you tell your father about me?

Krisztina I was really hurt then, but I realized since that it must have been even harder for you to say it. You only did it for me, so you wouldn't ruin my life, this was your way of getting me out of your system. I didn't quite get this when I went to see my father though.

Márta You're not the sharpest tool in the box, that's for sure.

Krisztina I know why you keep saying such things to me. I'm not mad at you.

Gyuri Stop it. Tell me what you told your father about me.

Krisztina I was really afraid. Of what he'd say. But I felt so alone that I knew that he was the only one I could turn to. And he forgave me. And listened to me. I told him everything, so he could understand how much I hated you. So much so that I wanted you to die.

Gyuri Really? So you denounced me to your father?

Krisztina I'm sorry! Okay? I'm really sorry!

Gyuri You don't say! Get the fuck out of here! Understand? Out!

Krisztina No! Your child is in my belly! I'll keep it and give birth to it. Get it? This will change everything. I'm not going anywhere!

Gyuri Not my problem! We did agree that it was over! There, it turns out they have come down on me because of you! They searched the place three times, and seized my manuscripts. And today I was even fired from the paper.

Márta Excellent, darling. As of today, I'm not allowed to work as a surgeon, only as a duty doctor. I thought this was because we had submitted our application to emigrate, but at least, now I can find out the real reason. But I don't care. I just want us to leave.

Annamari I don't want to! This is about my life, too! No one has ever asked for my opinion. So unfair!

Márta Annamari, go to your room. This is grown-up business.

Annamari This is my life, too. I'm not going anywhere, I'll stay here!

Márta Don't you dare!

Gyuri No problem, darling, I'll explain everything later.

Márta That will be delightful!

Krisztina I'll make it good, I'll tell my father to make it all go away!

Márta No need, thanks. I'm actually grateful to you, because had it not been for you, Gyuri would have never realized that there was no future for us here, and he wouldn't have agreed to submit our emigration papers. So we can finally leave this fucking country.

Grandma No. I'm not going anywhere. You can go for all I care, but I'll stay. (*To* **Gyuri**.) You know, sonny, I could have married someone in Italy and could have become a baroness, but I didn't because I chose your father and stayed with him. So I'm not going anywhere.

Krisztina No, this can't be, Gyuri, you can't possibly want this, you can't just go away, you can't dump me yet again, I won't allow that.

Gyuri (*to* **Grandma**) Please don't meddle with this, Mother. As for this bloody Italian saga, I don't want to hear it ever again, understand? (*To* **Krisztina**.) What did you say to your father? That I did what exactly to you?

Krisztina I told him the truth.

Gyuri What truth?

Krisztina *The* truth, what you promised, that you said you'd divorce and move in with me, and that you'd dedicate your book to me, seeing that you'd be able to finally write it by my side.

Márta Wow, this is amazing, my heart is about to break any minute.

Gyuri Darling, the situation is actually quite different, and far from being this straightforward.

Krisztina I also told him how you kicked me out. The sort of things you told me. Do understand that I thought back then that this was what you really meant. I didn't yet understand that you were doing all this for my sake.

Márta Well, baby, I can certainly see that Gyuri wasn't into you because of your sharp mind. Or were you, Gyurika? Did you fancy her for her intellect?

Gyuri Don't you call me Gyurika, okay?! I'm not Gyurika! (*To* **Krisztina**.) Did you also tell him that we agreed that you'd not get yourself pregnant because I already had a daughter? And that I was in no disposition for changing nappies.

Krisztina *keeps silent.*

Gyuri You didn't, did you? Thought so. (*Beat.*) And your father? What did he ask in return? What did he ask in return for finishing us off?

Krisztina Nothing! My father doesn't do that!

Gyuri Doesn't he? Fine. So what did you offer then of your own free will?

Krisztina Nothing! Understand, nothing!

Gyuri You must have promised that you wouldn't see me again.

Krisztina So? Can't you get it that I hated you?

Gyuri Your father won't be pleased to hear that you've come here.

Krisztina I don't care. I'm not afraid of him! Not afraid of anyone!

The bell rings, sharp, loud and long.

Gyuri Who the hell is this?

Márta I'll check. (*Goes to the door and looks through the spyhole. Meanwhile, the bell rings again, followed by loud knocking on the door.*) It's them. Here they are again.

Gyuri Dammit. Let them in.

Márta No. I don't want to go through this again.

Krisztina Who's there?

Márta Who do you think? Your father's secret police.

Gyuri Go, let them in for fuck's sake, you want them to crash the door? They can come in anyway if they want to. (*To* **Krisztina**.) At least you can see for yourself what a house search looks like. (*Goes to the door and jerks it open.*) Hello? Who are you looking for?

There are two men at the door, **Balla** *and* **Bajko,** *both plain-clothes police officers. They ignore* **Gyuri** *and charge straight in.*

Balla We're here to take a little look around.

Bajko We'll see if we can find anything.

Balla You never know.

Bajko Show me your IDs!

Márta Well, darling, at least you can see for yourself what you started.

Krisztina No, I didn't want this.

Balla IDs!

Krisztina Hold it. There won't be any house search taking place here.

Balla What?

Bajko What did you say?

Gyuri Krisz, stop it!

Krisztina Stop it, I said. Bugger off at once, boys.

Balla This is fucking hilarious.

Bajko This little slapper. And her going on about buggering.

Krisztina Are you deaf or what? Do you know who I am? Do you know who my father is?

Balla No, but he'll be pretty upset tomorrow.

Bajko He won't recognize his little daughter.

Balla He may no longer have a daughter by then.

Bajko Present your IDs at once!

Krisztina (*produces her ID, opens it and shows it to the officers*) There, see, fuck this shit! Can you read? Can you see my name? Does it ring a bell to you? Well?

Balla (*grabs it and studies it*) Fucking hell! Look, comrade captain! (*Throws the ID to his colleague.*)

Bajko (*takes a good look, then closes it*) Bloody good. (*Grabs* **Krisztina** *and starts dragging her towards the door.*) You'll come with me!

Krisztina Let me go!

Bajko As I say, you'll come with me!

Gyuri Leave her alone!

Balla Everybody stays where they are! IDs for inspection!

Gyuri (*wants to charge at him*) You bastard!

Márta (*holds him back*) Stop it, Gyuri!

Balla Do I need to say it again, IDs for inspection!

For a moment, they all stand there still, then everybody produces their ID, **Balla** *checks them one by one.*

Bajko (*in a soft muffled voice*) Sweetheart, I suggest you vanish from here like lightning, and go straight home if you don't want to get into trouble.

Krisztina If my father finds out, you'll be out of a job!

Bajko Actually, we'll be out of a job in case he doesn't. But he will, and then we also get to see where exactly you'll be heading.

Krisztina Excuse me?

Bajko Don't you get it? Comrade Veress is our boss. We are here because he sent us.

Krisztina Okay, I take your word, but this is no longer necessary. I'll call him and tell him that this isn't required any more.

Bajko You can do as you please. As for me, I'll do what I was sent to carry out.

Krisztina I forbid you!

Bajko Enough! You vanish from here at once, understand, or I handcuff you and take you to your father! You think this is the first time he puts us to the test? But he won't fool us, and won't send us to the quarries. We are loyal to him.

Krisztina You'll be sorry for this! I'll tell all this to my father!

Bajko Do as you please. As long as you are on the other side of the door. Beat it!

Shoves her out, and slams the door.

Balla What was this?

Bajko Dunno. A little test. You know what he's like, the old man. He doesn't trust anyone. He particularly seems to hate me. (*In a loud voice.*) Is everybody still here?

Balla Yes.

Bajko Good. Then we can begin.

Balla Your turn, last time it was mine.

Bajko Of course, but this is your speciality.

Balla Go fuck yourself.

Bajko Bollocks, you're talking to your boss! How much longer do you want to hang around here, fuck it?! Let's get started.

Balla Okay, okay, dammit, I'll get on with it.

Heads to the wardrobe, opens it and starts throwing the clothes out. Then opens the drawers of the dresser, and empties their content onto the floor.

Márta A bit more carefully, please.

Balla Sure, I'll pay more attention. (*Starts throwing books off the shelf.*)

Márta Thank you.

Gyuri There's nothing here – what are you looking for?

Bajko The question isn't what we are looking for but what we might find. (*Picks up a few sheets of paper scattered about on the floor.*) Such flyers, for instance.

Gyuri Stop fooling around, those are pages from a notebook.

Bajko Maybe yes, maybe no. You can tell all about it once you're inside.

Balla You can explain everything to Comrade Major. (*Keeps rummaging.*)

Bajko But first, we'll take this place apart. To make sure we don't overlook anything.

Balla Really? In that case, get on with the fucking job! Comrade Captain, stop giving me lip!

Bajko Okay, okay, I'll fucking get on to it. (*Kicks the coffee table over.*) Happy now, you motherfucker?

Balla Pleased to report, happy, fuck it.

Blackout.

Scene Three

Same location, later in the day. The living room in tatters. Enter **Márta**.

Márta Annamari, come here! Help me put this place back in order.

Annamari *comes over.*

Annamari Have they broken anything?

Márta No, except for the back of a dresser drawer. We'll glue it later. Let's put the table back in its place.

They move the table, slowly rearranging objects and tidying up. **Annamari** *is handing items to* **Márta** *who puts them away. The whole situation is pretty hopeless.*

Annamari They said they'd come back tomorrow.

Márta They always say that, but sometimes they do, other times they don't. We can't ever be sure.

Annamari   But why should we tidy up then?

Márta   Annamari, have you lost your mind? Our job is to tidy up.

Annamari   What for?

Márta   What do you mean, what for? Give me that shirt!

Annamari   Here you go.

Márta   We keep finding stuff we thought was long lost! Dad's wedding jacket, for example.

Annamari   It was at the back of the built-in wardrobe.

Márta   Goodness, how slim he used to be! Feel the fabric.

Annamari   So soft!

Márta   Italian cashmere. Grandma brought the fabric from Milan.

Annamari   Mum, why did they take dad away?

Márta   Have no idea, darling. My hunch is that they did it because they wanted to.

Annamari   When will he come home?

Márta   In a while.

Annamari   But they told us that we'd never see him again.

Márta   They only said that to scare us.

Annamari   But what if that's not the case?

Márta   He'll come back, don't be afraid.

Annamari   It's my fault, I shouldn't have let that woman in.

Márta   No, not your fault. It's no one's fault really.

Meanwhile, **Grandma** *appears, approaching really slowly.*

Grandma   Actually, this is all Gyurika's fault. He shouldn't have hooked up with that woman. And that family. He should have known what they were like. Always lying.

Márta   Sure enough, but you know Gyuri the best, so you also know what he's like.

Grandma   Of course I do. He's just like his father. When he's after a woman, he gets completely crazy. But why should I explain this to you? You've suffered quite enough as it is.

Márta   Grandma, please don't say such things when Annamari's here.

Grandma   She's up to speed with everything, don't take her for an idiot. You're up to speed with all this, right, Annamari?

Annamari   No, and I have no intention to be, either.

Grandma Fine, throw a tantrum then. (*Looks around.*) The mess these swines have left behind! They've almost cut open my expensive spring mattress. I just about managed to hold them back.

Annamari It may well be that this would have been more of a job than they bargained for.

Márta Annamari, don't be rude.

Grandma No, she's right, they wanted to make sure the blades of their pen knives don't get damaged by the springs. (*Notices the cashmere jacket.*) Goodness, you've still got this! (*Feels it.*) They no longer make stuff like this. Annamari, feel it, see how soft it is.

Annamari I know, I've already checked it out earlier.

Grandma Feel it again. They no longer make such fine fabric anywhere. We bought it in Milan for Pista, but it wasn't enough for an entire suit and he didn't want just a jacket. So it got handed down to your dad. Goodness, this was such a long time ago. In Milan, in such a different life . . . I was so beautiful, everybody kept asking who this amazing woman was . . . (*Cries.*)

Annamari Please don't cry, Grandma. All will be fine. We'll put the place back in order, won't we, Mum?

Márta Yes, but this won't mean that things will be in order though.

Annamari Mum, don't even go there.

Grandma . . . even at forty, I was so willowy that everybody kept asking who this amazing woman was. Annamari, you take after me so you'll see that you'll suddenly shoot up and will be just as slender as I used to be. Wherever I went, people would stare at me, wondering who this woman was . . . (*Stops talking.*)

Márta Alas, Grandma, don't start this again for God's sake, don't tell us about the Italian journey. I beg you, please don't make me listen to this saga one more time.

Grandma I could eat as much as I liked, and wouldn't put on weight. I could enjoy all the cheeses – we even asked the hotel reception to make sure I got thickly sliced ham for breakfast, forgot its name in Italian. Oh my goodness, if only we had known that we'd never be able to travel again . . . (*Stops talking, being on the verge of crying.*) Your mum has a point. Things will never be in good working order again.

Annamari They will. Mum, you did say all will be well, didn't you?

Márta Yes, I did. Except that they've never arrested your father before. He was summoned for cross-examination but not actually arrested.

Grandma My Pista was also arrested once. He never talked about it, perhaps you didn't even know this, but he was arrested and remanded in custody for two days.

Annamari And what happened next?

Grandma I went to visit him. I took Gyurika with me, too. I thought that this would help somehow.

Márta And what happened?

Grandma They got so scared of us that they released him. I could even say (*laughs*) that they shat themselves with fear.

Annamari Heard this, Mum? Let's go and bring Dad home.

Márta Oh, Annamari, you mustn't believe any old thing Grandma tells you.

Grandma You don't believe this? Yet it's true. I told them that if they didn't release him, I'd lie down on the ground, right outside the police station.

Márta Sure, I know. Next thing, the chief constable came out, apologized and brought you a bunch of flowers. Give me a break with these stories, Grandma, don't we have enough problems as it is?

Annamari Mum, this is actually true. I know it's true.

Márta Sure it is.

Grandma It really is.

Márta Fine, enough is enough! Annamari get dressed, we're going!

Annamari Where to?

Márta What do you mean where to? To bring your dad home.

Grandma (*heading back to her room*)   I've just remembered!

Márta What?

Grandma The Italian for ham. Pruh-shoo-tow.

Márta I'm thrilled. (*Beat.*) Annamari! How much longer do you need to get dressed?!

Blackout.

Scene Four

*The **Veress** mansion. Late afternoon. A more elegant living room than the one in the previous scenes, it even has a piano. The door opens wide and an infuriated comrade **Veress** appears, dragging **Krisztina** by her wrists.*

Krisztina Let me go, hear me, let go of my hand at once!

Veress (*pushes her into an armchair*)   What the fuck do you think you were doing when you just turned up at my office to make a scene? One can't just show up at my office – how can I explain this to comrade general? Huh?

Krisztina Couldn't care less. I want you to undo all this. I don't want you to harass Gyuri any further. I don't want it, get it?

Veress Nothing to worry about, comrade general, only my hysterical cunt of a daughter popped in to make a scene. It won't happen again, or in case it will, that won't amount to more than once a week at most. Can you even grasp the enormity of what you've done!?

Krisztina They didn't want to let me see you. They said you weren't in. I explained in vain who I was, they didn't want to let me in.

Veress They didn't? Of course not! What the fuck were you thinking? Even your mother was less stupid – she had her issues but she wasn't this stupid. Goodness gracious, you threw the bust of comrade general secretary on the floor, but luckily only two people saw. Fingers crossed I can make them keep this to themselves. What the hell is going on in your head, goddamit, I don't have a bloody clue!

Krisztina And this is reason enough for you to slap me in front of everybody, because of a stupid bust? It was just a fucking bust made of plaster, a wretched plaster cast. I don't understand why you're so carried away.

Veress It was the bust of comrade general secretary! What the hell is wrong with you – do you want to end up in a labour camp? Do you think this is some joke?

Krisztina Okay, okay, I'm sorry. But I had to speak to you at all costs, you see, it was a matter of life and death, and I absolutely had to be allowed in. I couldn't wait any longer, as I wanted to tell you what happened.

Veress I know what happened. The small matter of a house search. It was what you wanted, after all. Don't you recall blubbering and asking me to forgive you, throwing a tantrum about being hurt and having had enough, saying that they can't do this to you, and begging me to help you.

Krisztina Okay, you helped me but now it's enough, thank you, please don't help any longer. Now leave me alone, and leave Gyuri alone, too.

Veress You really imagine that this is some washing machine that you just switch on and off? When you denounce someone, that person is denounced, once and for all. If you want to finish someone off, that person will be finished off, there's no such thing as changing your mind.

Krisztina Yes there is. I thought it was all over, that I wasn't in love anymore, that I didn't want to have anything to do with him, but this wasn't the case.

Veress This is why you went to see him? What did you promise me, huh? Only to end up with my staff finding you in their flat? And you even made a scene and shouted at them, instead of shutting it and vanishing at once!

Krisztina I wanted them to stop doing what they were doing, and to leave.

Veress You still think this is some stupid game? You really think I have no enemies? Don't you realize I always have to watch my back?

Krisztina None of my concern. Get it. Not my problem.

Veress Trust me, there are enough people out there who hate me, and I know full well that they'd enjoy finishing me off. Several of my own staff included.

Krisztina This isn't about you, get it? So don't come up with such paranoid bullshit, okay?

Veress You'll see that they'll charge me with, say, skimming money, or with being biased, or with being a nationalist, or something else, whatever, and that will be the end of me. I should feel fortunate if they only send me into retirement and not to a stone quarry for fifteen years. But beware, that will also be the end of you, no more leading roles or French perfumes, you can become a cleaner or suchlike. In any case, you'll be finished, too, get it? (*Sighs.*) I'm too old for this.

Krisztina Spare me the shit that I've only become what I am because you are my father. I know it's not true, this is not the reason – the reason is that I've got talent, so give me a break. The perfume was a gift from my director – he was trying to make a pass at me and wanted to cajole me. In vain.

Veress It was me who had that perfume brought back from Paris in a diplomatic bag, together with your contraceptive pills. I wanted you to wear it because it was your mother's favourite. Your director got it from me, just so you know.

Krisztina Not true.

Veress Yes it is. So bear this in mind. You think you can simply turn your back on me, throw a little tantrum and that's that, you're no longer my daughter? I promised your mum that I'd take care of you. That I'd never abandon you.

Krisztina Don't you have any shame? How dare you bring Mum up here?

Veress You think you know the full picture? That you've always known everything?

Krisztina Right, only you can know everything, because only you have people whispering in your ear, snitching on others.

Veress There are certain things that I know, others I don't. The latter is mainly unimportant stuff. But it's best if you get it that if I weren't who I was, you wouldn't have become who you are, either.

Krisztina No way. Everybody says this, everybody reminds me that it's not down to me, that you are the one who made all this possible. But I know this isn't true, they're all lying. And you're lying, too. The bottom line is that I've got talent! Get it? Talent.

Veress Fine. You've got talent, indeed. I can only have a daughter who's got talent.

Krisztina Go get fucked! You don't know everything, far from it. Not even about me. No bloody way!

Veress No? And what is it that I don't know, huh? That you stopped taking the pill half a year ago? You think I don't know that you're pregnant? By this Gyuri? You think I don't know that you want to keep the baby? Actually, I know even more than this. I also know that you won't.

Krisztina That's not correct. I shall keep it. For the heck of it. I'll keep it and give birth to it.

Veress My daughter won't give birth to the child of a random man. And at the age of twenty-two at that! I won't allow you to ruin what I have built for you. I won't allow you to make a grandfather of me! Got it? I simply won't allow it.

Krisztina Fuck you! Fuck you! Fuck you!

Blackout.

Scene Five

Passport office. Looks like a waiting room. Several benches; in a corner there is a table with a phone. Nobody in sight. Enter **Márta** *and* **Annamari**.

Annamari Nobody here.

Márta (*whispers*) Don't say a word. They are listening to everything here. (*In a loud voice.*) Hello, anybody here? I've come regarding my husband.

No response.

Annamari Don't shout, Mum – as you can see, there's nobody here.

Márta (*whispers*) I told you to keep quiet! (*Shouts.*) I'm here to see my husband, I know he's here, I want to talk to him, I want to know what's going on with him!

No response.

Annamari Mum, there isn't anybody here, let's just go!

Márta (*whispers*) Do keep quiet! (*Shouts.*) I know you can hear me, I want to see my husband!

Still no response. Finally, a door opens and **Barta**, *the duty officer, enters.*

Barta How can I help you, comrade?

Márta I'm here to see my husband.

Barta Does he work here?

Márta No. He was brought here, following a house search at our place.

Barta Is that so? What makes you think he was brought here?

Márta Well, this is where people are usually brought, isn't it?

Barta Nobody is being brought here. This is the passport office.

Márta But I know that he was brought here. I know he's here.

Barta There's nobody here. Please calm down. Missy, tell your mum to calm down.

Márta No way. Leave my daughter out of this. I want my husband.

Barta How many times should I tell you that he isn't here?

Márta Yes, he is. I know it. I want to speak to him.

Scene Five

Barta   I told you he wasn't here.

Márta   We won't leave until he's released.

Barta   I'm telling you for the last time to leave the premises. This is the passport office, and there's nobody here.

Márta   Who's being issued with passports here? Nobody. (*Beat.*) I know he's here. I want to see him. At once. (*Lies down on the floor.*) Annamari lie down, too. (**Annamari** *lies down.*)

Barta   What do you think you're you doing? Get up at once! At once, I said!

Márta   No, not until you tell us where my husband is.

Barta   Madam, for the last time, this is the passport office, your husband isn't here. Get up.

Márta   No.

Barta   Don't make a scene here! Stand up. I insist!

Márta   No!

Barta   You'll get away with this if you simply get up and leave at once. If you don't, I'll be obliged to make a big fuss.

Márta   Not my problem, I want my husband.

Barta   Get up!

Márta   No!

Barta   Get up! Get up, for God's sake!

Márta   No!

Barta *is trying to make them move, tug of war, no result.*

Barta   For the last time, get up!

Márta   No!

Barta *gives up, goes to the phone, picks up the receiver, dials and speaks.*

Barta   We've got a situation here! Allow me to report that there is a situation! A lie-in! They're lying on the floor in protest!

The door bursts open, **Balla** *and* **Bajko** *enter.*

Balla   What's up, Barta?

Bajko   Need some help?

Márta   You're the ones, you took Gyuri away! Let me go to him, I want to see him!

Balla   Can't you handle a couple of women?

Bajko   They've even lain down for you!

Balla   Some people dream about this all their lives.

Barta Leave me alone, don't make fun of me.

Bajko Two women at once!

Balla But one's too old, and the other too young.

Bajko How picky you've become!

Barta Do something, I beg you, they can't just lie here on the floor. What shall I say to comrade major?

Balla Relax.

Márta You were the ones – tell me where did you take Gyuri?

Balla What are you talking about, madam?

Bajko It wasn't us.

Balla No, not us.

Bajko Who's Gyuri?

Márta I won't get up until you tell me what happened to my husband!

Balla Fine, don't bother, you are fine where you are.

Bajko You don't even have a husband.

Annamari Why are you doing this? Tell us what happened to Dad!

Márta Shut up, Annamari!

Balla We've had enough of this.

Bajko You're coming with us!

They haul **Márta** *up from the floor, and drag her towards the door.*

Márta Let me go!

Balla Up!

Annamari Mum!

Márta Annamari, stay there!

Annamari Where are you taking my mum?

Bajko Where she wanted to go.

Balla To your dad.

They drag **Márta** *to the door.*

Márta Let me go!

Annamari Mum!

Barta Missy, just go home.

Blackout.

Scene Six

Prison, a tiled white space, with white benches and bright white light. It feels like a hospital waiting room. **Gyuri** *is lying on a bench, staring at the ceiling. The door opens with a loud bang,* **Márta** *is shoved in.*

Márta   Gyuri? Can't believe you're here.

Gyuri   Why did they bring you here? They promised you'd be left alone!

Márta   They didn't bring me. I went to look for you. I wanted to take you home.

Gyuri   Great plan. And it worked out just fine. (*Laughs.*) It was madness to come here.

Márta   I had to, I had to do something.

Gyuri   I thought you never wanted to see me again.

Márta   Well, the day I actually want to leave you, I will. But I'll be the judge of that. And not them. If I wanted to, I could have put your suitcase in front of the door years ago, and hey presto, that would have been the end of it.

Gyuri   Perhaps this will be the end of it anyway.

Márta   No, it won't. We shall start again, we agreed that we'd start all over. So we'll just move away and start our lives over again.

Gyuri   They won't let us go. Even if they don't send us to prison, they'll never let us go.

Márta   They will. You'll see. The bright light and tiled walls are meant to make you feel that it's all hopeless, but it never really is. I had plenty of opportunity to learn this during those horrific eighteen months.

Gyuri   You've never talked about this.

Márta   Let's not go there now. It's not a good idea to talk about prisons while being in prison. But trust me, this isn't a proper prison yet.

Gyuri   What's up with Annamari?

Márta   Your mother is taking care of her.

Gyuri   Wonderful.

Márta   What did they say – how long would they keep you here?

Gyuri   They said all sorts. You know what they're like. But there was no cross-examination yet. I imagine that must be conducted by Veress himself.

Márta   Don't worry, you won't get into trouble.

Gyuri   Of course, I will. There is enough trouble already. I'm sorry about all this. Don't be mad at me.

Márta   You think I came to find you because I was mad at you?

Gyuri Yes, you wanted to finally send me to hell in private, just between you and me. (*Laughs.*) I'd deserve it.

Márta What in God's name is going on with you? This isn't like you at all! You never apologize, you never say sorry. You never regret anything!

Gyuri My father used to say that regret serves no purpose, and it's pointless to whine. Much better if everybody just drops dead wherever they happen to be, seeing that nothing can actually turn out any different from what was originally meant to be.

Márta Perhaps he was right. Don't worry, you won't get into trouble. See, they eventually allowed me to visit you. If they really wanted to send you to prison, they wouldn't have put me together with you.

Gyuri I'm sure all they want is listen to our conversation. (*Waves his hand.*) Oh, well, no idea what will happen.

Márta Nothing. They'll threaten us for a while, or perhaps for a long time, it makes no difference anyway, and then they let us go, then we pack our bags and leave the country. And that's that. We start our lives all over again. As we agreed.

Gyuri I don't want to think about this, but somehow I can't get the thought out of my head that it's perhaps already too late for us, we are too old for this and can't start again with a clean slate.

Márta Are you saying this because of that girl? And the child? Are you still in love?

Gyuri No. Definitely not. The first few months after I met Krisztina I felt that I was finally calming down, and I was no longer overwhelmed with this sense of inertia.

Márta Don't talk about it. You promised not to tell me anything about this.

Gyuri I don't want to tell you about this, just to say that it's all over, and that if I fell out of love with someone in the past, that was that, I simply stopped thinking about them. This time, I ended up hating this girl. Her voice, the curve of her mouth, the way she moves. I wasn't like this before.

Márta You've always been quite highly strung. Think about the fact that, sooner or later, we'll leave, you, I, Annamari and your mother, we'll all move somewhere else and start everything all over again. You'll be able to write about any topic you like. That alone is worth just about anything.

Gyuri At times, I feel that I don't actually want this. That I don't want to start all over again. That I want to stay here, be what may, I don't care, I'll just stay put. But I know this is impossible.

Márta Don't start again, please, we talked this over a hundred times, you know it's hopeless, you know we have to go, the sooner and faster the better, if only they'd just let us get out of here once and for all.

Gyuri I know, you're right. But ever since we agreed that we'd leave, that we'd really leave if they let us, I started to look differently at our town, and see it as if it was a foreign place, as if I wasn't born here, as if I wasn't familiar with every single bloody tile and goddamn doorway. And it's not working.

Márta You're in love. You're still in love, but this time with this town. (*Beat.*) You really don't want to leave this place.

Gyuri I do. And I also know what will happen next, I can feel that I'll end up hating all this, finally hating this fucking town, I'll be hoping that it burns down or there is an earthquake, anything just to make it disappear from the surface of the earth. This is horrenduous, you see, it's horrenduous to think such thoughts. I wished for the death of this Krisztina, too – this is why I didn't want to accompany her to the abortion clinic because all I could think about was that she'd die, and I didn't want to witness that.

Márta Come here! (**Gyuri** *doesn't budge, so she walks over to him.* **Gyuri** *stands up and they hug, holding on really tight to each other.*) This isn't like you at all. Fear is making you behave like this.

Gyuri Yes, you're right. I'm really afraid.

Márta Don't be, darling. You won't get into any trouble.

Blackout.

Scene Seven

The **Veress** *mansion. Evening.*

Krisztina *crying. Enter* **Veress***, bringing a glass of water.*

Veress Okay, okay, just drink this, no need to cry.

Krisztina Don't want it. I don't want anything from you.

Veress Don't start again, okay? Just don't! I have stuff to do, must go back to work, I have no time to hang out with you.

Krisztina What do you mean you don't have time? As you can see, it's evening.

Veress You know what my work is like. The time of day is irrelevant. I'm pressed for time regardless!

Krisztina What do you mean you're pressed for time? You kept saying this to Mum, too, and by the end, you didn't even visit her anymore.

Veress You're enjoying this showdown, aren't you? You're just like your mother!

Krisztina Don't you dare bring Mum into this!

Veress You started it!

Frantic knocking on the door; somebody is whacking the front door with a stick.

Veress What the hell is going on today?

Krisztina I don't want to see anybody.

Veress That's not the way to go about this. If somebody has the guts to come here at night, they must really be after something.

Krisztina Don't you open the door. I don't want to be seen in this state – get it?

Veress Then go to your mother's room. You know that I left everything as it used to be.

Krisztina Not there! It still smells of disease in there.

Veress Enough of this. You either go, or stay here.

Krisztina *leaves.* **Veress** *opens the door to* **Grandma** *and* **Annamari**.

Grandma Well, Lacika, do you recognize me? (*She's a bit unsteady, holding on to* **Annamari**.)

Veress No. Who are you?

Grandma Well, this is a little painful. (*Pushes* **Annamari** *to the front.*) Take a look at her. She's the spitting image of me at the time when you had first met me. Except a bit younger.

Veress Anna?

Grandma So you haven't forgotten all about me? I thought so.

Veress (*awkwardly*) You haven't changed one bit.

Grandma You, on the other hand, have changed a lot. You've aged. (*Waves her hand.*) Invite us in! I'd like to sit down. Because, you know, I'm finding it hard to stand.

Veress Sure. Do come in.

Grandma *heads straight to the first armchair and takes a seat.*

Veress Can I offer you anything?

Grandma A coffee wouldn't be bad. Annamari, what would you like?

Annamari Nothing, thanks.

Veress What a well-mannered girl. (*Shouts.*) Krisztina! Coffee!

Krisztina *sticks her head through the door.*

Krisztina What's going on? (*Surprised to see* **Grandma** *and* **Annamari**, *but doesn't comment.*)

Veress Make some coffee, sweetheart.

Krisztina Sure, straightaway.

Veress My daughter. (*Beckons her.*)

Grandma We know each other.

Veress Is that so. To what do I owe this unexpected visit?

Grandma Obviously, fate wanted this to happen. So we can meet again.

Veress   When have I last seen you? About fifteen years ago?

Grandma   Make it twenty-five. Or even thirty.

Veress   Well, well, how time flies.

Grandma   Makes no difference, the point is that I'm here again.

Veress   I must confess this isn't the most appropriate time.

Grandma   Sure. You have work to do.

Veress   Precisely. Somebody has to.

Grandma   No need to apologize. I know that you're a nice man. Or at least nicer than others.

Veress   Thank you.

Grandma   I'll never forget what you did for my poor husband.

Veress   Don't mention it.

Grandma   Do you still have that ring?

Veress   What ring?

Grandma   I see. Only asking because I would have liked to take one last look at it. Objects are becoming increasingly important to me as I'm getting older.

Veress   I don't know what you're talking about.

Grandma   Sure. Then I'd better tell you the real reason for my visit.

Veress   Indeed, please do, dear Anna.

Grandma   I'll tell you as it is. I'd like you to let my son go. Just let him go.

Veress   From where should I let him go?

Grandma   You know that all too well. From this country.

Veress   Dear Anna, you're overestimating my powers. I'm just a modest civil servant. How could I possibly let anybody go or make stay?

Grandma   Come on, stop playing this modesty card. You've always been a bit of a cheat.

Veress   What do you mean?

Grandma   You know exactly what I mean. (*Beat.*) Why was it the piano that your parents wanted you to learn?

Veress   Oh, this is what you mean? My poor mother obviously wanted to make me a gentleman. The way she imagined this to be, that is.

Enter **Krisztina**, *tray in hand. She places the coffee cup in front of* **Grandma**.

Krisztina   Here you go. Your coffee.

Grandma Thank you. In that case, perhaps it isn't my fault.

Veress What?

Grandma That you didn't end up a gentleman. Had I not slapped you then and sent you home, you might have actually learned to play the piano. And from then on, you would have been on to a winning cause.

Veress It was me, who shouldn't have touched your thighs. (*Laughs.*) Never mind, this is an old story that won't make a difference now. Drink your coffee and then head home.

Grandma The problem is that I'm a stubborn old hag.

Veress Yes, it's best if you leave. I did help your husband, but that was a different case altogether. This one is no longer in my competence, I couldn't help you even if I wanted to.

Grandma I told you I was stubborn. I know that you can sort this out if you want to. It's enough to just pick up the phone, and you have already made it possible for my son to be released and go home. And my daughter-in-law. They'd pack their bags and leave, you'd never see them again.

Veress Perhaps you're right. Perhaps I could do this. But why should I? That is the question. Why?

Grandma Well, I have no more jewellery. Haven't had any for a very long time.

Veress But you are still in possession of some treasure.

Krisztina Dad, what are you playing at?

Veress Stay out of this.

Grandma What do you mean?

Veress Well, for instance, you've got a granddaughter. What did you say her name was, also Anna perhaps?

Grandma *doesn't respond.*

Veress You're right, she's really the spitting image of you. (*To* **Annamari**.) Stand up, dear, so I can take a good look at you.

Annamari *doesn't budge. She's just sitting there, looking scared.*

Veress Do stand up, don't be afraid.

Grandma Lacika, leave my granddaughter alone.

Veress You're the one who brought her here.

Grandma I wouldn't have been able to get into a taxi on my own.

Veress Makes no difference, she's here now.

Grandma Leave her alone!

Veress You want me to help or not?

Grandma No. I don't know what I was thinking. Come, Annamari. We're out of here. (*Trying to stand up, she's leaning on her walking stick but keeps sinking back into the armchair.*) Annamari! Help me get on my feet.

Veress *snatches the walking stick from* **Grandma**.

Veress You've gotten rather sqeamish all of a sudden. A minute ago you were begging for help, and now you'd be heading off?

Grandma We shouldn't have come here in the first place.

Veress Why not? One should never give up. Every avenue must be explored. How did you put it, back in the day? You get what you pay for. Quid pro quo.

Grandma Enough is enough! Annamari!

Veress Or what would you say if I suggested somebody for somebody else?

Grandma Out of the question. Annamari! Let's go.

Veress This is your take on the matter. But let's see whether the little girl is also sharing this view. (*Points at her with the stick.*) No longer a little girl but a young woman, in fact. (**Veress** *starts using the stick rather creatively, at times pushing* **Grandma** *back into her armchair, other times holding* **Annamari** *back from going up to* **Grandma**.)

Grandma Leave her alone!

Veress What's your name, miss? Anna? Or Mari?

Grandma Don't respond to him, Annamari, hear me? Don't you even think about responding!

Krisztina Dad, leave them alone! Hear me?

Veress Don't meddle with this! This is none of your business!

Krisztina What? All this is because of me!

Veress You think so? (*To* **Annamari**.) Well, miss, what's your take on this? That they don't even want to allow you to answer a simple question? After all, this is a matter concerning your parents.

Annamari What do you want from me? What view should I share?

Veress It's enough to tell me your name, to start with. I didn't quite catch it. Are you called Mariann?

Annamari No. Annamari.

Veress Oh, yes. Annamari. Lovely name. Really beautiful. Are you afraid of me, dear?

Annamari *stays silent.*

Veress Don't be afraid! What did your grandmother tell you about me?

Annamari Nothing.

Veress She must have said something. She must have told you something about me, considering that she'd known me for so long. Ever since I was a child, nearly.

Grandma Annamari, stay silent!

Annamari Leave me alone.

Krisztina Leave her alone, can't you see that she's still a child?

Veress What child? I can't see any children here, all I can see is a beautiful young woman. How old are you, dear?

Grandma Annamari, don't respond!

Veress Come now, why shouldn't she respond to such a simple question? Let me ask again in case she didn't hear me earlier. How old are you?

Annamari Sixteen. I've just turned sixteen.

Veress Only sixteen? I thought you were at least eighteen. Fine, I won't hurt you. You're still a little girl. And far too beautiful at that. (*Gets hold of* **Annamari***'s hand.*) Let me see your fingers, are you also playing the piano?

Annamari (*tries to pull her hand away*) Leave me alone. Let go of my hand.

Veress But why? (*Doesn't let go of her hand, sighs.*) What a slender warm hand you have, what beautiful fingers! How long and graceful they are. Made for piano playing. Or caressing.

Annamari Let go of me!

Veress Do you have a piano?

Annamari No.

Veress What happened to that beautiful black concert piano?

Annamari No idea.

Grandma It was taken by the bailiff.

Veress What a shame.

Grandma This happened quite a long time ago, so I've more or less resigned to it. That's life. Come, Annamari, let's go.

Annamari Let me go!

Veress But you can play the piano regardless, can't you?

Annamari No.

Veress No? How come? (*To* **Grandma**.) Why didn't you teach her?

Grandma Because you have put me off teaching.

Veress But not also of playing the piano?

Grandma No, life itself has put me off that.

Veress Have you never played for your granddaughter?

Grandma None of your business.

Veress Reply to my question. Yes or no?

Annamari No.

Veress Have you never seen your grandma play the piano?

Annamari No.

Veress And would you like to? Of course, you would. Fortunately, I have a piano right here.

Grandma I can no longer sit on a piano stool!

Veress Of course you can, all you need is wanting to do it.

He lets go of **Annamari**. *He walks up to* **Grandma** *and grabs her arm.*

Veress I'll help you, come.

Grandma *stands up with great difficulty,* **Veress** *is guiding her along but doesn't return her walking stick.*

Annamari Can't you see that Grandma's ill – why are you doing this?

Grandma Annamari, don't interfere, just help me.

Annamari *helps her and, with great effort, they assist* **Grandma** *with taking a seat on the piano stool.* **Grandma** *is really struggling with her balance.* **Veress** *lifts the keyboard lid.*

Veress There, please play.

Grandma *is playing. It's a major effort for her. She's seriously struggling.*

Veress This is magnificent. Your skills haven't faded one bit. (*To* **Annamari**.) Miss? May I have this dance?

Annamari I can't dance.

Veress This isn't a question of ability but of wanting.

Krisztina Leave her alone. Dance with me.

Veress With you? I've already danced with you. You may leave the room.

Krisztina Excuse me?

Veress As I said, you may leave the room.

Krisztina *dashes out.*

Veress So then, will you dance?

Annamari Yes.

Veress Then come. (*To* **Grandma**.) Waltz!

They dance.

Veress Your grandma wasn't a great teacher but she managed to get me really interested in music. Do you like music?

Annamari I do.

Veress I find it wonderfully relaxing. After a long day, I just put a record on and forget about it all . . . Mind you, it's not easy to forget about my work. You wouldn't believe how stubborn some people can get.

They dance. **Grandma** *is finding it harder and harder to keep on playing.*

Annamari We've danced enough.

Veress Of course not, when I was young I'd carry on dancing till morning. I can feel the tension and unease in you. Let yourself go! (*Beat.*) Feel the music. (*Beat.*) Let me lead you.

Annamari Why are you doing this?

Veress I want to help. I want to help your family.

Annamari Then do help! Is this how you're thinking of helping?

Grandma *can barely cope.*

Veress As I say, I'd quite like to help but I can't. You, on the other hand, could.

Annamari Why are you playing games with us? You think this is so extraordinary? That you're doing this just because you can? Yes, I'm dancing with you, but you're still an old man smelling of mothballs. And that's that.

Veress Smelling of mothballs! This can't be your idea. Your grandmother must have put this into your head. Right?

Annamari *keeps quiet.*

Veress She said that you shouldn't be afraid of me because I was basically an old man smelling of mothballs. Right?

Annamari No.

Veress See, somehow people end up sharing their secrets with me. Often I don't even have to ask them, and they still do. I don't know why this is. Perhaps they trust me.

They dance.

Veress Do you know why your grandmother said this? Because my mother made me wear my father's old trousers. How tense you are again – let yourself go!

Annamari Please let go of me. Let's stop doing this. I danced with you, Grandma played the piano, now let us go home.

Veress You know, as people age, they start thinking about the past a lot more. And it's quite bizarre to see which moments keep cropping up in one's mind, these are not the major events that one would have expected to remember forever.

Annamari So you want me to promise that I'd remember this dance forever?

Veress This is precisely the point I'm making. You can't be sure. You can't know in advance what it is that you'd remember and what you'd forget, what you'd like to forget and what you'd prefer to re-live endlessly.

Annamari That's it, we've danced quite enough. (*Tries to break loose.*)

Veress (*refuses to let go of her*) There must be something seriously wrong with the world if such a young girl like you doesn't want to dance. As I said before, one should party till daybreak at this age.

They dance.

Once upon a time, when I was a young officer, I danced with an ugly girl at the ball of the secret police staff. She wasn't strikingly hideous, only her eyes were ugly. She had cow eyes. Such a small detail can seriously ruin an otherwise pleasant face.

Annamari And what makes you think this is my concern?

Veress It's an interesting story. (*Beat.*) Besides, she was aware of this, which made her entire body really tense, just like yours at the moment. But I held her close to me, as I wanted her to feel that she could trust me. (*Beat.*) And she did. (*Beat.*) And then, all of a sudden, she placed her soft lips against my ear and whispered something into it. A secret. Perhaps her biggest secret. (*Beat.*)

Annamari What was it?

Veress I'd never tell. A trifle. But the way she told it to me transformed her entirely. Every movement of hers ended up transfigured. She looked beautiful. And we danced till daybreak.

Annamari I don't have such secrets.

Veress Of course you do. Everybody does.

Annamari I won't tell you anything.

Veress Poor Annamari, nobody has taken you seriously so far. I'm the first person. (*Beat.*) This is an opportunity to help your parents. It only depends on you.

Grandma *is dragging her feet, but carries on playing.*

Veress You really love your father. I can sense it. Help him.

Annamari What are you after? What do you want me to do?

Veress Come on, you know that very well.

Annamari *doesn't respond. They dance.*

Veress But it's not enough to just do this. You also have to want it. Really want it.

Grandma *is struggling ever more with playing the piano; she gasps and her playing is now entirely erratic but the other two just keep dancing. Suddenly,* **Annamari** *leans in and whispers something into* **Veress**'s *ear.* **Veress** *is holding her tight, beaming.*

Annamari Let Grandma go.

Blackout.

Scene Eight

Prison. Same situation as before, but this time with a flickering lamp. It switches off, then on, then off again, and so on.

Gyuri How long have we been here?

Márta Don't know, maybe a few hours. Can't be more.

Gyuri It may well be morning already.

Márta No way this much time has passed.

Gyuri There's no morning around here.

Márta Don't think such thoughts.

Gyuri If only I knew what the time was.

Márta Do you remember your mum's clock on the wall?

Gyuri The one that struck with such a beautiful bonging?

Márta Yes, that one. What happened to it?

Gyuri Don't know. Wait.

The door opens. Enter **Balla**.

Balla Attention!

They stand up. **Veress** *comes in holding a bunch of folders, followed by* **Bajko** *and* **Officer 2**.

Veress Please sit down. But actually, why would you sit when you'd have to stand eventually anyway. I'm about to let you off. You can go home. (*Produces a piece of paper and starts reading.*) Do you still want to leave this country?

Márta Yes, we do. And we will.

Veress Be my guest. (*Smirks, and hands the paper to* **Márta**.) Here you go. Your emigration permit. Pack your bags straightaway, and you'll get your passports without having to wait for your turn, go through customs and slip away. You will have left the country within twenty-four hours.

Gyuri Excuse me?

Márta   Take a look. (*Hands the document to* **Gyuri**.) This is really it.

Gyuri   What's this, some kind of a cruel joke?

Veress   No. No joke. I'm letting you go.

Gyuri   You're lying.

Veress   Me? Never. You can go home. (*Beat.*) Say thanks to Annamari. Did you know how musically gifted she was? She can really sing and dance. Exceptionally talented. And skilful. Very, very skilful.

Márta   What do you mean talented, what do you mean we can say thanks to Annamari?

Gyuri   What did you do to my daughter? (*He's about to charge at* **Veress**.)

Veress *doesn't budge and the officers grab hold of* **Gyuri** *and restrain him.*

Veress   This is a question I'd rather ask you. So you'd better shut the fuck up. To be honest, I'm myself taken by surprise at the sight of such remarkable goodwill. (*Exit.*)

Blackout.

Scene Nine

Living room. **Grandma** *sitting in an armchair, all alone and silent. Nothing happens for a minute or so.*

The front door opens. Enter **Jánoska** *and* **Lajoska**, *carrying boxes. The same ones as before.*

Jánoska   See, if you refrained from making a scene, we wouldn't have to lug all this stuff up to the top floor again.

Lajoska   But we have to, dammit.

Jánoska   Why couldn't these people just move to the ground floor.

Lajoska   To make it harder for us. And then, to make us carry all this stuff down to the container.

Jánoska   They should go fuck themselves rather than move abroad.

Lajoska   Where are they moving to? Do you know which country?

Jánoska   Haven't got the foggiest. Let's ask the old woman.

Lajoska (*goes up to* **Grandma**)   Madam, where are you moving to?

Grandma *doesn't answer the question. She keeps staring ahead, as before.*

Lajoska   Where? Hungary? Germany? Italy?

Grandma *doesn't answer.*

Lajoska Jee, she's gone dumb.

Jánoska (*goes up to* **Grandma** *and leans in her face*) Hey? Can you hear me?

Grandma *doesn't answer.*

Lajoska I told you she's gone dumb.

Jánoska Madam, you should pack.

Lajoska Pack your stuff into these boxes.

Jánoska Everything you want to take away with you.

Lajoska Everything you think would get past customs.

Jánoska Other stuff is best to be left here.

Lajoska Not even worth packing because they'll be confiscated by the customs officer anyway.

Jánoska It's best to sell such stuff.

Lajoska Can you hear?

Jánoska Hey, madam?

Grandma *doesn't answer. Enter* **Gyuri** *and* **Márta**.

Gyuri Mother? Where's Annamari?

Jánoska You can ask her all you like. She's gone dumb.

Gyuri Mother? Mum? What's going on? Why won't you talk?

Grandma *doesn't answer.*

Gyuri Mother, what happened, say something.

Without saying a word, **Grandma** *turns around and grabs* **Gyuri**'s *hand.*

Márta Have you seen my daughter?

Jánoska There's nobody here. Except for the old lady.

Lajoska But she wouldn't say a word.

Márta And you, how did you get here?

Lajoska We were sent here.

Jánoska To help you. To help you get ready by the time the container arrives.

Márta By whom?

Jánoska You know who. Them. (*Whispers.*) Those above, y'know, madam doctor.

Lajoska The police. Y'know. To help you. We are doing this as a kind of whatsit work – what-d'ya-call-it?

Jánoska Social.

Lajoska That means, it's for free.

Jánoska Otherwise there's no more moonlighting.

Márta I see.

Gyuri Mother, don't do this, say something, tell us where Annamari is. What have you done to her?

Grandma (*looks at her hands*) I can no longer play the piano. I thought I'd never forget. (*Starts crying.*)

Gyuri Okay, okay. Stop it.

Grandma *stops crying.*

Gyuri Annamari? Where is she?

Grandma I forgot.

Gyuri Come, I'll take you back to your room.

He helps her stand up and walk to her room.

Jánoska Madam doctor, you should start packing.

Lajoska You should also hurry up, as everything needs to be boxed, numbered and itemized.

Jánoska But if I were you, I'd only pack the stuff that definitely gets past customs.

Lajoska Where are you going? It also depends on that.

Jánoska Indeed. Do you know the joke about the galoshes, madam?

Márta Yes, I do.

Lajoska So, then, are you taking your galoshes or not? (*The two men have a good laugh, then stop.*)

If you aren't taking your galoshes, you'd better sell them, together with anything else that wouldn't get past customs. It would be a shame to have all that stuff confiscated by the customs officials.

Jánoska It would be a complete waste.

Gyuri (*comes back*) Shall we bet that you happen to know some interested buyers?

Meanwhile, **Márta** *produces some paper from a drawer and is looking for a pen.*

Jánoska If we knew, would that be a problem?

Lajoska All we want is to help you.

Jánoska And for everybody to benefit from a good deal.

Gyuri Don't you have any shame?

Márta Leave it! Help me pack instead.

Gyuri How on earth can you just start packing? Doesn't it bother you that you don't know where our daughter is?

Márta Perhaps it's best not to know, and the packing needs to be done anyway, so at least we're preoccupied with something in the meantime.

Gyuri What do you mean, it's best not to know?

Márta When they arrested you, your mother kept talking about how, back then, she had engineered the release of your father.

Gyuri That's just a myth. I was four, don't remember anything. I don't think it's even true.

Márta Well, I didn't get this impression based on what your mother had said. Besides, she sorted this one out, too, didn't she? We were released, and made it back home, right?

Gyuri Right, but Annamari's nowhere to be seen. (*Beat.*) Stupid mother!

Márta She'll come home. Let's start packing.

She hands the pen and paper to **Gyuri**. *Opens one of the dresser drawers and starts throwing the clothes into a box.*

Gyuri Why on earth would you want to pack?

Márta So we can leave.

Gyuri And what should we do with all this shite? Let's just leave all this behind, for fuck's sake.

Márta No, we won't. Write here: fourteen pairs of black socks. For men. Two pairs of brown tweed trousers. A pair of suspenders. A knitted jumper in Scandinavian patterns. A stripy knitted jumper . . . (*Comes to a halt and looks at* **Gyuri**.) Are you making a note of this?

Gyuri (*sighs*) Yes, I am.

Blackout.

Scene Ten

Living room. Later in the day. Fully packed boxes, **Jánoska** *and* **Lajoska** *are wrapping the furniture into corrugated cardboard.* **Márta** *is still packing,* **Gyuri** *has filled up several pages with his notes.*

Márta An ashtray. Copper. Foldable shaver, in its case. Swedish steel, yellow case, bone handle. Three pairs of glasses. Horn frames. Two without lenses. A measuring tape.

Lajoska Wait, we'll have to tie this with a string on one side, the paper isn't big enough.

Jánoska We have to patch it.

Gyuri (*throws the paper*) Had enough. Why the fuck would we want to take a measuring tape?

Márta So we can measure. And have something to measure. When one moves to a new place, there's always something to measure. Don't you remember?

Gyuri We won't have a house.

Márta Of course we will. And a garden, and a round table.

Gyuri *laughs*.

Gyuri Never. And even if we did have them, what's the point? To sit around, just the two of us, without any children?

Márta He'll bring her back. Your mother said that Veress promised to bring her back.

Gyuri Yes. She did say that. (*They carry on packing.*) Except that she didn't say why he took her away in the first place.

Márta Let's not talk about this.

They pack.

Enter **Veress** *accompanied by* **Balla**; *they are bringing* **Annamari**.

Veress I brought your passports, as I promised. And also brought back what I borrowed.

Balla *goes over to* **Jánoska** *and* **Lajoska**, *takes a look at what they are doing. It's obvious that they know one another.*

Veress (*to* **Balla**, *in a low voice*) Give the boys a hand.

Balla *doesn't appear too keen, but gives a hand. From now on, the three of them are packing furniture in the background.*

Márta Annamari!

Gyuri My darling! (*Turns away.*)

Slowly, **Annamari** *goes over to her parents.*

Annamari This wasn't Grandma's fault, but mine.

Márta No need to talk. No need to say anything.

Annamari Dad, Dad, please look at me.

Gyuri (*looks at her*) I'm looking, darling.

Annamari But don't look at me like this, please not like this.

Gyuri How should I look?

Annamari Like you did yesterday afternoon in the kitchen.

Gyuri (*holds her hand*) Okay. I'm looking at you like that. Or I'm trying at least.

Annamari All I did was dance. I had no choice.

Veress As for the rest, it should remain our secret.

Gyuri Drop dead, secrets and all!

Veress You'd quite like that, wouldn't you? Huh? (*Waves his hand.*) You don't deserve such a daughter. Even though she loves you most in this world.

Gyuri Leave my daughter alone!

He's about to charge at **Veress**. **Annamari** *holds him back.*

Annamari Dad, no. Okay? Don't do this.

Gyuri Why not? Why shouldn't I?

Annamari Because I want you to help me.

Gyuri Help you with what?

Annamari Remember when we went ice skating and you let me drink mulled wine? It was really foggy, I sprained my ankle and you carried me home in your arms. You carried me all the way up to the fourth floor and then to my room.

Gyuri You were eight then.

Annamari No, almost ten actually. Makes no difference. The question is, do you remember?

Gyuri I do.

Annamari My ankle didn't even hurt. I just said that because I wanted you to take me into your arms and carry me home.

Gyuri I realized that. But I still carried you home.

Annamari I'd like you to carry me that same way now. (*Lifts a leg, as if she had sprained her ankle, leans against* **Gyuri** *and hisses.*) It really hurts. Very, very much. And I'm so cold.

Gyuri (*grabs hold of her, hesitates for a moment, then lifts her*) It's okay, my darling girl. Come, I'll take you to your bed.

Takes her to her room.

Veress Wow, this was quite some scene.

Márta Why, your daughter doesn't love you?

Veress Well, never mind. (*Produces four passports from his bag.*)

Márta *doesn't say a word, just looks at the passports as if she couldn't believe her eyes.*

Veress Here you are, I have four passports in my hand. (*Feels the documents, leafs through them, even plays cards with them.*) Stateless passports. You can go wherever you like with these. Or wherever they allow you in. Should such countries exist at all.

Márta They exist, don't you worry. We both know that.

Veress I hope you can look forward to an amazing future. Though I know for sure that you won't forget your homeland anytime soon.

Márta Well, you took care of that, didn't you? But still, we may only remember the good bits. (*Beat.*) What do you want from me?

Veress Nothing. Only to have a little chat in this cosy home of yours. According to regulations, I also have to ask you whether you really want to leave this country for good.

Márta Why are you only asking me? There's four of us.

Veress The others are in no position to respond.

Márta Cut it now. Tell me what you're really after.

Veress A last favour. You come with me at once and remove what your husband has put into my daughter. Then you return home, go through customs and bugger off.

Márta I'm a surgeon, not a gynaecologist.

Veress Cut this crap, okay? We both know why you did time, to the tune of eighteen months. So don't fiddle around.

Márta I'll never do such things again. (*Beat.*) Besides, I don't have any instruments.

Veress That's not an issue. I can get hold of anything that's needed.

Márta No.

Veress Why not? This could be such a beautiful revenge.

Márta I won't kill my husband's child.

Veress No?

Márta No. I know this will make you pocket our passports and leave. But I'll still say no. Never. Not for you.

Veress Is this your last word?

Márta Yes, it is. Because I'd never return from there. You'd take me straight back to prison.

Veress (*laughs*) You're actually a rather beautiful woman. Especially now that you're so desperate.

Márta Leave me alone.

Veress (*looks at the passports again*)   I always thought your daughter took after your husband, but now I can see that she actually takes after you.

Márta *stays silent.*

Veress   Well? Did you change your mind?

Márta   No.

Veress   Do you think that matters? You think it really matters whether you say yes or no? Make no mistake, this child will not be born. (*Opens one of the passports, looks at it and closes it.*) I'll make sure of that. (*Beat.*) But it no longer makes any difference. Go. (*Hands the passports to* **Márta**.)

Márta (*takes them*)   Is that it? You'll let us go? (*Leafs through the passports.*) I can't believe this. Don't play games with me please. I can't cope any longer, I've had enough.

Veress (*smiles*)   I played enough games for today. (*Beat.*) It's best if you aren't here. My stupid daughter's still in love.

Márta   Does everything really depend on such a wretched little book? Is this what I wanted so desperately? (*Leafs through it.*) This picture doesn't even look like me. (*Stares at it.*)

Gyuri *comes in, notices the passports, goes over to* **Márta** *who hands him one.*

Márta   Here you go.

Gyuri   So this is it. (*Examines it.*) Goodness, you were so young. (*Starts reading.*) Valid for a single journey. (*Closes it.*) We'll be able to leave. We'll get out of here at last.

Veress   You will. Have a safe journey. I wish you all the happiness in your new homeland. (*To* **Balla**.) Balla, let's go. (*Heads towards the door.*) Don't forget to send me a postcard once you get there.

The door bursts open. Enter **Bajko**, *accompanied by* **Barta** *and two uniformed officers.*

Veress   What's up, Bajko? You have no business here.

Bajko   I knew I'd find you here, Laci.

Veress   Since when are we on a first-name basis?

Bajko   We can carry on in a formal tone, if you prefer. (*Motions the uniformed officers to grab hold of* **Veress**.) László Veress, I hereby put you under arrest for plotting against our state and government.

Veress   On whose orders?

Bajko   You'll find out in there.

Balla (*goes up to them*)   Show me the warrant. (**Bajko** *hands it to him,* **Balla** *takes a look, salutes and hands it back.*) Comrade major, congratulations!

Veress   Nice one, Bajko, but perhaps you can also tell us what the charge is.

Bajko   I shouldn't tell you anything. You know it all too well. I should take you in without saying a word, so you could while away the time trying to figure it out.

Veress   I'm too old for this, son.

Bojko   Cosmopolitanism. Spying. Subversion. Conspiracy with the West. If I were you, I wouldn't even try to deny any of this.

Veress   Why wouldn't I? That way, your work is much more exciting, isn't it? Where's the fun if I just sign whatever you want me to sign?

Bajko   Here. (*Laughs.*) Do you want to know who denounced you?

Veress   You won't tell me anyway.

Bajko   I will. And you'll sign everything. And tell everything, too.

Veress   You think so?

Bajko (*moves over to* **Veress***, grabs his neck and pulls his head towards his own shoulder*)   Sniff my jacket! Well? Is it familiar?

Veress (*looks up, in a feeble voice*)   I'll sign everything. Take me away.

The officers escort him out.

Balla   And how about this lot? What should happen to them?

Bajko   They aren't going anywhere. Collect their passports.

Márta   No, I won't hand them over.

Bajko   They are crucial evidence in this case. (*To* **Gyuri**.) Tell your wife to stop this.

Gyuri   Darling, please don't do this. (*Takes the passport from* **Márta** *and hands it to* **Balla**.)

Balla   Here you go, comrade major. (*Hands all the passports to* **Bajko**.)

Bajko   Thank you. (*Pockets them.*)

Balla   So, can we go?

Bajko   You'll stay behind. I'll leave Barta here, too, so you can show him what a proper house search looks like. Understood?

Balla   Understood, you son of a bitch.

Bajko   You're in luck. I didn't quite catch that. But don't you dare speak to me on first-name terms ever again. (*Turns to leave.*) Off we go.

They leave.

All the others, **Márta***,* **Gyuri***,* **Jánoska***,* **Lajoska***, are still standing, staring at the boxes.* **Barta** *and* **Balla** *are also staring at the piles of boxes in silence.*

Barta Bollocks, so many boxes. (*Sighs.*) Comrade first lieutenant, this will be a massive job.

Balla Massive indeed, goddamit.

They keep standing there, staring at the boxes.

Jánoska And they will cut through all this precious cardboard.

Lajoska And tear these beautiful boxes apart.

Jánoska All this top quality cardboard.

Lajoska It really breaks my heart.

Blackout.

The End.

Note

1 *Securitate* (Romanian for 'Security') was the popular name for Departamentul Securității Statului (Department of State Security), the secret police agency of the Socialist Republic of Romania, in operation between 1948 and 1989.

The Man Who Had His Inner Evil Removed

Matéi Visniec

Translated from the Romanian by Jozefina Komporaly
(Original title in Romanian: *Omul din care a fost extras răul*)

4 Matéi Visniec: *The Man Who Had His Inner Evil Removed* – book cover design by Andra Badulesco Visniec for Cartea Românească, 2014.

Characters

Eric Nowicki – *celebrity journalist*
Vanessa – *TV presenter*
Mr Rat

The model family:
Dad – *Baldur*
Mum – *Erika*
Son – *Arno*
Daughter – *Hannah*
Grandma – *Dita*
Baby – *Laura*
Poodle – *Pacinto*

Mr Kuntz
Tony – *journalist*
Wanda – *journalist*
President
Spokeswoman
Butlers
Investigators
Old Man
Librarian

Rats
Siamese Sopranos (*one white, one black, conjoined at the back*)

Other characters passing by: **Journalists, Students, Tenants, Experts, Audience**, *etc.*

When entering the auditorium, spectators will find on stage a 'set' composed of say sixteen plasma screens.

The arrival of the audience and their taking a seat in the auditorium could be filmed from sixteen different angles, and these images could be projected via a 'live feed'.

Journalism without Hypocrisy: Lesson 1

For the first few minutes, the screens show live footage of **Eric** *on his way from backstage to the set. We see* **Eric** *in hair and make-up, getting ready for his appearance. An assistant gives him a head massage.*

He walks through several corridors. Someone gives **Eric** *a microphone, the director taps him on the shoulder, a few colleagues wish him good luck.*

Tango music.

Eric *appears, and is instantly placed in the spotlight. It feels as if a tango teacher burst onto the dancefloor.*

On-screen applause (or, a few strategically planted 'fans' could start clapping in the auditorium).

Throughout this scene, **Eric** *will be in dialogue with a group of 'fans' who absolutely worship him. We are already in the middle of the 'show', although it isn't clear whether* **Eric** *is in a TV studio or in a lecture theatre.*

Eric   Welcome to the Eric Nowicki course of journalism!

Students *applaud him.*

Eric   The only place in the world where journalism is being taught without hypocrisy! The Eric Nowicki School of Journalism!

Students *shout 'Eric! Eric!'*

Eric   And because this is a course of journalism without hypocrisy, I won't be a hypocrite either!

Students   No! No! No!

Eric   I'll tell you all.

Students   Yes! Yes! Yes!

Eric   You'll find out the truth about this profession!

Students   The truth! The truth! The truth!

Eric *produces a remote control from his pocket and switches on all sixteen screens. On each screen, there appears a different image from news bulletins transmitted by various international channels (BBC World News, CNN, Fox News, Al Jazeera, LCI, Euronews, Sky News, France 24, Rai, etc.)*

Eric   There's nothing I'd hold back from you!

Students   Nothing! Nothing! Nothing!

Eric *begins a striptease number. Spiralling mayhem.*

Eric   You'll find out the naked truth!

Students The naked truth! The naked truth! The naked truth!

Eric *throws off his hat, removes his tie, his vest, and then, wantonly, undoes the buttons on his shirt. He opens it suddenly to reveal the words 'BORN TO WATCH TV!' tattooed on his chest.*

Eric Look at the naked truth!

Students Aargh!

A great deal of excitement. A few female students want to touch **Eric**. *He turns his back to the audience and removes his shirt altogether. We see the following words tattooed on his back: 'BORN TO HAVE FUN!'*

Students Whoa!

Eric So what is journalism?

Students *A TV fucking bloody fun!*

Eric *Yeees!*

Students *Yeees!*

Eric *You've got it?*

Students *We've got it!*

Eric Journalism is a form of planetary show!

Students *Yeaaaah!*

Eric Pure adrenaline! Incitement! Sensation! Spectacle!

Students *Yes! Yes! Yes!*

Eric What is the eight o'clock news?

Students Adrenaline, provocation, sensation, spectacle!

Eric A slice of the world's misery! A sample of horror! A hovering flight over humanity's failure! Each and every news bulletin is ninety per cent human filth, moral repugnance, violence and cowardice, cynicism and existential diarrhoea, rottenness and abandon, ethical snot and civic disaster.

The **Students** *remain silent.*

Eric This is what you get on television, this is what you get in newsreels, this is what you get in news bulletins. A hymn to death, violence, money, sex and theft! This is what information has become in our world. A forum for showcasing death, violence, money, sex and corruption! Would you like to become good journalists? Here are your topics: death, war, crisis, famine, catastrophe, delinquency, blackmail, prostitution, trafficking, torture, theft. An interesting information is a negative information! Repeat after me, *you bastards*!

Students An interesting information is a negative information.

Journalism without Hypocrisy: Lesson 1

Eric An information that doesn't produce adrenaline is useless.

Students An information that doesn't produce adrenaline is useless.

Eric A train that arrives to destination on time is not an information.

Students Nooo.

Eric So what is an information?

Students A train that is delayed . . .

Eric Well done, you idiots!

Students A train that derails . . .

Eric May I call you idiots?

Students Eric! Eric! Eric!

Eric yanks the tattoo off his chest as if he removed his skin.

Underneath 'BORN TO WATCH TV' there is another text: 'FUCK THE PUBLIC'.

Eric Why does modern man need information?

Students For stimulation . . .

Eric How should a news bulletin begin?

Students With blood!

Eric Blood indeed, this is what modern man has for breakfast. As soon as he wakes up, modern man craves blood. And then, while shaving in the bathroom, he listens to the news. And he drinks his coffee watching the first foreign affairs programme of the day. And if the news weren't enough of a *scoop*, if the day didn't start with an adequate number of deaths, if nothing sensational had happened on the planet, our man is frustrated.

He turns down the volume on all TV sets (better still, one could freeze the on-screen images at this point).

So, then, what is our mission? If our modern man wants blood for his breakfast?

Students We give him blood.

Eric *Gooood.* Well done, you rascals. Now, we'll move on to a practical task. Task number one. Listen to this recording from 1952. There was a time when all news bulletins started like this.

The face of a newsreader from the 1950s appears on the gigantic screen composed of sixteen individual screens. The newsreader reads out the news: 'Belfast, Northern Ireland. An explosion in a Protestant neighbourhood leaves three dead.'

Eric Listen again.

Repetition: 'Belfast, Northern Ireland. An explosion in a Protestant neighbourhood leaves three dead and four injured.'

Eric Can you see how journalists started the news seventy years ago? First, they located the event geographically, then they defined it and only after that did they evaluate its consequences. Can we afford such a waste of time today, when we live in an era of *total* show, of information as spectacle, of topical news as entertainment?

Students Noooo.

Eric So, how do we need to transmit news today to raise adrenaline levels?

Students (*hands up, as if they were at school*)   Me! Me! Me!

Eric *approaches a student with his mic.*

Student 1 Three dead and four injured in an explosion that took place today in a Protestant neighbourhood of Belfast, Northern Ireland.

Eric *Very goood.*

He approaches another student with his mic.

Student 2 Three dead and four injured, one of which in serious condition, in an explosion that created panic in a Protestant neighbourhood of Belfast, Northern Ireland.

Eric *Very, very good.*

He invites a third student to the mic.

Student 3 Three dead and four injured, one of which needing both legs amputated, is the provisional death toll of an explosion that created panic and horror in a Protestant neighbourhood of Belfast, Northern Ireland.

Eric Well done! You got the gist. Any piece of news that isn't sold at its maximum potential for suggestibility is wasted. You need to learn, first and foremost, to broadcast news in a theatrical and sensational fashion, which should generate instant shivers upon reception. The butchers have already done their job, so your mission is to show these pieces of meat to their best advantage. On a set that should stupefy consumers. As paying consumers, they are entitled to news provided with competence and subtlety, akin to a bomb exploding in their brain or to drugs dispersing in their veins. This is what they expect from a piece of news, ultimate consumers and purchasers that they are! An emotional shock, a form of information-induced orgasm!

Students Yes, Eric! Eric! Eric!

Eric What shall we do now, continue?

Students Yess!

Eric The course of journalism without hypocrisy continues!

Students Yesss!

Eric Task number two. How does one begin a news bulletin?

Students With a scoop!

Eric Idiots, imbeciles, half-wits! A news bulletin has to begin with a bomb! When you start your news bulletin, you have to launch a news-bomb first and foremost. If you don't, then these idiotic and imbecile viewers simply switch to another channel, and discard you straightaway. When you begin the news you have to grab them by the collar and hold them tight, flabbergasted and hypnotized from the off. If the first item of news doesn't hypnotize them and turn them into loyal customers, then farewell, viewers will look for their fix at your competitors.

All **Students** *raise their hands.*

Eric What?

Students (*all together*) And how do we follow on from the news-bomb?

Eric After the news-bomb, you throw in a news-gun. And after the news-gun, a news-grenade. And after the news-grenade, a news-slap. And after the news-slap, a news-lightning. And after the news-lightning, you move on to a news-*horror*. An ideal news bulletin is a battlefield, a bloody expedition, a commando operation. And the key word is death. People watching or listening to us in the morning need death in order to get started with their day. So, you pack of hyenas, what does an ideal news bulletin need to contain?

Student 1 A terrorist attack in Iraq, Syria, Afghanistan, Libya or . . .

Student 2 Or, better still, in a Western country.

Eric Then . . .

Student 3 A *coup d'état* if possible, or at least a suppressed protest.

Eric *Yes.* Then . . .

Student 4 A natural catastrophe, if at all possible. Tsunami, earthquake, flooding, subsidence. With a relevant death toll, of course.

Eric *Bravo, vous êtes les génies de l'info. Et ensuite?*[1]

Student 6 A story about rape or paedophilia! Or incest. Or adultery, provided it has planetary implications!

Eric *You've got it!* You've understood everything.

Student 7 A story about high-level corruption. The deposition of a president. An *impeachment.*

Eric Yes, yes, yes! A news bulletin is only perfect when each and every word of it emanates death, violence, cruelty, barbarism, shivering, adrenaline, consternation, indignation, stupefaction, surprise, loathing, filth, fear and immortality. You've got what it takes! You'll be the best journalists in the whole wide world!

Students *Yes*!

Eric You can get started in this profession straightaway.

158   The Man Who Had His Inner Evil Removed

Students *Yess*!

Eric   On your marks! (*The* **Students** *get set on their marks as if they were running a race.*) Ready, steady, go!

The **Students** *set off, all running in different directions.*

Eric *remains onstage alone. Behind him, the screens are being switched off, one by one.*

Televisions 1

Eric *suddenly appears to be extremely tired. His facial expression changes, conveying a sort of disgust.*

He approaches the footlights, wipes his sweat with a towel, puts his shirt on and takes a sip from a plastic bottle. He addresses the audience.

Eric   The voice of rats is captured in the simplest possible manner, in the sense that we hear it in our brains. Each and every one of us can hear it if we pay attention. Some of us have heard it already in our childhood, without realizing it. Others start hearing it later in life, yet others only in old age.

A long black hand in a white glove stretches out from behind TV set 1 and pushes the button 'on'. It feels as if the TV set had a hand of its own and was switching itself on. Footage of a recently completed apartment building. The voice of a female correspondent (later the audience will learn that it was the **Spokeswoman***).*

Voice of the Counsellor   This is a pilot building, in which rats were invited to inhabit spaces especially designed for them. It used to house a weavers' workshop at the beginning of the nineteenth century, which is why the ceilings were so high. The looms were enormous. Given the size of the rooms, fitting in a second level of flooring, at about ten centimetres from the original ones, was not a problem. The loss of space, therefore, was not very significant for the human inhabitants of the building; meanwhile, the rats were also able to secure convenient *accommodation*.

Eric *turns around, looks for the remote control and switches TV set 1 off.*

A hand appears from behind TV set 2 and switches it on, pushing the button 'on'.

Journalist with a Slavic Accent   This is no good. Not right. First, you invent capitalism and consumer society. Then, for decades, you fill up your bellies, gorge on food, amuse yourselves and enjoy life, drive luxury cars, travel the world and live the high life, so to speak. And then, the moment we rid ourselves of the shackles of communism and also want a taste of real life, hoping to experience the orgasm of consumerism, you come over to warn us: 'Be careful, don't follow us, it's no good, don't copy our model, it's evil, it distroys the planet, pollutes the air and soils the oceans.'

The same game as before. **Eric** *switches TV set 2 off.*

Journalism without Hypocrisy: Lesson 1

A hand emerges from behind TV set 11 and pushes the button 'on'.

Mr Kuntz   Observe these jaws. A wonder of nature, no human technology has been capable of inventing a more efficient chewing mechanism. The rat's entire metabolism is astonishing, its boundless capaciy to absorb toxins, to breathe in carbon dioxide and live in polluted environments, both on the surface of the earth and under water. Of course, the proliferation of rats wouldn't have been quite so significant if our consumer society hadn't become so monstrous, if mankind hadn't covered the earth in such a layer of waste.

Eric *switches TV set 11 off.*

TV set 6 switches itself on with its own hand.

President   Remember the 2015 UN summit on the topic of sustainable development? Some of you must have attended it. What conclusions did you reach? One: a total rift between production and waste management. Two: mankind has no intention of changing its lifestyle and ways of consumption, even if it is drowning in rubbish and toxic waste. Three: there is no prospect of a global agreement between nations on any major topic of an economical or ecological nature, and there is no basis for shared values. As political caretakers, we carry on meeting each other to discuss matters, we tap each other on the shoulder and share the odd meal. Every so often, we even crack a joke and take a group photo at the end of our sessions, but all these . . .

Eric *switches TV set 6 off.*

TV set 2 switches itself on again, naturally with its own hand.

Journalist with a Slavic Accent (*chasing several rats with a shovel*)   This is what I do when I meet a rat. I'm sorry I'm not *politically correct*, I'm sorry I'm a barbarian, that I don't understand anything from the subtleties of universal values, but when I come across a rat . . .

Eric *switches TV set 2 off. TV set 15 switches itself on with it own hand.*

Dad   We opted for a *soft* version of cohabiting with rats, in other words, for a more limited contact with them. This means that the rats will work, roughly speaking, in our absence or at night. Thus, at least at the beginning, the operation will take place at reduced *stress* levels on both sides. We have to admit that this brings about an enormous change, but we are aware that the moment has come . . .

Eric *switches TV set 15 off. TV set 6 switches itself back on.*

President   . . . don't lead anywhere. Remember that 2015 was the year of the greatest surplus production since the Second World War. Hundreds of books have been written about the need to reform capitalism and to invest it with moral values. To what end?

Eric *presses the remote to switch off TV set 6.*

President   To what end?

Eric *repeats the movement.*

President   To what end?

Eric *presses the remote a few times, which only leads to the obsessive repetition of the phrase:*

President   To what end?
To what end?
To what end?
To what end?
To what end?
To what end?

Eric *gets up, walks over to TV set 6 and switches it off manually.*

Two hands appear at the same time. TV sets 2 and 8 are switched on.

Mr Kuntz   Even more astonishing is their ability to network. Each individual is in a continuous emotional rapport with the entire community, comprising billions of others. Consider the numerical reproduction of this jewel that is the rat's brain. All these magnetic fields practically link each rat to all its fellow beings. This is where the efficiency of acting in a group comes from. Consider the magnetic field of the tail. We don't quite realize this, but a rat's tail is a sort of Wi-Fi.

Group of Tenants (*appearing in what looks like a publicity clip*)   We recommend that a so-called *Space R* should be created for our friends, the rats in all our towns, buildings and dwellings, and in all industrial, entertainment and recreational units. We say YES to live rubbish bins! In order to have live rubbish bins, we need to create a parallel living space for rats. It's only normal. It's only human. It's only rat-like!

Eric *starts to fight with the hands behind the TV screens. Every time he tries to switch a TV off, the hands shoo him away or threaten him.*

Furious, he yanks out one of the long hands, from which a green and gluey liquid spurts out. The liquid trickles down several TV sets and then the floor.

On the surface created by joining screens 1, 5, 9 and 13 together, the face of the **Old Poet** *appears.*

Old Poet   One last poem and that's that. Time to depart for the sea. Enough water has gathered between the two drylands (death and life) for a reverse crossing. Everything seems to be possible again. Atoms pop like soap bubbles, their alchemy providing answers to questions. Imagination reverts back to motion, high above the waters. The bird that has the mission to herald the end of the flood is joyful . . .

All screens show an image of the sea. A sense of calmness is restored.

Eric *returns to the footlights and resumes his initial point.*

Eric   I was saying that the voice of rats is captured in the easiest possible way, in the sense that we can hear it in our brains. We can all hear it if we pay attention. Some of us have heard it already in our childhood, without realizing it. Others start hearing it later in life, yet others only in old age. At times, the voice has a musical quality to it – it's like a chorus echoing in our brains. We can hear it better when we are in the company of others. The more we are, the better the hearing. This is why we are gathered here together today.

All screens show the **Siamese Sopranos** *(one white, one black).*

Meanwhile, the TV sets move nearer to the audience.

Siamese Sopranos

> The rats' tails are soft.
> The rats' ears are soft.
> The rat's fur is soft.
> The rat's blood is soft.
> The rat's dreams are soft.
> The rat's life is soft.
> The rats' words are soft.
> The rats' feelings are soft.
> Our inner rats are soft.

The TV sets have advanced all the way to the stage lip. All the 'hands', growing from behind the TV sets, reach out to the audience.

Hands reaching out appear on the screens, too.

Long silence. **Eric** *covers his head with his hands, as if something was about to explode in his brain.*

Lights go down, the TV sets are gradually switched off and the entire TV wall is moved out of the way. Strangely, three live characters have appeared behind **Eric***, the two* **Siamese Sopranos** *and* **Mr Kuntz***.*

Mr Kuntz (*addressing the audience*)   Going back to the rats' tails, we, humans, detest them out of an instinctive fear. These tails provoke repulsion in us, above all because we can feel a mysterious force in them. It is true that rats make use of their tails, not only to maintain their balance or propel themselves forward when they jump, their tail is also a regulator of heat. When a rat feels too hot in its *habitat*, it sticks its tail out and explores the environment with it. The tail is a genuine information collector, a biological periscope, a broadcaster of intentions.

A gigantic rat's tail (slightly pink with tufts of hair) descends from the ceiling and parades itself onstage. In the forthcoming scenes, this live and fidgety tail will be brandished from time to time.

Mr Rat 1

A trapdoor opens. Loud noise and special effects (Dante's 'Inferno'). A platform appears, revealing **Mr Rat***.*

Mr Rat Good evening.

At this point, I'm just a voice.
A vague voice in Eric's brain.
It's almost midnight and Eric can hear me.
He can feel me in his brain.
Like a hint of intelligence.
He can sense a kind of warning coming from somewhere, a sort of unease.
At the moment, I'm just a source of anxiety in Eric's brain. An obstinate but luminous unease. There is no fear in this persistence. On the contrary. Only generosity.

The **Siamese Sopranos** *open the trunk and start dressing* **Mr Rat**. *They are getting him ready for a festive night out: white shirt, bow tie, tails, top hat, cane with a silver handle, etc.*

Mr Rat *Our* entire approach is rooted in generosity. This is why I allow myself to address you in such a direct fashion. After all, we are both species inhabiting a shared Earth. We occupy the same vital space. It's not *our* fault that you people prefer to look towards the stars rather than your neighbouring *species*. For a few hundred years, you were hoping to enter into contact with all sorts of intelligent extraterrestrial beings. Yet you know nothing about other intelligent beings inhabiting the Earth. You have never tried in all honesty to hold out a hand to us rats. Still, we can handle this. Now it is our turn to hold out a hand to you.

Here it is . . .

While **Mr Rat** *holds out his hand, tens of other hands burst out from behind the TV sets, waving flags (of imaginary countries).*

An enormous mic appears from behind TV set 1. The mic will pass from hand to hand until it reaches the last hand, that of TV set 16.

This move allows for countless mic checks, as whenever a character appears onscreen, they repeat: 'one, two, three, mic check'.

The platform that brought up **Mr Rat** *now descends with* **Eric**. *He's in a crouching position, covering his head with his hands.*

Siamese Sopranos (*singing*)

> We need a single voice
> We need a single light
> We need a single tongue
> We need a single sight
> We need a single heart
> We need a single dream
> We need a rat,
> The rat's dreams are soft.
> The rat's glance is soft.
> His scent is balmy.

The rat's tail is the extension of the rat.
Man is the extension of nothing.

Model Family 1

The model family enters on roller skates. **Dad, Mum, Son, Daughter, Grandma** *and* **Poodle**. *After a few dexterity numbers,* **Dad** *takes the mic from the 'hand' of TV set 16.*

Dad   Good afternoon.

Mum   Good afternoon.

Dad   Let us introduce our family to you.

Mum   We are an anonymous model family.

Dad   We live in Hamburg.

Mum   In the vicinity of the old port.

Dad   My name is Baldur. She is my wife.

Mum   Erika.

Dad   He is our son.

Son   Arno. Good afternoon.

Dad   She is our daughter.

Daughter   Hannah. Good afternoon.

Dad   And she is our grandma, my wife's mother whom we all call Mama Dita.

Grandma   Good afternoon.

Dad   This is our home. (*Images displayed on TV screens.*) A regular house in a regular neighbourhood of Hamburg.

Mum   Each child has a room of their own, and Grandma has her own room, too. This is our bedroom, mine and my husband's.

Dad   This is our living room, where we all watch television.

Mum   This is our fairly spacious eat-in kitchen.

Dad   We also have a generous basement, where we can play table tennis, and a garden where, weather permitting, we can go on the swing or have a drink.

All   We are all thrilled to participate in this ecological experiment set up by the federal government.

Dad   In this context, we are keen to stress that we have . . .

All   never ever despised rats.

164   The Man Who Had His Inner Evil Removed

From behind the TV screens, all hands emerge wearing white gloves and showing the sign of victory.

Dad   I've never laid rat traps in this house.

Mum   We don't even have a cat.

Son   We have a poodle called Pacinto though.

Poodle *barks at the gloved hands.*

Daughter   Who has never done any rat hunting.

Grandma   I don't think we've ever been inconvenienced by rats in this neighbourhood. In fact, the last time I actually saw any rats was during the war.

Dad   We are all aware that our consumer society will not be able to function as before without new allies.

All   And we wish to stress that we aren't allergic to rats.

Poodle *barks, but it's unclear whether it shares the family's views.*

Dad   So we decided to create a Space R for rats.

Mum   For experiment R to succeed, we need to have an open mind.

Son   We need to be generous.

Daughter   To be understanding.

Dad   To be visionary.

Grandma   To be R.

At each of the last few remarks, the gloved hands show a sign. The whole family applauds **Grandma**.

Dad   Rats are, therefore, welcome at our place, where we have a Space R especially reserved for them.

Mum   We'll have a second level of flooring built in at fifteen centimetres from the initial one.

Son   We'll have a second ceiling built in at fifteen centimetres from the original one.

All   Dear rats, welcome to our home!

Poodle *barks.*

Model family exits.

Grand Café 1

Mr Kuntz *descends spectacularly on a live and moving rat's tail, in the manner of a circus artist.*

He is wearing a strange robe, as if he worked in a science lab. Motorcycle goggles, which could also pass for magnifying glasses, are hanging from his neck.

He leads **Mr Rat** *into a 'Belle Époque' style café. It's quite like a museum.*

Mr Kuntz   Careful with the tiled floor, it can be extremely slippery. There are days and days on end, when not a single soul steps in here. The damp and dark form a slippery coat, as of varnish, that covers the floor. I'll wipe the floor straightaway, otherwise the hallway turns into a skating rink.

He turns on several lamps. He appears to be very agitated.

Well? Observe how to switch these lamps on. How delicate they are. These are gas lamps. You can't imagine you how hard I had to fight to keep hold of them. I had to fight for each and every object, each and every detail. Touch these curtains. Feel their texture, feel the weight of the fabric! I'll draw them for you. It's important for you to see this place in natural light. Please choose a table. Any table. There are forty-four tables here and another twenty on the balcony. The café can manage around three hundred covers at any one time, and another ten or fifteen at the bar. The billiard room can also cater for twenty or thirty people. For years, the café would be packed from first thing in the morning, fully booked for lunch, and after four or five o'clock in the afternoon, transform into a ballroom gathering the brightest minds in town. In a sense, everyone who was anyone in terms of intelligence, talent or feminine grace would pass by for a hot chocolate, a charlotte pudding or a glass of champagne.

He removes his attire and puts on a white apron. He turns into a waiter.

The President won't be long. I'm delighted to show you this place myself. Imagine that up until the war, the café practically never closed. There are very few cafés left in European cities that are open 24/7. I'm talking about proper cafés, with a tradition. What can I get you? Here are today's specials. May I recommend our strudel?

He starts to set the table for lunch. He lays out a starched tablecloth, brings cutlery, napkins, a candlestick, etc.

I'm glad that your discussion with the President will take place here, in this holy place. It breaks my heart that I had to take it out of circulation and close it down. But we couldn't take it anymore. It was far too overrun by mediocre and stupid people, and by tourists. In fact, I think it was the tourists who made me quit after all. I couldn't bear watching them trespass this sublime place in their trainers, dirty travel guides in hand, clutching their stupid cameras and rucksacks. Besides, I could overhear everything. From behind the bar, I could hear everything people were saying at their tables. It may seem strange, but after fifty years of uninterrupted service at this establishment, my hearing has developed like a funnel. Look at my ears. Can you see that they are somewhat enlarged? Thinned and enlarged. Well, let me tell you that I have a fragmented, and not a global, hearing. I was basically able to compartmentalize the reception of sounds. I would hear and register everything that was being said, at each and every table, and by each and every customer. Unfortunately, the quality of conversations has become unbearable. Before the war, there was talk of mankind, humanity, the paradox of our existence, the abyss of love and morality . . .

The **President** *appears, followed by his* **Spokeswoman** *and two bodyguards.*

Mr Kuntz   Good afternoon, Mr President. Careful with the floor tiles. Due to the wind that blows under the doors and the steam from the kitchen, a layer of ice forms on the floor at night, which transforms it into a skating rink.

The bodyguards are about to search **Mr Rat**, *but the* **President** *signals that it isn't necessary. The* **President** *takes a seat facing* **Mr Rat**.

The **President** *whispers something to the* **Spokeswoman**.

Spokeswoman (*to* **Mr Rat**)   The President apologizes but he doesn't have a mandate to talk to you direct. He is prepared to listen to you, however.

Mr Kuntz   Excellent, excellent! Please excuse me for a moment.

He disappears behind the swinging doors, as if he went to the kitchen.

The **President** *whispers something to the* **Spokeswoman** *again.*

Spokeswoman (*to* **Mr Rat**)   Be short and concise though.

Mr Rat (*stands up*)   Mr President, when will the human race realize that it is spreading all manner of untruths about us? For instance, the expression 'canal rat'. We can't help but laugh whenever we hear it. We can barely be revolted by the pejorative dimension of the term, taking into account how stupid it is. You take us for 'canal rats', as if these canals weren't of your own making. Who else but mankind has built these monstrous and dismal labyrinths? Not to mention that if it weren't for us cleaning them, your famous canals would clog up in a matter of weeks.

The **President** *whispers to the* **Spokeswoman**.

Spokeswoman (*to* **Mr Rat**)   The President would like you to take a seat.

Mr Rat *takes a seat.*

Mr Rat   Take, for instance, all these expressions that label us 'invaders'. What do your historians and scientists actually do? Everyone knows that we, rats, have appeared on Earth way before the human species. And, in fact, it is us who are witnessing an astonishing invasion carried out by mankind on the entire surface of the Earth. Are we the invaders? Well, this makes me laugh. Did you know, Mr President, that before the thirteenth century, we didn't even exist in Europe? And that we didn't have the slightest intention to 'invade' you, were it not for the Crusaders who came with their ships to free the Holy Land? Take it from me, that, due to our very nature, we don't like to travel. We prefer to stay in the vicinity of a regular source of nourishment. Mankind, however, has dragged us with them into the bowels of their ships, and scattered us all over the globe.

Mr Kuntz *returns from the kitchen with a tray on which there is a bottle of Champagne and a glass.*

Journalism without Hypocrisy: Lesson 1

Mr Kuntz Allow me to interrupt you for a second, so I can serve you. (*He opens the bottle, fills the glass and hands it to the* **President***.*) Gentlemen, to celebrate this event, we'll drink my last bottle of Dom Pérignon, vintage 1955!

The **President** *knocks back his drink. He holds out his glass, which is instantly refilled by* **Mr Kuntz**.

The **President** *drinks again, but this time he leaves a little liquid at the bottom of his glass. He gives his glass to* **Mr Rat**, *who empties it.*

Mr Kuntz *heartily approves and withdraws to the kitchen.*

Mr Rat If we didn't have an extremely well-developed sense of the ridiculous, I'd say that mankind is jealous of our qualities. Take, for instance, the expression 'the rats abandon ship'. In it, a sort of reproach, if not also disgust and contempt, have been recorded. And all this because we didn't have a sixth sense regarding the imminence of death or disaster. Yes, it's true that we are the first to abandon a sinking ship when it is wrecked and about to capsize. But how many times have we triggered the alarm ahead of an earthquake or a *tsunami*! No one has counted the number of human beings we saved in this way. Mankind was unable to spot a sign of intelligence in this instinct for survival, just desertion. Incredible, still . . .

The **President** *whispers to the* **Spokeswoman**.

Spokeswoman (*to* **Mr Rat**) Mr Rat, please don't get so worked up. Fortunately, you have in front of you a very special person to talk to, a man who understands that the moment has come for a genuine existential U-turn in our common destiny.

Mr Rat I hope, I do hope that mankind has finally understood that the moment has come to become our ally. At the same time, we don't want to be hypocrites, this isn't in our nature. We hold out a helping hand to mankind to save them, motivated by an instinct for survival, hoping to save ourselves first and foremost. Yes, we commit to look after all the waste produced by humans, on condition that we are acknowledged as a metaphysical measuring device of the humanity inherent in mankind.

Mr Kuntz *returns with a silver tray on which there is a small plate.*

Mr Kuntz Mr President, may I pour you some more champagne? (*The* **President** *indicates no.*) Then please help yourself to this appetizer, crostini with duck liver pâté soaked in . . . (*The* **President** *opens his mouth, and* **Mr Kuntz** *feeds him the appetizer. Several crumbs drop onto the plate.*) Well?

President Good. Very good. Excellent.

Mr Kuntz I can't tell you how happy I am that this site of memory is finally playing host to philosophical talks again. Oh, how I missed these topics and subtleties over the last twenty years! Can you imagine that my ears were literally bleeding at night due to the amount of endless shallow talk uttered by those wretched tourists?

He withdraws, leaving the plate with the crumbs on the table.

The **President** *pushes it towards* **Mr Rat** *who picks them up and eats them.*

Mr Rat I think you agree with me that mankind didn't evolve much on a philosophical level since the invention of this discipline. I'd say that it poses more and more questions and provides fewer and fewer answers. Well, Mr President, we are capable of offering mankind some metaphysical certainties. Mankind has been wondering for four thousand years about the reasons for its existence, whether it is the carrier of a divine message or just a consequence of basic biological facts, whether it is free or manipulated by destiny. There are thousands of undeniably subtle questions, but how frustrating not to have clear answers for any! Well, we rats can offer you a compass. We can suggest a way out of your existential dilemma! To recap, we offer you what you have been always lacking: an existential scale, a measuring device for interiority. It is astonishing that you have invented measuring units for everything, you measure distance in metres, time in seconds, weight in kilos, temperature in degrees, electricity in volts, traction in horsepower, and so on. But how about yourselves? How about your inner humanity? How about your inner *existentiality*?

Mr Kuntz *returns with a bowl and a tureen. He dishes out some soup to the* **President**.

Mr Kuntz Spinach cream with green papaya zest. I agree wholeheartedly that humanity must *be reflected* by an undisputed measuring unit. This is our sole chance of escaping this uncertainty that has been haunting us ever since we gained consciousness.

Mr Kuntz *leaves. The* **President** *starts eating his soup and whispers to his* **Spokeswoman**.

Spokeswoman (*to* **Mr Rat**) What are you suggesting exactly?

Mr Rat I suggest that inner humanity should be measured in rats. Given that we are guaranteed to clean, swallow and make disappear all filth generated by mankind, I believe that we are the only suitable measuring device for man. The mass of inner humanity could be clearly expressed in rats. Remember Marx's point that the value of a product is equivalent to the time needed to produce it. In the case of our relationship, one could claim that the metaphysical mass of a man will equal the number of rats needed to dispose of the rubbish and waste generated by said man. I'll provide some examples. Let's say that a man generates rubbish, dirt and filth that require the intervention of a hundred rats. In this case, we could say that the metaphysical weight of this person is a hundred rats. Suppose that another person produces debris, leftovers and filth that require the intervention of one hundred and thirty-two rats. Well, in this case, the metaphysical mass of this citizen-human-being is one hundred and thirty two rats. Measuring the metaphysical weight of mankind in rats, seems to me to resolve one of the essential problems of philosophy, if not all of them. Mankind can finally rely on a certainty, and contemplate themselves in rats as in an *alter ego*.

The **President** *has finished eating his soup and hands the bowl to* **Mr Rat**. *The latter starts licking the leftovers (helping himself with his fingers when his tongue doesn't reach the bottom of the bowl). The* **President** *whispers to the* **Spokeswoman**.

Journalism without Hypocrisy: Lesson 1

Spokeswoman (*to* **Mr Rat**)   Interesting.

Mr Kuntz *returns from the kitchen.*

Mr Kuntz   Brussels sprouts and quail with mushrooms with a light truffle sauce. Allow me to share an opinion with you: adopting rats as a metaphysical unit of measurement for mankind, is not only a matter of urgency, of common sense and survival, but also a sign of acknowledging the goodwill of rats towards us. I believe, Mr President, that we owe rats this gesture of public acknowledgement and gratitude. After all, they don't ask for anything in return, but we can extend to them this symbolic social recognition. Do excuse me if I was too outspoken.

Mr Kuntz *leaves, the* **President** *starts eating and as he devours his quail, he places the plate with the bones in front of* **Mr Rat**.

Mr Rat   Yes, Mr Kuntz spoke perfectly on our behalf. We insist on being acknowledged not only for our practical usefulness but also for our contribution to clarifying the metaphysical mystery of mankind. This will help our public image, too. It's unbearable what the West has made of us. In the East, rats were considered on a par with gods, and some communities worshipped them outright. In the West, we were identified with the devil and the very essence of evil. There is no greater insult than being told that you have a rat face. This is why our historic rehabilitation is a necessary act of justice.

Mr Kuntz *returns with a bottle of wine. He pours some to the* **President**.

Mr Kuntz   Saint-Émilion, *grand cru* 1998. Absolutely! No one knows that rats are a factor in maintaining biodiversity, because they contribute to pollenization. The University of Princeton published an astonishing study on his topic. Only that the general public has no idea, doesn't know that rats pollenize flowers and that some plant species would have perished a long time ago if rats hadn't taken care of their perenniality.

He leaves. The **President** *whispers to the* **Spokeswoman**.

Spokeswoman   How could we contribute towards this process of rehabilitation?

Mr Rat   We need, first of all, the help of the media. Without them, we can't achieve anything. We need to mount a media campaign, a *lobby* in the visual media. An enormous pedagogical campaign is required, and only the press can take this mission onboard.

Mr Kuntz *returns with a tray on which there is some dessert, a cup of coffee and a bottle of mineral water.*

Mr Kuntz   I know, Mr President, that you aren't into sweets, but you really must try this walnut cake. It's still tepid and fresh. Look, one might say it's basically fidgeting on the plate. May I pour you some Güssinger?

He pours the **President** *some mineral water. The* **President** *tastes the cake, then hands it to* **Mr Rat** *together with the leftover wine. The* **President** *whispers to the* **Spokeswoman**.

Spokeswoman Could you evaluate right now, the approximate metaphysical weight of the President?

Mr Rat Yes, 872 rats.

The **President** *coughs, stands up and holds his hand out to* **Mr Rat***.*

Televisions 2

Tony Yes indeed, Wanda, you've put it right. A few minutes ago, I was notified of an incredibile event that took place this morning in Italy, in a place called Ventimiglia, where rats devoured all counterfeit products at the local flea market. The operation was co-organized by the Italian and French customs authorities, to highlight the major contribution played by rats in the rehabilitation of global trade.

Wanda The question though, Tony, is: how come the rats were able to tell the fake brands from the genuine ones?

Tony No idea. However, in less than half an hour, an immense army of rats managed to devour tons of counterfeit products: fake Lacoste T-shirts, fake Louis Vuitton bags, fake Nike and Adidas trainers, fake Swatches, fake spare parts and so on.

Wanda The question, Tony, remains: how come the rats were able to tell the fake brands from the genuine ones?

Tony Well, the media footage leaves us perplexed, the rats haven't spared anyone, neither sellers nor buyers, and after they *cleared* the marked at Ventimiglia, they continued their operation on the regional train service from Ventimiglia to Toulon.

Wanda In Luxembourg, the European Commissioner in charge of negotiations within the framework of the World Trade Organization has already reacted favourably to this incident. Counterfeit products make up about a third of world trade, and if rats manage to eradicate this scourge, then the entire world economy could be relaunched on a much healthier foundation.

Mr Kuntz I'd like to add something, if I may. All the scientists who studied the patterns of social organization practised by rats have been astonished. In rat society, the leader is naturally instituted. No elections, no hereditary power, no conflict in the process of selecting a leader. The rats, being organized into a republic of sorts to protect their common interests, simply have a special intuition for a genuine leader. Meanwhile, the leader is in charge and leads on the basis of information received from the entire group.

Eric I'm the first human on the planet to be contacted by Mr Rat. And I'm not ashamed of this. I was the first journalist to throw up on live television on the eight o'clock news. Millions have seen me throw up live then. Following this, the footage was on a loop for days and days on end. Over three millions views on YouTube. Over seven million *likes* on Facebook. Among those watching and listening to me right now, there are perhaps some who saw me vomit live last night.

President   Dear citizens, we shall issue a code of mutual tolerance that everybody will need to observe if we want this project to succeed. The rats have promised never to exceed twenty kilos in weight. This is a crucial point. We can congratulate ourselves on this compromise. Dear fellow countrymen, each and every apartment, therefore, will need to be supplied with scales. Dear fellow countrymen . . .

War Veteran   No one had a clue that in the winter of 1942, in the midst of the siege of Stalingrad, about a hundred of General von Heist's tanks were blockaded because the rats had chewed the electric wires. This *act* of sabotage has never been reported. No one has ever thought of mentioning this in history books, or to dish out medals to reward the rats.

Angry Passer-By   Poetry is something utterly useless that only drags people down. That's poetry for you. A human indulgence, a futility, a great nullity, a mask, a sort of refuge from failure, a cowardly escape, a luxury, an incredible masquerade, a danger for the future, a form of paralysis, a blessing, a drug, a metaphysical distortion, a wound, an expression of the pathological narcissism that has spied on us ever since we gained consciousness, a swelling of dreams, a canker we can position between two shores to cross non-existing rivers, a scam. Personally, I detest poetry, I refuse to listen to poetry, read poetry or allow myself to be invaded by any poetic sentiment. Plato put it right when he argued that poets should be banished from the city. Poetry is an abyss for mankind, something that can poison the soul. It is the most harmful of religions, an ontological illusion. Poetry, go to hell!

Talk Show 1

The TV wall splits in two, as if the city gates opened, making way for a set.
Vanessa *appears in an extravagant outfit, mic in hand.*

Spotlights focus on her, music, special effects, fireworks, etc.

A live talk show is about to begin.

Vanessa   Welcome to *Talk-talk 24 hours talk-talk show live*! The most cracking *talk show* in the whole wide world!

All the screens show an audience of overexcited fans. All shout 'Vanessa! Vanessa! Vanessa!'

Two special guests today, two colossal guests! Two really fascinating people: biologist, researcher, poet, philosopher, futurologist and master chef Kuntz. Please welcome William Kuntz!

Everybody welcomes **Mr Kuntz**, *who takes a seat on a tall chair on* **Vanessa**'s *left.*

Vanessa   Beside him, someone who needs no introduction: the journalist, columnist, commentator, decipherer of news and animator Eric Nowicki!

Fans in genuine ecstasy. **Eric** *greets his fans, hugs* **Vanessa**, *shakes hands with* **Mr Kuntz** *and takes a seat on a tall chair on* **Vanessa**'s *right.*

Vanessa   Eric Nowicki, the man who vomited live on consumer society!

Frantic applause. A downpour of tissues over **Eric**.

Vanessa   Eric, I should stress that this is your first public appearance since you vomited on live television while presenting the eight o'clock news on our national channel Total News!

Fans clap enthusiastically. **Eric** *takes the mic.*

Eric   Indeed.

Vanessa   Tell us why you decided to offer this *comeback* to us, and not to someone else?

Eric   Because I think that you are simply tremendous, unique, credible and amusing.

Vanessa   Applause for Eric! And for *Talk-talk 24 hours talk-talk show*!

Fans clap again, unleashed. Some shout 'Eric! Eric!' Others shout 'Vanessa! Vanessa!'

Vanessa   Many thanks. You are an amazing audience and in this moment in time, we are being watched by 23,564,877 people! Hugs to you all. Tonight, we'll talk about a fascinating theory regarding a species that would appear to want to establish rational contact with us. I'd like to address our specialist, Mr William Kuntz, this clear and radical question: can rats actually talk?

Mr Kuntz (*gets hold of a mic*)   No, individual rats are not capable of speech. But owing to their amazing head count, they managed to achieve what in Hegelian and Marxist dialectics is called the transformation of quantity into quality. In this particular case, the proliferation of rats on Earth has led to a qualitative *leap*. Or rather a *biological leap*, which has made it possible for their species to establish an *emotional resonance* with us.

Vanessa   We shall return to the idea of *emotional resonance,* but did the rats really try to establish contact with us?

Mr Kuntz   Yes.

Vanessa   Why?

Mr Kuntz   Because we humans have created a suicidal industrial model, and rats are in a position to save us.

Vanessa   How?

Mr Kuntz   By turning into living waste bins.

Vanessa   Are we facing a new revolution?

Mr Kuntz   Following the industrial and information revolution, we are now facing a biological and relational revolution. We can foresee a profound symbiosis with rats. Researchers agree that this species is our trump card for the future. May I remind you that there are no more utopias left for mankind?

Vanessa   What utopias?

Mr Kuntz   The last but least was communism, which triggered hundreds of millions of deaths, and the very last was globalization, leaving in its wake a billion people in utter poverty. The 2008 financial and economic crisis also *impoverished* us, as far as our future is concerned. Consumer society has shown its limitations, globalization revealed its sterile and mercenary dimension. You still recall, I imagine, the 2014 suicide wave, a dramatic expression of the existential void generated by the crisis and the lack of social and moral visibility.

Vanessa   And you think that rats will help us regain our taste for life?

Mr Kuntz   More than that, they'll help us solve a philosophical problem, I'd say. The problem of evil. Because in its current phase of development, mankind is hampered by this problem. We need to humanize evil. We need to introduce rules in the evolution of evil. We need to slow down the progress of evil. As a matter of fact, a new branch of science is in the making, and even if it sounds bizarre, it derives from the indisputable observation that evil is a form of energy, deeply ingrained in us.

Vanessa *turns to* **Eric**.

Vanessa   Eric, what happened on the evening of 3 September?

Eric   No idea.

Vanessa   Did you have a stomach ache?

Eric   No.

Vanessa   So then?

Eric   I felt a total metaphysical disgust.

Vanessa   Have you thrown up since?

Eric   No.

Vanessa   I hope you aren't going to do that now on live television!

Fans laugh and clap.

Vanessa   What is, in fact, metaphysical disgust?

Eric   How shall I put it? Well, first of all, I'm sick and tired of hearing certain phrases and words uttered by politicians. For example, the phrase 'to do everything we possibly can'. When I hear someone say this, I feel as if my brain was falling apart. I can almost hear it go 'bang'. *Decisive action.* Bang! *Crucial summit.* Bang! I simply get knocked out for a moment or two. And then I go 'bang'. It's not my mouth throwing up but my brain.

Vanessa   When have you first noticed these symptoms?

Eric   When I started as a newsreader on the 8 o'clock news.

Vanessa   Do you know roughly how many people were watching the show at that point?

Eric   Yes. 10,546,854.

Vanessa   10,546,854 viewers witnessed Eric throw up on live television out of disgust! Let's applaud him! This is a world record, Eric! You threw up on 10,546,854 viewers.

Fans clap, whistle, show signs of excitement, stamp their feet.

Vanessa   Eric Nowicki, our special guest on *Talk-talk 24 hours talk-talk show*!

Screens switch back to the programme logo, fans scream 'Eric! Eric! Eric!'

Vanessa (*to her fans*)   Those who have witnessed Eric throw up on live TV, please stand up!

About a third of the fans stand up, some even climb on chairs.

Vanessa   Perfect! Eric, many thanks for this *comeback* on our show, and not on any other . . . because we are the best!

Unleashed fans endorse this point.

Vanessa   This marathon edition of *Talk-talk 24 hours talk-talk show* is watched at the moment by 5,654,987 fans! *Thank you! Thank you* all! (*To Eric.*) Eric, I imagine that you were immediately sacked after throwing up.

Eric   Yes.

Vanessa   So you are unemployed at the moment.

Eric   Yes indeed, I'm an unemployed journalist.

Vanessa   Eric, the most famous unemployed journalist on *Talk-talk 24 hours talk-talk show*!

Raving fans.

What Is Poetry 1

The set transforms into a library, either through images projected via the TV screens or by a redeployment of props.

Mr Rat *is looking at the poetry books on the shelves. Every now and then, he pulls out a book, leafs through it and puts it back.*

His movements, though seemingly not menacing, make the **Librarian** *talk feverishly and show signs of panic.*

Librarian   I don't think I could define poetry.

Poetry is being silent and looking at silence and silence turning into two large but ragged eyelids.

Poetry occurs, when a child comes up to you, shows you their hands and says 'done'. And you realize it's your child.

Poetry happens when it starts to rain and you speed up and your umbrella gets turned inside out by the wind. And you step into a puddle and get annoyed. And a wet cat meows from under a fence.

But why do you want to know what poetry is?

Poetry is when your daughter says, 'I'll take your voice away'. And you reply, 'Don't take my voice'. But she takes it regardless and says, 'I took it'. But you can't say a thing because you have no voice. She then understands your plight and says, 'Ask me to give your voice back'. And then you ask her, *inaudibly*, to give your voice back. But she says, 'Ask me *loudly* to give your voice back'. And then you ask her *loudly* to give your voice back and you give her a kiss. 'Here, I give your voice back,' she says, and takes the stolen voice from her lips and plants it on yours. In the meantime, however, the voice falls on the floor. 'It's raining again,' your daughter says. 'The lights are on again,' someone adds.

Why do you want to know what poetry is?

Or, better still, poetry is when you go to a café in the morning, order a cup of coffee and watch the world go round. And you see two or three passers-by, a still closed cinema, an insurance company (also closed), a long green worm-like bus, a motorbike and a bike chained to a tree right in front of the café, as if abandoned for a long time, and then you suddenly burst out, 'This is happiness'.

I'm sorry to disappoint you. I talk nonsense. But why do you want to know what poetry is?

I'm really sorry I'm unable to explain to you what poetry is. Federico García Lorca said that poetry is the meeting of two words that nobody could have imagined together. But this is not all . . . Poetry isn't only a formation of words; there is *something*, an *absence* between words, between the lines from which poetry emerges. Poetry, according to Raymond Queneau, is the impulse that claims that it rains when, in fact, it's a nice day and that it's nice when it rains. But still, this isn't quite enough. No definition can sum up poetry.

I have clearly disappointed you, I'm afraid, haven't I? Why do you want to know what poetry is?

Journalism without Hypocrisy: Lesson 2

Eric *enters, rolling in several bizarre gadgets: smilometers.*

Eric   What I feel is much more complex, but in the absence of a more suitable term, I shall call this state *disgust*.

I can't be precise about how it all began. *Disgust* has settled in me gradually, without me being aware of it. Initially, I felt a sort of unease whenever I found myself in front of cameras, it was a sort of twitch mixed with guilt. I attributed this feeling to stress, although I've always been comfortable with mics, audiences and cameras. Journalists covering the news or moderating *talk shows* have to take a degree of pleasure in what they do, otherwise they are lost. I have always felt like a performer, if not a ham actor on TV sets. After having presented thousands of news programmes you develop a certain style, you become more self-assured, you start to indulge in small personal delights, you begin to enjoy the attention you receive from people and take pleasure in alerting them to important events and essential news. You start to believe that you have become indispensable, that millions of people are awaiting you at eight o'clock to sum up the essence of their day, and that you convey to them not only words but also inflections and small subliminal messages.

Many times my first piece of information would have been a warm, welcoming smile, a signal to my viewers that the news would be easy on the ears, bringing some light and relaxation.

This is the kind of smile I mean.

He demonstrates the smile.

Look . . . My eyes feel slightly moist, my face relaxed, my mouth half-open and curved up.

To mark the beginning of the ten o'clock news, I have ten different facial expressions to choose from, graded from 0 to 9.

He points at the ten smilometers displayed on trolleys. They look like ophthalmological devices used to test vision, but also like miniature guillotines.

Ten actors, each placing their chin on a smilometer. Moving from one to the other and making use of a wand, **Eric** *sets their respective smile levels.*

This is a *smilometer*, also known as an *expressionometer*, invented by myself, a device with which I can select the relevant smile for each occasion. With this device, I can set the expression that corresponds to the first two or three news items of the day, or even to the entire news bulletin.

Level 0 is an almost audible laugh, I use it on festive occasions, for New Year and Christmas, or when our country wins the football World Cup or when it attracts global attention for some amazing achievement. It is absolutely essential that no catastrophe or murder attempt should disrupt such a day.

He 'models' the expression corresponding to level 0.

Level 1 is a massive smile, accomplice, even witty.

He resets the expression on the actor's face to make it correspond to level 1.

Level 2 is a calm and soothing smile, a sort of slide through which words flow straight into listeners' ears.

The same procedure. He sets the relevant expression for level 2.

Level 3 is a formal, flat and straightforward smile, which doesn't give much away about the mood of the forthcoming half an hour. To put it differently, viewers can be prepared for pretty much anything.

He sets the face attached to smilometer 3 to the relevant expression.

Level 4 is a censored and repressed smile, as if it alerted viewers: 'I'm a warm and open personality but what I have to tell you unfortunately forces me to adopt a sombre tone.'

Fine tunes the face to reflect subtle details.

Level 5 is just a shadow of a smile, a passing glimpse at old friends, meaning, 'Oh, how I'd like to spend some time with you but this breaking news won't allow me'.

The face in smilometer 6 might repeat: 'Oh, how I'd like to spend some time with you but this breaking news won't allow me.'

Level 6 is reserved for professional sobriety. The expression I adopt is still humane but could barely be classed as considerate, as if I wanted to warn viewers, 'Sorry, what you are about to hear isn't pleasant but you have to learn about it regardless'.

He resets the expression with his wand.

Level 7 is an expression of controlled concern. It is the expression I might adopt for announcing a plane crash, an earthquake or a terror attack. Level 7 conveys the message, 'Let's keep calm and assess things together, responsibly and in dignity'.

Resetting the next expression. Wand in hand, **Eric** *remodels the face and adjusts the expression at the corner of the mouth.*

Level 8 is almost a frown, an expression of obvious refusal regarding the enormity of the forthcoming announcement. With this, I warn those who have tuned in just to see me that I will talk about things I consider abhorring, events that repulse and sadden me, and that in addition to the information I'm about to broadcast I also invite my audience to join me in condemning these events. How is it possible that on an island in the Mediterranean, where thousands of people spend their dream holidays, the sea should bring to the shore the bodies of hundreds of African immigrants, drowned while attempting to make it to Europe?

He keeps adjusting the face in expressionometer 9 until the dead bodies of illegal immigrants can be glimpsed in reflection.

Level 9 is the expression that corresponds to national mourning. It heralds a piece of disastrous news, it's a warning that after watching my broadcast nobody would be able to carry on with their usual activities, have dinner, watch a film or go to bed in peace. It's the expression I adopt whenever there is a nuclear explosion and the radioactive clouds are heading towards us. I made use of this expression when the Chernobyl nuclear plant exploded back in April 1986.

He sets the same expression on his own face as the one in expressionometer 10.

See? All done!

Awakening 1

The **Spokeswoman** *together with two or three aides wake the* **President** *from his nap.*

President Why are you waking me up? I told you not to wake me when I don't want to be awake. What's this smell? What could be so urgent? Where's my coffee?

Spokeswoman (*handing him his coffee*) Something strange is going on, Mr President. We don't yet know what exactly but three journalists, three major TV stars, have thrown up live on television while presenting their shows to large audiences.

President Why did they throw up? What happened to them? Why is it my business that they threw up? Why do you wake me up just because three idiots have thrown up? Which TV channels do they work for? Any of them from public service broadcasting? Why didn't you put sugar in my coffee?

Spokeswoman One of them is our employee, the other two are from independent channels.

President And what do you expect me to do now? Why did you have to alert me that these people threw up on live television? Did you interrogate them? Was this a joint action? Are they insane? Is this a conspiracy? Do I have anything to do with this? Does the fact that these three morons threw up concern me in any way? Do I know them?

Spokeswoman Yes, Mr President. You do know them. You have been interviewed by all three lately. And all three are invited to the summit.

Awakening 2

Eric *and a team of* **Investigators**.

Investigator 1 Eric Nowicki, it is very important that you try to tell us all there is to say. Even what you think you don't know.

Eric I'm doing my best to say it all. I have nothing to hide. On the contrary, I am very pleased to be in a position to tell you what I think is happening to me.

Investigator 2 So what's happening to you, Eric?

Eric Something has cropped up in my brain. For a while now, two voices have taken refuge in my brain. In fact, everything started from a rat. This is what I think, at least. My sense of disgust began then.

Investigator 3 Eric, try to give a single response to each question. Do you understand what I mean?

Eric I do. Except that I don't have a single brain any more, or to be precise, my brain is host to two separate voices. I have been chosen to act as a messenger. I have something very important to transmit. This is the reason why I wrote to the President.

Investigator 1 Eric, let's go back to your sense of disgust. What is the connection between disgust and the rat?

Eric The rat started to pay me visits in my make-up booth. Every time I'd sit in front of the mirror, I'd see it there. In fact, I could see it through the mirror. I have even told Anita the first time I saw it: have you got rats around here? But Anita said: no, what rats? I didn't think much of this at the beginning. I don't really spend a lot of time in make-up, perhaps five to ten minutes. Anita gives me a head massage to relax me before I start my show.

Investigator 2 Has the rat appeared in other places, too?

Eric Yes, at my home. The same rat. It was this that threw me, I think. It's a rat with a red mark on its eye. One of the eyes. Can't remember which one. The first time I saw the rat it was in the mirror, and it seemed to me that the mark was on its left eye. But when I saw it climb on the keyboard of my computer the mark was on the right eye.

Investigator 3 Eric, have you ever had the impression that the rat was trying to get in touch with you?

Eric Oh yes, absolutely. It wasn't any old rat. It was rather large, for a start. The size of a small rabbit or so. And it started to rummage in my paper bin. It displayed repetitive gestures. Probably to show me that it's capable of reason. Anyway, my sense of disgust started at that point.

Investigator 1 Disgust for what?

Eric Everything. Myself. Towards every word I uttered. This is why I threw up. But there is a solution. I know that other journalists have thrown up, too. Globalization won't succeed without a pact with rats. The problem is that we'll need to be convincing. Public opinion is moronic. If some extra-terrestials appeared here tomorrow, everybody would be bending over backwards to get in touch with them. But no one is prepared to shake hands with rats. No one.

He starts to cry. The three **Investigators** *hand him a tissue each.*

Grand Café 2

Music. Preferably Anton Bruckner's Locus iste. *We are in the Grand Café. Important figures enter guided by the two* **Siamese Sopranos** *and take their seat at the tables.*

The Man Who Had His Inner Evil Removed

Mr Kuntz *greets the new arrivals while mixing something in a large bowl; perhaps he is preparing homemade mayonnaise 'à la mamma'. He tastes the mix every now and then, and continues stirring.*

As the various characters, couples, highflyers and celebrities take their seat, **Mr Kuntz** *walks up to them and offers them a taste of this 'mayonnaise', whispers something in their ear, laughs and continues to stir.*

Mr Kuntz We have to change our outlook on evil.

Evil is a staple of our world, so it has to be integrated into our lives, and not excluded from it. There is nothing worse than trying to oppose evil.

Those who confront evil are annihilated by it.

Evil is a facet of our existence with which we can establish a dialogue.

Evil is something we can negotiate with.

Evil is something unavoidable with which we can cohabit.

Evil is not something fatal, it's rather a frontier.

Evil should never be seen as an opposite of good; all concepts we use to make sense of the world are relative.

Evil is like a substance lining human existence: in some way or other, in smaller or larger quantities, it is present in all our actions and destinies.

Evil is like an animal that has to be domesticated, tamed and persuaded to take man's side.

Evil is not like an arrow laden with hate that is heading towards us; under no circumstances should we feel that we are its *target*. Evil is rather our power that launched the arrow.

Evil needs to be tackled with wisdom and politeness, with patience and caution. We must learn to accept defeat, and under no circumstances should we posture in case we win.

Evil is an ally of good, in the same way as death is allied with life.

When we are asleep, good and evil play dice together.

Evil is like our own skin: we can never escape it; it's our ultimate frontier, a prerequisite for our being.

Evil is unbiased; it is pointless to solicit favours from it.

We can enter into dialogue with evil, but only if we all manage to invent a language for this purpose.

There is a science dedicated to the art of living with Evil, called *evilology*.

Up until now, no one has catalogued human knowledge regarding our dialogue, cohabitation and complicity with evil. I am the first genuine *evilologist*.

Don't be afraid of approaching evil with trust; there is always a solution if you respect evil's status as a primordial force.

Never confuse evil with other negative concepts such as stupidity, cruelty or cynicism. Evil is honest in its approach.

Never confuse evil with the idea of accident, blight or curse. Evil is pure in its approach.

Evil is not a rite of passage we need to undertake by all means; it is rather a dashboard display that shows the speed of the car we keep learning to drive throughout our lives.

One can sign an agreement with evil.

Everybody can hold out a hand to the evil nurtured by themselves.

How stupid to confuse evil with the devil – please get this out of your minds!

With a little good will, one can establish a collective dialogue with evil.

Please close your eyes and repeat after me, in silence, the following question: 'Why are we so evil?'

Now you can open your eyes, you'll probably realize that you have already been relieved of evil.

I recommend to carry out this exercise again, this time in a loud voice. Let's close our eyes and repeat together, 'Why are we so evil?' One, two, three . . .

Now you can open your eyes; as you can see, the sense of relief is stronger still.

Evilology is a science that should be freely publicized in schools so that all citizens know how to live with evil.

Our institute of therapeutic evilology proposes strategies for initiation in the communication and cohabitation with evil. Don't hesitate to try this experience, it is easier to establish a group dialogue with evil.

Should you feel anxious or assaulted or provoked, please note that this is a good sign, only in this state can you begin your first genuine conversation with the evil in you.

He offers a taste of his mayonnaise to each guest.

What Is Poetry 2

A bench by the seaside. An **Old Man** *is scribbling into an old notebook. Next to him, there is a rat.*

Old Man No, I'm not a poet. Yes, I did write poetry as a teenager, like everyone else. Now I write because my hand is shaking. My doctor advised me to keep on writing. To keep fighting. So I come here every day and I write. I make a note of various words and thoughts. I also draw at times. Unfortunately my hand shakes so much that even I can't really make out what I wrote. Everything appears shaken.

No, I don't know what poetry is. I have never thought about this.

But now I think that poetry is something that is shaking. It is possible that this is the real nature of poetry. Something that vibrates . . . And there are so many things that vibrate in the universe . . .

No, I can't tell you any more.

In fact, I have no idea why I'm telling you all this. As if I was hallucinating.

Where are you from, Mr Rat? The sea? Are you a sea rat? It is true that the low tide washes out all sorts of creatures and . . .

You are wet, you must have just come out of the water.

Do you want to sit on the bench? Do you want to join me? Do you want me to show you my notebook? This one here, shall I? Have you hurt your eye by any chance?

There. I told you that nothing makes sense.

No, honestly, I cannot tell you what poetry is.

Although, when I look at these people who seem to emerge out of nothingness after the low tide . . . They are all wearing wellingtons and have plastic buckets. They're all crabbing and collecting shells. There is the odd dog running up and down with them.

In any case, why do you want to know what poetry is?

Talk Show 2

Live transmission of a talk show. 'I'm the best!' presented by **Tony** *and* **Wanda**. *This evening, their special guest is* **Vanessa**.

Tony Welcome to a new edition of 'I'm the best!'

Brisk reaction from the audience.

Wanda 'I'm the best!' with Tony . . .

Tony And Wanda . . .

Wanda 'I'm the best!' because we have the courage to make promises we can fulfil.

Tony 'I'm the best!' because we have an actual influence over politicians!

Wanda 'I'm the best!' because we provide the most sensational footage.

Tony 'I'm the best!' because we not only provide information but also clues to decipher it.

Wanda This is our 863th show.

Tony Today's special guest is . . .

Wanda and **Tony** (*together*)   Vanessa!

Journalism without Hypocrisy: Lesson 2

Vanessa *appears on the set accompanied by music and light effects, while the already 'warmed up' audience sings 'I'm the best! / I'm really the best. / Because I believe in me. / Because I believe in humanity. / Yes, I'm the best because I don't believe in what I see. / I believe only in I'M THE BEST!'*

Tony   And...

Wanda   And...

Audience   *And we like* Vanessa!

Tony   Good evening, Vanessa!

Wanda   Good evening, Vanessa!

Vanessa   Good evening, Tony, good evening, Wanda.

Tony   Can we move on straightaway to what we really want to find out?

Wanda   The audience wants to know...

Tony   How was it when you threw up on live television...

Wanda   With the President there...

Tony   Who was your guest...

Wanda   For the last three days, social media has been innundated by these images...

Tony   Almost two million views on YouTube.

These images are now relayed by the TV screens in the background, too: **Vanessa** *throws up while asking the* **President** *a question; the latter quickly produces a tissue from his pocket and wipes* **Vanessa's** *mouth, and then her tears.*

Wanda   I hope you aren't pregnant, Vanessa.

Tony   In any case, many thanks for making your first public appearance after the incident on our show.

Wanda   It's already been three days and you haven't yet issued a statement.

Tony   We're listening, Vanessa.

Wanda   Is the fact that you threw up on live television connected in any way to the President?

Tony   Or is it a chain reaction, considering that three days prior to your throwing up you had a guest on your show who had himself thrown up on live television?

Wanda   The entire world is listening to you, Vanessa.

Tony   *Go,* Vanessa, do tell us!

Silence. **Vanessa** *produces a tissue from her handbag and wipes her nose. (The tissue is branded with Mickey Mouse images.)*

Vanessa   I have some really serious stuff to tell you. I want to speak to you all, whether you are listening to us or not, hoping that those who do listen will share this message.

We have always blamed rats for being the main culprits in spreading the plague and other diseases. But this isn't true. Rats could have never spread any disease if humans hadn't been continuously producing squalor and rubbish, ordure and filth.

Rats have always been scapegoats of sorts and we have always tried to eradicate them. We, humans, have invented tons of ways to get rid of them: traps, poison, deratization . . . Even our language is infected with offensive remarks on rats and mice. 'When the cat's away, the mice will play.' How stupid! How moronic! 'I'll find you even in a mousehole.' How stupid! How moronic! It's high time we take action and decontaminate our language.

Freeze-frame. Everybody stands still, all on-screen images freeze.

Mr Rat 2

A well-behaved army of **Rats** *makes its appearance onset. The group moves forward to the very front of the stage.*

Rats (*altogether*)   Don't be afraid.

We talk to you as a group because we have a shared brain.

Please allow us to tell you that we, rats, appreciate you very much.

Yes, we do, without a doubt.

It's a fact, you are a very successful species and we are capable of appreciating the real successes of nature.

This fact has to be clarified from the very beginning, because it will form the basis of our code of conduct.

An essential basis, shall we say.

So don't be afraid.

We talk to you as one because we, rats, have a shared brain.

We respect and admire your evolution, although, we must admit, we also find it a form of folly.

Your species has undertaken a labour-intensive and large-scale operation to transform the world, and we find this impressive.

Yet we must stress that you have no chance of success without our help.

We talk to you as a chorus because our species is equipped with a unique and shared brain.

You, humans, will never succeed with globalization without our help.

You, humans, need *us*, you need our skills, you need our strength.

The moment to acknowledge this fact has arrived. The moment for clarification has come.

It's high time to talk openly about all these matters and, above all, to do this via information media.

Humans need rats.

This is the thought of the day.

Humans and rats must progress together, hand in hand so to speak, helping one another.

Humans and rats are made to survive together, as joint custodians of this planet.

The **Rats** *withdraw. Presenters and audience start fretting on set.*

Tony   Vanessa . . .

Wanda   Vanessa . . .

Tony   Vanessa, what's going on?

Wanda   Vanessa, why have you suddenly stopped talking?

Model Family 2

Darkness. **Dad** *and* **Mum** *in bed.*

Dad   I don't know why but . . .

Mum   I'm also a bit . . .

Dad   Do you think they . . .

Mum   No idea what . . .

Dad   Still, up until now it seemed . . .

Mum   Is it perhaps a . . .

Dad   Could it just be something in . . .

Mum   No idea, but I . . .

Dad   I'll go and check if . . .

He goes to check whether the children are asleep. He returns to bed.

They are both sleeping like a log, so I think . . .

Mum   Do you think they might also . . .

Dad No, let's not . . .

Mum Do you still want to . . .

Dad Yes, it would . . .

Pause. They try to make love.

Mum No, I'm afraid that . . .

Dad Still, isn't it natural to . . .

Mum Yes, but neither is . . .

Dad Where do you see that . . .

Mum This is how . . .

Dad Sure but . . .

Mum As a rule, no . . .

Dad No idea what . . .

Mum Not in this way in any case . . .

Dad And yet it will be necessary to . . .

Mum Can't you see that it doesn't . . .

Dad We have the obligation to . . .

Mum I'd rather . . .

Dad Please . . .

Mum Some other time, as soon as . . .

Dad Calm down, perhaps we can try to . . .

Pause. The same game.

Mum Impossible to do such a. How could you want to. All this situation of. I don't believe that. And don't know if. Perhaps we should. I think we are entitled to. Since we are not. Why don't you say something more. We are both worrying about. But nothing seems to. How could it when. Everything seems to me. And it isn't even where. But if not why. Or I not. Really, perhaps. Nearly. But if not and not. Perhaps that even others who. Let's talk to. Around who knows where. You can say wow. I'm not crying only hiccupping so.

Dad Let's not still really. There is until perhaps. Who knows if not. And anyway I want some. Perhaps we can take a. Don't cry because. Important is that we love because. We shall get used to until. After all they are also. And if it's our turn to. Why should we that ones that. Everywhere even here. All that can ring really. No.

Mum No idea until where which.

Dad It is perhaps rings where.

Mum If not and is comes.

Dad The most which although know.

Mum So that no or perhaps a little.

Dad Good how and tomorrow or.

Mum Tomorrow if or why.

Dad Sure no or what to more.

Mum Good night.

Dad Night.

Grand Café 3

Strange mood, somewhat disturbing music. There is something erotic in the air. The set could look like anything from a members' club to a palace or even the ceremonial hall of a masonic lodge. The atmosphere and suspense is reminiscent of the orgy scene in Kubrick's film Eyes Wide Shut.

Men and women appear in elegant and exquisite outfits. Sublime cleavages, extravangant hats. A few guests are casually smoking long cigarettes held in cigarette holders. The characters, in pairs or alone, walk up and down as if they were in an art gallery. **Eric**, **Vanessa**, **Tony** *and* **Wanda** *are among them.*

Mr Kuntz *shows guests around his lab for experiments on rats.*

Mr Kuntz If rats weighed thirty kilos, they would be masters of the universe, Einstein observed.

He points at the enormous tail hanging from the ceiling.

Rats have adapted their anatomy to our consumer society. This is astounding. Let's begin by looking at their tail, this 'specific feature' that generates so much disgust. Long and pinkish, occasionally ribbed and with tufts of hair, rats' tails have inspired plenty of negative fantasies.

In the Middle Ages, people believed that rats, whenever they are squeezd into a tight space, mistake others' tails for theirs and thus end up tied to one another. Medieval etchings depict tens if not hundreds of rats with their tails tied together, forming a kind of gruesome colony, a moving and monstrous ball. This disgusting ball, covered in faeces, urine, mud, hair and straw is called *Rattenkönig* in German. The French call it *un roi de rats*, because due to the welding of tails, often using dried faeces, rats appear to form a superior being, a king . . .

Short pause. The presentation by **Mr Kuntz** *can be accompanied by visuals.*

This *Rattenkönig* or *roi de rats* is a powerful metaphorical image. The interconnection of rats through their tails is an amazing attempt on behalf of isolated individuals to form an ensemble that is superior to each and every one of them. No other animal on

Earth, with the exception of humans, has felt the urge to develop such interconnection.

Pause.

I suggest we hold hands.

They form a large 'interconnected' group.

The technological advances of the last twenty years involving the Internet are, in fact, mankind's chaotic attempt at interconnection. Yet there is a form of organic interconnection that is superior to this. Please hold hands . . .

The images displayed on the TV screens begin to shake, and the protagonists experience a state of trance, of transfiguration.

If rats weighed thirty kilos, they would be masters of the universe, Einstein observed.

There is evidence that rats are the first vertebrates who managed to achieve radical mutation through interconnection, through a process of adhesion and organic joining. Some *Rattenkönig* have led to the appearance of a new species . . .

Rattenkönig . . . Rattenkönig . . .

All Together (*in a trance*) *Rattenkönig . . . Rattenkönig . . . Rattenkönig . . .*

Mr Kuntz *removes his hands from the 'group' and the tension immediately decreases. The group disintegrates and the lights are switched back on. Jazz music or any other kind of music that creates a sense of conviviality.*

Several **Butlers** *roll in a long table on wheels, covered with a white tablecloth that reaches the floor. The table is laden with platters, bottles and glasses of champagne.*

The scene transforms into an exhibition opening or a showroom. **Butlers** *serve champagne to guests, while old Mickey Mouse cartoons are shown on TV screens.*

Spokeswoman (*appears with mic in hand*) Yes, we could make the point that Walt Disney was a visionary.

The audience laughs.

Ladies and gentlemen, welcome to the presentation of the government programme 'Rats, our partners'.

Applause.

Yes, Walt Disney was a visionary because he created Mickey Mouse, the only positive, popular and likeable rodent character.

In this phase of our history, when we are preparing for an absolutely unique event, the first genuine and rational *interspecies* pact, we should pay tribute to Walt Disney and draw inspiration from his approach. We need to do for rats what he did to *humanize* the image of mice.

Butlers *return dressed as rats, as if they were in Disneyland. Everybody claps.*

Spokeswoman Initially, our target audience should be children and young people. They represent our future, and they will be the first beneficiaries of the *interspecies* partnership. We will have to educate the next generation to love rats.

Advertisement shown on TV screens. A range of games focusing on rats as characters.

We shall distribute a broad range of cuddly toys in the shape of rats. These will be made of fur, plastic and other touchy-feely materials. Rat-toys, rat-stickers, rat-magnets, rat-cut-out-books, rat-colouring books, rat-logos will have to be familiar to all families and become part and parcel of children's lives. Naturally, we shall relaunch cartoon and electronic game productions focusing on rats as the partners of humans, rats-as-our-best-friend, rats-as-robots, rats-as-companions, rats-as-cuddly-toys, rats-as-superheroes . . .

The image of rats will have to be vindicated at the level of interior *design* and decoration, too. We shall release prints, tablecloths, curtains, wallpapers and carpets featuring rats. Our textile industry will also make a contribution, so why shouldn't we print rat images on T-shirts, baseball caps, jackets and capes?

To give you an example of what I mean, I took this initiative:

The **Spokeswoman** *turns her back to the audience, two* **Butlers** *unbutton her dress and reveal a spectacular tattoo on her back: two images in fusion, a rat and a human, and the words 'TWO SPECIES – A SINGLE DESTINY'.*

Everybody claps. Balloons of various sizes, decorated with images of rats, are released from the ceiling. **Butlers** *disguised as rats or mice hand out rat-shaped sweets, etc.*

Butler 1 (*turns to* **Eric**)   Mr Eric Nowicki?

Eric Yeah . . .

Butler 1 The minister requests the pleasure of your company to share a glass of Champagne with her and the President.

Eric With the President? Where?

Butler 1 Follow me please.

Eric *follows the* **Butler** *among the tables laden with platters and bottles.*

Butler 1 Please be very circumspect. But, first of all, let me give you your *badge*.

Butler 1 *produces a badge attached to a lanyard and hangs it around* **Eric**'s *neck. He reads what is says on the badge.*

Eric What does PS mean?

Butler 1 Parallel Service.

Butler 1 *lifts a corner of the tablecloth and gestures to* **Eric** *to get under the table.*

Eric Seriously?

Butler 1 *nods.*

Eric enters a new spatial dimension. From this point onwards, everything that takes place under the table can be seen projected onto the screens. The words uttered by the characters under the table are amplified by loudspeakers, but even so, they come across somewhat muffled.

The **President***, the* **Spokeswoman, Vanessa, Tony, Wanda** *and* **Mr Rat** *are all huddled together under the table, champagne glasses in hand.*

Spokeswoman   Thanks for coming, Eric. Let's squeeze in a little. I'm so pleased you could join us. As you can see, from this vantage point, the world looks like a different place.

Mr Rat (*laughing*)   I'd be tempted to suggest that the change of perspective is radical.

Spokeswoman   Let me introduce the President.

Eric   Mr President, I'm honoured.

President   I know, Eric. But here is the hard part. Persuade me that I'm doing the right thing.

Vanessa, Tony, Wanda   Welcome, Eric.

Eric   Hello.

Spokeswoman   Well, now that we are all here together, let's share a glass of Champagne with Mr Rat. He has chosen to remain silent so far.

Mr Rat   There's a time for everything.

As it's so crowded under the table, the **Spokeswoman** *can only fill the glasses with great difficulty.*

Spokeswoman   Eric, let me have your glass. Who else needs a top-up? Mr President?

President   I still have some.

Mr Rat   Let's drink for our irreversible partnership!

All drink.

Spokeswoman   So, to begin with, Mr Rat will explain or clarify a few details. Then, we shall prepare the summit.

President   Go ahead. Let's talk about other rubbish.

Mr Rat (*assumes all of a sudden a formal stance*)   We can clean up moral excretions, too. We can wash, lighten or remove altogether any kind of moral squalor. Anything that's ugly in you, for instance. You, humans, have made two major ontological errors. You have created a globalized consumer society without having initially provided an efficient system for handling refuse. This was your first act of insanity. And then, you burdened your being with moral contamination without having set up an efficient system for handling inner refuse.

President   I agree.

Mr Rat   Fortunately, we rats are right here, with you and beside you. There are many of us and we are prepared to eat away all your mental filth, or, in other words, all 'other rubbish' (to quote the President). The situation is far from desperate. Nowhere near. The situation can be controlled because we are able to actually wolf down all your food waste but also your dirty thoughts, all the filth generated by your lifestyle, and all spiritual residue left in the wake of your gruesome passions. We are capable, therefore, to clear up all public rubbish heaps on the planet, as well as the subhuman sediment that has appeared in the universe. You could already witness how efficient we are with all the expired food thrown away by supermarkets. This represents about 30 to 40 per cent of all goods, so I think the overall percentage is in fact higher. Well, we can carry out the same thing with your outdated and feeble ideas, right at the source. Slops and any vile stuff produced by your brain and your subconscious can be erased. All we need is a *metaphysical mandate*. Your subconscious is, please forgive me, an unbearable cesspool that endangers every other living being on Earth. Trust me, you must let us enter into your mental cellars, the basement of your grey matter, your dreamways, your existential slaughterhouse and your cognitive cemeteries. Yes, we can cover a lot of ground provided we are well organized and, above all, acknowledged for our capacity as public service moral filters. We require a *long-term* pact with you that we sign at a biological level. Are you with me, Mr President?

President   I am. We are witnessing a historic moment. We are saved.

Mr Rat   We have always known that you are one of us.

President   Iris, get me another drink.

The **Spokeswoman** *tries to open another bottle of champagne, but she doesn't manage due to the overcrowding;* **Eric** *takes over the operation, the cork pops, and a few drops of champagne flow down* **Vanessa***'s throat.* **Tony** *produces a tissue and wipes* **Vanessa***'s throat. The* **Spokeswoman** *takes the bottle and fills the* **President***'s glass and then all the others'.*

Mr Rat   Cheers! We are all in the same boat.

All drink. The **Spokeswoman** *passes round a small basked of rat-shaped cookies. Everybody takes one and starts nibbling. A mobile phone rings, the* **President** *tries to find the device but fails.*

President   Iris, can you please . . .

The **Spokeswoman** *asks* **Eric** *to hold her glass. She then searches for the* **President***'s jacket and produces the mobile.*

President   Who's there?

Spokeswoman   The presidential press office.

President   Ignore them.

Mr Rat So, as you can see, we rats trust your elite. This is the reason why we're here. I don't think there are any further issues with the elite. We need to deal with public opinion now. The fact of the matter is that it is *you* and *us* who'll survive on this planet. In other words, we'll need to work together and to *fuse* together. The genetic mutations we experienced over the last few years allow *us* to work in the field of ideas and reflection, in the ethical and axiological field, where behavioural values and norms are being forged. We are ready for a cosmic spring clean. We, rats, can be found wherever humans live. There is no country or region, city or village, without a strong *rat*-presence. Would you like to know how many of us are there at the moment? Well, about a million rats for each human inhabitant.

President That's a lot.

Mr Rat *It's a fact.* What matters is that we are all prepared to work hard. We need to organize an interspecies summit. This is the next news-bomb that the journalists who have recently thrown up can aptly transmit to international platforms, public opinion and political parties. Journalists, the news-bomb is yours. Please take care of it straightaway, and make use of all your talent so that it explodes as it should.

Tony Yeah, we'll need to launch this bomb, the rat-bomb . . .

Mr Rat We want an equal partnership, of course.

Wanda Right.

Spokeswoman It goes without saying.

Mr Rat And all this needs to be registered in the constitution.

What Is Poetry 3

Mr Rat *is in the library, followed by the two* **Siamese Sopranos**, *one white and one black.*

Each of the **Siamese Sopranos** *carries a sort of first-aid kit. They open their kits and begin to fit* **Mr Rat** *out as a surgeon preparing for an operation (or a torturer preparing for a torture session?) They give him thin rubber gloves, a magnifying glass, a leather apron, etc.*

One of the **Siamese Sopranos** *produces a few instruments that appear to be more or less suitable for surgical interventions. (Some are really delicate, such as a scalpel and a forceps.) The other produces small jars of various sizes and a container with a blue lid.*

The **Librarian** *carries on talking just as zealously as in the previous scene.*

Librarian Poetry is a form of dandruff that appears not on our heads but in our brains, it's an incendiary cosmic beat, a quest without a compass, an untranslatable outcry, an endless wake, a bitter taste in one's mouth, an absence guarded by hundreds of inner frontiers, black water dissolved in black water, a hereditary immune disaster, a simulated sexual phobia.

Why do you want to know what poetry is? How did you get in here?

Poetry is something invented by mankind, so that people can break off from their inner selves. An attempt for stepping out of our initial misery and nothingness, our subsequent mediocrity and boredom and the trap of life and death, joined, as it is, at the hip.

Mr Rat *gestures to be given a poetry book. One of the* **Siamese Sopranos** *brings it to him.* **Mr Rat** *examines the book as if it were a diseased organ.*

Librarian   The idiot inherent in people believes that poetry can give them wings to escape the cage of their own being and fly above eternity.

The idiot inherent in people is right, it is possible to fly above eternity on the wings of poetry, provided your eyes are shut.

Why do you want to know what poetry is?

Poetry is like a legless horse, a neckless giraffe, a crocodile queueing in a dentist's waiting room, a cloud without a sky, a day without morning, a pair of wings without flight, a smile without eyelashes, an answer without a question, a bridge under a river bed, a parachute that brings down the sky itself, a beautifully wrapped box full of apples under a Christmas tree.

Mr Rat *leaves through the book and affixes it in a bookchair (he almost shackles it). He begins to pull out something from it with the aid of a pair of tweezers.*

Siamese Sopranos (*address the audience singing*)

> Don't be afraid.
> We had to get here.
> To this point.
> Everything will be simple.
> You won't feel any pain.
> Everything will be like a long sea voyage.
> On a sea without waves.
> On absent waves, that is.
> On a sea without depth.
> On a narrow strip of water.
> In other words on a fake sea.
> On a very small sea.
> On a sea the size of a shell.
> On a shell without waves.
> A long journey on a shell.
> It's paramount not to shout.
> It won't hurt.
> So please don't shout.

Mr Rat *pulls out a fairly long worm from the book. It waggles, being caught in between the teeth of the tweezers. One of the* **Siamese Sopranos** *opens a jar,* **Mr Rat** *deposits the worm and the second* **Siamese Soprano** *pours some blue liquid over it.*

If the director finds it necessary, **Mr Rat** *can repeat this procedure.*

Summit 1

*Eric and **Vanessa** in front of cameras, ready to present the show 'I'm the Best'. Hustle and bustle. We are in the press room of a major summit.*

*Eric and **Vanessa** are interviewed live by **Tony** and **Wanda**. While Eric and Vanessa are being interviewed, two groups of **Rats** position themselves behind them: a smaller one behind **Eric** and a larger one behind **Vanessa**.*

Tony   Good evening, Eric. Good evening, Vanessa. You are in Luxembourg, where everybody's experiencing a historic day today, due to the fact that the agreement with rats has finally been signed.

Eric   Yes, Tony, and the entire international community salutes this initiative that represents an enormous step forward.

Wanda   The ecological, economical, sanitary, and, let's stress, metaphysical consequences of this partnership are enormous.

Tony   Eric, Vanessa, please clarify for 'I'm the Best' this latter aspect, the metaphysical dimension of the man–rat alliance.

Eric   Well, Tony, things are rather simple: taking into account that rats will engulf from now on all human excretions, rats will be officially acknowledged as an essential component in the definition of man.

Vanessa   To be precise, this summit will confer rats the status of being a unit of measure for the human being, or for the human 'brand', so to speak.

Tony   Could you be more precise about how these relationships will be quantified?

Eric   Just like a car's power is measured or expressed in horsepower, the degree of humanity inherent in each individual will be measured in rats.

Vanessa   We shall say that a person is *worth* ten rats when the filth produced by that person requires the intervention of ten rats to clean it all up.

Eric   When a hundred rats are needed to clean up the excretions and filth produced by someone, we shall say that this person *weighs* or is *worth* a hundred rats.

Vanessa   *The metaphysical weight* of each and every human being can be calculated *in rats*, in the same way as liquids are measured in litres and solid matter in kilos.

Wanda   Shall we celebrate, therefore, that for the first time in its history, mankind has a genuine instrument to evaluate the human condition?

Eric   Let's celebrate in moderation . . .

Tony   Viewed from here, we have the impression that you are experiencing a moment of high emotion over there. I'm getting a sense of this just by looking at what is taking place right behind you, and I think our viewers can pick up on that, too.

Wanda   Today, Eric, we could see disturbing images of rats walking up and down the official dinner table, surrounded by heads of state and government of the G7. The symbol is very potent indeed, and I wonder whether everyone's quite prepared to accept it. How about the G20, not to mention the G30.7?

Tony   Because we need to acknowledge that rats have a very bad image.

Eric   Yes, Tony, yes Wanda, this topic has been widely explored here, both in official discourse and behind the scenes, by the almost 2,000 journalists gathered to report on this first summit dedicated to good neighbourly relations.

Vanessa   I should add that, in parallel with all this, we've started to mobilize public opinion regarding the forthcoming World Summit of Good Neighbourly Relations.

Eric   But just to return to the initial question: yes, it's true, rats have a bad public image. What does a bad public image actually mean these days? Well, we, journalists can produce bad publicity simply by *omissions*. What, Somalia has a good public image? How could it possibly have a good image when we only talk about Somalia through the lens of civil war?

Vanessa   And piracy.

Eric   Or Iraq, or Madagascar, or Colombia. What image does Colombia conjure up in you? Drug trafficking and perhaps guerillas hiding in the jungle. What image does Greece have these days?

Vanessa   A country engulfed in debt crisis, selling its islands . . .

Eric   Countless other countries and communities have a bad public image only because journalists treat them through the dominant lens of negative images.

Vanessa   Take, for instance, the case of Romania – we only talk about it in conjunction with three negative topics.

Eric   Orphanages and abandoned children, stray dogs, the miserable life of the Roma.

Vanessa   It isn't fair to only label countries with a few negative connotations!

Eric   Each country can offer, in fact, a much broader range of negative topics.

Vanessa   Which transforms them instantly into a normal country.

Eric   An increasing number of governments demand the same thing from the Western press: talk about our entire range of negative issues.

Wanda   I see. So, in fact, Eric, this claim also reveals the mechanism of producing media clichés and labels.

Eric   Yes, Wanda, today I attended the colloquium 'Why do we hate rats?'. Its conclusion was that rats have always been the victims of an ongoing hype of clichés.

Wanda   Carriers of infections and diseases, especially the plague.

Eric   Clichés, clichés, clichés. This is the conclusion of today's debate, a debate conducted with our friends the rats and a number of prestigious scientists. Has anyone mentioned so far that rats have an amazing spatial memory and are capable of escaping from any maze?

Tony and Wanda No.

Vanessa That rats never forget a painful experience, and that they avoid for the rest of their lives any product that has caused them harm?

Tony and Wanda No.

Eric Or that the female rat is able to receive the sperm of several males at the same time, and give birth to six to twelve babies fathered by different individuals?

Wanda Incredible! As you pointed out earlier, Eric, we have got used to information as spectacle, and therefore to sensational negative topics.

Tony I'd like to remind our viewers that Eric Nowicki and Vanessa Imperiali are the special envoys of 'I'm the Best!' at the Summit of Good Neighbourly Relations currently held at Luxembourg.

Wanda Tomorrow lunchtime we shall broadcast another special edition of our programme dedicated to this new and unexpected form of inter-species partnership. By the way, Eric, if I'm not mistaken, you are currently being surrounded by a number of rats, aren't you?

Eric I am indeed . . .

Tony How many?

Eric I don't know exactly. I can count if you like . . . At least fifty or sixty.

Wanda And you, Vanessa? Don't take this the wrong way, but what is your metaphysical weight?

The **Rats** *turn towards the cameras and take a respectful bow.*

Summit 2

Eric *walks across the set, followed by his 'metaphysical group' of* **Rats**.

When he stops, the **Rats** *stop, too.* **Eric** *takes a few steps. So do the* **Rats**.

Eric *turns around and gazes at the* **Rats**. *The* **Rats** *look at the floor respectfully, even bashfully, as if they didn't dare to 'disturb'.*

Eric *takes a few steps towards them. The* **Rats** *step back in an orderly fashion, reminiscent of a Macedonian phalanx.*

Eric *signals to the* **Rats** *to disconnect from one another, so he can count them. The* **Rats** *concur and* **Eric** *counts.*

Eric Ninety-five?

*The **Rats** indicate that he is wrong. **Eric** scans the group again and realizes that he missed a **Rat**.*

Eric   Ninety-six?

*The **Rats** nod.*

Eric   Shall I take it that you are determined to follow me everywhere?

*The **Rats** nod.*

Eric   Shall I take it that this is my metaphysical weight?

*The **Rats** nod.*

Eric   My metaphysical weight is precisely ninety-six rats? (*Yes.*) No more and no less? (*Yes.*) How did you arrive at setting my weight at exactly ninety-six rats? (*The **Rats** shrug.*) Look, if you want us to have a long-term partnership, I need to know. (*The **Rats** avoid his gaze and look to the floor.*) Does it say ninety-six on my forehead? (*The **Rats** look to the floor, meaning no.*) Why then ninety-six? (*The **Rats** tilt their heads humbly to the right.*) How do you know my lifestyle and how much rubbish and filth I produce every day? (*Ninety-six heads meekly tilted to the left.*) Have you been keeping an eye on me for some time? (*Silence, stillness.*) How long have you been observing me for? (*Silence, stillness.*) From birth? (*No, with immense respect.*) Shall I take it that you can look through me? (*Yes.*) I can't hide anything? (*No.*) You know what I think at all times? (*No.*) You mean this? (*Yes.*) I hope you won't want to sleep in my room though . . . (*No.*)

*A terrified **Vanessa** dashes in, followed by a group of **Rats**. She tries to chase them away or get rid of them, but the **Rats** are adamant to 'stick' with her, keeping a distance of about a metre or two but determined not to abandon her.*

*The **President** appears, dictating something to the **Spokeswoman**. They are both followed by compact groups of **Rats**. The **President**'s 'escort' is much more numerous that that of the **Spokeswoman**.*

*Other characters also appear, in various states of panic and followed by compact groups of **Rats**. In performance, this theme could be expanded through choreography, for instance.*

Summit 3

*Film footage: **Vanessa** followed by her group of **Rats** in a hotel corridor. Smaller or larger groups of **Rats** are planted in front of each door. **Vanessa** stops in font of a door ('guarded' by approximately ninety **Rats**) and knocks gently. **Eric** opens. The **Rats** adopt an attitude of immense politeness and secrecy as **Eric** talks to **Vanessa**.*

*ced, like the thaeracters also appear in ostates of panic, followed by compact door. The two groups of **Rats**, **Eric**'s and **Vanessa**'s, will remain at either side of the door.*

Vanessa   I had enough. Give me something to drink.

Eric Vanessa, you've been warned.

Vanessa I hate them. I feel I'm going crazy.

Eric How can you say such a thing?

He pours some whisky. **Vanessa** *drinks.*

Vanessa Take me into your arms. Hold me.

Eric Vanessa, get yourself together. We are about to add a new page of history to the adventure of life.

Vanessa How many have you got?

Eric Ninety-six.

Vanessa I have two hundred.

Eric Two hundred?

Vanessa Yes, two hundred. I counted them five times. There must be a mistake.

Eric Rats never make mistakes.

Vanessa No, no, there is a mistake. Believe me. I don't generate so much rubbish. Impossible. Look I have to throw up again. Every time I think about them, I have to throw up and hiccup.

Eric You'll get over it. Right now, we are in an experimental phase.

Vanessa Don't be stupid. We shouldn't have agreed to be used as guinea pigs.

Eric There was no other way. Somebody had to start.

Vanessa Can you hear them? There are swarms of them everywhere. They contaminated the entire hotel.

Eric Nothing is 'contaminated'. The hotel was especially *kitted out for rats*. It has double flooring and double ceilings everywhere. Rats need vital space and passageways so they can carry out their work.

Vanessa *examines the room, opens a few drawers and the bathroom door, and looks under the bed.*

Vanessa Do something so my headache goes away. Fuck me.

Eric Vanessa, repeat after me: rats are our friends. Rats respect us. Rats are our saviours. Rats are a providential solution for a wretched and idiotic mankind that is unable to come up with another industrial and trade model. Unlike humans, rats are friendly, useful and indispensable.

Vanessa Thanks, Eric, thank you.

Eric But we humans, we need to make an effort, too. We have to improve ourselves and become worthy of them. Vanessa, make an effort and improve yourself. (*He pushes her towards the door.*) Goodbye.

Vanessa Nobody wants me tonight!

Eric We are in the midst of a biological revolution, Vanessa. It's a blasphemy to think about sex.

Vanessa (*in desperation*) Nobody wants me. Why not? I knocked on countless doors. How do I look? Do I look that bad? Could it be because of the hiccups? Let me show you something. (*She turns around, lifts her blouse and lowers her skirt until the top of her thighs start to show.*) See?

Eric No.

Vanessa (*she lowers her skirt further*) And now?

Two names are tattooed onto her thighs: 'Eric' on the left thigh, 'Nowicki' on the right thigh.

Vanessa See? See, blockhead? I was crazy about you. God, how I loved you! Everything I know, I've learned from you. (*She offers herself to him.*) Come on, try me!

Eric Vanessa, at this moment in time, I'm a messenger between two species. I have no time for anything else.

Vanessa Come on, you'll see that I'm all *organic* and *ecologically sound.* Have you ever tried an *organic* woman before? There are still very few of us about but we militate for an *organic* sexuality. Everybody wants a *green* industry and an ecologically sound behaviour. We have come up with the idea of *green* sex. I've been eating only *organic* products for the last two years. Everything I wear is a hundred per cent natural. Look, everything I wear is *handmade*, in the spirit of fair trade, without any artificial colourings. Everything I buy is made in poor countries by correctly paid craftsmen. You should really appreciate this. How can something like this not get you into the mood! For the last two years, I've only been using entirely *organic*, natural and edible moisturizers, shampoos and shower gels. (*She takes her lipstick out of her handbag.*) Here you go!

Eric What shall I do with it?

Vanessa Taste it! At least that.

Eric (*sticks his tongue out*) OK, but only a lick, and then each retires to their own bed.

Vanessa (*applies some lipstick*) You dumb-ass, this isn't the way to taste it! Taste it from my lips. I swear it's edible, it's made of raspberries from New Zealand.

Eric *hesitates, but then sticks his tongue out and gently touches her lips. Two large tears roll down* **Vanessa**'*s cheeks.*

Vanessa You can taste my tears, too. Come on, you fool, drink my tears, they are *organic*.

Eric *sips up one of her tears.*

Eric Vanessa, I'm sorry, I've lost my sex drive.

Vanessa I knew it. I had a feeling. It's because of them. Of course. How could you possibly get a hard-on with these rats all over the ceiling? How could you have an erection with rats swarming under your feet? This is already a collateral damage of this shit partnership. Farewell erection! Farewell sex drive!

She bends down and puts her ear to the floor.

Vanessa They claimed that they'd keep quiet and we won't hear a thing. But I do hear them. I can hear them all the time. Let me show you something.

The pair steps out on the corridor. The two groups of **Rats** *react immediately, as if they came to attention.*

Vanessa This is where our home secretary stays.

Eric Impossible! How many?

He starts to count the rats positioned in front of the home secretary's room.

Vanessa There are 467 in total. Everybody has made a detour here out of sheer curiosity.

Eric What can I say, 476 is a respectable figure.

Vanessa Absolutely, but if we take into account that the Italian prime minister has 6,875 . . .

Eric Really? Who has counted them?

Vanessa *gets her iPad out.*

Vanessa Everything is out there in the open. On Twitter, on YouTube. Look Eric, we've entered an era of horrible transparency. Nobody can pretend their rats don't exist. *Everything* has been laid bare. We are facing a moral explosion of cosmic proportions. Many will be unhappy, politicians, businessmen, artists, especially since it isn't clear whether the number of rats refer to physical or moral filth . . .

Eric In my case, it's physical.

Vanessa Really? Eric, don't be so naive! With ninety-six rats, it's obvious that you're a pig.

Eric Let's sleep at least two or three hours. Come on, good night.

Vanessa (*talking to her* **Rats**) Still two hundred of you? To clean up what exactly? Take a good look at me. I eat and live in an *organic* way, I'm a vegetarian, I hardly throw anything away and I don't even have rubbish bins at home. What exactly have you got to clean up in my case? Even my erotic fantasies are *organic*!

Grand Café 4

Ambient piano music. **Mr Kuntz** *is about to demonstrate how his device that eradicates evil from humans works. The model family is waiting in the lobby.*

Mr Kuntz We've found the evil inherent in man. The inner evil in man has been identified. It's neither located in the heart, nor the brain, not even the soul.

Well, ladies and gentlemen, I shall put it as plainly as possible. The evil in man is located in the liver, in other words, in the very organ that filters out all toxins and harmful substances from the body.

Please take a look at this image, scaled up from one to a million. This tiny dot, which has been invisible so far, is an appendix to the liver. It is here that evil resides, in a sort of pocket, a sort of niche, surrounded by a protective membrane that the liver cannot penetrate to clean up. We have no information as to when this anatomical *bunker*, this refuge to isolate and shelter evil, first appeared.

One thing is certain though, this *pocket* withstands the liver's healing actions. This pocket can be emptied through surgical intervention, however. The only drawback: if the *pocket* is emptied surgically, the patient dies.

Yes, ladies and gentlemen, the experiments I conducted in my lab, with the aid of rats, led me to this certainty. I pinned down the location of human evil, I know where it is, I can remove it, but when I do, the person in question dies.

Note: directors may wish to include a few actual demonstrations at this point.

However, if a small live rat, say a baby rat, is placed into this *infected* pocket, the situation is sorted. The rat feeds on the evil generated in the human being, and the latter becomes a hundred per cent good or, in other words, is freed from evil.

The **Siamese Sopranos** *start singing while the model family make their way to the operating theatre.*

The operation will be carried out on the baby. The 'bunker' of its liver will be opened, the evil removed and, in its place, a baby rat installed. The rat is so tiny that it doesn't even have eyes yet.

The **Siamese Sopranos** *carry on singing throughout the operation and hand* **Mr Kuntz** *the necessary instruments.*

Siamese Sopranos

> Rats are the friends of humans.
> Rats help people attain perfection.
> Only rats can remove evil from humans.
> The person freed from evil is happy.
> Rats keep watch over the happiness of mankind.
> The person who has a rat inside is happy.
> Nobody should refuse the opportunity of having their inner evil extracted.
> Nobody should refuse cohabiting with an inner rat.
> An inner rat is our moral compass.
> An inner rat is cheerful and alive.
> An inner rat is the best friend of the human in us.
> We should be grateful to our inner rat.
> The inner rat plucks us from the night of nothingness.

The inner rat is a beacon.
It's our polar star. It's the horizon.
Let's go on a journey with our inner rats.
For all our journeys, the ideal destination is our inner rat.

A conveyor belt brings new babies that **Mr Kuntz** *positions, one by one, into the device that extracts evil. The two* **Siamese Sopranos** *remove baby rats from a nearby cage. They hold them from their tails, and then* **Mr Kuntz** *places these tiny, eyeless rats into the opening created on the babies' bodies.*

Dad   Gentlemen, there's a solution for mankind. Soon, we'll all have an inner rat. Together, our inner rats will form a republic. Together, our inner rats will organize society games and Bach chorals. The origin of evil has been cauterized.

Daughter *comes up to the footlights. She is neatly dressed in a sort of uniform, wearing a knee-length skirt, black boots and a spotty tie. She is about to recite the following tribute.*

Daughter (*takes a bow and utters the title*)   The Rat.

She adjusts her tie a little and 'tackles' the text.

Our inner rat never sleeps
it is soft and alert
happy and with its mouth full
it's always chewing
our inner dreams
our longest silences
and our words left unspoken
our inner rat helps us slowly traverse
to the other end of the night
far from the placenta of evil
our inner rat never rebels
and is never scared
it's not afraid of death because he
keeps ingurgitating us from within
even beyond death

Everybody claps and kisses her.

Summit 4

Several **Journalists** *appear in their pyjamas or dressing gowns, and start running up and down the corridors. Several* **Bodyguards** *also run up and down, talking on their earphones.*

The entire hotel is caught up in a flurry of excitement, people abandon their rooms, and humans and **Rats** *bump into each other. Every so often, people in a massive rush end up treading on* **Rats**, *who then scream in pain.*

Journalism without Hypocrisy: Lesson 2   203

A group of journalists (some still in their underwear) gather in front of the **President**'s *door. The latter comes out, also in pyjamas, with a toothbrush in one hand and a glass of water in the other.*

Several Journalists   Mr President, we want an explanation right now.

President   Perfect. But don't take notes or record anything.

Journalist 1   We want to know if they have access to our brain.

Journalist 2   How can they communicate with human beings?

Journalist 3   Mr President, we want to know what did you sign exactly and on whose behalf? The European Union?

Journalist 1   Did the entire G20 sign?

Journalist 4   Did you sign on behalf of the human species? Under what mandate? Did the UN authorize you?

President   Well, let's take these points one by one. I appreciate that you are concerned. I'm concerned too. Mankind will soon take a socio-biological leap. We have genuine reasons to be concerned.

Journalist 2   Why do we need to be transparent?

President   Do you have any idea how hard we fought in the first few decades of this century to obtain fiscal transparency, to redress the banking system and to eradicate tax havens? You all wanted transparency then. Well, now we are moving from institutional to individual transparency.

Journalist 1   Meaning?

Journalist 2   Why is it important to see at a stone's throw how many rats a particular human being weighs?

President   Because from now on we'll be experiencing an ongoing crisis. And perhaps it's not such a bad idea to be obliged to be accompanied day in day out by our *personal* rats. This way, it's all clear.

Journalist 4   What's clear, Mr President?

President   We can measure up against one another, see what lifestyles people lead, figure out people's excesses and even their hidden vices.

Journalist 5   Thank you very much, dear rats!

President   You can adopt an ironic tone if you like. I believe that rats are doing us a major favour, an essential anthropological and social favour! They force us to pay more attention to our moral, civic and institutional filth. Have you ever contemplated the fact that there is such a thing as a squalor of democracy? Or . . .

Journalist 3   What are the chances of this scenario working out and this method being adopted at a global scale?

President No idea. The *Summit* of Good Neighbourly Relations hasn't finished yet. The technical details of our collaboration will be discussed only tomorrow, with the agreement protocol scheduled to be signed in the evening. This is a project in its early stages, so beware, the game is far from over. Since we live in a democracy, all these revolutionary proposals will be publicly debated by the European nations and our partners on other contients.

Journalist 1 Will Parliament have anything to add to this?

Journalist 4 My impression is that rats are a touch too keen to start actual 'collaboration'. Why are they in such a rush?

President They are in a rush because they are more rational than us.

Journalist 3 Mr President, since I'm a journalist represented by only thirty-two rats, which means that I'm a more modest generator of filth than others, am I entitled to a promotion?

Journalist 2 Mr President, if the rest of the world doesn't accept this radical proposal of transparency, will Europe go ahead with it regardless?

Journalist 5 Aren't you concerned that Europe will be fooled yet again?

President Just by organizing this summit and thus demonstrating courage, Europe emerges as a shining example for the entire planet.

Journalist 1 Mr President, we'll become a laughing stock with all these rats following us.

President Who else could I rely on if you aren't prepared to help me introduce a new way of thinking to this planet? Please try to understand, should you have any brains whatsoever, that this is our last chance. You know very well that all ecological summits from the previous decades have failed miserably. The various countries on this planet have never managed to find a common platform to save what can be still saved of our shared home, the Earth. But Europe has never yielded, and now demonstrates an instance of courage, ingenuity and, above all, remarkable imagination.

Journalist 4 Mr President, we want to help you, but we did a vox pop which indicated that seventy per cent of the journalists accredited here loathe rats.

Journalist 5 More than that, we'd like to crush them.

President Do make an effort to earn your status as European intellectuals. Think about the fact that Europe has reclaimed its former vocation. In parallel with the initiative of establishing individual transparency with the aid of rats, Europe has found itself in its element. Don't forget that industrial civilization was born in Europe. The model of consumer society also appeared here, and so did that of capitalism. We mustn't be afraid of acknowledging these facts. It was natural, therefore, that the task of finding a long-term solution to surviving the system should also come from Europe.

Journalist 3 Perfect, *Mister President*. We shall put a hard sell on this madness that Europe assumes its *leadership* in the search for a *long-term* solution. But do you really think that rats can solve the nuclear issue, too?

President No idea. Like you, I attended a few demonstrations that have stunned me. Rats claim that they are capable of clearing up nuclear waste, and this leads us to confront a revolutionary solution. If it turns out that rats, to be precise mutant rats, can really engulf radioactive spills and pollution, then we can justifiably cry out loud, 'Victory!'

Journalist 2 Mr President, I hope that after the summit we can all return to our hometowns accompanied by our personal rats.

President Why would you be bothered by this? I believe that it is beneficial to have a permanent moral and biological thermometer. We shouldn't hide behind our words. Let's get out in the open with our rats, so people can evaluate at any point our *moral weight*. Rats will help us to sublimate and become zero error. We'll be able to Google at any point the moral weight of any leader on the planet, any businessman, opinion leader, writer or journalist. You are the first journalists chosen for the pilot. Have you counted your rats yet?

Rumours and various responses: 'yes', 'somewhat', 'sure', 'no'.

Okay, let's move on to a quick comparative exercise. Raise your hand if you weigh less than a hundred rats from a metaphysical and hence moral point of view.

A few hands are raised.

Journalist 1 Only fifty-six . . .

Journalist 2 I have seventy-eight . . .

Journalist 3 Ninety-nine . . .

President Who *weighs* between a hundred and two hundred rats?

Other hands are raised.

Journalist 4 167, if you don't find that excessive...

Journalist 5 109!

President And you?

Journalist 6 197.

President Perfect. Let's split into two groups. All those weighing more than two hundred rats should move over to my left.

A few **Journalists** *relocate.*

President Very interesting. Those who *weigh* more than four hundred rats please move a little sideways.

Five or six **Journalists** *proceed to move.*

President There you go. This is transparency. I don't want to blame anyone, but I do think that those of you who weigh over four hundred rats should be ashamed of yourselves.

Stupor. The **Journalists** *not targeted by this remark clap and start booing. They throw plastic cups, balls of paper and slippers at their 'immoral' colleagues.*

President (*joking yet serious, to the 'immoral'* **Journalists**) How did you manage to amass so much filth? There's no doubt that you must cheat on your partners, and you must be selfish, envious, flattering and profiteering. You must be taking bribes and, most probably, whatever you write is rubbish. All you do is please someone more powerful than yourselves.

Booing, insults, menacing gestures. The 'clean' **Journalists** *shout at the 'filthy' ones:*

– You scumbags!
– You stink!
– You've got a double chin!
– You've really sold out!
– You thieves! You rascals! You nonentities! Shame on you!
– The scum of society, that's what you are!
– And you, moral dregs!
– Out with you! On your knees!
– That's it, return your accreditations with immediate effect!

As in Laurel and Hardy films, or in the silent comedies of the 1920s, the 'moral' journalists throw themselves at the 'immoral' ones and begin to rip their clothes, pyjamas, etc. The scene becomes more and more hilarious and lynching is imminent. The 'immoral' journalists try to defend themselves the best they can and run on all fours, etc.

Journalist Weighing More than 400 Rats I hope you're joking, I hope . . .

President (*ends the scene with a gunshot*) I don't know whether this is a joke. Perhaps it is, perhaps it isn't. (*To the 'immoral'* **Journalists**.) This is really serious. Either because you live like beasts, consume in excess and soil the planet more than your colleagues do, or because, from a moral point of view, you are filthy pigs and you thought you could conceal this fact. Under normal circumstances, you should be handed over to the police straightaway.

Attempts at laughter, but it all comes out rather alarming.

Journalist with a German Accent As far as you're concerned, Mr President, do you consider yourself worthy of office?

President (*suddenly whining*) Don't know . . .

Journalist 5 May I point out, Mr President, that yesterday your metaphysical and moral weight was 872 rats, and by today it increased by 16 rats?

President You had the insolence to count my rats!

Journalist 4 Why should your rats be a state secret?

Journalist 3 Do you realize what shit we're getting into, Mr President?

All **Journalists** *get their cigarettes out.*

President (*lights the cigarettes, one by one*) And yet, right here and right now, we have to accept this last judgement. Just think how evil, cynical and hypocritical we all are. We don't care about anything, we only talk ill about one another. I know it won't be easy, but I believe in total transparency. We shall all bear the cross of transparency. Think about the fact that our children have no ideals left. There are no utopias for them to be inspired by. But now, thanks to the rats, we can behold a new horizon.

Journalist with a Russian Accent Long live the transparency between nations! Long live the ideal of total transparency! Our ideal: rat weight zero! Our model: zero rats! Long live rats, our moral liberators!

Journalist with a German Accent Sergei, stop it!

Journalist with a Russian Accent You motherfuckers!

Several Journalists Fuck you!

President Enough, go to bed now. I'm deadbeat.

Several Journalists Mr President, Mr President . . .

Temptestous discussions among **Journalists**. *A bottle of vodka appears from somewhere, and two or three Russian* **Journalists** *start singing 'The International'.*

Russian Journalist *Na zdarovie!*² You've never wanted to work with us or be our genuine partners, and now you team up with rats. You've got what you deserve!

Mr Rat 3

Pacinto, the **Poodle**, *on a bench by the sea. A* **Rat** *approaches.* **Poodle** *barks. A second* **Rat** *appears.* **Poodle** *barks. A third* **Rat** *appears.* **Poodle** *leaves.*

A few **Giant Rats** *appear. They are about a metre taller than the humans.*

The screens zoom in on the audience.

Giant Rats We, rats, wish to transmit this Declaration of Intent to the Human Species.

We, rats, as a species equipped with reason, would like to establish communication with humans.

The **Rats** *keep stirring something in metal bowls as they talk. They resemble chefs making a cake.*

We have accompanied *humans* for a very long time, only that our species have separated due to us following different, and we could even say, divergent routes.

Mankind has followed an evolution guided by the principle of absolute individualism, in the sense that each human individual has their own brain.

We, rats, have chosen another path on offer from nature, the path of a shared brain for the entire species.

Despite our fundamental differences, we believe in the possibility of dialogue between us and *mankind*.

Taking into account our ability for *reasoning*, we believe that the scenario with an individual brain has had catastrophic consequences for our planet.

What's the purpose of each individual having a brain of their own, a judgement of their own, not to mention emotions and an evolution of their own?

*A **Chief Rat** passes by all the others and pours some liquid in their bowls. They all continue to stir.*

Nothing, is our answer.

Ever since they've chosen this path, individuals belonging to the hominid species haven't stopped killing one another and exterminating all other forms of life on the planet.

We'd like to suggest to humans to reflect more seriously on the advantages of a single brain shared between the entire species.

A shared brain allows to eschew emotional and behavioural fragmentation.

A brain shared between the entire species is the very expression of reason. A single emotional centre for all individuals, a single centre for handling information, a single centre for taking decisions on the survival of the species: this is the only way to avoid existential, ontological and metaphysical *waste*.

*The **Rats** taste what they've been stirring in their bowls.*

What Is Poetry 4

*Morning. The **President** is in his hotel appartment. Hundreds of people seem to be coming and going to the room hosting his office, various secretaries bring documents for signature, all sorts of files land on the **President**'s desk, etc. A photographer comes to take the **President**'s picture, an aide gets him to try on a new jacket, sporting a collar suspiciously looking like rat-skin, etc.*

*Is the **President** talking to an invisible rat? Even when the phone rings and the **Spokeswoman** hands the receiver to the **President**, the latter carries on reciting his reflections on poetry.*

President I don't know what poetry is and don't think you'd ever need to know that, either.

Thinking of it, none of us humans seems to know what poetry is, so I can't really tell *you* either.

For me personally, poetry doesn't mean a thing, it has neither been of any assistance, nor has it hindered my progress in life.

I did enjoy some poems when I was young though, when I had to learn poetry by heart at school. There is even a line that has stuck with me all this time, a stupid little line written by a Dadaist poet called Tristan Tzara. The line is as follows: 'Dogs cross the air in a diamond'.

I don't think anything more stupid than this could ever be imagined. In fact, this isn't even verse just useless whim.

And yet, I have never forgotten this line, it has remained screwed on to my brain ever since I was seventeen.

I have often astounded my girlfriends with this line. I have even used it in political discourse.

The image is astonishing, above all because it's about dogs. It's as if the poet claimed that only dogs have survived on the planet. And then, the dogs decided to cross the air. Why would they do such a thing? We don't know. In any case, there are no humans, so the dogs leave too, but they need to cross the air. However, the air can only be crossed 'in a diamond'. Seas can be crossed on ships, forests on foot or in a car. But the air can only be crossed in a diamond. Why, we don't know.

I think this is the essence of poetry, it troubles your mind without explaining anything. I think this is the role of poets too, to disrupt the order of people's thoughts. Yet nobody is in need of such a thing. If poets had other skills, such as leading an army or running a city, they would have carried on with those, but they are good for nothing and all they do, as a rule, is to disrupt other people's minds and thoughts.

I can't add anything else on poetry. I'm not the person to make you understand poetry, since I don't understand it myself. Sometimes I wonder though whether the only thing left behind after the disappearance of mankind might be this line: 'Dogs cross the air in a diamond'. I don't know why, but it seems to me that this line travels the universe, it has managed to detach itself from Earth and now is in motion. It's like an invention of sorts. While the line 'dogs cross the air in a diamond' crosses the universe, towards other minds capable of vibrating in response.

All this, however, is far from conclusive. You've made me improvise. This is the first time it has occurred to me that poetry could survive in the universe after the disappearance of mankind.

Summit 5

A strong smell of coffee in the air. All **Journalists** *have a cup of coffee in their hands. The* **Spokeswoman** *joins them, also cup in hand, and is immediately surrounded by the group.*

Spokeswoman Please make sure you switch off your voice recorders, mobiles and other devices. Everything that happens in this room should stay in this room. Okay?

The **Journalists** *nod. Members of the security team check whether the devices are indeed switched off, using mobile scanners that look like mine detectors.*

Spokeswoman Everything said here is off the record, and we'll talk informally. I think I know your questions, so I'll try to explain what's going on.

Chattering amongst the **Journalists***.*

I can confirm that you've been chosen to take part in the first ever inter-species cohabitation experiment. We are facing such a radical behavioural change that we decided to evaluate its shock impact on journalists first.

Journalist 1 So we are the guinea pigs.

Laughter.

Spokeswoman In a manner of speaking, yes you are. But at the same time, we are relying on your cooperation. Whoever feels that they don't wish to continue are free to leave right now.

Silence. No one budges.

Spokeswoman This, how should I put it, society project has to be tested by someone . . .

Journalist with a German Accent Madam Government Advisor, please allow me to introduce myself. I am Max from Canal XXL, weighing 512 rats. Is it true that our leaders are also contemplating the 'long-term' decontamination of language?

Spokeswoman You crossed your Ts, Max. This is a possibility we are looking into at the moment, but I wouldn't like to put the cart before the horse. At this moment in time, we are analysing the proposal for an ethical association put forward by rats, and we have just signed a public statement acknowledging the importance of their work deployed in the service of mankind. It wasn't an easy task, our experts have been up all night . . . Well, I can let you in on the secret that rats are not prepared to compromise. They want to insert a *metaphysical* clause into the constitution.

Journalist 2 Why are they so obsessed with the *metaphysical* aspect?

Spokeswoman We have no idea. In any case, we don't have any objections to placing the rat–human partnership under metaphysical consideration. We don't mind acknowledging the *eternal dignity* of rats, both from a symbolic and a practical point of view.

Journalist 2 Why are they so obsessed with symbols?

Journalist 3 As if we weren't ourselves...

Journalist with a German Accent Madam Advisor, let's not beat about the bush, please. Are we about to be subject to a linguistic purge? Have the rats proposed to simplify our communication system? Are they asking us to reduce our vocabulary by fifty per cent?

Spokeswoman   By ninety per cent actually. For the good of reasoning.

Tittle-tattle among the **Journalists***.*

Spokeswoman   Don't even try hypocrisy with me, it won't work. We all know that we've been talking for years without actually saying anything. Rats believe that we need to unburden our brains from the tyranny of language.

Journalist 1   And what's their plan, to remove certain words from our brain?

Spokeswoman   Think of the abyss between words and action that we humans, as a race, are solely responsible for. We kept on developing our language like a gangrene, until we've got entirely engulfed in it. We have allowed the proliferation of thousands of synonyms, we have indulged in adjectives and adverbs, and invented trendy words and expressions. As a result of this pathological temptation to juggle with words, we have in fact ridiculed *sens*e and *meanin*g. We are being swamped by a linguistic bog, a labyrinth of perversions. Imagine a juggler who has long lost his eight or ten juggling balls, but who continues with his hand gestures regardless. This is the situation of mankind today. Keeps rattling on.

Noises, interjections, half-baked questions.

Journalist 1   Don't say that . . .

Journalist 2   This would be the last straw . . .

Journalist 3   No, no, still, well . . .

Journalist 4   To really . . .

Journalist 5   Madam spokes . . .

Journalist 6   *Shit.*

Spokeswoman   Our moral purification can't be achieved without a purification of our language. There is no doubt about that. Unacceptable semantic contradictions are deeply ingrained in our brain. It's high time for us to clean up our linguistic cesspool. To simplify everything. To ease ourselves. To degrease ourselves on a conceptual level. To disinfest our sham subtleties. To get rid of stuff that paralyses us.

Journalist 4   Down with verbs. Nouns will suffice!

Journalist 5   To give up grammar? Are they really asking us to give up grammar?

Spokeswoman   Anyway, we are about to compile a list of useless words together.

Journalist 6   Mother? Father? Homeland? Origin?

Spokeswoman   All major revolutions have been painful at the beginning. The French Revolution was achieved at the cost of hundreds of heads being chopped off. Ours will be carried out by cutting back a few instances of linguistic outgrowth here and there. This is the only way in which we can invigorate our ability for reasoning.

We have stopped thinking, by now we're outright delirious. Rats will infuse oxygen into our vocabulary, so that we develop a newfound ability for positive thinking.

Five or six **Journalists** *sing: 'Aaaaa'.*

Spokeswoman   Moreover, in the course of this evening, heads of state and governments will attend a demonstration on ways of decontaminating language. If you are well behaved, you may be allowed in, too.

A few other **Journalists** *join the group singing 'Aaaaa'.*

Journalist 1   Brainwashing until the bitter end. Aaaaa . . .

Journalist 2 (*hysterically*)   Gentlemen, I'm not prepared to give up my words. Gentlemen, don't take words away from me!

Journalist 3   Yes, no . . . Yes, no . . . *Google. Facebook. Microsoft.*

Journalist 4   A, e, i, o, u. I think it's really sufficient to retain the vowels. Seriously. We can express a great deal just with the aid of vowels.

Journalist 1   Oi!

Journalist 2   Aiee, aye-aye.

Journalist 3   Eye a, eye euoi.

Journalist 4   Eye you, eye I . . .

Journalist 5   Yea, ya, yo.

Spokeswoman   Words have paralysed us, words have soiled us, words have driven us away from nature! Words have. Words have. Paralysed. Driven away. Nature. They have. They have. They have. Us. Us. Us. One. Two. Our brain to. Easy until. Now without. Again us with. And will yes. But they what. So that not. Or if until. All that.

Summit 6

Mr Kuntz *officiating the mysterious operation of decontaminating language.*

Heads of state and governments seated around a semi-circular table in the reunion room of the summit. **Mr Kuntz** *places a helmet-aquarium on the head of everyone in attendance.*

Journalists *observe the scene. They behave like paparazzi.*

Mr Kuntz   Ladies and gentlemen, dear guests. Our experiment is just a simulation. Nothing that takes place here tonight is irreversible. Please relax. Please smile. You are witnessing a historical moment. Disinfesting language will open up a pathway towards true essence. We will separate the wheat from the chaff. The first phase is to provisionally break up our vocabulary. Imagine that you are at the barber's and they are applying shaving foam on your beard. Ha-ha . . .

The screens located in the background flash and display the word 'CRISIS'. Vibrations, various sound effects, spectral or meditation music, visual suspense.

Mr Kuntz *pulls out a long, algae-like thread from each helmet-aquarium.*

The word 'CRISIS' flashes up and splinters into smithereens.

All world leaders involved in the experiment utter an 'Aaaaa' in relief.

Another word appears onscreen: 'NATIONALITY'. **Mr Kuntz** *pulls it out from under the helmet-acquariums. Unanimous sighs of relief: 'Ooooo', while the leaders move closer to one another.*

Mr Kuntz *pulls out another word: 'PAST'. Prolonged sense of relief: 'Eeeee'. A further gesture of closeness among leaders.*

Mr Kuntz *pulls out the word 'LIE'. An 'Uuuuu' of relief. During this act, the leaders start levitating, as if, having become lighter, they lifted into the air and formed a compact group.*

Mr Kuntz *pulls out the word 'SEX'. A prolonged 'Iiiiiii' of relief.*

Mr Kuntz *pulls out the word 'FREEDOM'. Cracks and burps. A leader throws up. They wipe each other's mouths and cram further into one another. A human ball lifts up in the air.*

Giant Rats *return with their bowls in which they continue stirring an unknown substance.* **Mr Kuntz** *continues to pull out words: 'DIVERGENCE', 'CONTRADICTION', 'DOUBT', 'FABRICATION', etc.*

Giant Rats (*all together, as if singing in a choir*)   We, rats, are convinced that our model is the only viable way of preserving life on Earth and in the universe.

A single centre of pleasure, but billions of receptacles for those same pulsations and a single dream for a billion of sleeping specimens: these are just some of the advantages of preserving life in this way.

While humans exhaust themselves in the process of multiplying their vices and sources of unhappiness, we, rats, in a tacit and collective effort, have created the ideal matrix for survival.

Some of the advantages of a shared brain are: it doesn't develop any fear or anxiety in relation to death or dying; it doesn't fancy itself as a divine figure and it entirely preserves our collective memory.

The **Chief Rat** *removes some liquid from the helmet-acquariums and mixes it with the content of the bowls. All* **Giant Rats** *continue to mix energetically, while* **Mr Kuntz** *pulls out words such as 'DEATH', 'FEAR', 'DARKNESS'.*

Giant Rats   A brain shared between an entire species is never aggressive.

You, humans, are in the best position to observe that despite your obsessive attempts at hunting us down and exterminating us, our species hasn't developed any form of hatred towards your species, no form of violence or instinct for revenge.

It's obvious that our shared brain doesn't contain the seeds of violence and aggression.

A shared brain also makes any interest in politics impossible, or, if you like, leads to the eradication of any potential need to exercise such activities.

By its very nature, the shared brain of our species controls the very idea of social organization.

The rapport between individuals and the shared brain is so clear and frank that there is no space whatsoever for mutual manipulation or personal ambition.

No one wishes to rise above others in situations of brain-sharing.

Other advantages: even though pain will continue to exist as an individual experience, it is easier to handle owing to the shared brain that also plays the role of a centralized and universal *healer*.

The shared brain is incompatible with the idea of ownership and stinginess. What communism failed to achieve for you humans has succeeded for us rats, through the organic sharing of our neurons and grey matter.

*Each **Rat** sets fire to the content of their bowl with a lighter, as if they were to serve a flambé dish to the audience.*

We also have an entirely different relationship with time, pleasure and creation.

Time is no longer an *endured* existential dimension, but a sheer spectacle of duration.

As far as pleasure is concerned, let me tell you that we have been following human evolution (or rather involution) for a long time, and we are astounded by your approaches, according to which pleasure implies a suffering of sorts (and at times, the pleasure of some triggers the suffering of others).

Comrade humanoids and dear neighbours, you really have to sample the shared brain to understand the sense of intense pleasure experienced in togetherness.

You should know that we support artistic creation but not as an infinite multiplication of useless objects. We swear by a single line that constitutes the essence of poetry and universal beauty: 'Dogs cross the air in a diamond.'

*Darkness. The **Rats** circulate among the spectators, holding their bowls in which the flames slowly die out.*

Mr Kuntz *pulls out the word 'POETRY'.*

Siamese Sopranoes (*singing*)

   Where? When? Why? How?
   Whereto? Until when? How much?
   From whom? From what?
   Until when? Until whom? How?
   Let's yes? Let's no? Let's be? Really?
   Let's no? Let's yes? Let's how?

From where? From how much? From really?
Really until? From how what? Since how?

The human ball floats gracefully above the stage.

Model Family 3

The model family is at home. **Dad**, **Mum** *(holding a baby)*, **Son**, **Daughter**, **Grandma** *and dog. The model family has just started to experience the disintegration of language.*

Dad Good morning. Let me share a piece of good news with you.

Mum Family our has expanded model.

Dad We have a girl baby . . .

Mum May Laura introduce you . . .

Dad Who all be her life a morality paragon.

Mum ZERO evil, ZERO selfishness.

Dad This is room we prepared Laura for . . .

A film (eerily reminiscent of an ad) is projected onto the screens. The entire space is decorated with images representing likeable rats.

Mum We've chosen Laura wallpaper representing rodents of all shapes and sizes.

Dad For Laura chosen lamp this as you can see how in fact rat-mole natural which size seems road lights up with a torch. Humour observation kindness, curiosity, rat-mole . . .

Mum This cradle Laura with maintained as you can see rat-kangaroos two . . . Slippers these for when starts Laura walking on the toecaps mice two head.

Daughter Mum, with also want slippers mice . . .

Poodle *barks.*

Mum Yes Hannah will a tomorrow pair slippers of mice get.

Son And a I want live hamster for pet.

Seemingly disgruntled, the **Poodle** *barks.*

Mum and Dad *(together)* Yes Arno will get you birthday hamster pet.

Grandma For I'd like a Christmas muff ground squirrel . . .

Dad But let's with some continue other news. Observe our floor is higher and the ceiling is lower . . . From our family benefits the partnership with rats.

Mum, Dad, Son, Daughter and Grandma *(together)* Be like us. Trust the biological symbiosis. Our species are complementary.

Mum   As with result partnership rats have to throw away foodwaste . . .

Daughter   This our is the after meal evening kitchen . . .

Images of leftovers in plates, bowls, etc.

Son   And this our is next kitchen morning.

Images of clean plates.

Grandma   Ja, ja . . . Danke shön . . .

Mum   Contribute no longer we to nature of pollution.

Son   Longer no we the environment pollute.

Mum   Everything deal with rats.

Dad   Everything clean up rats.

Mum   I no longer a mum throw am soiled happy nappies.

Dad   Eat rats them.

Mum   And are see feel rats efficient, discrete, polite, invisible, presence, never.

Daughter   Them to will we unless visit invite.

Son   For this a purpose we flute utilize.

Dad   This is how we starts come it see whenever us flute someone rats works.

Dad *plays the flute. Rat heads, claws and tails appear pretty much everywhere: under the furniture, emerging from drawers and books, from under cushions and wardrobes.*

Dad   We when withdraw playing stop rats.

Mum   We can a lot learn from rats.

Son   Them improved we have owing to.

Baby   I shall as for me better world in a live.

Mum, Dad, Son, Daughter and Grandma   Ha, ha, ha . . . It look already talking.

Dad   It's today Eve Christmas.

They all sing 'O Tannenbaum'. The **Rats** *lug in a decorated Christmas tree and place six beautifully wrapped boxes underneath.*

The **Poodle** *barks.*

Dad   Oh Father us all brought Christmas presents. (*Reading a gift tag.*) A Dita present for Grandma . . .

Grandma   Father Chri than.

Dad (*reading the gift tag*)   An Erika present for mum . . .

Mum Than Fath.

Dad An Arno present for.

Son Than Fath Chri.

Dad A pre fo Hannah.

Daughter Oh, oh, than Fath Chri.

Dad A pre fo Baldur . . . Than Fath Chri. And a pre fo Pa.

*The **Poodle** barks. Frantic opening of boxes. They all find an apple inside. Everybody shouts, 'Oh, thank you, Father Christmas!'*

*All members of the model family come up to the footlights and eat their apples. Behind them, the **Rats** demolish the boxes, the wrapping paper, the ribbons and gift tags.*

*As soon as they've finished with their apples, all family members throw the cores right behind them. These are caught in the air by the **Rats**.*

*The **Rats** make the cores disappear in an instant, and move on to demolishing the Christmas tree.*

Ending Level 1

Old Man *surrounded by several* **Rats**.

Old Man Ah, you're back. I'm glad you've come to see me. I was wondering where you were.

I see you're in company, you're with your mates. And you're all wet. Have you been bathing in the sea? I may have asked you this already. Are you sea-rats? I didn't know there was such a thing as sea-rats.

Would you like to know how I'm getting on? Well, I'm very pleased. I've lost my eyesight, so can't see the sea or the stars. And I can't hear a thing. Can't hear the roaring of the sea or the breathing of the wind.

I can hear you though, I can feel you. Thanks for coming. Since I died three days ago, forty-seven people have gone past me. No one stooped to check how I was, no one tried to shake me up. Everybody assumed I was just lying here admiring the sea.

I can no longer stand myself, though. I've started to stink.

Please help me and eat me.

Ending Level 2

*The occassionally stirring tail that has been sprawled all over the stage begins to lift up. The audience realizes at this point that it belongs to a **Giant Rat**, which has been hiding above the stage all along.*

As the tail lifts up, the **Giant Rat**'s *whiskers, snout, head and body are also revealed.*

The **Giant Rat** *has a bloated face and its features are surprisingly human. It has an expression genuinely concerned with the problems of humanity.*

As the lights fade, the **Giant Rat** *opens the trapdoor and tries to disappear inside, without success though.*

Giant Rat   Coming, wait for me, I'm coming. If I said I'd come, I come. I know it wasn't easy for you. I know you've been torn between contradictory options. I know that you hate one another, that you can't stand each other, that you despise one another, that you insult each other most of the time, that you are allergic to each other. I know you don't have it easy. I know that you experience every now and then a sense of loathing for everything that happens to you and for how you've lead your lives.

Come on, stop crying. Thanks to these monstruous ears, I can make out the hustle and bustle of your inner contradictions. I can hear your increasingly heavy breathing, can hear you choke, and hear you torture yourselves as well as one another.

I can hear all your questions, your bewilderments, your doubts. You are a really awful race! Quite astonishing . . .

Come on, stop crying. I said I'd come.

I can find a solution . . . a solution . . .

Ending Level 3

All the characters reappear onstage in a kind of religious procession. They carry the **Giant Rat** *on their shoulders, as if it were a relic.*

They are progressing at a measured pace, in perfect discipline.

As one, they utter the followings:

He wasn't obliged to come, yet he did.

Let's salute him.

We were on our own, but we no longer are.

Let's kneel in front of him.

All our windows were boarded up, but now we can see the light.

Let's sing for his glory.

We used to be a rubbish heap and now we are a green meadow.

Let's declare our eternal gratitude to him.

We had no moral compass yet now we are transparent like tears.

Let's cry for him.

We had no idea who we were, but now we all know the extent of our humanity.

Let's cherish him with all our might.

We were clueless about the horizon and now we can behold it.

Let's pray on it.

The End.

Notes

1 In French in the original: *Well done! You're the masterminds of news reporting. And then, what's next?*
2 In Russian in the original: *Cheers!*

Stories of the Body

Artemisia
Teresa
Eva
Lina

András Visky

Translated from the Hungarian by Jozefina Komporaly
(Original title in Hungarian: *A test történetei: Artemisia, Teréz, Éva, Lina*)

Introductory Notes to the Series

The series entitled *Stories of the Body* comprises of texts rooted in the technique of open dramaturgy. The texts can be staged with one or with several performers, and theatre makers are free to experiment with actual numbers. My aim was to differentiate clearly between characters. In case the play is staged with several performers, it is needless to say possible to skip the narrative stage directions or sound effects necessary for clarity when we are dealing with monologues (e.g. 'she said').

In my view, theatre companies would put on various combinations of the plays and, therefore, spectators would be able to watch two different productions each time, on occasion perhaps even in a different order. In this way, the plays – and their approximately fifty-minute stage versions – would gain new meanings in each other's light and context: illuminating the stories of the body in the most varied refractions, as a variation of a single theatrical space (set design).

The plays can also be staged in their own right, as full-length performances.

All plays are based on real life stories of remarkable women, and are connected to various cities, including Budapest, Cluj, Kolkata, Rome, from the seventeenth to the twenty-first century. The plays themselves are works of fiction.

Stories of the Body
Artemisia

András Visky

Translated from the Hungarian by Jozefina Komporaly

5 András Visky: *Stories of the Body: Artemisia* – Theatre Y Chicago (directed by Melissa Lorraine and Andrej Visky). Premiere: 25 May 2018. Poster design by Péter Szabó.

Introductory Notes to *Artemisia*

This play is based on three paintings by Artemisia Gentileschi, and examines the influence of a personal and personality-defining trauma on the way in which the artist relates to the world, and how this influence can be identified in her work. I encountered Artemisia's story at the time of writing my play *Caravaggio Terminal*; her life and court deposition on 18 March 1612 in front of Judge Hieronimo Felicio had left such a deep impact on me that I carried on researching her life for years.

Artemisia was the daughter of the renowned Orazio Gentileschi, and she had shown great talent at drawing and painting from a very young age. Her father took Caravaggio's side in the infamous trial against Giovanni Baglione, and their close relationship is well documented (Caravaggio would regularly borrow props for his paintings from Orazio Gentileschi). Orazio Gentileschi was responsible for the wall paintings of the Palazzo Pallavicini-Rospigliosi – Casino delle Muse – together with Agostino Tassi, one of the best perspective painters of the time, who was generally inundated with commissions. Orazio asked Agostino Tassi to teach Artemisia the art of painting; however, Agostino took advantage of the situation and raped the girl. (Artemisia's three younger brothers were ear witnesses to the rape.) It was by reading Caravaggio monographs that I came across material on the trial between Artemisia and Agostino. These documents present a vulnerable yet extremely courageous young woman, who submits herself to torture by thumbscrew in the course of the process and – in a fashion unique for her time, when women would normally be found guilty – she wins the case.

In Artemisia Gentileschi, we honour the first professional female painter in Western culture. Her body of work, despite comprising only about thirty paintings, some of uncertain origin, reveals not only a significant artist but a genuine creator, who interprets some of her most intimate experiences in her paintings. When it comes to stylistic features as well as the personal treatment of themes, Artemisia is one of the most significant 'Caravaggisti', who had actually surpassed her master in the representation of the world in dark, dramatic and illusion-free tones, and, most importantly from our point of view, overtly bears the hallmarks of coming to terms with trauma. She had painted the story of the biblical Judith several times, highlighting her slaying Holofernes and her safeguarding the people of Israel from annihilation. In addition, the amazing dramatic qualities and blood-soaked naturalism of her first and clearly identifiable 'Caravaggist' work on display at the Uffizi Palace, and her Judith, painted a decade later, also commemorate her court testimony and torture.

The play follows two strands: the trial – as far as it can be traced back in documents (edited and compressed) and an episode in Artemisia's life (only minimally fictionalized in places) – the untimely loss of her mother and her relationship with her father, followed by her departure from the parental home, seizing the opportunity to embark on a life of her own.

Three paintings will be projected throughout the performance, ideally onto the entire back wall of the performance space: *Susanna and the Elders* and two versions of *Judith Slaying Holofernes*.

The role of the Judge and of the Confessor can be played by the actor playing Orazio Gentileschi; the role of the silent Bailiff, who carries out the torture on the orders of the Judge, is recommended to be linked to Agostino Tassi. Prudentia can be played by the actress cast as Signora Tuzia, but she can be represented by sound alone, as well. The barber Giuliano Formicino can appear in the production; however, it is possible to bring the character to life through Artemisia's narration. All these stage directions are only initial suggestions: directors and theatre companies are invited to take their own decisions on merging or separating parts as they see fit. The play can be staged as a piece of theatre for one or for three performers (in the latter case, Artemisia and two men). Passages not attributed to anyone in the dialogue belong to Artemisia's monologue. The story of *Susanna and the Elders* could be pre-recorded and integrated into the production by way of playback, or could be narrated by Orazio Gentileschi and Agostino Tassi taking turns. Performers switching from one character to another in full view of the audience could also underpin a potential approach to the production. Notwithstanding these decisions, it is Artemisia's sentences, (inner) voice, gaze and imagination that fill the entire stage.

When writing my play, I relied among others on Marry D. Garrard's monograph and the catalogue *Orazio and Artemisia Gentileschi*, edited by Keith Christiansen and Judith W. Mann, including a variety of studies by several excellent researchers.

Characters

Artemisia Gentileschi
Orazio Gentileschi, *painter, Artemisia's father*
Prudentia, *Artemisia's mother*
Agostino Tassi, *painter*
Caravaggio, *painter, Orazio Gentileschi's friend*
Signora Tuzia
Formicino, *barber*
Confessor
Judge
Bailiff

Trial I/Petition

Orazio Gentileschi Most Holy Father, Orazio Gentileschi, painter, most humble servant of your Holiness, respectfully reports to you, how, through Madame Tuzia his tenant, and as a result of her complicity, a daughter of the plaintiff has been deflowered by force and carnally known many, many times by Agostino Tassi, a painter and close friend and associate of the plaintiff. Also taking part in the obscene business was Cosimo Quorli, your orderly. By this I mean that, besides the rape, the same orderly Cosimo, through his intrigues, took from the hand of the same young woman some paintings, and in particular a large-scale *Judith*. Thus, kneeling at your Holy feet, I beseech you to take action against this ugly intemperance by bringing him who deserves it to justice, and I will forever pray to God for your most just reward.

Scene One

Artemisia Aaaaaaaaart . . . Aaaaaaaart . . .

The scent of our mother's death has crept into our wardrobes, our clothes. If you open the wardrobe, the sweetish smell of death just pours out. Let's sell mother's clothes or strew them out of the windows, so beggars can have them! But no, no, I keep saying and repeating over and over again, all is in vain.

Orazio Gentileschi You're just imagining this! Your mother was perfectly embalmed for the funeral by Master Formicino. Her scent was just like the one I recall from the time she was my bride.

Artemisia Yet it is the scent of death that was left behind here, and not that of her being a bride.

I've never smelt such a death scent before. Not even when my brother, Giovanni Battista, died. Soon after this, I had another brother and father had him baptised Giovanni Battista, too.

Orazio Gentileschi So that he carries my name forward! Carry my name forward! Let someone carry my name forward!

Artemisia Your name will survive, don't you worry, by way of your paintings and frescoes. You are an aaaaaaartist!

Orazio Gentileschi But I want my real name to survive, too. Giovanni Battista.

Prudentia The little boy had already carried your name off, way beyond the realm of the possible. Let's give this new baby another name, please!

In vain. He was baptised Giovanni Battista, too. And he died. He carried father's name off, except that we don't know where to. Giovanni Battista and Giovanni Battista. I can't remember their faces or voices, I can't remember anything.

I keep doing the laundry at all times, I'm washing mother's clothes and bedding. And I keep airing . . .

Orazio Gentileschi We won't give these to anyone, we'll keep them, one and all. And you'll grow into them anyway, one by one.

Good God! To grow into my mother's death!

Our father in heavens, cleanse our house of the scent of death, or help us move away from here, so I can get a bedroom of my own, and a place full of light and your kind soul where I could paint.

Aaaaaaart!

Artemisia Do you have any idea what our mother had actually died of?

Orazio Gentileschi Fever.

Artemisia Sure, fever. Ignominy and constant humiliation more like it. She died of this pushy and bloodthirsty city, of this mandatory hatred and hostility. Of this ongoing shit-stirring, yes, and your cowardice, too. Not to mention your endless commands! She spat blood, not her own though, as there can't possibly be that much blood in a human being! As if you didn't notice! She had spat the whole city out. Hoooooly city! Exactly!

Orazio Gentileschi Artemisia! Darling! You know that I loved your mother . . . You inherited all your beauty and kindness from her.

Artemisia Okay, okay. I know.

Orazio Gentileschi I have concealed your mother's gaze and the emerald sparkle of her eyes in every single Madonna that I painted.

Artemisia I know, I know. Sorry. How about me? Am I beautiful?

Orazio Gentileschi You are the most beautiful of all, Artemisia. You are so magnificent, I can barely set eyes on you. I didn't even notice that you have grown into a big girl, my belle, my one and only!

Trial II/Deposition

Artemisia It was a rainy day, and I was painting a picture of one of Tuzia's boys for my own pleasure. Agostino stopped by and managed to come in because the masons, who were working in the house, had left the door open. When he found me painting, he said: 'Not so much painting, not so much painting,' and grabbed the palette and brushes from my hands and threw them on the floor, saying to Tuzia: 'Get out of here.' And when I said to Tuzia not to go and not to leave me alone, just as I had previously also asked her, she said: 'I don't want to stay here and argue, I want to go about my own business.' Before she left, Agostino placed his head on my breast, and as soon as she was gone, he took my hand and said: 'Let's take a walk together, because I hate sitting down.' While we were walking two or three times around the room, I told him that I was feeling ill and I thought I had a fever. He replied: 'I have more of a fever than you do.'

Scene Two

Artemisia Mummy, please don't die.

    Prudentia I'm leaving, my darling daughter, not dying.

    Artemisia Don't leave. There's nowhere to go, Mummy!

    Prudentia Perhaps there is, darling, perhaps there is somehow. In a place where Giovanni Battista and Giovanni Battista are at the moment. They must be so lonely . . . the angels will come and take my soul away, don't be afraid!

    Artemisia They'd rather cured you! Tell them that if they take the trouble to come here they should look after your body first, and your soul second. When I tell them so.

    Prudentia Okay, you tell them that.

When she was unable to speak, she'd just hold out her feverish arms to me, and I'd wash her body with a soft wet cloth. Her skin would crack at times, and such hairbreadth cracks would spread all over her body, covering her face, arms, breasts, her two trembling thighs, as white as snow, all the way down to her feet. I found her magnificent, and a sense of shame took over me. Light was pouring out of her, as if she were a marble statue. I sent the boys out of the room: Francesco, Giulio, Marco, hurry up, get out of here.

Let us stay, Artemisia, Mum wants us to be with her.

Vanish!

The boys kept weeping in front of the house, constantly asking when they could come in. Meanwhile, I wiped the entire body clean, and Mum kept humming some tune to make it easier for me.

Can we come up yet?

The little ones, this is how our mother called them.

> **Prudentia**   Look after the little ones, Artemisia.
>
> **Artemisia**   How could I look after them? How? I can't even look after myself. Don't even task me to look after a dog! Mummy! Mum!
>
> **Prudentia**   Yes, darling.
>
> **Artemisia**   Can I ask you something?
>
> **Prudentia** (*laughing*)   Me? Sure, go ahead.
>
> **Artemisia**   Look after me once you are gone, promise?
>
> **Prudentia**   Promise. If I can't, I'll stay with you.
>
> **Artemisia**   Good, let it be so. Stay with me once you're gone.

I washed her, and dressed her. A naked and cold mother. A minute ago, she was hot as a furnace, now she's ice cold. Who can keep up with this?

Led by Francesco, the little ones went over to San Giacomo to call a doctor. The three boys ran all along the Via Paulina, then down on the Via dei Greci, all the way to the hospital. Once there, they all kneeled down and burst into a loud prayer, asking for someone to be sent over to heal our mother.

Who should be healed?

Our mum.

Who are you?

Giovanni Battista Lomi's sons.

And who might that be?

Well, Orazio Gentileschi. Our father.

The painter?!

Yes.

Go home, we can't cure her.

What! Isn't that your job?

We've told your father a thousand times that she's incurable.

We don't care, just cure her! Send someone! Meanwhile, we'll kneel here and sing to you, till morning if need be.

Francesco, however, didn't cope for long, so picked up a stone and threw it at the windows of San Giacomo.

See, this is why our mother had no shroud. Father punished us in this way. The damage had to be paid for. It was your fault. And not just fault but sin, sin, sin. So much money!

Giovanni Battista Lomi, known as an artist by the name of Orazio Gentileschi.

Scene Three

Artemisia Aaaaaaart!

Our father didn't even bother to stay at home while mother was on her deathbed. He'd turn up every now and then. Ask whether she was still alive and then dash off again, as if he'd been chased by someone.

Orazio Gentileschi Is she still alive?

That is the question indeed. I've been asking this too, ever since she died. Is she still alive? Is she? Are you alive, Mum? Are you? Send us a sign!

Orazio Gentileschi The plastering is wet, so I must paint. Once it dries, I have to start from scratch. Besides, they'd deduct from my wages. I'm off. Oh no, Prudentia, what will happen to the kids if you leave us? I'm off, I must go.

Our father adored Mum, but his fear of death was greater than his love.

A coward, that's what he is. At times, this can be seen in his paintings, too. His fear.

Father's plastering is wet at the most unexpected moments, and at such times, he dashes away from home. At times, the plastering stays wet for days, in various places across the city. At times, the entire Rome is wet. The whole of Italy is wet because of our father's frescos.

Wet? – I asked father as he was about to leave.

Orazio Gentileschi What? Yes, they've sent word that it's wet so I must rush to paint!

He always came up with the same response. At times angrily, at times sadly, at times with sparkly eyes, at times like a teenager, and at times with a dark complexion, as if he were a murderer.

He held me tight before he left.

Meh, I can feel my breasts!

Father doesn't always lie. Father doesn't lie at all times. It's impossible to get by without lies. But he confesses them, perhaps not every single one of them, so he can start anew from the beginning. In Rome, commissions are the new god. Everyone adores them and pays homage to them. If you are being commissioned you exist, if not, even dogs can sense it and just wee on your legs.

Orazio Gentileschi   The Pope has already given me his blessing! He has, so bite your tongue! The Pope himself! He kept shouting this whenever he had an argument with Mum. Clement VIII, not just anyone! The Holy Father! He came up to me in San Giovanni in Laterano as I was finishing the nave, and gave me a personal blessing. To me, in person. With his beautifully fleshy hands!

Mum would never raise her voice.

Aaaaaaaaart!

Trial III/Deposition

Signora Tuzia My name is Tuzia, the tenant of Signor Orazio Gentileschi, the painter. I have known Orazio Gentileschi for about a year, since I was living in Via Margutta and he lived across the street from me. He had a daughter named Artemisia whom I had never seen or known nothing about, and because the said Artemisia was alone, she called one of my daughters who asked my permission to visit her. Having been told that the said Artemisia was a respectable young woman, I allowed my daughter to visit her. Later on, my older daughter, who is sixteen, also began to associate with her, and so did I. And we began to enjoy each other's company very much, so much so that when her father Orazio met me in the house, he seemed pleased to see that his daughter and I were friends, and she could enjoy herself a little, as she was always alone and didn't have anyone. A few days later, he asked me if we would like to rent a house jointly and live together. Finally, we agreed with my husband to move to the Via della Croce, where we would live together in the same house with them. Signor Orazio had a door and a staircase fitted, so that we could go down to their apartment. Signor Orazio had many friends but he associated with two in particular, and loved them very much. One of them was called Signor Agostino who, they said, was a painter and together with Signor Orazio was decorating and painting a room in the Palazzo del Quirinale. Whenever Signor Orazio would leave, he'd always entrust his daughter to me to take care of her, and he warned me not to speak to his daughter about husbands, rather, that I should persuade her to become a nun, which I tried to do several times. Agostino, the painter, came very often too, and when Artemisia was in her apartment, he'd go downstairs through that door that leads into her rooms to see what she and her father were doing. He showed great affection to Artemisia, he loved her very much, and for her and her father he would have given his life. I opened the door to him whenever he came. In short, we couldn't take a single step with Artemisia without Agostino always being nearby. Agostino was, so to speak, obsessed with Artemisia and he tormented me when he couldn't come and talk to her. Agostino sometimes pushed his way into the house while Signor Orazio was out. One time in particular he came while Artemisia was painting a portrait of my son, and right after he arrived, Artemisia stopped painting. I left and went upstairs to my apartment, leaving the said Agostino with Artemisia, while her brothers were also there. Later on, I saw Signor Agostino's face scratched and his eyes bruised. Many times I have seen the said Agostino alone in the room with the said Artemisia; she was undressed in bed and he was dressed. Sometimes Agostino would throw himself on the bed with his clothes on. I don't know whether carnal copulation had occurred between Agostino and Artemisia. Artemisia told me that Agostino wants to marry her.

Scene Four

Artemisia When Mum came down with fever, our father was in the middle of painting the angels on the dome of the Madonna dei Monti. I went to take a peek at him. He painted large, helpless angels, the dome barely able to bear their weight. Their eyes were not yet painted but they could sense that I was there, so all four of them started to shake. As far as our father was concerned, they could have taken flight all over the city. He kept pouring the powder paint into the whitewash, then put his hand into the bucket, drying and checking the paint, looking at it at length, smelling and licking it.

Angels, will you come for my mother? – I asked in my heart.

We will, don't worry, Artemisia, but we are still blind at present – they responded. Don't let her die until we are ready and able to see.

What am I, the god of death?! What could I possibly prevent, my little purblind friends?! Get yourselves together and hurry up. If you are blind, then just get on to it and do it blind.

Fine, fine, we'll come, be it blind, we promise.

That's more like it!

Aaaaaaaaart! Aaaaaaaaaart!

Scene Five

Artemisia Come boys, come, Francesco, Giulio, Marco! We have to lift Mum off the bed and put her on the floor.

Have you lost your mind, Artemisia?

Come, come now, don't be afraid.

As we touched the still warm body, we all burst into tears. Mum, darling Mum! She was light as a bird. Her soul hadn't departed yet, that's why.

To die on Boxing Day, when the whole of Rome rejoices . . . as if the Holy City was celebrating our mother's death. We should say something, delay Christmas, the Pope should know about this! Why doesn't he know about our mother, our mother, our mother, about Prudentia? Why not? Why not?

Never mind, he who knows it all, can't know it all.

It's okay, one cannot undo what may not actually happen.

Let it be! The bells toll, the naked little god has been born. He's going to grow up fast, in spring they'll already have him killed. He allows that, he allows everything. People are so resourceful! We are the best at torture and killing, I swear. I wouldn't allow this to happen. I really wouldn't.

We are singing Christmas carols with Mum and the little ones. Death-Christmas. I'm not crying, not crying, not crying.

She left. She departed from her own life. But not mine, I won't let that happen. We take her to the cemetery. On the left hand side, it's the resting place of Giovanni Battista, on the right hand side, the resting place of Giovanni Battista, in the middle, our mother. Our mother underground, beautiful snow falling onto your grave, blind angels mourning you. Amen.

Scene Six

Artemisia Giuliano Formicino was a barber by trade, but he accepted any job that he got paid to do. Provided there was a need, and provided he got paid, he sutured wounds in the middle of the night, gave false testimony, and revamped the faces of wanted criminals to make them look unrecognizable. And he did get paid. Everyone knew him and, sooner or later, everyone needed his services. He'd also do modelling, even naked if need be. He'd even model for women, although women were forbidden to partake in the life drawing of naked models. Haggard old model, his cells overflowing with soiled time.

I confessed about Formicino. But not the fact that I draw. And paint.

> **Confessor** Formicino! Formicino! There's nothing to see in him, my daughter, I swear by everything that's holy! There's no sin in this. Anything else? he asked, as if he were at the fish market.

I like to go to confession at the Santa Maria del Popolo. I adore the grid that separates me from the priest. The priest looks at me as if he were a tired prisoner, sentenced for life. He's on the other side, and so am I.

> **Artemisia** Does God know about time, Father?
>
> **Confessor** Whatever do you mean, my daughter? What would you like to know?
>
> **Artemisia** Does God have a body?
>
> **Confessor** God is an eternal soul, and our souls are fashioned out of his . . .
>
> **Artemisia** Does he have a shape?
>
> **Confessor** Yes, in fact, no, I mean . . .
>
> **Artemisia** Then he can't know what time is.
>
> **Confessor** Well, my daughter, a thousand years for him are just like a moment, and a moment like a thousand years.
>
> **Artemisia** I told you. He has no idea, I knew it.
>
> **Confessor** What are you on about? I can't absolve you, understand? Go, you aren't allowed to partake in Holy Communion! Get out of here!
>
> **Artemisia** Not so loud, Father, don't scream, don't create a scandal in God's house, I'll go, I'm out of here, it's fine.

But I just couldn't do it. So I hid in the Cerasi Chapel to pray. I told God that he had particularly stupid priests, and asked whether he was bothered by this. And that I felt for him. He smiled.

In the painting situated at the left of the chapel, three men are busy crucifying the Apostle Peter with his head down. The picture is dominated by the enormous bottom of one of the bailiffs. He squeezed himself under the cross in order to push it up with his back. All of his body parts are making a major effort, but above all his bottom. It isn't really a bottom, it's an arse. It's a giant orange formation that lights up the altar. Terrified little old Peter, don't be afraid, they'll kill you, just as you want it.

Large zealous arses are busying themselves with the fate of the world.

Trial IV/Deposition

Artemisia After we had walked around two or three times, each time going past the bedroom door, we got in front of it again, and this time he pushed me in and locked the door. He then threw me onto the edge of the bed, pushing me down with a hand on my breast, and put a knee between my thighs to prevent me from closing them. Lifting my clothes, which he had a great deal of trouble with, he placed a hand holding a handkerchief on my throat and mouth to prevent me from screaming. He let go of my hands, which he had been holding with his other hand, and, having previously put both knees between my thighs, with his penis [*membro*] pointed at my vagina [*natura*], and began to thrust it inside. I felt a strong burning sensation as it hurt very much, but because he held my mouth, I couldn't cry out. However, I tried to scream as best I could, calling Tuzia. I scratched his face and pulled his hair, and before he penetrated me again I grabbed his penis [*membro*] so tight that I even managed to scrape a piece of flesh off. All this didn't bother him at all though, and he continued with his business which kept him on top of me for a while, retaining his penis [*membro*] inside my vagina [*natura*].

Scene Seven

Artemisia Formicinio, the barber, is about to prepare our mother's body for the funeral. There is a knock on the door. I thought there were father's angels from the Madonna dei Monti. Come, come, you purblinds, and take her away with you!

But no, it was only father's friend, Caravaggio, who came to pick up some props: angel wings, a wooden sword with a long blade, some blood red velvet backdrop fabric and such like. Let him take these. He also asked for a few of Mum's clothes to be used as costumes. Why not, let him take them.

This Caravaggio barely said a word, and when he talked, he only uttered a word or so at a time. The gap between words was such that I found it impossible to put them together. Meanwhile, he appeared to be constantly talking to himself in interminable sentences, without any break. Uuuummmmvzsvzs . . . As if there was a storm unleashed in his being, or some kind of an ice drift. Every now and then, the odd word would come to the surface of this flash flood, just the odd shard. Uuuummmmvzsvzs . . .

He leaned over our mother, then lied down on the floor and took a long look at the soles of her feet. Linear perspective, indeed. Shortening. Our mother's perspective – well, this can no longer get shortened any further.

    Caravaggio Is this? Uuuummmmvzsvzs . . .

    Artemisia What?

    Caravaggio I didn't ask you.

    Artemisia Yes, you did.

Caravaggio Uuuummmmvzsvzs . . . This is. The one.

Artemisia No.

Caravaggio I don't know. Soul? Was there? Did you see it? Is there still?

Artemisia What still?

Caravaggio (*lying on the floor*) The soul?! Does she still have one? Did she? Uuuummmmvzsvzs . . .

Formicino Where is that by now!

Caravaggio Where? Where indeed? (*To* **Artemisia**.) Did you see it? Were you here?

Artemisia I was here, but I didn't see it. When we lifted her with the little ones, she was light as a bird. But now she's very heavy. We can't lift her anymore.

Caravaggio Bird.

Artemisia Bird.

Caravaggio What kind?

Artemisia Well, I have no idea. A kind of empty and, yes, blind bird.

Caravaggio It's still swirling. Come down here, next to me, lower. Can you hear me?

Arrtemisia Goodness! I'm scared.

Caravaggio I'm not. Haven't been in a good while. Uuuummmmvzsvzs . . . What should I be scared of?

Next, Caravaggio tried to lift the body on his own. It was hard, but he managed. Eyes shut, he kept holding on to the stiff body for ages, turning around and harking about as if he was measuring something.

Caravaggio There is no more.

Artemisia What?

Caravaggio Prudentia.

Artemisia But she's here. My mother.

Caravaggio She isn't here. This isn't her.

Artemisia Draw a picture of our mother for me, Caravaggio.

Caravaggio No. I don't draw the dead.

Artemisia What is the soul, Caravaggio?

Caravaggio Movement. And moment. Uuuummmmvzsvzs . . .

Artemisia Will you teach me to paint?

Caravaggio   Artist? You want to be an artist?

Artemisia   No, not an artist, no way.

Caravaggio   Then yes. It's possible. We can talk about it. I'll talk. To your father, yes. He's an artist. But he has sold out. He's doing the rounds at the holy market. Like blowflies. There's nothing to learn from him. Nothing. And there's Agostino Tassi. And Giovanni Baglione, the chief informer. Accademia di San Luca. A fragrant cemetery. Monkeys. Avoid them at all costs.

Artemisia   I've learned a lot from him – why are you offending him?

Caravaggio   Whom?

Artemisia   My father.

Caravaggio   As for that, not yet.

Artemisia   What?

Caravaggio   That. That it's a no. That nothing matters. Only the soul. What doesn't exist.

He left, without taking a single look at me. I couldn't be his wife. That much is certain.

Aaaaaaaaaart! Aaaaaaaaaart! No.

Caravaggio disappeared without a trace from Rome. He killed Ranuccio Tomassoni, the luxury pimp. The best procurer in the Vatican, and the purveyor of the freshest meat, as they said. He had to flee from Rome.

I learned nothing from him. I learned everything from him. But that wasn't enough.

I miss him. We used to mock his speech with the little ones. We pretended to act out his inaugural lecture at the Academy: Gentlemen! Uuuummmmvzsvzs . . . Uuuummmmvzsvzs . . . Uuuummmmvzsvzs . . .

Formicino   I stitched Ranuccio together, but it was already too late – Formicino said. – His blood is still there on the Piazza Navona.

I inspected the bloodstain. It was a large stain on a slab of stone. Human stain? Soul stain? Is there such a thing? No idea. Rome is a giant bloodstain.

I'll manage on my own then. I shall learn to paint all by myself.

Trial V/Deposition

Artemisia When I saw myself free, I went to the table drawer and took out a knife, and moved toward Agostino saying: 'I'd like to kill you with this knife because you have dishonoured me.' He opened his coat and said: 'Here I am', and I threw the knife at him but he shielded himself, otherwise I would have hurt him and might have easily killed him, too. However, I did manage to wound him slightly on the chest and some blood dripped out, only a little, since I had barely touched him with the point of the knife. And the said Agostino then fastened his coat. I was crying and suffering over the wrong he had done me, and to pacify me, he said: 'Give me your hand, I promise to marry you as soon as I get out of the labyrinth I'm in.' He added: 'I warn you that when I take you [as my wife] I don't want any foolishness,' and I answered: 'I think you will be able to see if there is any foolishness.' And with this promise I left a lot calmer, and with this promise he later induced me to yield lovingly, many times, to his desires, since he would reconfirm this promise many, many times. This is all that happened between Agostino and me.

Scene Eight

Artemisia I received a virginal from my father. A present! Brand new. Magnificent and still a virgin! A virginal is always a virgin.

 Orazio Gentileschi So?

Artemisia I'm happy.

 Orazio Gentileschi See! Try it. Come on!

Artemisia Magnificent! It's sufficient to touch it and music is already pouring out of it. And then it all vanishes, leaving nothing behind. Yes, this is it! Something perfect that leaves nothing behind. Echo, echo, nothing. Perfect.

 Orazio Gentileschi You shouldn't get married, Artemisia, we'll get by as it is.

Artemisia But I have no one, what are you talking about?

 Orazio Gentileschi Nor should you have. This is just fine as it is, right? For my and the boys' sake. You are the heart and soul of our household.

Artemisia Indeed. We'll get by. Shall I take Mum's place, is that what you want? To take a wow of chastity? Shall I be a virgin mother to the little ones?

 Orazio Gentileschi We'll be happy, you'll see.

Artemisia And how about my life?

 Orazio Gentileschi I fear for you! I shall secure your future.

Artemisia No, please, no! Not my future! At least that you shouldn't decide.

I have never feared the future, only the present. Those who're afraid of the future, don't know the present. Do we actually exist at all?

I'm afraid of you!

Reading, writing, virginal, painting. Cooking, washing, cleaning, window cleaning – this is the only chore I like.

I wanted a lute, but he refused to get me one. That's so sluttish, he said. The lute that is. He knows what he's talking about. The virginal is virginal, and will stay so.

Father seems to like this word, he doesn't grasp anything from what's happening to me.

Aaaaaaaaaaaaaart! That doesn't exist, for sure. According to our father, art makes us better and truer – well, that's pushing it. No way. I haven't seen that anywhere. Caravaggio is no artist. Fortunately.

Could it be that there has never been such a thing as genuine art? Except for the theatre perhaps? Those embodying God or Satan, angels or devils are actual people! I must try this once!

These aaaaaaaartists surrounding our father! The way they're murdering one another. I've never heard any of them say a good word about anyone else. Unfathomable hate was sent onto the world by artists . . . denunciation, theft, plagiarism, war on top of war to win the favours of a god-known success.

Scene Nine

Artemisia I paint. Whenever I can. I only concentrate on the light, nothing else. On light and movement. When I paint, I feel alive. As if I was alive. My life . . .

My father's new partner is Agostino Tassi, a large beast of a man. The markets are booming, and commissions keep flowing in. I cook for the boys and do their laundry whenever I'm not painting. Or the other way round. And I draw. I'm always drawing, even when I'm not. I have learned to draw and paint in my head. I'm already quite good at reading, less so at writing.

I reveal myself in front of the blank canvass. I open myself up. I let the universe penetrate me. Come, darling Mum, come here, too. Come, brothers, you story-less Giovanni Battistas.

I'm a genius according to my father, but it's a shame I was born a woman. Never mind, he won't give in.

I can't make sense of his words.

Well, that he'd insist at the Academy that women should also be allowed to do life drawing. And nudes, too! Indeed. He will demand that! He'll go as far as the Pope if need be! He'll open his mouth!

He doesn't go. He doesn't open.

Tassi visits us often, and at our father's request, teaches me about perspective. He claims that father doesn't know about that, either. Father agrees with Tassi, but forbids me to be alone with him. Under any circumstances. I must be careful.

Fine then.

Artemisia Please model for me. Both of you.

Orazio Gentileschi Don't jest with us, Artemisia!

Agostino Tassi I'm already taking my clothes off!

Artemisia No need to do that, don't rush. Sit down there, Agostino, and be as old as you possibly can.

Agostino Tassi Even older than I actually am!?

Artemisia Old, evil and tiny.

Orazio Gentileschi Old and evil is no problem, but tiny . . . that's difficult.

Agostino Tassi I'm growing just by looking at you . . .

Artemisia Ha-ha-ha! These celebrated below the belt jokes of yours! As they're echoing in the empty churches while you are painting the Madonna. Calm down, small will also work for you, all you need is courage!

Agostino Tassi Is this good?

Artemisia Almost. Let's do it like this.

Agostino Tassi Shouldn't there be some lust, too? Lust is really cool nowadays. People pay the highest price for lust.

Orazio Gentileschi Behave, Agostino!

Artemisia In your case, it's sufficient to be yourself. That alone is lust enough.

Orazio Gentileschi How about me?

Artemisia I'll position you, come. Like so.

Agostino Tassi I'm already positioned. Ouch!

Orazio Gentileschi (*turning bright red in the face*) Hold your horses, Agostino.

Agostino Tassi If only you could see my other head!

Orazio Gentileschi Tassi, stop it! I'll kick you out of here!

Agostino Tassi Perhaps I'll kick you out . . . of the next commission, that is. If you prefer.

Artemisia Calm down, I can't work like this.

Agostino Tassi Lust? How much? Just to let you know that we haven't clarified this!

Artemisia Fine, Agostino. More is fine. Like so. Anyway, in the end it will be me who'll decide when it comes to the canvas. And evil, too. Perfect. Honesty is really important.

Aaaaaaaaart! Acccccccademy! Ooooooooh!

Scene Ten

Projection 1. Artemisia Gentileschi: Susanna and the Elders *(1610) Schloss Weißenstein Collection, Pommersfelden, Germany.*

Artemisia Every day Susanna would go into her husband's garden to walk. The two elders used to see her walking about, and they began to lust for her. They were both wounded by her beauty, but were ashamed to talk about their lustful desire to seduce her. Suddenly one of them said: 'Let us go home, for it is time for lunch.' So they both left and parted from each other, but secretly they both sneaked back into the garden and found themselves facing one another. Then together they arranged for a time when they could find her alone. One day Susanna wanted to take a bath in the garden. 'Bring me olive oil and ointments, and shut the gates of the garden so I can bathe.' The servants did as she ordered, and left through the back door to get what she had asked for. They didn't see the elders because they were hiding. When the maids had gone out, the two elders got up and ran to her: 'Look, the garden gates are shut, and no one can see us. We are burning with desire for you; so give your consent, and lie with us. If you refuse, we will testify against you that a young man was with you, and this was why you sent your maids away, so they will stone you.' At this point Susanna cried out for help, and the elders also started to cry out protesting against her. Then she was taken in front of judges, and the elders were amongst them, too. Then the two elders stood up before the people and laid their hands on Susanna's head and said: 'While we were walking in the garden alone, this woman came in with two maids, shut the garden gates, and dismissed the maids. Then a young man, who was hiding there, came to her and lay with her.' Because they were elders, the judges, the husband and all the people believed them and condemned the adulterous woman to death. Just as she was being led off to be stoned, a young judge by the name of Daniel shouted with a loud voice: 'Return to court, for these men have given false evidence against Susanna!' When they all got back, he said: 'Separate them far from each other.' When they were separated from each other, he summoned one of them and said to him: 'Tell me under what tree did you see them naked?' The elder said: 'Under a eucalyptus tree.' Then, putting him to one side, he ordered them to bring the other and asked him, too: 'Under what tree did you catch them being intimate with each other?' The elder replied: 'Under an oak tree.' 'Take them away, and deal with them in accordance with the law,' Daniel said.

Scene Eleven

Orazio Gentileschi Spellbinding! Goodness, Artemisia! We must deny in front of everyone that you painted this.

Artemisia Why should we?

Orazio Gentileschi Who's this woman?

Artemisia Susanna.

Orazio Gentileschi I meant the model, Artemisia. Who modelled for you?

Artemisia (*posing as Susanna*) Look more carefully...

Orazio Gentileschi Who's this?

Artemisia I won't tell you.

Orazio Gentileschi It is forbidden for you to paint naked models. Women are strictly forbidden to paint! It's a papal ban. The last thing we need is to be denounced by someone!

Artemisia Did you raise this at the Academy? You promised...

Orazio Gentileschi Where? How does the Academy come into this?! Mindboggling!

Artemisia And what if there was no model?

Orazio Gentileschi No way! Just like that, such a perfect form based on imagination? No, impossible. And the movement! Goodness! Magnificent!

Artemisia I've stolen that from Michelangelo, for instance. The left arm, look! I thought you'd spot it at first sight.

Orazio Gentileschi Even I could be recognized in the man on the left-hand side! The other is that godforsaken Agostino, visible to all including the blind. Good God! Looks like a denunciation! If anyone sees this, we'll say I painted it. Goodness! I have never spied upon you, Artemisia, I swear!

Artemisia Well, you didn't...

Orazio Gentileschi Agostino has? Answer me!

Artemisia Can't you see what's happening right in front of your eyes? Or you just don't want to see it?! He sends this monstrous Cosimo to make me yield to him. So he can come into my bedroom. Or that at least he can watch me while bathing. These are the kind of messages he's sending me with that monkey, that papal courier. They are friends of yours, aren't they?!

Orazio Gentileschi Artemisia, as long as he promises that he'll marry you...

Artemisia Marry me? Him? Has he placed an order for me? I asked you a question! Have you reached an agreement over me? There! He's now asking me to draw a naked picture of myself and send the drawing to him with Cosimo. Cosimo Quorli, the papal courier, Agostino Tassi, the greatest aaaaaaartist and shit-stirrer, and me. Nice work.

Orazio Gentileschi Did you do it?

Artemisia What do you think? When I was playing quoits with the boys after lunch at Cosimo's place, you joined in the laughter at Tassi's idiotic jokes. Is the ring going to land on the pale, or the pale penetrate the ring? And how talented I am at hitting the pointy rods! Why on earth should I paint since I'm so good at this?! And all three of you just carried on guffawing with laughter. Cosimo's wife was squealing with delight, as if she were a suckling pig.

Orazio Gentileschi We'd been drinking, you know, quite a lot. I'm sorry, forgive me.

Artemisia You don't have to look after me, understand?! You can't anyway.

Orazio Gentileschi Artemisia, darling, marry Agostino, he's a great artist, the most influential in Rome, I myself am dependent on him, please understand! Be his wife, and all will be well!

Artemisia Have you lost your mind? It will be well? All?

Trial VI/Torture

Judge Having been ordered to tell the truth and nothing but the truth, and to swear under oath, I'm now asking whether you voluntarily wish to add anything to what you had testified in your statement, and whether you intend to add or withdraw anything?

Agostino I don't need to say anything other than what I have said in my other testimony, nor do I have anything to add or withdraw.

Judge Are you willing to tell the truth about whether you raped and had sexual relations with said Artemisia, Orazio Gentileschi's daughter?

Agostino Sir, I have spoken the truth and I am telling you that not only have I not raped the said Artemisia, but I have never had sexual relations with her either.

Judge Artemisia Gentileschi, do you know the person standing in front of you?

Artemisia Yes, I do know him, sir.

Judge Who is he?

Artemisia His name is Agostino Tassi, who raped me and promised to marry me after dishonouring me.

Judge Your testimony about the accused here present was and is true.

Artemisia Yes, sir.

Judge Do you intend to confirm and substantiate now, before the witness here present, that what you had testified was true?

Artemisia Yes, sir, what I said in my deposition before Your Lordship about the person Agostino Tasso here present is the truth, and for the sake of the truth I am ready to confirm and substantiate it right here in front of him.

Judge Artemisia Gentileschi, are you prepared to confirm your aforesaid deposition and statement, as well as everything contained in it even under duress?

Artemisia Yes, sir. I am ready to confirm my deposition even under duress and whatever else might be necessary.

Judge In order to remove any mark of infamy and any doubt that might arise against the person of the said summoned woman or about the things she said, from which she could appear to be a partner in crime, and most of all, to corroborate and strengthen her statement, as well as to ensure all other good ends and results, and, moreover, to affect the person of the said summoned woman, I decree and order that the summoned woman, in the presence of the witness, be subjected to torture with the thumbscrew.

The prison guard comes to proceed with the torture; he affixes the cords upon **Artemisia**. *The guard begins to tighten the cords with a string.*

Artemisia *while being tortured, repeating over and over.*

Artemisia It is true, it is true, it is true, it is true! (*Shouting*.) This is the ring that you gave me, and these are your promises.

Judge *during the torture.*

Judge Are you confirming your testimony?

Artemisia It is true, it is true, it is true, everything I said was true. It is true, it is true; it is true, it is true! Miserere!

Agostino *showing a piece of paper to the judge.*

Agostino Don't let her go! I want to ask her some questions.

Judge Ask your questions.

Agostino (*roaring to her*) Who made you testify against me?

Artemisia Nobody has induced me to testify against you.

Agostino Tell me exactly how and on what occasion did I first have relations with you?

Artemisia I have said so much about it this evening. It should be enough.

Agostino Have you ever written letters to anyone, and if so, what did the letters contain?

Artemisia I cannot write and can barely read.

Agostino To what end, and with what hope did you give this testimony?

Artemisia In the hope that you would be punished for the wrong that you did.

Agostino How did you protest? Did you shout? Why didn't you make any noise?

Artemisia Because you gagged me, so I couldn't shout.

Agostino What are the signs that a virgin shows when she has been deflowered? Say it, and say how you know it!

Artemisia I said in my testimony. When you first raped me, I was having my period.

Agostino Have you told anyone that I raped you?

Artemisia I told Stiattesi and his wife. And you also told Stiattesi.

Agostino Were you hoping to have me as a husband?

Artemisia I was hoping to have you as a husband in order to restore my honour, but now I don't, because I know that you have a wife. It's been two or three days since I've learned that you have a wife. (*She faints.*)

Scene Twelve

Projection 2. Artemisia Gentileschi: Judith Slaying Holofernes *(1612–13) Museo Capodimonte, Naples.*

Orazio Gentileschi Where have you been? You scare me to death! Don't roam alone about the city.

Artemisia I can do what I like, I'm no longer afraid of anyone or anything. I took another look at the Caravaggios at San Luigi Francesi and at Santa Maria del Popolo. I want to take them away with me in my heart.

Orazio Gentileschi Artemisia, do you realize that no talent like yourself has yet been born in Italy?! You'll end up in the midst of wolves, they'll tear you apart and annihilate you no matter where you'd go! Stay by my side and I'll protect you.

Artemisia Somehow, this didn't quite work out in Rome.

Orazio Gentileschi Don't be angry! Forgive me. Please don't move to Florence! Don't go anywhere! I beg you, I'll look after you.

Artemisia Is he still alive?

Orazio Gentileschi Of course he is. He's in prison. This is why he's begging you to marry him.

Artemisia Not him! Caravaggio.

Orazio Gentileschi They say he's still alive. I don't really know. He keeps writing letters to the Pope, asking for forgiveness and to be allowed back to Rome because he didn't kill, only participated in a duel. He knows that duelling is forbidden, but he was coerced into it and there was no way out. This is the rumour . . .

Artemisia Why should he return to Rome if he had already managed to get away? Never mind. Yes. He knew everything a painter needed to know. Except for one thing. And this is now certain.

Orazio Gentileschi What's that?

Artemisia Do you remember his *Judith*? You showed it to me.

Orazio Gentileschi Yes of course, I remember it well. We were looking at it for so long that it grew dark around us.

Artemisia And the blood, do you recall the blood? It's pouring out of his neck all the way down to the pillow and the bed. Not a single drop touches Judith herself. I was wrong. I thought Judith can remain clean. I thought that blood cannot taint the victim. But no. Not even the victim can remain clean. This is what Caravaggio didn't realize. Terrible! And this backdrop . . . can't even bear to set eyes on it. Back then I didn't know who I was. Not in the least. They stretch you out and all the world's past and future evil enters you . . .

Orazio Gentileschi I'm not blaming you, Artemisia. You weren't found guilty on any counts.

Artemisia Who? These? They would have quite liked to, though. Why do you think they didn't torture Agostino?! Because he is an 'emeritus' member of the Academy? Accademia dei Virtuosi al Pantheon! Virtuosi! Good God! He's indeed a living image of the 'virtuosi'. This is out of this world! Or why else? I've won nothing, you understand, absolutely nothing! Aaaaaaaaaart!

Orazio Gentileschi Artemisia, darling, come!

Artemisia I won't throw up, don't worry, I'm past that stage. I don't vomit – I paint. How many colours can possibly co-exist in a single human being?! The full spectrum of evil and cowardice, erupting like a volcano!

Orazio Gentileschi You want me to kill him?

Artemisia Could it be that you didn't understand anything from what had happened to us? Fine, leave it, I'm out of here! I shall paint it one day, and then blood will squirt towards Judith. (*The image morphs into the second* Judith *painting; she takes a long, hard look at it.*)

Projection 3. Artemisia Gentileschi: Judith Slaying Holofernes *(1620–21) Uffizi Gallery, Florence.*

Something like this, yes. (*Very slowly, the image morphs back into the previous one.*) I shall leave this first *Judith* here, for you. Look, Holofernes is still alive. There's still life left in him. And that's the way it will continue to be. So take a look at it. Look at that head. And at the other, too, mine. Leave it! I don't need anything. I'll only take the virginal with me. It will remind me of you. And do make sure the boys won't become artists. Come here, give me a hug. (*She leaves.*)

The End.

Stories of the Body
Teresa

András Visky

Translated from the Hungarian by Jozefina Komporaly

6 András Visky: *Stories of the Body: Teresa* – Theatre Y Chicago (directed by Melissa Lorraine and Andrej Visky). Premiere: 25 May 2018. Poster design by Péter Szabó.

I will continually be absent from Heaven . . .
                                        (Mother Teresa of Kolkata)

I received a long letter from my elderly mother.
She has just learned about our mission, after all this time.
She had been convinced that I had long perished.
I didn't respond – after all, she wasn't far off.
                                        (Zsuzsa Takács)

It occurred to me that perhaps it is harmful for the soul to have faith without experiencing any emotion.
                                        (Szilárd Borbély)

Characters

Teresa
Father
Father Jambreković
Voice
Saint Peter
Homeless Man
Tempter
Officer
Sister Beata
Girl

The male parts and, respectively, the two female parts, can be combined in various ways. It is also possible to stage the play as a three-hander (Teresa, a man and a woman).

Scene One

Teresa Yes. Yes. A voice . . . The same one. Yes, I'm coming.

Look, look there! Can you see, Dad? There . . . and there . . . The surface of the earth is speckled with unburied bodies. Nobody can gain as much as a foothold in Skopje. Can't you see?! Dad!

Father Come here, darling, come to me. Calm down, don't you cry, I'm right here. It's okay, it's all fine.

> Waves, waves, toss and turn,
> Steam arise, and make me yearn,
> Silent angel, grab me tight,
> Gleaming ocean, shine out bright . . .

Scene Two

Teresa I was twelve when I first became aware of it. It was then, I can remember most vividly. Yes, twelve. It was then that I first knew I had a calling. The poor, the have-nots. Yet it's not them but the dying on the streets, the people rotting alive, yes those. I know I'll have my work cut out for me, but they are calling me. We tread on them, stepping from body to body, this is how we move, onwards and upwards. Each and every one of us!

Well, no, not quite, not me.

This is my body, the body whispers as I'm treading on it, I can hear it. Can you hear? We forge ahead, body to body, one body at a time.

It isn't true that people die, I've never seen anyone die. And the soul doesn't slip away either. The soul is waiting for something, not sure what, perhaps the final judgement, and it's prepared to hold on for a very long time. It would be good to know, but it can't be known. Best of all would be to believe: in the final judgement, when the trial of unburied bodies is finally conducted. The body is no shelter for the soul. No, never.

I've seen all those bodies and didn't dare to leave the house. I won't tread on them for anything in the world. For a long time, I've thought that this was a recent thing, but when I read *Antigone* at school, because it was compulsory reading, my doubts vanished. I can't remember anything except that Antigone, that virgin immersed in sisterly love, wanted to bury her brother, and for this, she had to die. It didn't occur to me when I read the play, though I was the same age as Antigone, that I had the same name as her, too: Antigone and Gonda.

But Antigone would talk in beautiful verse, something I was unable to do.

The deceased, or rather a lifeless body, a corpse, was condemned to rot unburied in front of everyone's eyes. So that the birds of Satan can take its flesh and entrails apart, and stray dogs can chew on its bones. But Antigone put up a fight for him. For the dead body. So she can return to earth what duly belongs to earth. There is no greater truth than a dead body.

I lifted my gaze from my book, and found myself overwhelmed by the sea of unburied bodies.

Scene Three

Teresa My dear maiden sister Antigone! You are magnificent, the most beautiful of all sons and daughters of men! Let me look at you, fairest of all! Let me go blind by staring at your radiance! Let me help you get dressed, you, queen of unburied bodies.

She said nothing, but didn't accept my help. Now I can see. She stood there right before me, in my room, naked. I've never seen anything as beautiful as this.

Everyone is beautiful when in love. And a virgin, too. Only my father thought I was beautiful, no one else.

Could it be that Antigone was born ugly? The ugliest of all, like me? A frog? And she suddenly turned beautiful when she started to fight for her unburied brother? Could it be that only the ugliest of all turn truly beautiful? If only I knew who I'm talking to.

I asked my father to take me to the sea, hoping that the sea, at least, may have retained its purity.

Teresa I need to urgently see the sea, Dad.

Father Urgently?

Teresa I haven't slept for days, I need to see it.

Father I know you can't sleep, Gonda, I hear you sing.

Teresa Sing!?

Father And you are talking to someone, in quite a loud voice. You're saying, you're saying?

Teresa Forgive me, Dad, but this means you aren't sleeping either, not just me.

Father I can only hear your voice though. Does the other person respond to you? Who are you talking to all night?

Teresa Talking?! Don't be mad at me, Dad . . . I feel so embarrassed.

Father I'm not mad, how could I be! Come, let's go, poppet.

Teresa I like it when you call me poppet.

Father Me, too. Let's go.

Scene Four

Teresa Dear me! Unburied bodies are floating in the sky-dark Aegean Sea! On the horizon, where sea and sky join together, bodies are bashing into the hard sky only to fall back into the water in a flash. Good God!

I gazed at my father to make sure he could also see what I see.

His face was beautiful, like that of a helpless god. Rejoicing, tears in his eyes, in the spectacle of the Greek sea tossing and turning. My poor ignorant and blind father, can't you see? But I stayed quiet, without saying a single word.

My body is taken over by wild hatred, unsure for whom.

Teresa Let's go, let's be on our way! I want to go home now, I've had enough.

Scene Five

Teresa I went to confession, to father Jambreković, though I gave away nothing of what I'd seen.

He could tell I was lying, he could sense that I kept the most important thing hushed up: the sea covered in bodies. It's none of his business. If it were, he could see it too. But since he can't, it's not.

Teresa Father, I'm a sinner. Sins I've not committed keep weighing on my mind.

Father Jambreković You have not committed them, my daughter?

Teresa No, Father.

Father Jambreković What is it that you haven't committed?

Teresa I'm in love.

Father Jambreković You are?

Teresa But still a virgin.

Father Jambreković A virgin and in love?

Teresa Yes and yes.

Father Jambreković And this is your sin . . .

Teresa Yes, this is it.

Father Jambreković Who are you in love with?

Teresa Not sure, many people . . . thousands, tens of thousands, hundreds of thousands . . . Men, women and children. I want to give myself to them. I want to be all things to all people.

Father Jambreković To all people? Isn't this a bit much?

Teresa All things to all people, yes, precisely. Father, can I ask you something?

Father Jambreković Of course, ask me, my daughter, fire away.

Teresa Father, are the sins we haven't committed mortal sins?

Father Jambreković Whatever do you mean?!

Teresa Don't know . . . I'm just thinking that Antigone could have held on to her purity and lived happily ever after, but she went for the dead, not for the living. She shooed away the birds feasting on the corpse and lifted the body up, taking it with her as far as she could. She didn't listen to anyone, or if she did, I don't know who that was. Father, could it be that sinlessness, I mean that purity is in fact the sin of all sins?

Father Jambreković Gonda, do you want to drink the chalice to the last drop?!

Teresa I can't allow my uncommitted sins to strangle me.

Father Jambreković Indeed, do not.

Teresa What should I do?

Father Jambreković Get going, and do what you have to do.

Teresa He didn't absolve me. There was nothing to absolve me from.

By the time I stepped out onto the street, it was already dark. I walked slowly, minding every step. I got home at dawn, before daybreak. I didn't notice the pack of dogs following me. I didn't notice the silence pouring out of them. They were gazing at me, in stillness and in silence, expecting something to happen. Blood kept dripping down my body, all the way home.

Have I killed?

I gave the dogs a blessing, not knowing what I was doing. Upon this signal, they dispersed, in silence, as before.

Scene Six

Teresa Hatred flared up in my heart, right there on the beach. Could this be love? Antigone's silent fire flamed up in me. This was the very first time I felt this thing called happiness, the existence of which I had no inkling about. 'I was *born* with love enough to share: no *hate* for anyone': Antigone, yes. With love, well, for a corpse . . .

For the first time in my life, I loved myself.

Scene Seven

Teresa My father left. He didn't leave as such, he passed away. I found him lying on the cold kitchen floor. I wasn't at home when he left. I was sitting in the empty church. Alone in a church: there's nothing more heartbreaking than this. Churches are brimming with sound. They stream from somewhere, everywhere. And those glances! Terrible! Don't look at me, can you hear? Can anyone hear me?

Sounds or echoes? I can't really tell them apart, though I should.

My voice is an echo, I know that much, and it harks back to the beginning of time.

I lied down under the pews, and listened to the sea echoing in the floor stones. And to the footsteps layered in them over thousands and thousands of years. Silence! The sky is being echoed in the stones: I would have never expected anything like that.

Father Come home, Gonda, hurry up, I'm thirsty.

Teresa Who's this? My father?! It's him, oh my!

I'm not coming until you call me 'poppet'.

Father Poppet!

Teresa Are you thirsty?

Father Thirsty like I've never been before.

Teresa Coming, coming. Wait for me, you hear?!

Teresa I ran across town, as fast as I could. I can't recall the moment I started crying. But soon I was sobbing so hard that I had to come to a halt at an iron post. People thought I was throwing up. Fountain of pain, this is what I am.

Water and blood. Go away, let me be alone, I'm fine.

He left. He didn't leave: he's right here in front of me, his body that is. He didn't wait for me, he did. He left me, he's with me. I'm kneeling by his side, candle in hand, like a tired murderer.

No echo, but no silence either. He's come to an end, my father. From here to there. Nine hand spans and a bit. Let's say two fingers. There should be some golden ratio involved, but can't remember the formula. Should know about formulas. That's that, all the same now. How dreadful. I didn't close his eyes, so he could carry on looking. A dead God who keeps looking, looking and looking. And cannot see.

Thirsty. Eternal thirst, my father, you.

> Waves, waves, toss and turn,
> Steam arise, and make me yearn,
> Silent angel, grab me tight,
> Gleaming ocean, shine out bright . . .

Scene Eight

Teresa I decided to leave home. People think I'm mad because I'm about to take on tasks that are most likely to cause me pain. At the calling of whom? Antigone? I hear hysterical laughter, but it's not coming from outside. From inside, rather.

From within me.

I joined the Sisters of the Loreto. I took the name Teresa and waged unconditional obedience. On 6 January, our ship sailed from the sea to the River Ganges, also known as the Holy River. Strewn with dead bodies, I should have known. I didn't say a word to anyone.

The calling, yes, I understand.

The heat of India is simply burning. As I walk around, it feels as if fire was burning under my feet, which then sets my whole body on fire. Yet for me, this was complete and utter happiness.

Fire consumes me, while love always consumes the other. Could it not be the other way round? No, it couldn't.

I'm finally alive, oh, my, I feel dizzy. I made an eternal pledge and started teaching.

Scene Nine

Teresa The Hindu–Muslim conflict broke out in Kolkata. The Day of the Great Massacre. Life came to a standstill in the city. I left the school building. There were three hundred girls in our hostel, and we had no food. We were forbidden to go out, but I went anyway. Then I saw human bodies on the street, stabbed, beaten up, lying in strange postures, in their dried blood. People had been jumping over the walls of our school, first a Hindu, then a Muslim. We took both of them in, and helped them get away in safety. I was not confronted with death, the death that was chasing them, until I ventured out onto the streets. I was stopped by a truck, loaded with soldiers.

> **Officer** You're not allowed on the streets, no one is allowed! It's forbidden.
>
> **Teresa** Don't touch me! Don't you lay as much as a single finger on me!
>
> **Officer** Okay, my poppet...
>
> **Teresa** I'm not your poppet! Understand?
>
> **Officer** Sorry... On my honour as an officer...
>
> **Teresa** Don't say that. You don't have to say that.
>
> **Officer** I understand. But you have to go back, you can't stay out on the streets.
>
> **Teresa** I had to come out, you understand?! I have three hundred girls who have nothing to eat. Plenty of soldiers have checked me out.

Teresa The soldiers had some rice – they gave me a lift back to the school and let us have several sacks of rice.

The unburied. The seen and the unseen. So many of them, my God! Who are you? Come, they call me, and wave at me. What's this? I'm so afraid, so terribly afraid.

Scene Ten

Teresa A letter came: my mother's dead. It's her silence that I remember the most. As she looks into the distance, in silence. Why does a mother have to die? How is this business thought up, my Lord?! She was still so young when I left home! And now, she will remain young for me, forever.

Sister Beata Cry, Teresa, cry.

Teresa I can't.

Sister Beata You have to.

Teresa I can't.

Sister Beata You won't be able to bury her unless you cry.

Teresa They'd already buried her by the time the letter arrived. They couldn't possibly leave her out there in the open air?!

Sister Beata You have to bury her, too. You can't drag her along with you for the rest of your life. Let her go wherever she needs to.

Teresa I can't. I'll take her with me. Go, let me be.

Scene Eleven

Teresa Yes. The Voice addressed me, at night, on the train to Darjeeling. A male voice. I got up from my seat, and looked around to check whether anyone else could hear. No-one. Everyone was rocked to deep sleep by the train. What an invention, these trains! There's no love in them. Entangled bodies, billowing to the rhythmic clacking. Perhaps we won't even arrive. Ever, anywhere. Darkness densely swirling in the open carriage. Every now and then, an ice cold light flashes in from the outside. Faces harden for a moment, and then relax. As if they all died for an instant.

Voice I'm thirsty.

Teresa Father, is that you? Who are you? Answer me!

Voice Leave everything behind.

Teresa Everything?

Voice Everything.

Teresa But I have nothing, no belongings.

Voice Leave the convent. Dress in simple, old and worn clothes, rather like my mother dressed. Live, eat and sleep like those living on the streets.

Teresa I'm afraid.

Voice Will you turn me down? My intended, my poppet!

Teresa Poppet?! Dad?!

Voice Do what I ask.

Teresa What did you say?! Poppet?! Only my father called me by this name.

Voice Allow me, too. Don't be afraid, I'll always be with you.

Teresa Did you say your intended? Say it again.

Voice Some religious orders have plenty of nuns caring for the rich and wealthy, but for the poor, there are absolutely none. These orders are too rich, and receive more than they give away. For them I yearn, for those living on the streets, the unburied. Chase the birds of Satan away from them.

Teresa Don't go! Continue, tell me more! Can you hear? Can you hear me? Don't go, stay! Promise me that you'll always stay with me and talk to me! Promise!?

Voice I want free nuns shrouded in my poverty. Will you turn me down?

Teresa I'm so afraid, terribly afraid. This fear tells me how much I love myself. I'm afraid of the suffering that would touch me once I led the lives of those living on the streets. Don't let me make a mistake, you hear me? Wait, I'm coming. But why won't you promise?! Why won't you answer me?!

Teresa The voice didn't promise a thing. My poppet, my intended – what's this? Me?! Should I be satisfied with this, with absence? Fine, you keep quiet, but I promise I won't. Don't rely on that. Who am I in love with? Myself? Don't you even think about that! Let the honeymoon commence!

I took the decision to leave the order. To step out from the confines of goodness and perfect purity. I'll live on the streets, together with the people nearing the end and dying on the streets. I'll abandon purity, never to return. European orders are too rich, including the Loreto. They receive more than they give away, including the Loreto.

I didn't set out to arrive at this place when I'd left home. And I didn't arrive at the place where I'd set out to.

Scene Twelve

Teresa I left Loreto at 8 o'clock in the morning. The doors of a life lived safe have closed behind me. I take my leave, I'm on my way. It's much better not to look back. I head off in search of the unburied.

The Order is concerned that I'm a great danger to the Sisters of Loreto. They forbade them to have anything to do with me. They go out of their way to prevent any help and assistance being offered to me. For the Order, I've become something truly horrible, on a par with Satan, and they brand my work Satan's work so I can't get any help.

Fine, I'm on my way.

I spoke very little, just did some washing of sores and bandaged a few wounds, and gave out some medication. I disinfected the wounds of a stark naked, ill and dying man, lying on the streets, and I gave him a drink of water. He was so strangely grateful. At the market, I came across a poor woman, dying of starvation more than illness. I gave her something that would help her to sleep, but she asked me to look after her instead. She'll go to sleep in due course, when the time comes. Her body temperature was only 35 degrees. I see . . . Go, go, you're ready! I did everything I could, but had I been able to give her a mug of warm milk, her cooling body might have come back to life.

I found two people eaten alive by worms. The eldest asks for a cigarette after I finish caring for him. I happened to have two packs of the finest cigarettes in my bag, received that same morning from someone on the street. I accepted them without a second thought, which made us both burst out in laughter. Was it you?! Billows of finely smelling smoke shrouded the unwanted old man – a sight of utter delight!

I got to my lodgings late at night, tired though not weary. I checked myself out: I've never worn such dirty clothes in my life. Bloodstains, grime, fingerprints, even the mark of a perfect palm. How beautiful! Who could it belong to? Suddenly a forceful surge of heat overflew my entire body: I've never felt greater happiness! I don't want to return to purity, ever.

No.

Scene Thirteen

Teresa There are more and more girls wanting to join me. They walk the streets, too. They're actually flying, hovering in fact, rather than walking. They're beautiful, brave and happy. I should be concerned about them, but I'm not.

And how about you? Did you address them too? And then left them to their own devices, like you did with me? Did you light the flame of darkness in their hearts?

It felt as if he had given himself to me. Entirely. Six months' worth of joy and unbroken union of love felt short lived. The darkness is such that I cannot see a thing. At times, all I hear is the sobbing of my own heart.

Scene Fourteen

    Teresa   I dreamt that I was standing at the gates of Heaven and Saint Peter wouldn't let me in.

    St Peter   You can't come in.

    Teresa   Why not? I asked, feeling a little edgy.

    St Peter   Because.

    Teresa   But I'm personally acquainted with the son of the big cheese!

St Peter Drop this, the son of the big boss seems to be known to everyone who makes it here. Don't name-drop the big cheese here! And don't shout, I'm not deaf.

Teresa I did have that impression . . .

St Peter Everybody takes me for a deaf man. Can't make sense of it. Strange . . .

Teresa You should at least turn the music down if you want to talk to me.

St Peter It's you who wants to talk to me, not me with you.

Teresa Yes, but don't shout.

St Peter All right, I'll try, but I'm not really in charge of the music. That's coming from within, from the angelic hosts, you should know about that! Rather boring, but this is what they can come up with.

Teresa Finally. Well: I'm not only acquainted with the son of the big cheese but . . .

St Peter But what?

Teresa Lean over. Closer. Even closer. Like so. I'm involved with him, too. It's all quite private, I should add.

St Peter How private?

Teresa Well, you know . . . Very . . . Positively intimate. It couldn't be any more intimate. The rest is none of your business.

St Peter Oh, it's you?! The 'poppet', of course. Why didn't you start with that?

Teresa I didn't want to involve him straightaway.

St Peter Don't you worry about him. Holy moly, the son of the big cheese has some strange tastes judging by the look of you! Listen up! I have a message for you, hang on, where is it, right here. Yes, it's kind of an order, listen carefully. You're not allowed in.

Teresa And why exactly would that be?

St Peter Because there are no slums here in Heaven. It's not your kind of place. You'd want to leave here sooner or later anyway. This is the order. It's done. And: dusted.

Teresa This is the reason?

St Peter This indeed.

Theresa Done and dusted?

St Peter Done and dusted for good.

Teresa Well, in this case I'll send you enough misers to make your ears burn. I'll fill up the sky with slumdogs.

St Peter You've got a problem with my ears again.

Scene Fifteen

Teresa The natives, on the outskirts of Bourke, lived in tin and cardboard shacks. I entered a random shack and said to the man living there:

Teresa Let me make your bed, launder your clothes and tidy up.

Homeless Man Don't bother I'm fine, I'm fine. Trust me.

Teresa You'll feel much better if you let me do this.

Homeless Man But I don't want to feel any better, understood?

Teresa He pulled out an old envelope from his pocket, then another and another. He kept opening them one by one, until he got to his father's photo. He showed it to me. I looked at the photo, then looked at him.

Teresa You're the spitting image of your father.

Homeless Man Really? Am I?! Of my father? People! Can you hear me? I'm the mirror image of my father!

Teresa I blessed the photo and gave it back to him. He put it into the first, second and third envelope, and then into his pocket, close to his heart. As I tidied up, I found a dirty lamp.

Teresa Why don't you light this lamp? It's so beautiful.

Homeless Man For whom? No one has come to see me for months and months and months. Who should I light it for?

Teresa Will you light it if the sisters come and visit?

Homeless Man If they come, I will.

Teresa The sisters came to visit daily, only for about five to ten minutes, but they always lit the lamp. After a while, the man got into the habit of lighting the lamp himself. Two years later, by which point I have forgotten about it all, he sent me a message.

Homeless Man Let her know that the light she lit is still shining bright.

Teresa By then, I was living in complete darkness.

Have I killed?

Scene Sixteen

Teresa (*letter*) Father, please pray for me because there is such horrendous darkness in me as if everything had died. I cannot really put into words how alone I feel in my heart. I find it harder and harder to talk. Before, I used to get a lot of help and consolation, but from the time the work has started, nothing. More than that, it would seem that I myself have nothing to say either. I'd really like to have a good chat, but the thought of having to reveal all about the Voice holds me back, so I decided not to speak to anyone. The more I crave him, the less I'm wanted. I want to love him as he's never been loved before, and yet there is that separation, that terrible emptiness, the feeling of God's absence. For more than four years, I haven't been able to find any help. The agony of desolation is so great, and yet at the same time the longing for the Distant One so deep . . . If only you knew what I'm going through. He has destroyed everything in me. But I ask for nothing. He can do as he pleases with me. Pray for me, so I'll always smile at Him. There is such contradiction in my soul. Such a deep desire for God, so deep that it hurts. Constant suffering, yet he doesn't really need me, he rejects me. I'm empty, have no faith, no love, no zest. Souls don't attract me, Heaven has no meaning, it's just like any other place to me. Thinking about him means nothing to me, yet there is this excruciating longing. I'd like to say it, but I can't. I can't find words to express the profundity of darkness. He went away, and left me on my own. Despite all this, I'm His poppet, and I love Him. Not for what he gives, but for what he takes away. He thinks it's best for me to be in a tunnel. He left me on my own . . .

Scene Seventeen

Teresa I'd like to build a town for the lepers, one that is theirs alone. I shall call it Shanti Nagar, the city of Peace.

Our friend, the Punjabi girl is in terrible pain. She's crying loudly. I only leave her when her mother arrives. What a contrast between the rich and the poor. The poor are living martyrs, they never complain. A young boy, who suffered unbearable pain, said at last that he was sorry to die because he'd just learned to suffer for the love of God.

We picked up a man from the sewer, half-eaten by worms, and brought him to the home. His last words were: 'I've lived like an animal on the streets, but now I'm going to die like an angel.' He was truly happy. He raised from his bed, holding out and up his arms chewed to the bone, as if someone had come to collect him.

Let the AIDS patients come to me!

Was that you? And what shall become of me? Are you coming to get me? I've just come to love darkness. When your dark light scatters over the faces of my dying people, I'm prepared to forgive you everything.

Scene Eighteen

    Tempter Come with me to the mountains. I want to show you something.

    Teresa Who are you? What's this light? Are you an angel?

    Tempter Yes indeed. Come, I'll show you the city.

Teresa I know it, I'm not coming. My foot throbs, I'm in pain all over.

Tempter Come, please come. I'll help you, you won't even feel the walk, don't be afraid. Look at those shiny buildings, aren't they just like palaces!

Teresa Loreto?

Tempter Yes, that's right. You used to live there too, in happiness, love and comfort. Look at that shiny light – heavenly, isn't it?

Teresa Magnificent! Oh, how I love it!

Tempter You only have to say one word, and all that will be yours again.

Teresa Get away from me, verminous light! Leave me alone. I want nothing, understood? Nothing, nothing, nothing!

Scene Nineteen

Teresa I gave birth to a child. Brought a child into this world. It slipped out of me, merrily, and it was still drenched in blood when it asked me not to kill it because it will come to my aid. I didn't take notice when it was conceived. How could this happen?

One shouldn't wake up at all. How could one carry on dreaming, and live this life with a child? A girl!

Teresa Whose daughter are you my dear?

Girl Yours, no one else's. You love poverty more than anything, even more than the poor – she said, bursting into loud laughter.

Teresa Even more than the poor?

Girl More indeed.

Teresa Is this possible? Everything I'd done is equal to nothing? I'm lost!

Girl You will be happy, just don't redeem by means of other people.

Teresa But I don't want to be happy.

Girl You must. You must be human to hear me out.

Teresa Am I not human?

Girl No.

Teresa And you?

Girl Me neither.

Teresa Dream?

No.

Dream?

No.

Dream?

No.

Scene Twenty

Teresa   Who am I that you'd choose to forsake me?! No one . . . Darkness is skin deep and I'm all alone. Unwanted, abandoned. I have no faith, I have no courage to utter the words and thoughts in my heart that cause me unspeakable pain. Love – this word has no meaning. The reality of freezing cold and emptiness is so distressing that nothing can touch my soul.

Why do I toil? If there's no God, then the soul can't exist, either. If there's no soul, then you don't exist. Heaven – what emptiness!

Always smiling – the girls keep commenting on this. Little do they know that my cheerfulness is the cloak under which I conceal all emptiness and hardship.

There, I'm laughing. Lo and behold, I'm here. I'll always be smiling whenever I think of your unseen face.

Let's see your next move, the moment I'm unable to walk.

Scene Twenty-One

Teresa   They put me to bed. Me. They think I'm about to die. Nurses, there is nothing left in me that has yet to die! If I step on the scales, the arm turns left from zero, not right. Had it turned right, it would show my weight, but turning left it measures my God-deficit. I stand on the scales until the arm comes to a halt. But it doesn't stop, it keeps turning faster and faster, in circles. Showing a negative sign.

Let's make it clear: I haven't come to this world to fill in for your absence! Your job is your job.

Scene Twenty-Two

Teresa   My back hurts. No wonder: I've been carrying your absence around all my life. You've worn me out. This is what's known as unbearable pain. Yet it isn't the pain that's unbearable. I'm pregnant with your absence. I cannot give birth to you.

These hospital lights are blinding me. The breathing machine breathes. Or inhales rather.

I take a breath.

Come for me.

Light! Help!

Scene Twenty-Three

Teresa Darkness. Inside and outside, everywhere. Finally. The nurses and doctors are running around. They keep leaning over me, listening. What happened?

Power cut.

Miracle!

The breathing machine doesn't breathe. It doesn't even sniffle. Great. I motion my girls not to start crying, because I'll get up from here and won't be held accountable for anything. I've always been accountable for them, not so much for myself. A chubby priest turns up, panting, he must have come in a hurry. Where was he heading in such a hurry? And why are these people always late if they're in a perpetual hurry?

The silence of my machine does me more good. I beckon him to leave me alone. And to take the candle with him, too. Light pollution. I don't need light, not now, my aim is to see, finally.

What's this? The whole of Kolkata is shrouded in darkness!

I knew it! I knew that you'd clad yourself in darkness and come for me. That you'd conceal the whole world with yourself on this day.

No, leave it, you don't have to apologize.

Will you bury me? Promise?

Into your own self? You mean you'll bury me into yourself? Much better! This is the best! Let's leave heaven to others. I, for one, don't want it.

I'm right here.

I'm on my way, take me.

> Waves, waves, toss and turn,
> Steam arise, and make me yearn,
> Silent angel, grab me tight,
> Gleaming ocean, shine out bright . . .

The End.

Acknowledgements

An earlier version of this translation was first developed in 2016 in the course of the translation mentorship programme run by Foreign Affairs theatre company (Foreign Affairs Translates!) and further refined for the stage productions entitled *The Unburied: The Saint of Darkness* (directed by Camila França and Trine Garrett for Foreign Affairs London in 2017). Many thanks to all creatives for their input in shaping the translation, and to Peter Sherwood for his suggestions regarding the lyrics of the recurring song.

Stories of the Body
Eva

András Visky

Translated from the Hungarian by Jozefina Komporaly

7 András Visky: *Stories of the Body: Eva* – Theatre Y Chicago (directed by Melissa Lorraine and Andrej Visky). Premiere: 25 May 2018. Poster design by Péter Szabó.

I must confess that I don't know exactly what that is: human dignity.
(Jean Améry)[1]

Scene One

I turned twenty-seven. . .twenty-seven, indeed, and he threw me a birthday party.

Yes. No one had done this for me these twenty-seven years. Not once. And then, he invited people I hadn't seen in a long while, and they all came and sat here. He invited a great many people, and there were twenty-seven candles on the table. I could have never imagined anything like this. They were all very happy to see me, I could tell.

I was at my wit's end, I really had enough of it. Besides, they suggested that we travel to Italy or somewhere. Perhaps Germany? Us five girls. I was pleased, it should be great and I could at least save up for a deposit for a place of my own. So I gave up my spot on the street. That busy corner with such a massive footfall. They came, took me with them, I came back, they took me again. I've resigned to this now, and will be gone within a week. Can't wait to have a place I can call home, and a life, to come back at night to kids waiting for me, and suchlike. I wanted to break this news here, on my birthday. To let everyone know. To blow the candles out. I didn't want to carry on in this line of work forever. To stand on street corners and live like this.

No.

The care home is better. Like in the old days, when I first ran away from my mother.

Scene Two

I rushed to one of those offices and said that I'd like to go back to the care home. How about your mum, where is she? Well, she's at home. They told all this to Mum, and she just hit me, mercilessly. Take this for a care home! So I stayed with her, and she hit me as hard as she could.

When I finished school at the end of year eight, they immediately sent me to work on the fields. My mother didn't give me anything proper to eat, and this was by far the worst. I was always hungry. She'd always give me something small though, but only at certain times. Twice a day, in fact. At one o'clock, and then around six in the evening. This was barely enough. There was nothing for breakfast. I don't know why. She hated me for sure, she really did.

She'd wake me up at six in the morning, come on, do the washing up from the night before, tidy up, light the fire, and I would jump up and down as she ordered because this was clearly what my mother wanted me to do. The others would just carry on sleeping, and Mum would go back to bed, too. I don't know why. I did think about this a lot, but have got nowhere. I couldn't explain it, and all this just made me feel ill at ease.

I'd take the dirty dishes one by one, and lick them clean. Then I'd drink plenty of water. I'd throw up, the vomit burning my throat, so I'd wash it down with some more water, and hear it tossing about inside me while doing the dishes. An entire sea billowing in my belly.

Scene Three

I broke my leg, and she just left me behind in the forest.

We'd been collecting firewood, quite far out in the thickets. It was only us living there in those parts. No one else. One had to follow a dirt road to get there. It was a forest, on the flood plain, not sure what it's called. I've been always quite scared of it. That day I was picking up branches, mainly acacias, put them on my back, but by then she was already far ahead. I rushed after her, and fell over. Snap. Not the tree, my leg. She just left me there. I screamed, but in vain, she didn't come back. Mum, Muuum! No one except for my screams. My voice. Auuuuuch! I was unable to stand up, walk or carry the firewood. And she just disappeared before my eyes, without as much as looking back. She was a tough woman, my mum.

Never mind, I said to myself, the roes and wolves will come soon, they'll lick my leg and heal it, they'll teach me how to walk again and I'll just stay with them. I don't know how long I had been there for, sitting and lying on the ground. I was no longer cold, and my leg didn't hurt either. Could it be that the roes and wolves came to me while I was asleep? I simply don't know. It feels as if I had a second knee growing into my shin. Having two knees on the same leg isn't such a bad deal, is it? I'm no longer in pain, it's over. Happiness, finally. But no, not quite. I came round at some doctor's surgery because these idiots had woken me up. Mum's younger sister had come to fetch me from the forest, she was the one that saved me. She saved me from happiness, this sister of my mum's.

Scene Four

Whenever I feel a little happiness, I know that they'll come for me and save me and bring me back. To my own life. That's where you belong, they say. Yet I don't actually have a life of my own. Where are they bringing me back to? No idea. They are healing me, and treating me by removing happiness from me. Something drips into me, and happiness is all over.

I don't know, yes. Okay, let it be: I don't know. A life of my own is about to begin, yet I, for one, don't have such a life.

I don't know how old I was. I haven't yet started school. I remember it though. Happiness that is. I haven't forgotten about it. I thought that this was the reason why grown-ups existed. That Mum beats happiness out of me, because it will be easier when I grow up if I don't know what it's like. This must be education, I thought. I'm the one who's bringing you up, nobody else, my mum bellowed, you are mine, and mine alone. Yet when they told me off at school for being badly brought-up, I knew they were right. What are you grinning for, you moron?! I had no idea that it can be so wonderful to hear the letters on the page come to life to the sound of my voice when I was reading aloud in class. I always had to laugh then. Every time I managed to read out loud a whole sentence. Moron, idiot! Why does everyone have to scream? Back then, there was still happiness in me. Quite a lot, in fact.

Whatever isn't beaten out of you at home, it falls to the school. There, they continue with the job. There, they beat out the rest.

She left me there, at the edge of the forest. Yet I have seen worse. She used to hit me on the head, because it is there that happiness resides. Understandable, really. Until I come into being again, stillborn. One has to get born out of happiness, and then everything will be fine.

Scene Five

I left home as the festive season was approaching. It was the run-up to Christmas Eve and suddenly a sturdy bloke turned up from the blue and asked if he could go out with me. I wanted it too, yes I did. Then Mum said that we should bring her something to drink. So we did. Then the bloke said that a relative of his lived nearby and we should pop round to see him. I said, fine, let's get to know this man. But we should hurry up to get back home on time, I said. Sure, he agreed. I trusted him. We arrived at his relative, who offered me a drink, and I accepted. The sturdy bloke first took me outside, touched me up and sucked my neck. At first, I didn't even realize that he was sucking. What on earth is he up to? This must be it when people are going out with one another, I thought, one just has to put up with it, they go straight for the neck, it seems. Then the bloke brought me back into the house, groping and hugging me there, too. He wouldn't stop, though the relative was watching us from a dark corner, breathing and moaning heavily.

Ouch, ouch, ouch, let me be, let me be, let me be, no, no, no, I don't want this.

A few knocks on the door, then full-on banging. There was a large wardrobe in the room, so they put me inside. Hide in there, who knows, who's at the door. I could hear that it was my mum, charging in. She immediately had a go at yanking the door of the wardrobe open, while I was holding on to it from the inside. I was pulling at it and so was she, but then I let go, after all why should I pull. As soon as I let go, she started hitting me with a belt she had brought along for this purpose. She was hitting me straight in the face. She was hitting me hard, real hard. Perhaps she was right in asking what I was actually doing in that wardrobe. She kept hitting me with that belt, my face and all over, and then, as I was standing by the window, I suddenly jumped through the glass. I jumped out into the snow, shards of glass flying left, right and centre, and then I legged it straight to the woods. I kept running, and running, and running, constantly hearing my mother's voice in my head. Just come out, just come home and then you'll see! But nothing, not a single sound. She thought I died, since I had cut myself with the window pane. I was covered in blood yet felt no pain, only got a little sleepy all of a sudden. I felt warmth when I fell asleep in the snow. Finally, this is it. This is the feeling of happiness again, it's here, I recognize it, come, please do come now! Don't you even think about saving me!

Scene Six

The bloke is in a rush, wakes me up, I knew it.

Your mother left, he says.
And where should I go now?
Home.
No, not there.
Then I'll take you to my mother.
I'd rather stay here.
Where?
Here, in the snow.
Come, that's not an option.

We made it there late at night, her mother got out of bed and brought us some rags. Lie down and sleep. But I couldn't sleep, so ended up listening to the mice as they were chewing on everything. I didn't sleep a wink, just sat there. It was only in the morning that I became aware of the state of the place, full of filth and dirt, with soiled clothes galore. Goodness gracious, where have I ended up!

After three days, the sturdy bloke says that it's high time we slept together. I didn't understand what he meant. Okay, let's sleep, I said. What does he want from me? Am I not living here with his mother and these mice already? In this filth, with no room to swing a cat! When night falls, I go to bed.

And then, he says to me, bloody hell, is this the way you're going to sleep?
I say, yes, I always sleep like this.
Take your clothes, knickers, everything off, and sleep like that.
How?
Well, so that you have nothing on.
Oh, no, I can't do that, I wouldn't dream of such a thing.
Why the hell wouldn't you? Why the hell?
Just so that I wouldn't.

I didn't let him touch me. I kicked him off with all my might whenever he tried to lie on top of me. I didn't let him, so he was really angry with me, of course he was. I kept listening to the mice. In the morning, he said to me, let's gather some firewood, let's go to the forest. We're walking in the snow, without ever saying a word. Then he just trips me up and pushes me into the snow. I fall over. Next he's pulling his trousers down, and says, take it in your mouth! Me, taking this in my mouth? No way, I'm not doing that! So I ran as fast as I could, but he grabbed me by the hair, wanting me to do that again, but it didn't work out for him. He kept hitting me all along the way home. It doesn't hurt, I'm not letting him. This is just another way to drive happiness away.

Scene Seven

An elderly woman would drop by every once in a while. She had an old chair tied to her back. She carried it round at all times. She could see how I lived there. They'd beat me up, barely giving me a bite to eat. One day, this woman with the chair said to me, would you like a new place? I said yes, I would. She said, put your nicest clothes on, and pack the rest away. Come. So I went. She left some money behind on the table.

It was a beautiful day. We walked and walked until we got to a clearing in the woods. A great many people were gathered there together, I've never seen so many in one place, and all of them were of our kind. The elderly woman removed the chair from her back and told me to step on it. As I did, she started to shout out loud:

This girl is for sale!
Please don't sell me!
Shut up, you have no clue.
Please don't sell me!
For sale!

No one heard me. Plenty of people came over. I'll buy her, no I will, I, I, I. They could see that I was a new girl. That I haven't yet been with anyone. Guaranteed. I swear by all that is holy, the woman with the chair pointed out. New, yoo-hoo, beautiful, brand new girl. Top quality, the woman with the chair explained.

A tall woman came over. Give her to me, she'll be mine. She paid, the others conferred in a low voice, and then shut up. And there was silence. This tall woman had a daughter at home, and I was meant to look after her. So I lived with them, reasonably well. They didn't beat me, and they fed me, too. I was sixteen when I was sold off. I know it's a nice age. Really mighty.

Scene Eight

One day, the tall woman's husband came home early. He locked the door. He came up to me, grabbed me by the hair and began to tear my clothes off. No, no, I don't want this, please no, leave me alone! He slapped me, pushed me to the floor, ready to pull his trousers off. I kept kicking and screaming, saying no, no, no, leave me alone! He never said a word, just carried on working his way down.

They were men of few words, used to just taking a long look and then turning things over and over in their mind.

Meanwhile, the tall woman was dashing home, as if she'd known what was about to happen. I couldn't have been more pleased to see her. She never said a word, just put the boot into her husband. Then she said that I can't live with them anymore. She'd pass me on to her brother and I should live with him and their mother.

He was one of those simpletons, you know, how should I put it, he had his nerves in pieces. I don't really know, but he was such a half-wit, and a proper one at that.

I gathered my clothes. The little girl was crying, but I wasn't. I mustn't cry. I've always been afraid whenever I felt even a tiny bit happy. The little girl helped. I told her, take my happiness on, I'm not allowed any. And she did. Is there any more? Yes, there is. We hugged and danced, this was how I let her take on all that was still left behind. This was our game, and it was full of happiness. Those who cry can be happy, too, but I have to drive out what's still left behind. Crying included.

The tall woman took me to her elderly mother, and I started my new life there, with the mother and the half-wit. He was harmless, so I had nothing to fear. The old woman never said a word. I'd clean the house, do the laundry, gather firewood with the madman, chase the mice away. I brought a fresh scent along with me, the loony used to say and would laugh like a squealing horse. I didn't mind him, let him have his laugh. Let someone be happy to see me, too. Another human being.

I was with him, with this loony, that I did it for the first time, in bed. Something love-like. We were hovering and billowing above and beneath one another. But not only that. I gave it to him, he deserved it. No happiness, I simply gave it to him, so they don't sell me off again. I just got rid of it, to cut back my market value.

Scene Nine

My sister found me. I didn't even know I had a sister. Yet she found me and took me with her to Budapest where she had a splendid home. It has to be said that by then she was already working on the streets, this was her livelihood. I didn't know that this was her work.

The flat didn't belong to her but to the bloke she was working for, and with whom she lived. There were others too, all girls. On the evening of my third day there, they told me to get some bread. And they explained where exactly to go. So I went.

I could see all the girls standing there. Gorgeous dresses, lipstick, mirrors, hair curlers, short hemlines. Beautiful but somehow not quite. Somehow not quite.

We've been expecting you, they said, laughing.
I was sent to get some bread, I said, I'm in a hurry.

Come, you'll be standing here, this is where you'll earn your bread. They'll help, they said.
No, I won't.
Yes, you will.

They all surround me and explain that they are working for my sister's bloke, he's their go-between. Yet there was no one going anywhere, they were all just standing and waiting. Occasionally, cars would arrive and take the odd girl somewhere else. But I have no such dresses, my hair isn't styled, I've got no lipstick . . . You don't need any of this, you're beautiful as you are. Top quality. You'll be free as a bird.

Out of the blue, I see a police car coming. Nee-naw, nee-naw. These girls have all vanished from there at once, every single one of them. I was the only one left standing there, of course. They caught me, yes, it was me that they caught.

Well, the policeman said, what are you waiting for? Get in the car sharpish!
I was sent to get bread, I say. They didn't let me go.
Have you got any papers?
What papers? I have no papers, never had any.
They'll take me to the care home then.
So be it.

As we were driving out of town, one of the policemen, a large porky bloke, kept staring at me.
Let's strike a deal, he said.
What do you mean, I asked.
If you don't want to go to the care home, you can be with all of six of us instead, and we'll let you go.
Baby, the porky said and touched me up. Baby, me.
You want me to be with six policemen?!
You've heard it right.
I'd rather go to the care home, I said.
Okay, the care home it is then.
Your father?
Mother, I said.
All the same. Where does she live?
I give them her address.

They didn't take me to the care home, but to my mum's. This wasn't what we agreed or what I wanted. To my mother's?! We made it there, my mother got out of bed and came to the door, why did you bring her here? Bring her back where you brought her from. So they took me back to Budapest.

Bye, baby, you'll give in one day, I know you will.

Scene Ten

I found some work for a week. As a cleaner. Not much money, but still some. This is my life. It is what it is, but still mine.

No one says hello to me, but never mind. No one greets a gypsy. I simply don't hold my head high, and this is best. They come up to me and grab my bottom or my breasts. I hit them, and they hit me back. How do I dare to hit back, they ask. They scream, turning all red in the face. I didn't hit back, I simply hit, I say. I hit if people touch me. It is them hitting back, not me. Fancy that! They grabbed me, so I hit them, and they hit me. I don't understand how they can't understand.

There was a bloke there, he was Roma, too. They stopped hitting me after that. I lived with him for three full years. He's the father of my son. I got pregnant, no idea how that could happen! Because we couldn't be together say in a bed or suchlike, only in the woods or places like that. He wasn't allowed into my hostel. Nor I into his. We'd stand by our windows and wave at one another. He lived opposite, in the other block, together with the boys.

This was the first time I felt it was good. Just this one time. Love. Being loved. Dear me, what's this? That's when I got pregnant. Yippee! It happened in the toilets, I didn't mind. I sat down, and he sat on me, somehow. This happened when it was good.

I was one month pregnant and said to him, let's go home. To Mum. I thought this was a reason for happiness, me being pregnant. So we went. We lived at my mum's, but only as long as we had money to hand over. I was around three months' pregnant when we ran out. Get out of my house, get out of here at once. I said, where should we go with such a belly? Wherever you like. Nowhere.

Mum's dad let us stay at his place. That was yet another filthy dump, but I was happy enough with it. I tidied up. When the mice came, I just slapped them hard, bang, and that was that. I brought in water and firewood, while my man returned to Budapest. He sent money for a while, but my mother's father took it all. Meanwhile my belly got bigger and bigger. I stole whatever I could lay hands on, cucumbers, onions, sweetcorn. Even chicken. I wrung its neck, then took it home and cooked it. This is how I lived.

The festive season was coming up. Christmas. And then something was suddenly pressing hard on my belly, more and more often. I said to myself, it can't be true that I wet myself, can it? I had no idea how children were born. I went in haste to a relative, asking what's this? What's wrong with me? Oh, we have to call an ambulance. An ambulance? I don't need such a thing. But they did call for an ambulance. I had no nighties or suchlike, nothing at all. They took me to hospital still wearing my filthy clothes.

As I'm sitting there, they tell me that the time has come. My time hasn't come, no way! I wake up in the morning and they bring in all sorts of scissors, for this and for that. What on earth can they want from me? I jumped off the bed, running and screaming that I won't give it away, I won't give it to anyone. They restrained me, put me back in bed, gave me a gas and air mask, but I tore it off, I don't need any of that, leave me alone. The doctors started to panic, oh no, they were here to help. I don't want anyone to help, that's the last thing I need. I was always afraid of people wanting to help. They held me down. Well then, give strength to the baby, push and help it along its way. And then it suddenly slid out. On 22 December. Ronnie.

Scene Eleven

I walked home. It was snowing, and I was very cold. They didn't let me take my son with me, and I wasn't allowed to stay at the hospital any longer. Go, they'll bring him home later. I went. I had nothing. My man didn't earn a penny, but he drank. And he hit me. I hit them, too. My man and my mother's father. The old man. I gave them what for. I didn't drink at all. I was expecting my son.

Little Ronnie was finally allowed home. One had to be happy now, there was no other way. To wake up and breastfeed him. This was a must. I didn't know that there was such a must as to be happy. This will cause a lot of trouble someday. Then to give him a bath. We play a game where I give him all the happiness. But then, my son gives it all back, to the very last drop. And more. Keep it, don't you give it back. He laughs, and gives it all back straightaway. There will be trouble, no doubt about that. There will be punishment, because I was so happy. I tore up my only bedsheet, and put that as a bedding for him, washing it around the clock. This is how we lived until Ronnie was nine months old. He was already pulling himself up into standing with his hands. I couldn't cope with this life, just couldn't. To start stealing again, I didn't have as much as a shoe or anything really . . . How on earth is one supposed to manage?

I take the child and go up to Budapest, I'll find some work and leave all this behind. I heard that there are some jobs in the meat industry. I see a doctor to obtain a health card so I can be hired.

Go for these check-ups and then come back, the doctor says. Fine, I go, I'm in a rush but all's well. I go back to the doctor and ask for my card. That's not possible because the chest X-ray result is missing. I'll go and get it myself if it takes this long to send it through.

The radiologist tells me to take a seat.
I've got no time, this is the only thing I need, the X-ray, and then I'm done.
Do take a seat, the doctor insists.
I sit down.
Where have you been living until now?
Why does it matter? What business is it of yours?
You aren't allowed to work.
Why not?
You have an infectious disease.
How come? I don't get it. I lived the way I lived.
Go get a nightie and take the child to your mother. You have tuberculosis. You need a year to recover.
A year? That can't be true.
If you don't seek treatment, you'll be dead in six months.

I went home and told all this to my mum. And asked her to look after Ronnie until I recover. She was kind enough to agree. So I left my child behind. But I won't die, not least because he's waiting for me.

Scene Twelve

My mother sent word that if I don't let her have twenty thousand, she'd put Ronnie into care. I didn't want Ronnie to be put into a care home, just the thought of him there, no, no way, that's not possible, I don't want that. I ran away from hospital and went to a relative, she was already out on the street. I told her about mum's message, and asked her to lend me twenty thousand, I'd give it back later. This is the place, you can stand here, too and earn it. To stand here, too? Why not stand here? You'd get the money in no time and you'd be able to pay your mum for looking after Ronnie.

And then a bloke showed up. He said, will you come with me? I give you a thousand. I said, no. I give you two thousand. No. I give you three thousand then. Three thousand was worth an awful lot then . . . I started to cry, how could I possibly live like that? No, not me. It was very hard there, but I've become smarter and smarter over time. That was the last time I cried.

There's no such thing as happiness, this is the secret truth, so I've become very strong.

And I've been standing there for eight years. They tried to kill me, put knives to my throat, took me to the woods and tied me to trees, everything, absolutely everything. Yet I lived.

Forget, everything. Hand over everything. Work till dawn, then forget.

Scene Thirteen

A German bloke showed up. He'd always come to me. He kept coming until I got together with him. He had a fabulous house. I lived at his place. I didn't hope to be happy, by then I knew that this wasn't even possible. Whips, chains, handcuffs, and lots and lots of needles. For six hours. He'd tie me to the bed and whip me, this was his idea of pleasure. I decided that I wouldn't feel a thing, but it didn't really work out. I often fainted, or coughed up blood. He absolutely loved it when blood was pouring out of me. He forced me to do all sorts of dirty deeds, and got his dog to lick my blood up. He was happy with me. I'm off, I said, I can't cope anymore, I'm too weak. He won't let me, he said, I'm very good, the best he'd ever had, I must get this out of my head. My disease has become infectious again, I said to him. I have TB, I yelled screaming my lungs out. The dog started to whimper. This finally scared him and he let me go.

At that time, I'd also be drinking, yes, that was the only way I could cope. I'd usually be fairly wasted by the time he got back home. I got really addicted to drink. My relatives would also keep saying, drink, drink, drink, you've made it big, you mustn't leave the German! I was legless most of the time, the German didn't mind. I left him.

After this episode with the German, I returned to the streets. I spent all my earnings on drink. Another German turned up, Olaf, I really loved him. He loved me, too, he'd always pick me, every time. He was gentle with me, and I could see the look of love in his eyes. At times, he'd wash me and dry me from head to toe, give me lots of money and leave. I don't want your money, Olaf. Take it, it's yours. I didn't drink a single drop after that, I was waiting for Olaf. Once I was together with him, I'd have somewhere to take my son to, away from the care home. He stopped coming one day. It was over. One mustn't love. Or hope. Somehow, I keep forgetting this. I always screw up this love-business, always.

Scene Fourteen

I cried for him. Yes, I did! It was a long time ago when I last cried, and now again. This will lead to trouble. I was standing on the street, crying. I mustn't be like this, no, no, no! I could only cope using drugs. Money came, I bought some drugs, money went, nothing. A social worker visited and said he'd help. Don't help, I said, there's nothing you could help me with. I shouldn't be ashamed of what I do, he said, I'm a sex worker and he's a social worker. Work and work. He laughed about this for quite a while. See, I'm such a cool guy, he said.

Okay, let's leave this, I said.

I should watch my health, that's very important, he'll help, this is his job. He can give me drugs, too, if I'm desperate, because he does understand.

Don't help, I say, this can lead to nothing good.

I'm clever and still very beautiful, he said, he'd help, I shouldn't be afraid.

I'm not afraid of anyone, I said to the social worker.

Slowly but surely, he ended up handling my money. By the time I took note, he was already hustling me.

We moved in together. He never said that I should get out of all this, why on earth he didn't, I have no idea. All he said was that I shouldn't be ashamed. He isn't ashamed of being a social worker, either. He'd always laugh about this.

So he got in, rather than me getting out.

I screwed up again.

He rarely hit me, though he did that at times, too, and I gave him all the money I made. I told him that I want a flat, I want to get my child out of the care home. Fine, he said, I'll help you save up. And soon, there was enough money for a flat. I'd be lying if I said that he was bad. Those few blows were nothing to write home about. And I serviced him whenever he felt like it.

He bought the flat and I stood on the streets working from morning till dawn, but still got round to furnish it and keep it tidy. I also managed to come off the gear, somehow it was really easy. The social worker, however, carried on with the drugs. To be fair, this only happened every once in a while.

Flat. Mine. It was clean as a whistle, and nice too. Not a speck of dust in sight. I'm now ready to get out of this, I said to the social worker, I'll bring my son home, look for a job, this was enough. I'm bringing Ronnie home.

Don't get out just yet, he said, adding that it's not only me he's trafficking, two other girls would also move in here and live with us for now.

Everyone get the hell out of here, I said to the social worker. You're free to join the girls, I'm out and that's that. I haven't had the slightest inkling about the girls, none whatsoever.

They won't set foot in here, this is my home.

Hold it, hold it, the social worker said.

My mum called me home, asking for money. She heard about the flat, and figured there must be some money, too. She wanted sixty thousand. Well, I said, I don't have that, but I can give you thirty thousand. She took the money and threw it to the floor. I should take Ronnie away with me then, he was at her place at the time. She'd taken him out of care so she could demand more money.

I let her know that this was the reason why I'd come, I'm taking Ronnie with me to Budapest. He was stick-thin, and all covered in filth. But that was that, I'm taking him away now. I've given them plenty of money to mind him and to keep him clean, and yet they couldn't care less, only squandered the money.

Once back in Budapest, I can't get into the flat. What's going on? The lock has been changed, various voices coming from inside. I bang on the door, open up. The social worker opens the door, but leaves it on the latch. The girls come to the door, too, staring at me.

What's going on here, I ask.

Go away, the social worker says, and don't make a fuss because he'll have no choice but call the police then.

He doesn't have to call the police, I say, I will and kick him out of the flat.

The flat is only in his name, the social worker said at this point, so I'd be better advised not to cause problems for myself.

I banged on the door until I got covered in blood. It wasn't the police that took me away, it was the ambulance.

I thought the flat was mine. It wasn't mine, but his. I really thought that it was mine. I earned the money for it, on the streets. And now, nothing.

I didn't take a single thing away from there. Perhaps the social worker will get back on the right track one day. It can't be good for him, either, to be as he is. Perhaps he'll think of me one day, and remember that my place should be in that flat. They'll fuck up the whole place. I've done such a great job on it, yet not a speck to take away with me, not even that. It must be hard for him though, the social worker I mean. It's hard to get out. But I'm getting out, I swear I am.

I stand on the street corner again, and start saving for another flat. Just in case. In case he didn't remember me. There's a boy without a mum or a dad. He has to leave care. My mother. She doesn't really exist. And I've never had a father. Neither had Ronnie. There are no fathers, only pimps. Pimps are running the country, baby.

Scene Fifteen

It doesn't work. I can't go back. If I do, the girls chase me away on orders from the social worker who doesn't want to see me anymore. There is no room for me on the streets, all the spots have been taken. I am not needed anymore.

I have a drink of water, the sea billowing in me. I'd rather sing, I have a lovely voice. Don't I? All the same. For whom should I sing? The wolves and the roes. So they look after Ron until I buy another flat, where we can be together after all. So they look after him until he grows up, to look after me.

> There are so many worlds I stumble into
> And only a few words I can say
> 'Hello', 'I'm fine', 'goodbye'
> are the ones I know in every language
> resting on the tip of my tongue
>
> I draw red lines around the places
> I never want to go back to
> but I never see them in the dark
> I become less and less as I leave myself behind
> In every corner in which I fall asleep
>
> I've built a prison for myself
> So that I don't slip through my fingers
> But soon I have to go
> To find another corner
> Where I can feel invisible again.[2]

No one, never mind. So, what else have I got? I have myself to myself. How rich I am! Here's my arm, help yourselves, it's up for sale. My nose and ears are both especially fine, as you can see. My ankles: up for grabs! *Osso bucco*, magnificent, tastier than lamb, I swear. Please take your pick, it's all delicatessen on display. My eyes have seen some dreadful horror – they're only for the toughest of the tough! Can I take a look? Yes: no one has had the guts to look me in the eye. Ronnie! Where are you? Come and look me in the eye. The sea is billowing in me, I've won, I've won, I've won . . .

The End.

Notes

1 *At the Mind's Limits*, trans. Sidney and Stella P. Rosenfeld (Bloomington: Indiana University Press, 1980), p. 27.
2 Lyrics by Bence Visky.

Stories of the Body
Lina

András Visky

Translated from the Hungarian by Jozefina Komporaly

8 András Visky: *Stories of the Body: Lina* – Theatre Y Chicago (directed by Melissa Lorraine and Andrej Visky). Premiere: 25 May 2018. Poster design by Péter Szabó.

For Attila Demény

Introductory Notes

This play was inspired by the music of Pēteris Vasks and, for this reason, I indicate scene by scene the works I could hear in my head or I was actually listening to while writing. Future productions based on the play, however, do not have to necessarily follow these musical impositions. I kept them in the text because Vasks's compositions conjure up the mood and spatiality of the various scenes.

Lina was written in response to music, and comprises visions and fairy-tale elements, yet it is not mere fantasy. A friend of mine with whom I had often collaborated on theatre productions in the 1990s had lost both his legs and, in this way, I was closely confronted with such a trauma. I started to make enquiries regarding the specificities of perceiving the world from the perspective of a mutilated body: such as the shifts in the relationship between reality and fiction, or the journey we tend to follow in the course of losing and rebuilding our own self.

Human beings are always whole, because they are always aware of their own incompleteness.

Lastly, I would like to reiterate that stage directions to my plays are mere suggestions, and this text allows for a merging of parts. In this play, the male and female parts are interchangeable. Moreover, the animal heads should not be scary but rather easy on the eye, colourful and friendly, and, in any case, should be imagined and manufactured on a very large scale.

Characters

Woman
Man
Female Doctor with a Bird's Head
Male Doctor with a Stag's Head
Female Doctor with a Bear's Head
Little Girl (*voice-over*)
Policeman
Fireman

Scene One: Anax imperator

Brakes creaking, sound of a collision, a firework of sparks, metal pierces metal, sound of sirens, flashing lights of police cars and ambulances. At first, the sounds and lights seem realistic, then they become increasingly long-drawn and morph into a dream, eventually gaining musical characteristics. Meanwhile we hear people talk ('Alcohol level in blood?' 'Zero.' 'Drug test?' 'Negative.' 'Sedatives?' 'None.' 'Medical history? Have we got any information on this?' 'Nothing', etc., etc., other relevant medical terms.)

This cacophony leads on to the sound of monitors in the intensive care unit, which in turn morphs into the prolonged whistling sound that heralds the imminence of death.

Woman (*wakes with a start*) Whoa, what the fuck! Almost! Just short of a small step . . . less than twenty centimetres. (*Back to the daze for a short while, then startles again.*) I knew it! I did! I'll have another go. Like so. (*Slurring her words.*) Body: Anthropod (Arthropoda). Class: Insects (Insecta). Order: Dragonflies (Odonata). Infraorder: Large dragonflies, or dragonflies with uneven wings (Anisoptera). Family: Aeshnids (Aeshnidae). Genus: Anax. Species: Anax imperator. Goodness! What's this? Who are these? Hey, who are you?! Can't you hear me?! Are you deaf? I won't allow this, no, no, no!

Scene Two: Tala gaisma

Dream-like long-drawn light and sound effects again, which give way to Pēteris Vasks's concerto Tala gaisma (Distant Light) with Gidon Kremer.

Woman 33 minutes 28 seconds . . . 33 minutes 28 seconds . . . 33 minutes 28 seconds . . . 33 minutes 28 seconds . . . 33 minutes 28 seconds . . . (*Slightly awkward and hesitant sounds of applause and encores audible in the distance.*)

Scene Three: Pas de deux

Only the concerto can be heard. Hospital ward, rehearsal room, hospital ward; quick changes in lighting.

Woman (*dances to the music, by moving her hands about and counting the rhythm; suddenly stops*) I knew it! My leg . . . legs?! Goodness gracious! They are no longer there. Have been entirely bitten off. Someone had devoured them both altogether! Yum-yum-yum. Let's see what's this: Andante – Cadenza 1. What does this actually mean? Falling, perhaps diving. Yes, we've had that for sure. 7 minutes 52 seconds. Cadenza. Have I danced to this? Impossible, they said, one can't dance to such music, it's not meant for this.

Rehearsal room.

Man Up, higher, fly, take to the air! And now turn, and, and, and: fall, clink-clank! Is there a problem?!

Hospital ward.

Woman   Got it: Tala gaisma. Yes, this is the title. Concerto? No, no. Oh, yes! Tala gaisma. What does it mean? Don't know. How come I don't know? Tala gaisma! And yes, let's get on with those steps. Let's get on with those damn steps!

Rehearsal room.

Man (*in a dull voice*)   Pas de chat = cat's step; Pas fouetté = fouetté turn; Pas des anges = angel step; Pas des ciseaux = scissor step; Pas balancé = balancé; Pas de chassé = chassé.

Woman   I hate this! Can't stand it! I hate these steps, step after step. Art, yes, that's what I hate!

Man   Okay, okay. Try again! One last time! This is no way to fall, you anthropod! Just land softly and silently. Well?

Hospital ward.

Woman (*searching*)   Tala gaisma. Yes, this is it: Distant light. Yes, I can see, there it is. 33 minutes 28 seconds. And Gidon Kremer. Got it! There's the distant light! Coming, on my way . . . Goodness gracious!

Rehearsal room.

Woman (*hysterically*)   Don't touch me! Don't touch me, understood?!

Man   I love your body.

Woman   Don't! Love me instead!

Hospital ward.

Woman (*trying to find her legs*)   Where could they be? Hey, where are you? Legs?! I can't feel them! And they can't feel me either! I can feel that they can't feel. There! I've lost them, I must have lost them both! What the . . .! I dashed out of the theatre and, and, and I must have forgotten them on the underground. Yes, that must be it, I keep losing everything! The city is chock-a-block with my lost property, they are in search of me. Bags, buckles, scarves, gloves, a tooth or two . . . (*Tries to playfully copy them.*) Sir, have you seen Lina? And a separate tooth filling, too. Lina! And shoes! Those, too. I've lost an entire shoe shop in town. Lina! Lina! Haven't you seen them? A minute ago, they were still here. Of course! Oh, darling legs, please don't weep, I'll place an ad straightaway, offering a reward to those who find you. My legs! Didn't you feel anything?! Me neither. But at least you have some shoes on, I hope . . . Look after each other! Yes, yes, yes . . . that's it: I flung the doors of the dance hall open and screamed out loud that I'd never ever set foot in there again. I clearly recall this, yes. I also broke a mirror, yes. This is what happened. I won't set foot here again! Not my legs, never. Neither of them, I think. This must be true indeed. Clink-clank . . . I dashed out of the theatre. I'll never ever set foot there again. Yes, I jumped into a car and headed straight into the night! Clink-clank . . . Were you with me?! With me? With me? (*Faints.*) (*Alternatively, she keeps going round in circles, endlessly.*)

Scene Four: Pas des anges

Pēteris Vasks: Presences. Cello: Sol Gabetta.

Female Doctor with a Bird's Head, **Male Doctor with a Stag's Head** *and* **Female Doctor with a Bear's Head** *cross the stage, run off and then come back again. When they are about to run off again, they pause, come back, and look at the* **Woman**. *Then they start sniffing and getting to know one another, trying to dance in an awkward yet cute fashion, as children tend to dance, letting out a range of very soft sounds. Finally, they start twirling, sharing a kiss, until* **Man** *appears. Then they stop and withdraw to the back of the stage, from where they watch the scene. At times, they nod, offering a running commentary on proceedings by way of their bodies. This is all very well considered and hardly ever overplayed.*

This tableau is not so much an independent sequence of actions but rather a 'response', an 'accompaniment' to Scenes Four and Five.

During this scene, a **Litte Girl** *is reading from an etymological dictionary. She is struggling with the text. This sequence could be pre-recorded on video; however, in case the* **Little Girl** *is actually present on stage, voice-over should be used. (In the event of productions in other languages, the text to be used should be based on a relevant etymological dictionary for the respective language.) The length of the text should be determined by the overall duration of the scene.*

Little Girl (*voice-over*)

stump (n.)

the part of a limb or tooth that remains after the rest is removed; the remains of something that has been cut off; especially the remains of a tree, the remains of a limb.

maim (v.)

c. 1300, *maimen*, 'disable by wounding or mutilation, injure seriously, damage, destroy, castrate', from Old French *mahaignier* 'to injure, wound, muitilate, cripple, disarm', a word of uncertain origin, possibly from Vulgar Latin **mahanare* (source also of Provençal *mayanhar*, Italian *magagnare*), of unknown origin; or possibly from a Germanic source, from Proto-Germanic **mait-* (source of Old Norse *meiða* 'to hurt', related to **mad** (adj.)), or from PIE root **mai-* (1) 'to cut'.

In old law, 'to deprive of the use of a limb, so as to render one less able to defend or attack in fighting'. Related: *Maimed; maiming*. It also is used as a noun, 'injury causing loss of a limb, mutilation' (late fourteenth century), in which it is a doublet of **mayhem.**

maimed (adj.) having been mutilated.

Scene Five: Guillotine

Man *sitting by the side of the sleeping* **Woman**, *holding a giant bunch of roses that look unreal. Bright red rose heads, long stems. The* **Man** *is wearing a smart black suit* *with a black T-shirt; he is barefoot like dancers. He is looking at a photo, smoking. He stands up, sits back, walks up and down, tries to dance, but he's getting nowhere with the dance despite trying, etc.*

The **Woman***'s even but occasionally interrupted breathing is enhanced by a loudspeaker (no voice-over!) – it fills the whole space; the* **Man** *tries to listen to the rhythm of her breath.*

Man Not a single scratch. On me. Goddamit. Who will finish me off if I get away with murder? Nothing can touch me. We betrayed my father, clink-clank . . . This must be the reason why. Everyone in this crazy family. This is why it fell on me. It's a good job you remember everything, Dragonfly. I don't recall a thing. I'd forget you, too, in case I weren't with you every day. It will fall on someone in the end. I ran after you and jumped into the car, right next to you. This is what they said. This was their reconstitution of events. Not mine though. That's still work in progress. He wanted a rough plank coffin, this was his final wish. My father's, that is. He wasn't condemned to death though, not any more than you or me. Those, who. Are born. Come into this world. Everyone. He wanted that his body. Rough plank, doesn't matter what kind of wood. The cheapest in the lumberyard. There's always something cheaper. This was his stipulation. And sackcloth. No clothes, just a sack. No need to iron anything. Chinese patent shoes made of paper and such like. He's not going to a reception after all. But the cowardly family. What will people say, and so on. They said. Father was familiar with the Greek alphabet. The letters look great, have to admit that. All of them. They said. It has to be shown. Respect has to be shown. And the Hebrew alphabet, too. Those letters, too. He was familiar with them all. Personally. He was forced into a varnished coffin. His body. They couldn't force him though. I told them not to turn his body into a beautiful corpse, at least not that. I screamed in whisper: beautiful corpse, not that! Forgive me, dear Father. Well, I don't know. It's no longer possible, for sure. There's no forgiveness. I waited so that the body. In a final effort. But no, no. Clink-clank . . . The body can't manage a final effort. We've desecrated it with that varnish. At least the sun. Could have not shined. Like an animal. You came in order to be with me. You even held me back on one occasion. Didn't you? Don't make a scene, there's no one from the press here. This is what they said. Not you. You didn't. You kind of love me, I thought. Do you love me? I could feel your breasts as you held me, asking me not to throw tantrums . . . I remember this. Your breasts. Or was that just pity? My father is lying there. Not breathing. Just his body, as one of my brothers put it. I think he wanted to comfort me. What do you mean by just; what do you mean by just, I screamed in whisper. And then. Then the 'just'. Well, yes. A sharp flashing guillotine blade has just broken loose somewhere. It has just been. Released. It's on its way, plummeting. What's that just. What's that just the body. Clink-clank . . . You were too close to me. There's nothing showing on me. Not even a scratch. It hacked you down instead. The instinct for self-preservation. Forbearance. A near miracle, they wrote. I sat next to you. Don't spare my feelings. Too late. I'm coming, so I don't forget you. Otherwise, everything else. Dance, what does that actually mean. But I'll come, always. I'll go, sorry. This is the term needed. Dance, Breath, yes. I can't bear this, I'm so sorry. Bye. (*Leaves.*)

The doctors with animal heads go up to the **Woman**, *listen to her heartbeat and pulse, then stop to think things through, and finally leave.*

Scene Six: Save As

At first, city sounds (ambulance, firefighters, warning phrases used on the underground, cars, traffic jams), then typical sounds from a well-known cartoon, say Tom and Jerry.

Policeman   Obvious case of speeding. They were trying to flee from somewhere.

Fireman   The question isn't where from, but where to. (*Laughs, on his own.*)

Policeman   Or who from.

Fireman   That's another bet, see. You're right.

Policeman   These people were not being chased by anyone though. Because in that case they would have made it here by now.

Fireman   Maybe they overtook them somehow.

Policeman   Maybe.

Fireman   But they can't stop, for anything in the world. So they keep going, going, pushing on blindly, fleeing. It's enough to watch the course, everyone chases someone and everyone is being chased. But whereto, that is the question.

Policeman   Love. There is some sort of a love story here. That's always the case.

Fireman   The man got away. He was the guilty one, though.

Policeman   We don't actually know this.

Fireman   What?

Policeman   Who's the guilty one.

Fireman   But he got away.

Policeman   We don't actually know that.

Fireman   Just fainted, that's nothing. I can see. At a quick glance.

Policeman   Maybe. Possibly. Will come round somehow.

Fireman   I'll cut the girl out of the car. I won't wait any longer.

Policeman   They said they'd come. Bloody ambulance crew. We are the ones saving them, and yet it's them after all (getting the credit).

Fireman   I'm going to cut her out, otherwise she'll die. Her legs are done and dusted anyway.

Policeman   Go for it. Meanwhile, I'll try to resuscitate her somehow. The other one's doing well. Has already forgotten everything, I can tell.

Fireman Yeah. He's in the middle of forgetting. Whoever comes across us changes the channel.

Policeman Yet we are live.

Fireman They still change channels, goddamit. They can't wait for such a blood-drenched flight rooted in some love story, and yet they still end up changing channels. Opting for Hollywood, what else! Because they aren't after blood, just ketchup. (*Looking into the distance like a sad romantic poet.*) The live broadcast carries on in the dark, I don't know whereto, onwards and upwards . . . (*Angrily, again.*) Well, I don't know, goddamit, don't have a clue why this is the way it is.

Policeman And that goes on.

Fireman What?

Policeman The broadcast. That goes on, I said. Non-stop.

Fireman Right. But why, can you tell me why?! No one knows.

Policeman My wife watches me on TV. She records everything. Saves it all. I call her when I'm on TV, and she watches it. This time, too. And then she saves the recording.

Fireman This seldom happens to me. No one wants to watch. As far as I know. It would be good, though. A different kind of saving, I really like that. One document to another. There are these fucking folders: they are the size of my nail and yet you fit into them. In one piece.

Policeman Into them, yes. Quite easily.

Fireman But no one saves me, not at all. As I carve people out of the tin, like a god. At times, they are all in one piece, but no longer alive. Or the other way round, that can happen, too. Or everything in bits and pieces.

Policeman This one is alive, but no longer in one piece. The legs are gone.

Fireman It happened to me once that someone kept singing while I was cutting them out with the cold chisel and the flex. Sang all the way through, in a high soprano voice, like at the opera. I had one of these cases, too.

Policeman Just about anything's available. Everything is within reach these days. In the olden days, there wasn't, but today, there is. Then, for example, I wasn't around either. Not that long ago, let's say. But today, I'm around, too.

Fireman Me too, yeah. But in the past, not really.

Policeman Yeah, you too.

Fireman But no one saves me in a file, goddamit.

Policeman My wife does. You, too. She's watching the broadcast and saving it. You, too. Told her to watch it.

Fireman But she isn't watching me, not me. What will happen to those who are not being saved by anyone? See, this is what I can't understand.

Policeman   Yeah. And to those, who are being saved. What will happen to those?

Fireman   Something for sure. They've been saved. Into that ball-sized folder. And then there is that other kind of saving. That's the real deal. I'd like that one. Her legs are lost forever.

Policeman   Yes indeed. Don't cut them off, leave them. The doctors will deal with this. It's their job.

Fireman   I could do it, I swear. With the flex. Yeah. We are the ones saving them, and then it's the ambulance (getting the credit). They are uncovering the love stories. No one even looks at me. What will happen to me, I ask.

Policeman   Yeah, yeah.

Scene Seven: Cut Flowers

Pēteris Vasks: Vox Amoris

Woman *wakes up, notices the roses.*

Woman   Cut flowers! They cut the flowers, down to the very last stem. Clink-clank! Where are you? Will I ever dance? These still have legs. I had an actress friend, she was French or perhaps Armenian, I think she fled from some war zone and came, well not quite here, to Chicago. This is how she got into theatre. Away from her family, I think, from them. Her family was the war zone and the humanitarian catastrophe. She worked at a florist's, this was her day job. That woman was excellent at cutting the legs of flowers off, good God! Her boss, Luke or Mark, the author of one of the gospels in any case, a Latvian, kept bringing the flowers to her, and she'd just cut and cut, using one of those flower-leg cutting scissors, clack, clack, clack, clack . . . Then she'd sweep the chopped-off legs and flower blood from the worktop into a tin bucket. As soon as too many legs had piled up in the bucket, Luke or Mark, but Luke more like it, he was the Latvian florist, would take the bucket behind the mall and throw the flower-legs out. I don't know what would then happen to these flower-legs, no idea. Major oversight, a really major one. I should have asked him . . .

Scene Eight: Opera miseria

*The **Doctors** return and the amputation-opera begins, or rather the amputation-ceremony, yet they aren't operating on the **Woman** but keep offering explanations making use of plastic limbs (hands, ears, fingers, genitals). At the end, the two legs also appear.*

Female Doctor with a Bird's Head   Amputation entails the loss of a body part (organ or limb). It can be the outcome of an accident or surgical intervention. In some countries, the mutilation of hands, legs, tongues or genitals is utilized as a punishment. In wars or terrorist activities, amputation is used for tactical considerations. The shortened limb is called a stump.

Doctor with a Stag's Head Muncus, mutilus, muticus, defectivus.

Female Doctor with a Bear's Head Amputated are a British brutal death metal band from Bristol, England. Studio albums: Enjoy the Slaughter; Gargling with Infected Semen; Wading through Rancid Offal; Dissect, Molest, Ingest. Video albums: Live Amputation! Lyrical themes: Gore, Rape, Sickness, Perversity, Pathology. Amputated appeared on the BBC show 'Singing with the Enemy', in which they wrote a song together with the all-girl pop group Fallen Angelz. Pa-pa-pa-pa-pam-pam.

Doctor with a Stag's Head Amputatio extremitatis superioris sinistrae propter traumam in pes sinsitrae. (*Holds up the left leg.*) Ecce primus! Amputatio extremitatis superioris melior propter traumam in pes melioris. (*Holds up the right leg.*) Ecce secundus!

Female Doctor with a Bird's Head/Doctor with a Stag's Head/Female Doctor with a Bear's Head (*singing the colophon of the Handel chorus*) Hallelujah, hallelujah, hallelujah! / For ever, and ever, and ever, and ever. / Hallelujah, hallelujah, hallelujah, hallelujah!

Scene Nine: Leg selfie

Pēteris Vasks: Lidzenuma ainavas (Plainscapes)

The first part of the scene is an imaginary and farcically sad funeral, while the second transforms into Lina's wait. It is a matter of directorial decision, but if the production requires, the animal-headed doctors can be present as long as they are silent; and the older woman can be played by any of the characters with an animal head.

Woman I asked the doctor not to throw away my severed legs. I want to bury them. To pay them the final respect. After all, I'm the leg, too. The doctor didn't get it. First, I invent a religion with all its ceremonial rites, and then I bury them. The doctor didn't get it at all. (*Performs an imaginary cemetery scene, in clowning mode.*)

Who are you mourning, miss?

My two legs, madam.

Two at a time?

Yes, they were identical twins, and very beautiful. And now, they are both gone together.

How moving. Please allow me to weep.

This is forbidden here in the cemetery. You know, we are in America. Except that this is the theatre.

Forgive me, I lost my self-control. Are the deceased your relatives?

Yes, they stemmed from my body. Both of them. A right and a left. Would you like a selfie with the leg? Well?

Oh, yes. Very much. You can read my thoughts, miss. You can see through me, as if I were a glasshouse.

There, madam, take your time.

Left. Right. Brilliant. Could we take another one with you on it as well, miss? Yes?

Wonderful, thank you. My sincere condolences to you.

Thank you, madam, this is really kind of you.

There will be a stone, too, a gravestone. Here lie a pair of legs, that is two. Two legs. The right leg on the right, and the left leg on the left. May they rest in peace.

Not allowed, the laws won't let you, said the stump-doctor. A proper stump-artist, everyone goes to him in the area, and he doesn't let anyone return home on their own feet. I don't want to think about what will happen to my legs. Stump: I learned this word. I've been aware of it but have never used it. This is the ugliest word in my mother tongue. In Hungarian. (*Says the word in Hungarian:*) *Csonk. Csonk.* I thought that this word wouldn't be used to refer to people, only countries. But it is. Hello stump, introduce yourself to me. Nothing? Then introduce yourself to yourself. Hello, hello, I'm Stump, and you? I'm also Stump, hello.

(*As if it was a funereal speech at the grave.*) After the Great War, Hungary was called a maimed stump.[2] The war amputated its limbs. Hands, legs, everything. It was amputated all round. It lost the war, so this is what happened, it got punished. My family didn't remain in the main body, in the half moon-shaped torso, but ended up in the Eastern stump. 'A maimed Hungary is not a country, / A whole-Hungary is Heaven.' There was such a poem after the first war. Stump-poem. Despite the fact that Hungarians are good poets, I swear, the best poets in the world. Stump-experience, with lots of phantom-pain. Then, it was time for the second war and for another amputation. There is no whole, the whole had vanished from the surface of the earth for good. No one. Nothing. A whole-Hungary is Heaven, says the poem. Well, yes. Then there are phantoms in whole-Hungary. Phantom-maps. A single glance at the map suffices: one stump next to another, stumps all over. And roaming phantom pain everywhere. Well, somehow pain has no boundaries. And yet, we aren't experiencing pain together, not in it together. (*Throws a fistful of soil or flowers onto the grave.*)

Where are you by now?

Stump is a word that refers to several things. There is the stump, and there is me, the other, who's pretty much the same. Clink-clank. Would it have occurred to you that my legs won't live to see my death? Only the pain has remained of them. They are no longer, yet they ache. Only pain can makes us whole. These legs will surely carry on dancing wherever they happen to end up. How about you? You? You?

Scene Ten: Es mīlu Tevi or On Forgiveness

Pēteris Vasks: Vientulais Engelis (Lonely Angel)

Woman   You're here.

Man I haven't left.

Woman But you said goodbye.

Man But I didn't leave.

Woman I fell asleep.

Man Me, too.

Woman Because of the medication.

Man No, not me. Because of the music.

Woman What music?

Man Lonely Angel.

Woman Vientulais Engelis? Vientulais Engelis! Good God!

Man You danced to it. You said it was impossible, and yet, you still danced to it.

Woman Those days have come to an end.

Man Can't be, that's what you said.

Woman Kitsch! I'm kitschy, you said. Everything has come to completion. The impossible, and the possible, too.

Man But not you.

Woman Indeed, a stump can't be complete. Shall I laugh?

Man Don't be angry.

Woman You were right. I don't know what kitschy means.

Man Neither do I.

Woman I've known it for ages, but now I don't.

Man Me neither.

Woman 12 minutes 50 seconds.

Man What?

Woman Vientulais Engelis. That's all. This is why I started to learn Latvian. Because of these two words. And because of these 12 minutes 50 seconds. That's how long the piece lasts. This is the time of eternity. Can you hear it?

Man/Woman (*together*) To be honest, I thought it would never be brought to completion.

Man What?

Woman What?

Man Well, for Gidon Kremer it's no big deal.

Scene Ten: Es mīlu Tevi or On Forgiveness

Woman Oh, no, it's not him. It's Alina Pogostkina. Can you hear? This was on then, too.

Man Where?

Woman Where, yes. But not as a question. Where: is no longer a question. Always there. Well, in the car, or in the rehearsal room? Es mīlu Tevi – what does it mean?[1]

Man Must be some swearword or curse. First thing, we always learn to swear in a foreign language. Swearword-tourism, very lucrative. Forget it.

Woman Or?

Man Or . . . I don't know. Swearwords, for sure. And the names of genitals. Come on. Laughable. Es mīlu Tevi – sounds very funny.

Woman I can't.

Man What?

Woman Forget it.

Man Right, I'll help. Wasn't it you who put it on?

Woman What? (*To the music.*) Not me. I don't listen to music. I took a vow. This was the first thing I did when I'd come round.

Man Yet the music was playing, and I fell asleep before I could have left.

Woman It's still on.

Man Someone outside, I'm sure. They might be busking . . .

Woman You should have left.

Man I can't leave when I'm sleeping.

Woman I was sleeping, too.

Man Then even less so.

Woman Did you stay for the night?

Man I can't leave, when I can't leave.

Woman Who was driving?

Man When?

Woman When, yes. Not a question. When. Well, then . . . Zsiiiiuuuucsattzszszsbrrrdurrrspang . . .

Man You . . . Don't be mad.

Woman I am, but don't know who I'm mad at.

Man No one to blame.

Woman No. Only the dead. Or my legs perhaps? They've certainly had their share of punishment!

Man Not even them.

Woman You didn't see me then.

Man No.

Woman Me neither.

Man I actually did. I saw you.

Woman Me, too.

Man We were looking at the same thing then.

Woman What? Tell me what that was.

Man You first.

Woman The fall? The impact? The pier of the iron bridge as it wouldn't budge for anything in the world. And we crushed into it, gently. . . Zsiiiiuuuucsattzszszsbrrrdurrrspang . . .

Man No, not that. The dragonfly flying motionless above the water.

Woman We were looking at that?

Man I was.

Woman The river?

Man Creek, mountain creek, but abounding in water.

Woman Right. I saw that fish, that wild, Schubert-faced trout.

Man Then it's not.

Woman What's not?

Man Not the same thing.

Woman Perhaps not the same thing, but each other.

Man As for me, the dragonfly.

Woman Me, the trout. That Schubert-faced one. How I hated it!

Man I liked what I saw. I kept watching that motionless flying. I was looking at the impossible.

Woman Dance. That's dance. Not all the same.

Man Dance, fine, all the same. Motionless.

Woman Hey, why did you start calling me Clink-clank?

Man Me? It was you who called me names!

Woman Really! I can't recall this.

Man Yet for everything . . .

Woman Yet everything. . . .

Man Where were we?

Woman That it was motionless. And dance.

Man Right. Yes, there's the abundant creek at the bottom, like a blind storm, and above, the motionless dance of the dragonfly. And the trout . . .

Woman . . . that obnoxious Schubert-faced one . . .

Man . . . that is to say: I, personally, in a beautiful somersault . . .

Woman . . . Tsukahara double vault one and a half right twist . . .

Man Why would you have such an idea? How does this Tsukahara relate to this?

Woman I remember it all, you know. I remember my parents' memories, and my parents' parents' memories. I remember the horrible memories of the whole country. Ever since I was born that is.

Man That's true.

Woman The 1972 Olympic Games in Munich, the twentieth. Then the terrorists of Black September turned up, occupied the Olympic Village and slaughtered eleven sportsmen. And . . .

Man . . . now this, too . . .

Woman Pommel horse jump, gold medal: Tsukahara. Doesn't come back to me. (*Points at her head.*) It's all here, everything. I'm not a tabula rasa, that's for sure.

Man Arvo Pärt.

Woman What?

Man Tabula rasa. Arvo Pärt.

Woman 10 minutes 54 seconds: Ludus, and 10 minutes 21 seconds: Silentium, which together . . .

Man But which one? It's not all the same! The one for two violins, string orchestra and prepared piano, or the one for violin, viola, string orchestra and prepared piano . . .

Woman All the same.

Man No, no, no . . . 27 minutes 16 seconds . . . altogether!

Woman Yet they said that one can't dance to that, either. Well, I showed them. For God's sake, these motherfuckers!

Man Don't swear, really don't do that now!

Woman I didn't swear. I just showed them their mother's god. The most beautiful god, the god of mothers . . . Why aren't you laughing?

Man This is rather kitschy. Clink-clank . . .

Woman You're right. I won't do this again, I promise.

Man Is he Latvian, too?

Woman Who?

Man This Pärt?

Woman No, he isn't. He's Estonian. Small countries hovering above the cold earth: who's going to protect them? (*Cries*.)

Man Don't cry, don't cry! You promised . . .

Woman Not crying.

Man Good. If you're not crying, then you can cry a little . . .

Woman (*cries*) Okay. In America, for example, you're not allowed to cry. Except in the theatre. It's especially forbidden at funerals. There, it is compulsory to take selfies with the deceased. Those who don't take selfies with the deceased are denounced for abusing the dead. In case you didn't have a laugh with the dead, the police will come and get you, as if you were a snake or crocodile on the loose, and that's the end of you.

Man What made you think of America?

Woman The dead. Did you know that the dead are only beautiful in America, nowhere else?

Man If you cry again . . .

Woman Small countries . . . they can't do anything except for singing and dancing motionlessly. Who's going to protect them?

Man Who? Where? What?

Woman . . . that country no longer exists . . . and Munich . . . maybe that doesn't exist either.

Man Oh, it does! Can you still hear it?

Woman Zsiiiiuuuucsattripproppripropp . . . Zsiiiiuuuucsattripproppripropp . . . I can always hear this. The impact, the squeaking of metal, the crackling and creaking sound of sparks. And the silence. Silent violins are protruding towards the sky. I can always hear that. Kitschy? Seriously?

Man No, not this. Silent violins. This is nice . . . not bad, that is . . .

Woman . . . and then that Schubert-faced trout shoots up from the water and . . .

Man . . . the dragonfly dancing motionlessly . . .

Scene Ten: Es mīlu Tevi or On Forgiveness

Woman . . . why doesn't it flee? Why doesn't it finally move? Why not?!

Man It doesn't. It dances. It scatters the colours of the rainbow with its wings. It cannot move, as it is lost in the dance. Whoever dances, can't actually move off.

Woman Okay, agreed! And the trout and the Tsukaharadoublevaultoneandahalfrighttwist bites all its legs off.

Man . . . only the leg . . . the legs . . . yes, I remember, all of them . . .

Woman Hey, how many legs do dragonflies have? Clink-clank, I asked you a question.

Man . . . can't remember. I swallowed it. Yum-yum-yum. Six? Maybe. That Schubert-faced trout. That was the one that swallowed them. All.

Woman Yet it wanted to swallow the entire dragonfly!

Man Got it wrong. The Tsukaharadoublevaultoneandahalfrighttwist didn't work out to perfection. It was bewitched by the dragonfly's beauty.

Woman Not a back handspring?

Man No, Tsukahara, as you said.

Woman It didn't work out.

Man No. Besides, the landing was catastrophic. It splashed into the water like a ridged blue whale.

Woman But why? Well?

Man Because that Schubert-faced trout wanted to be noticed by the motionlessly dancing dragonfly. Before devouring it, that is. Before making it its own. Had no idea about being in love. Realized it too late. When it ridiculously fell back into the water like an overweight frog.

Woman Common frog or ridged blue whale? Decide!

Man Whale. Let's go for the blue whale, it has nice stripes.

Woman So? And then?

Man Clink-clank, clink-clank . . . Yes, very much so . . . The dragonfly had no other option but flying away. The motionless dance above the water . . . Ever since then, it has been unable to touch down, so it's only hovering above the fast creek.

Woman Yes. Time was bitten off it. It's present in the where and then. In always, never, nowhere and righttthererightthen.

Man This is what happened. And the dance carries on in this way. Motionless. In the heart.

Woman You, you, you . . .

Man Yes, me, Clink-clank.

Woman . . . did you know, Clink-clank, that the insect of the year 2018 is the giant dragonfly? Did you know that? Did you, you, you?!

Man This is a joke. A stupid joke, for sure. It's geared towards this. They gear everything in such a way to make it easier to sell. At least you shouldn't aim everything as an ultimate joke, at least not you! We are living our own lives, we're not in the theatre, Clink-clank!

Woman But I'm not, I'm not, I'm not . . . 2018! Anax imperator! That's the name. Of the dragonfly of the year!

Man Isn't that Es mīlu Tevi?

Woman It could be that, too, you're right, you Schubert-faced trout. But it isn't called that, just simply dragonfly.

Man So this is your year, tabula rasa.

Woman I'm no tabula rasa, told you.

Man Spāre then.

Woman What?!

Man Spāre . . .

Woman What's that?

Man I thought it was beautiful.

Woman Yes, but what?

Man Dragonfly in Latvian.

Woman No tabula rasa.

Man Well, no.

Woman Nice one. I like this spāre. And in Estonian?

Man Liblikas. Isn't it nice?

Woman Liblikas . . . yes, yes, liblikas . . . And in Lithuanian?

Man Wait a second . . . got it: laumžirgis.

Woman This, too! How nice!

Man Superb. Beauty can't just be cut off, Clink-clank . . . or amputated just like that. Can you imagine?

Woman No?

Man No. Yours certainly can't.

Woman I remember it all, you understand, all. When I get started, I remember everything like a machine. Though I thought that they had cut this off, too.

Man   What, Clink-clank?

Woman   Well, remembrance . . . And all this that I am . . .

Man   No, definitely not.

Woman   Look! (*Speaks rapidly and funnily as if answering questions in a biology class.*) 'The German *Wasserjungfrau* (water maid, water virgin) or the French *demoiselle* (maid, girl, damsel) and the fullofmusic Romanian *libelula* can be easily aligned with the relevant Hungarian term (*szitakötő*), because these are all terms carrying positive emotional content. The English dragonfly is not so commendatory, as it highlights the sanguine and predatory nature of the species. The also English damselfly refers to small dragonflies in specialist literature.'

Man   The Schubert-faced trout knew about the water maid and water virgin, Clink-clank, this is why it threw such a Tsukaharadoublevaultoneandahalffrighttwist like a lunatic . . . crazy-crazy in love . . . (*Cries.*) . . . Es mīlu Tevi.

Woman   Es mīlu Tevi.

Man   Es mīlu Tevi.

Man   Es mīlu Tevi.

Woman   Stop it. You promised you won't cry. The Americans don't like it.

Man   Except in the theatre.

Woman   Only in the theatre.

Man/Woman   In this case: we won't cry! Forbidden! Dance!

The End.

Note

1. I love you (Latvian).
2. 'Stump' (used here as an equivalent for the Hungarian 'csonk') is an allusion to the loss of territories by Greater Hungary after the Treaty of Trianon. The phrases 'maimed Hungary', 'rump Hungary, 'dismembered Hungary', 'truncated Hungary' have been used to refer to this situation, and Visky plays with the complex associations inherent in 'csonk'/'csonka'.

Acknowledgements

Many thanks to Melissa Lorraine and Theatre Y for commissioning and helping me shape these translations for their production *Stories of the Body* (directed by Melissa Lorraine and Andrej Visky for Theatre Y, Chicago in 2018).

Sexodrom

Giuvlipen Theatre Company

Translated from the Romanian by Jozefina Komporaly
(Original title in Romanian: *Sexodrom*)

9 Giuvlipen Theatre Company: *Sexodrom* – National Centre of Dance, Bucharest, Romania (directed by Bogdan Georgescu, produced by Giuvlipen). Premiere: 7 May 2019. Poster design: Andrei Ionita.

Texts by Mihaela Drăgan, Bety Pisică, Nicoleta Ghiță, Oana Rusu, Zita Moldovan, Antonella Lerca Duda, Raj A. The project was developed as part of the Active Art workshop 'Politici în privat' (Private Politics), coordinated by the playwright-director Bogdan Georgescu.

Original performers: Mihaela Drăgan, Nicoleta Ghiță, Oana Rusu, Zita Moldovan, Antonella Lerca Duda, Raj A.

Concept of the play and director of the original production – Bogdan Georgescu. Set design and costumes – Irina Gâdiuță, music – Alex Bălă, choreography – Paul Dunca, make-up and hair – Marina Ioniță, production – Andrada Roşu and Anca Nica, PR – Lavinia Ionescu.

World premiere – 7 and 8 May 2019, hosted by the National Dance Centre in Bucharest, Romania. Producer: Giuvlipen.

Note: Some of the performers use their own names, while others prefer to use stage names. As if at a hippodrome, the performers are fighting for the spotlight, to get to share their story.

The performers enter the stage and form a circle. **Nico** *takes charge of the counting-out game, to determine who gets the spotlight first.*

Nico   Let's do the Crow[1] rhyme.

Nico (*starts counting*)   On pole, big claw

Caw caw caw

A crow's taking a crap

Slap bang into your yap![2]

The game is repeated until only **Nico** *and* **Zita** *are left. One by one, all the other performers take a seat behind the stage.*

Zita (*interrupts* **Nico**)   No, no. I count. On a pole . . . (**Zita** *cheats and eliminates* **Nico** *and takes the spotlight.*) I'm the queen. (*They start playing* Stop! I'm Queen. **Zita** *covers her eyes.*) One, two, three, stop. One, two, three, stop. One, two, three, stop.

Zita (*talking to the audience*)   I'm about to turn forty and am still hot! I like myself more now than I did at the age of twenty, when I was a model. Hashtag *self-love.* Hashtag *birthday girl.*

Men claim that women tend to become more and more hysterical and crazy as they get older. The innocent woman, highly 'shagg-able' at twenty, turns into a sourpuss by the time she's forty. That's because, the *MILF* doesn't take their *bullshit* anymore!

These dickheads keep dishing the dirt on various blogsites that they regret the 'Eternal feminine' and the innocence of young women, only to bury us as soon as we're past the age of thirty-five.

(*Game resumes.*) One, two, three, stop.

Women at forty are fed up with all the bullshit they had to take from these wankers, who had passed through their lives, beds and thoughts. I have no more time and energy for these sad blokes, who have nothing to say! All they want is to keep hearing their own voice, ignoring my time and my nerves, and conducting conversations in which they pretend to be smart, barely giving me a chance to squeeze in the odd, 'Wow, that's really cool! Wow, super cool! Yes, that's correct! Yes, you're right.'

But why don't they simply pay someone, whose job is to rubber-stamp all the bullshit they come up with? I'm no longer buying this crap.

(*Game resumes.*) One, two, three, stop.

When you're twenty and they tell you that 'It's not your fault, you're too good for me, I'm sorry, I fell in love with someone else', they essentially write you off. You go on about 'What does she have that I don't?' for a year, continue with 'I'm a free woman' for another year, then you drink 63,673 shots of vodka straight from the bottle and pull another sad bloke to get your revenge. At forty, it's different though, really different. At forty, I say: 'Get the fuck out of here!', I pack his bags, throw a party for my girlfriends and go on holiday without a care in the world.

(*Game resumes.*) One, two, three, stop.

When I used to get invited to parties in my twenties, I'd spend two months getting ready, I'd buy a new dress, wax a couple of times, post about it on Facebook, complete with check-ins, selfie taken alone in the club toilets, selfie with my friends at the club, selfie when drunk, selfie the morning after, singing with joy. Thank God there was no Facebook when I was twenty!

(*Game resumes.*) One, two, three, stop.

These days, if I'm invited to a party, wedding or baptism, I spend a week figuring out an excuse for not going, I take a selfie with Theraflu, put my phone on airplane mode, open the package of my latest mail order vibrator and spend a quiet night in with myself. This is because a woman at forty knows how to choose what's best for her, with no false regrets and no major compromises. Some call this being a 'sourpuss'. I call this freedom and believing in yourself.

(*Game resumes.*) One, two, three /

Nico (*taps her on the shoulder*)   Stop! I'm Queen! (*She takes* **Zita**'s *place on the stage.*)

Beat, scene change.

Nico (*sings, punctuated with comments by the* **PE Teacher** *played by* **Raj**)

> We all went on a school trip, yay, with everyone in class,
> Our tutor couldn't make it, nay, had leaking pipes, 't was gas,
> That's how we went without her there, PE teacher in tow,
> Who sadly failed to grasp this rule: girls' knickers are a no.
> Who the hell's now at the door, honking louder than a goose,
> Do get it no one is at home, you'll make these hinges loose!

PE Teacher

> Hey gypsy bitch, where is our Teo? Am I not talking clear?
> Don't make me say this all again, you'd better stay in fear.

Nico

> Hello, hello, are you all right, a tarot reading, sir?
> Oh, she's just being sick right there, the poor luckless girl.

PE Teacher

> What's with this yucky bathroom stench, tell me you lil' Crow,
> A good hiding is on the cards, as I'm quite sure you know.

Nico

> Whatever is the problem, sir, you seem ready to flip,
> Plus, you're kinda drunk and spent, please do forgive my slip.

PE Teacher

    You've all been smoking grass and weed, how come you're acting smart,
    You'd better watch your own foul mouth, or I'll disclose your part.

Nico

    What would you say, sir, just in case – this is of course a test,
    You found that your own wedding ring was 'bout to hit your chest?

PE teacher

    You'd better leave my fam'ly out, you bloody brownie lass,
    What happ'ns in Vegas stays in Vegas, you goddamn pikey ass!

Nico

    You smell like rotting garbage, you smell like marshes' slime,
    I'll snitch on you, I'll do, I swear, just hit me one more time.

PE Teacher

    You'd better keep your muzzle shut and hold a common front,
    Should Mum get wind of this somehow, you'll have no teeth in front.

Nico

    This is a catchy title, see: teacher gets pupils drunk, all five,
    And rubs their clits till they pass out, he rubs until they jive,
    Here's some good news for tabloids, for we've filmed by mistake,
    We've got what you had done to them, indoors and by the lake.

PE Teacher   Who, me?

Nico   Yes, you.

PE Teacher   Me?

Nico   Yes, you! You, you!

Raj (*taps her on the shoulder*)   Stop! I'm Queen. (*Takes her place onstage.*)

Beat, scene change.

Raj (*singing*)

    I am a flawless woman, perfect in every bit
    You fantasize about me; you know I'm super fit
    You know I am amazing
    A super-bitch, admit!

(*Talking to the audience.*) Well, I've only shaved my upper chest now, the corset hides the rest. Hope he won't really mind. I was about to get the blade out, but he's just coming round.

> Kiss, kiss, make space – boss lady is around
> Hasn't been tuned, as you can see,
> Check her right out, real as can be.
> Attractive shapes, from head to toe.
> High sex appeal, exterminating ho.

(*Talking to the audience.*) I haven't been fuckeeeed . . . for aaageees.

Sings, keeping the same beat as the following piece.

> I'll keep fucking until the walls come tumblin' down.

> No drug, I really know this, feels harder than does sex . . .
> Because I've tried them all, E, LSD 'n' the rest
> All men are always drooling and crazy 'bout me
> My eyes are peeled for expats, so why don't we just see.

Raj (*notices him*) He's really cute. Tall, well above 1,82 metres tall, dark hair, green eyes, casually dressed.

He's sexy . . . (*Starts singing.*)

> He's a male model, women must be dying for him
> I'll fuck him like crazy, to show him the woman I am

He What are you up to, cunt? Here! Suck my dick.

Raj (*singing*)

> Hold on, hold on, no need to rush!
> You must first keep away.
> In case you really want me though . . .

(*Talking to the audience.*) I'm horny, but he should have asked me in another way. I'm more the romantic type, you know? Foreplay, kisses, caresses, music and suchlike . . . I'm desperate for a good spank. Really itching for it.

He (*rapping*)

> Away, away with this gum, it's time to spit it out
> Must get ready to blow me
> My cock is in your pout.
> Beware of my curses,
> Mean words, and rude remarks.
> I have some good intentions, you mustn't make mistake,
> Say sweet nothings to women, there's no such thing as fake.

Beat.

> In just a single moment, your day is all but strife,
> Another coupl' of seconds, and I'll make you take your life.

Raj He grabs me by the hair and slams me down onto the floor. Holding on to my hands, he kneels on my chest. He's forcing me, trying to stick it all in, then he spits in my face /

He   What would you say if I killed you, huh? (*Pause.*)

Shall I? You fucking whore!

Raj   I can feel his hands pressing harder and harder on my throat. I can barely breathe. I'm fighting for breath.

He (*rapping*)

> When you move, it looks as if you were about to piss,
> But you're so elegant, it's much closer to bliss.
> You're a genetic barrel organ, a rare hurdy-gurdy,
> Bewitching us with your walk of an epileptic birdie.

Raj   I'm running out of air. I can't breathe.

He (*rapping*)

> The point of your existence, bitch, is relative,
> Feel free to drop dead of your own initiative.
> But, seriously, and I beg your pardon,
> I need you as I need holes in a condom.

Raj (*talking to the audience*)   He grabs a pillow and is charging at me. I struggle, so he slaps me again in the face. He busts my lips open, and blood starts to trickle down my face. He places the pillow on my face and presses it down really hard. I would like to howl, but have no air. I have a pain in the chest. I can't breathe. All sorts of images flip through my mind, for instance that I'll be found dead in the house, only shaven down to my nipples. As for him, nobody knows who he is, and he won't be found, ever. Who the fuck made me ask him to come over? All I wanted was a long night of sex, kisses and tender touches. I'm trying to push him off my body. I'm lying on the floor, shaking, and he's on top of me. All I want is to stay alive. If he slaps me one more time, I faint. Let me faint then. I pretend to faint. He slaps me twice more, not sure whether to check on me or to kill me. I'm not moving. I'm no longer moving. I'm holding my breath. He gets up, spits on me, pulls up his trousers without closing his fly, lights a cigarette and is about to leave. He realizes that I'm faking it. I'm trying to breathe as little as possible. I don't dare to open my eyes. I can't.

(*Sings with his eyes closed.*)

> Why don't you give a damn thing about my feelings, huh?
> Why can't you see how hurtful you can behave to me?
> All you can do is cause pain, cause harm and misery,
> To hell with fate, I must say, never had luck, not me.

He   You got what you deserve, you fucking transvestite. What do you want me to do with you, huh? You thought that if you pretend to be a woman, you can get it up faster? You bloody doormat, you fucking slapper, you can't! I want to fuck a man, not such cross-dressing sluts. I could set you on fire, and all of your kind. I could burn you alive. You were laughing like crazy at my cock, you thought you'd caught the golden fish. Into the fire with you, you trash.

Raj He opens the door and leaves. I stay behind, lying on the floor. My whole body is in pain. I feel like throwing up. I can hear the sound of his lighter. It doesn't work. What if he returns . . . He's outside, by the window, I can hear that he's smoking, and I can feel him looking at me through the window. I don't have the courage to open my eyes. I don't want to die. I can't hear any more movements. Quiet. I wait. I keep waiting. I open my eyes.

He I'll catch you one day and finish you off, you bloody worm!

Raj I close my eyes. I close them very tight. I stop breathing.

(*Sings quietly.*)

> You've got no clue what it takes to be man
> To charm and please a woman, at least a day or two
> You've never even tried
> Or had a go, just so.
> My argument is silent
> It's for my eyes alone.
> Got no idea what's it to be a man
> And there's no one out there, to ever teach you, damn.

(*Cries out for* **Zita**'s *help.*) Zita!

Zita (*comes forward slowly, and gently taps him*) Stop! . . . (*Long pause.*) I'm Queen! (*Takes* **Raj**'s *place onstage.*)

Beat, scene change.

Zita (*to the audience*) My mum has called me today: 'Congratulations, finally God has given! Come on, gal, I've seen your belly picture on Facebook, how could you not tell me?' 'I'm not pregnant, only a bit bloated. Since last year.'

My mum is one of those people who keep throwing up slogans, such as: 'Come on, get yourself together', 'It's in the way of things' or 'So you have something to live for' and my favourite, the fabulous: 'The jug of water in old age!' Children as carers and nurses! Why would I – or anybody else who isn't desperate for external validation – take a decision as important as that of having children based on the requirements of the world? Just because some people feel that their life has no meaning, and decide to have a child only to fulfil the role of *entertainer* (a sort of amusement) and to post pictures. How about pictures of me? Because in exchange for my *miracle* child, I'd also end up with cellulite, stretch marks and dark circles. No, thanks! Give me a break with this beauty of being a mother! What a great achievement!

(*Game resumes.*) One, two, three, stop.

And don't tell me that I can't possibly know about this until I'm a mother myself, because I actually have friends who are mums.

A friend told me: 'It's really lousy to be pregnant, you feel like pissing all the time, you're bloated, you have the urge to shit and piss, and everything ends up stinking around you. Those wretched hormones make you cry and keep getting on your nerves. Halfway through the pregnancy, you feel a bit better, that must be the *glowing* stage. The worst, however, is just before giving birth, your bones between the legs are hurting so badly that you're seriously concerned about dropping the child on the floor. You can't sleep properly, seeing that there are only two positions in which you can rest, either on one side or on the other, you can't bring your legs close to one another. And when you finally fall asleep, your baby starts moving and all your plans to have a good night's rest go to hell at once.'

(*Game resumes.*) One, two, three, stop.

I want to have children. Though my husband wants kids more than I do. Oh, no, I'm not on my own, that's not the reason why I don't have children. I want children by my own choice and not that of others, at a time that suits me. I want to adopt, I'm not a narcissist.

(*Sings.*)

> Wonderful lashes, just like a flower,
> You melt when y'adopt them.
> And you're in their power,
> Love is all healing; love is an anthem!

What if this trend of adopting Roma children as *kale* as possible makes it to us, too? Could it be that white people adopt so it's visible to the naked eye how open-minded and tolerant they are? What if this is nothing more than a form of therapy against their own racism?

> Let's whiten up and run away
> Take to the world, today
> We'll suffer and will cause dismay
> Blackness can't fade away!

Well, wouldn't it be better if we adopted them? I mean, if we were to adopt children of our own kind. I'll turn into the saviour of saviours, so that your white lot can't make itself a laughing stock with adopting the most *kalo* Roma child. Still, if you do take these children anyway, take them altogether, with their culture, their history, their *background*. Don't bring them up to be whiter than the whites themselves.

(*In the mirror.*) Look, how black I am! How exotic!

(*Game resumes.*) One, two, three, stop.

Nico Stop! I'm Queen!

Beat, scene change.

Nico (*rapping*)

> Today's the day: I come of age, it's time to have some fun
> My family and friends are here, I know we're all as one
> It's an important day today, I can now do all sorts
> Passing from my adolescence to what maturity imports.

Now I can do what I might want, no need to self-explain
Can come and go as I see fit, to clubs, to entertain
I'm really free, I have a job, and get by pretty well
I need nobody's help these days to make my life go swell.

I'm now at my own sister's place, the huge house with the yard
They're all out sunbathing tonight, the moon is on its guard.
By now they're all quite off their face, they're legless one could say,
I've come by with some speakers, yay, and get pints as my pay.

I feel fulfilled with my loved ones, all blissed out in our shack,
Come quick, pals say, 'He's wild again, you'd better watch your back!'
My man lashed out, punching around, quarrelling with his mate,
Jealous again, makes fun of me, oh, why's he in such state.

Come now, let go of him, we'll talk some other day,
You're drunk again, completely smashed, this makes you go astray
What's wrong with him, he kept away, I stayed with you all night,
He sticks his fingers down my throat, 'You're a slut, alright!'

I cannot breathe, I have no air, I choke yet try to flee,
With a strong punch, he strikes at once and takes the wind of me,
Without a pause, he carries on, he hits so I can't react,
He grabs a chair, which makes me freeze, and in the end retract.°

I see the chair fly 'n the air, then held by someone's hands,
As it's my perplexed bro-in-law, straight in the wall it lands.
I beg 'let go!' but he wants a fight and kicks him out, this bloke,
I'd wail in pain, but hold it in and go instead for a smoke.

To soothe my pain, I take a drag, to put myself at ease,
A girl is groaning next to us, she cries, 'Let go, let go, oh please!'
The noise is loud, as I look 'round, and getting more intense,
And there she is, I've found her now, right by a concrete fence.

His hairy arse is now exposed, all I can see is skin,
Her clothes ripped off, and all he does is shout 'must stick it in'.
He holds her hair, to make her suck, the girl's in quite a shock,
She knocks him down, he gets right up, hopin' she'd ride his cock.

This makes no sense, I was drugged-out, why do I need such tests,
My face's been punched, this one's undressed, or so I would suggest,
Nothing makes sense, I dash to help, I'm on a mission now,
I punch him in the mouth at once, knocked out he is, oh wow.

He staggers, and I strike him down, just so I can prevent
Him hurting this young lassie here, I kind of represent,
I grab his hair and thrash his hard, again, again, oh my,
His head against the fence does fly, as he's all drunk and high.

Please stop, she cries, please stop she begs, do stop and don't cause harm,
I fail to see and fail to hear, but know I must leave marks.

When in the end I look around, there is a pool of blood,
The girl was nowhere to be seen, 'n' the dude was dead and gone.

It's hard for grown-ups, is it not, if that's the common start,
Hoping to see some better days, and not the same old fart.
I wished for something fresh and new, but all I found was skewed,
I never knew what I'd go through and get so badly screwed.

I'm still a child with my daydreams, still wishing on a star,
Not grown-up facing courts and laws, gaol sentence, behind bars.
Too much abuse in secrecy, it's all behind closed doors
They do their best to cover up, no truth can ever soar.
That's why I wish it dawns on you, and hope you'll get a clue!

Nico I need a break.

Mihaela Stop! I'm Queen! (*Takes the spotlight.*)

Beat, scene change.

Mihaela *and* **Pavel** *are actors. The character of* **Pavel** *is always played by a female performer –* **Oana** *in the original production.*

Pavel Have a sandwich. My wife has made enough for you, too.

Mihaela Oh, no, you know I don't eat meat!

Pavel Wow, you've turned into a proper hipster girl! Have a beer then. Or hipsters don't even drink beer?

Mihaela Exactly. They drink cider.

Pavel Crikey! You drink no alcohol, eat no meat, not to mention fucking, which is entirely out of the question, hahaha!

Mihaela You must know this colleague, if not from the theatre then at least from this Romanian soap that was on TV. He even has a joke on this topic: 'I went to bed as an artist, and woke up as a TV-slut.' The conductor asks him for an autograph, so he asks for a separate compartment just for the two of us, so we can take a rest. We'll have a show the next day, and must absolutely stand out at this festival. It's the very first in my career, so I'm understandably nervous, so much so that I'm shitting myself. But I have this colleague by my side.

Pavel Come on, you'll be a great actress, and that way you can experience some joy in life.

Mihaela Sure! So that I'll also be offered my own private compartment.

Pavel *takes another sip of beer.*

Pavel Hey, why don't you have faith in yourself? It's clear to see that you don't.

Mihaela What do you mean?

Pavel You're . . . inhibited on stage. Why are you so wild? (*Laughs.*) One can see everything on stage, y'know: who you are, your level of education, if you come from a shanty or from a good family, if you are unfucked or a slut. One can even see what you've had for breakfast. (*With self-conscious tenderness.*) So, to come back to my question, why don't you feel good in your skin?

Mihaela You can really see all this on stage? And you're only telling me now?

Pavel Well, it is only now that I feel we're getting close. Besides, there are things you must already know yourself. You know that you'll never play Juliet or Ophelia. You don't have the face for that sort of thing.

Mihaela Really? What faces do Juliet or Ophelia have?

Pavel White ones! (*Laughs.*) Hey, you must be aware of your assets. You don't have a face for an ingénue, but to be fair, you have the coolest mouth I've ever seen. You're smart, you have a sense of humour. You can drive any man crazy with these tits. So why don't you believe in yourself? You could be a brilliant actress if only you got rid of your inhibitions.

Mihaela (*to the audience*) Why don't I have faith in myself? And his hand touches my shoulder. He has never spoken to me like this before. Slowly but surely, his hand is sliding down my back, to help me relax. Bit by bit, it's under my breasts, on my belly, so I can be a better actress. Next, taking its time, his hand makes it to my thighs, because I can't be an actress if I have inhibitions and don't feel comfortable in my skin. Carrying on at a steady pace, it lands down there, so it doesn't show on stage that I'm an unfucked wild creature.

Only after I realize that he has stuck his tongue down my throat while rubbing my crotch do I finally say: it's NOT OK what you're doing! I have nothing else on my mind, I feel that if other words were to come out of my mouth, they'd pour out like poison, they'd roll over me, roll over us just like his hands rolled over my body, and all the water in the world wouldn't be able to wash this filth and shame away. I recognize this situation, there's something familiar in this sensation, I've experienced it before. I don't touch him at all, but still abandon my body in his hands. Why don't I react?

Pavel What are you thinking about?

Mihaela Pappy. It's summer, and I'm at the countryside. I'm six or seven years old. Or maybe five? I'm with Pappy, an uncle twice removed, who has only two fingers and three stumps on one of his hands. The thumb and the index fingers. He doesn't have children, because his wife Dodie couldn't have any, so he really loves us, his nephews and nieces. We keep asking him to show us his stumps and to tell us how he had lost his fingers. We laugh. Pappy breeds pigs and says that they are his children. And us. We're really fond of him. He keeps inviting us to visit so he can see how much we've grown. Every so often, I avoid visiting and come up with all sorts of childish lies. But the adult is more cunning and plays tricks on me. I'm embarrassed to say no or to annoy Pappy. Why is Dodie never home? He's calling us to show us the piglets? Each has a name: Georgie Porgie, Lexi, the white one's called Minister, the spotty ones Scabby 1 and Scabby 2, the black one Big Cheese. Each time, after checking the piglets out, we go inside. I know already that I don't like being in the house and keep telling him that I want to stay with the piglets, as I was missing them a lot. Not to mention that he promised that he'd soon let me have Minister, and Grandma told me that I could keep it in the house, in the summer kitchen. Pappy says that he'd let me have a piglet just to myself, but I'm naughty and, above all, ungrateful. I don't want to annoy him, so I go inside.

He takes me in his arms, sits me on his knees and starts wiggling. He keeps swinging like this with me for a few minutes, holding me real tight with his stumps and two remaining fingers.

'A bit more, come one, just a little bit', and when I can no longer take it, I explode: 'Please, Pappy, I want to go home, take me home.'

'Come on, Alex, stay some more – he'd always call me by a boy's name – you're like a daughter to me, I love you as if you were my own child.'

For me, as for my sisters and cousin, he was indeed like a father, which is why we called him Pappy. I've never mentioned this business to them. I've never said anything to anyone, as I didn't know whether it was right or wrong. But my body did know and would tense every time he took me in his arms and started wiggling as if he wanted to thrust something towards me. He'd never undress me or touch me down there, only keep swinging with me in his arms.

I had forgotten about Pappy. I really wanted to forget. You made me remember.

Pavel Hold on a second, I think there's a misunderstanding here. What's your point? Why are you telling me this story?

Mihaela I told you to stop, it's not OK.

Pavel Excuse me?

Mihaela I told you it wasn't OK. Not to mention that you have a wife and children. I don't know how to tell you so I don't offend you and make you feel rejected.

Pavel Well, first of all, leave my wife and children out of this, you're heading into a danger zone and that's not correct. I have no idea what sort of games you're playing here with me, but let's not forget that I have been as correct and generous as possible with you! I agreed to be in your shoestring show, being paid a pittance, I threw in money from my own pocket to help you and countless others, not sure how many others in my shoes would have done that, I even found a director and a venue. Let's face it, I don't want to show off with being a hotshot actor but you've said it yourself that you didn't expect me to agree to work with you. You'd just left drama school at that point. By the way, did you actually graduate?

Mihaela Yes.

Pavel Well done! In this case, how shall I put it, I feel somewhat taken advantage of, to make use of a euphemism rather than draw attention to having been 'fucked and robbed'.

Mihaela I haven't said that I don't acknowledge what you did for me. I shall always be grateful to you for everything, but this doesn't mean that I'm obliged to do something I don't want to do . . .

Pavel Have I ever obliged you to do something you didn't want to do?! Have I ever put a knife to your throat? Have I ever put pressure on you?

Mihaela No. But I did tell you that I didn't want this.

Pavel Are you sure? Why didn't you actually do anything then? You didn't lift a finger. As far as I know, women tend to put up resistance and scream if they don't like something. You did nothing. 'It's not OK, oh no, you have a wife and children', whereas your body just kept telling me to ride you. Let's get real, we are adults.

Mihaela This isn't true!

Pavel Not true? In that case, why are you wet between your legs?

Mihaela Sorry?

Pavel Feel it, if you don't believe me! You know what? I'll take the next train back to Bucharest, because it's clear that you take me for a fool. Bloody hell, I've never had to face up to the claim that I'm a 'rapist,' when all I've ever wanted was to do good, only a woman sick in her head is capable of inventing such an aberration!

Mihaela Come on, please . . .

Pavel Please? What please?! (*Beat.*) Come on, say it, what do you want to ask me to do?

Mihaela (*screams*) Please, don't leave! (*Long pause.*) I return to the hotel, get into my room, still feeling the sensation of his hands all over my body. Disgust. His tongue that has entered my mouth. I look in the mirror and see a short and stocky body, of almost a woman, with far too large breasts and a pelvis that has only been touched a handful of times. I get into the bed and start shaking, my body and I are no longer one, we haven't been ever since he started touching me. My body has left me, the way it used to stiffen when I was little. I cry for a while and the most natural thing I think I should do to reclaim my body is touch myself.

I shall forget you, the way I managed to forget Pappy. Because I want our show to be a success, because I want to be a good actress, because I'm ashamed of what you did and I don't want you as my enemy, because I'm sick of becoming one of these abused women. An abused woman, who doesn't even scream or put up any resistance.

That evening, the show went really well.

Antonella (*taps* **Mihaela** *on the shoulder, interrupting her, and takes the spotlight*) Stop! I'm the Queen!

Beat, scene change.

Characters: **Antonella**, **Doctor** – *played by* **Nico**, **Nurse** – *played by* **Raj**.

Antonella (*talking to the audience*) 14 October 2005. Saint Parascheva. I studied theology for a year, just so you know. Oh, one second, I forgot to make the sign of the cross. (*She makes the sign of the cross over the entire upper part of her body.*) A rainy autumn day in Iași. The consulting room of an endocrinologist, white walls that haven't been repainted for ages, medical appliances and cables galore. The doctor is a pot-bellied man with stubbles and glasses, dressed in smocks over a blue shirt, wearing a badge. The nurse, with straight blonde hair tied in a bun, is wearing a cap. Her short smocks are blue, worn over a tight-fitting dress with heels. She has striking green eye make-up, gold creole hoop earrings and black frames. I'm wearing a long, colourful pleated skirt and a basic, low-cut vest in pink. Black hair, no make-up. I knock on the door. 'Good afternoon! I'm here for /' The doctor interrupts me.

Doctor Yes, take a seat, I know what you're here for.

Antonella Gingerly, I take a seat. The doctor, looking inquisitive, is leafing through some medical notes.

Doctor When have you started to display such deviant behaviour?

Antonella Well, you know . . . I don't like what I see between my legs, it upsets me!

Doctor What does your mother say?

Antonella She's outside, she came with me!

Doctor Yes, but isn't she afraid that you could end up impotent because of these pills? Bye-bye grandchildren then!

Antonella (*proudly*) No! Really, she has already spoken to that Moroccan doctor!

Doctor (*interrupts*) Silman. Yes. I didn't know that back in his country they practised such bullshit.

Antonella (*to the audience*) The door opens. Not bothering to knock, the nurse enters, holding a folder. Hands it over to the doctor and glances at me. Then asks the doctor, as if I weren't even present.

Nurse Consta, please sign this after you finish with . . .

Doctor She or whoever . . . doesn't like what she has between the legs! To make matters worse, Silman encourages such people by saying that in his country they can have an operation that turns them into women.

Nurse (*visibly irritated*) And you get involved in such a thing? Goodness me, sonny, what's going on in your head?! How can you dislike girls? You'd rather do the dishes? Cook? Do the laundry and hang it to dry, instead of doing pretty much anything that might take your fancy being a boy? Chill, drink a pint at a match and have as many girls as you like? Haven't you got a girlfriend? Take that skirt off at once.

Antonella (*somewhat scared*) No. I was supposed to . . .

Doctor (*interrupts* **Antonella**, *smiling at the* **Nurse**) Wait, hear this one! You know those gypsies in Păcureț, that neighbourhood in the middle of nowhere. He came to us because he couldn't get a hard-on on his wedding night, clearly . . .

Antonella (*to the audience*) The nurse is pulling me by the sleeve.

Nurse Now, son, do be honest. You had no idea what to do with this girl, seeing that your lot tends to get married at the age of twelve and nobody shows you the ropes!

Antonella Not quite, Alina and I are best friends.

Nurse Her name is Alina. See, Consta, what a lovely name for a bride. Have you at least tried to kiss her or hold her in your arms? What did you do with her all night?

Antonella We put on make-up, we talked, we did each other's hair . . . I tried on the dress.

Nurse Goodness gracious! Have you seen the priest yet?

Doctor In this case, it would take the Metropolitan bishop.

Nurse Listen up, one of these days you go to the holy Metropolitan Church, take a pair of knickers with you and rub them over the holy relics. You'll not only have amazing luck in bed with girls and have children, but you'll also cure this illness you have, this 'travestitism'. (*Beat.*) How about a psychiatrist, have you seen one?

Doctor Well, he's just been there and was diagnosed with 'gender' dysphoria. My job is to write a prescription.

Antonella (*to the audience*) The doctor skims through the medical records on his desk, makes some notes, then opens a drawer and produces a medicine box, a blister pack, takes out a pill and hands it to me.

Doctor Swallow!

Antonella (*to the audience*) I throw the pill in my mouth.

Doctor EASY! Have some water.

Nurse Hold on, son, let me give you a glass.

Doctor Where do you think you're going? You think this has magic powers, huh? You swallow it and you've already completed your transformation? You think we're dealing in magic and casting spells here, like your lot does?

Nurse Come on, Consta, what the heck? You make me take part in such stuff.

Doctor Let it go, Irina – what if one of these days you want to become a man and take my place? (*To* **Antonella**.) Take one a day to start with, and we'll see how the disease progresses.

Nurse (*to* **Antonella**) Heaven forbid, to embark on such a thing, kid. You're out of your mind.

Antonella Listen, Miss or Mrs Irina! With due respect, what would happen if you minded your own personal business? I refrained from commenting on the fact that you dye your hair, even though it is against the teachings of the Bible. Not to mention that you are wearing a skirt so short that one can see your knickers. Did you not know that we are made in God's own image? Why are you defiling your eyes with this loud green make-up that, by the way, doesn't even suit you? If I were to scrutinize you more closely, I'd say that with your lips injected with fillers, you look more of a 'transvestite' than I do. (*Beat.*)

Nurse And this mum, waiting outside, tells me that this must be it if God lets her be this way . . . Such mad people! See where poverty can lead.

Antonella Go fuck yourself! You make me sick. (*To the audience.*) And I make my exit triumphantly. Suck it up!

Oana (*interrupts*) Stop! I'm the Queen!

Beat, scene change.

Characters: **Gabriela** *– played by* **Oana** *– and* **Florina** *– played by* **Zita**. *They are both actresses, part of the ensemble of a theatre in Bucharest.*

Gabriela Who told her to make such a scene?

Florina She didn't kick up such a fuss at the TV station for nothing.

Gabriela Sure, but what started it? And, most importantly, who?

Florina Well, it's dead simple, he wanted revenge!

Gabriela Aha! What for?

Florina To take revenge on her, seeing that she no longer wanted to . . . I've seen some messages she shared with me, messages from him. I'm a friend of hers, you know.

Gabriela But she made it public – perhaps she was the one that wanted revenge. Besides, she's used to such scandalous publicity appearances. Good or bad, all the same, what matters is that people hear about you.

Florina Give me a break, girl, she's in no need of such publicity, everybody knows who Vanda is! She's a TV presenter, brought out albums . . . Let's face it, she doesn't have to rely on this to market herself!

Gabriela Great! But then why did she make this public? Why didn't she just sue him? Wasn't this for the sake of publicity?

Florina No! She did sue him, and appeared on TV in order to publicly shame him so that other women could also hear what happened at that theatre and no such things could happen to other women.

Gabriela It was reported in the media that she had in fact been his lover for some time, and their arguments were entirely dependent on the outcome of their sex sessions. She was apparently sending him nude pictures and he was only responding to her messages. She was used to all this, having posed for *Playboy* in the past . . .

Florina And what if she had posed? That was a long time ago, when she was twenty. But he made use of his powers as a director and fired her.

Gabriela Wasn't he the one to give her the job?

Florina Yes, he was, but that was only for a fixed term.

Gabriela The truth is that I'm unsure whether she was properly employed. You can ask HR. In case she was employed, there had to be an application process. I had to apply, signed all sorts of paperwork, there was a contract and various clauses. You can't be fired at the drop of a hat. On what legal basis was she actually fired?

Florina Can't you see?!

Gabriela Aha, so she wanted a job and could have indeed gone to his office, seeing that he was the director of the theatre. 'Good morning, I'd quite like to work here long term, maybe we could put on a show . . .'

Florina (*doing an impression of the manager*) 'Sure, Vanda, why not! Pop on my desk for fuck's sake!'

Gabriela Yes, the girl knew what side of her bread was buttered. She got the job, appeared in a show, and then no longer wanted to lie with her back on his desk.

Florina You mean that she was expected to lie on this desk indefinitely? Before we know it, we'll end up with people claiming that she was the one harassing him. Based on the harassment cases that you're aware of, who tends to be the one being harassed: the woman or the man?

Gabriela The woman! But this doesn't mean that they never display any harassing behaviour. She did what she wanted with him! Right? Until she had the deal in the bag, so to speak.

Florina What are you taking about, what bag? While she was employed, she only appeared in two parts, minor ones at that, so she was nothing but a *stand-in for a stand-in* . . .

Gabriela Yeah, that's correct!

Florina You see? He literally kicked her out of the theatre, and made fun of her!

Gabriela If we take a look at the facts, we find that she goes to see the director, gets herself hired, appears in shows, and, after a while, no longer wants to carry on . . .

Florina Fucking shit! He fired her! And it's still her fault!

Gabriela Was it not her fault?

Florina NO!

Gabriela Shouldn't he think that he had been taken advantage of?

Florina It was he who had taken advantage of her! He fucked her, and when she no longer wanted to carry on fucking, he fired her!

Gabriela Didn't they both take advantage of each other?

Florina NO! Because the victim here is Vanda, not him!

Gabriela Guilt never belongs to just one party. I don't deny that he has this . . . slimy look . . . I don't deny her *sex-appeal* and that she had probably asked for favours more than once. They are both aware of their *sex-appeal*, and since they are adults, this problem has to be solved by them, in one way or another . . .

Florina So what if I made use of my charms? Does this mean that you are entitled to fuck me whenever you want? The poor thing only wanted to do her job, she wanted to belong to a company and to act, while he . . .

Gabriela I'm also doing my job and work at a theatre but nobody has asked me to lie on a desk, I applied for my job, signed a contract and followed a certain protocol. Except that she was employed for a fixed term. During this probationary period, she was kept in this mockery, as a *stand-in for a stand-in*. And when the permanent contract was about to be drawn up . . . No, no, that can't be! You know, the thing is that the current trend is to show that she's the victim in this situation, just because she's a woman . . .

Florina Because she's the only one who had the courage to speak up.

Gabriela She had already acquired this image of an exposed woman before coming to the theatre. And he thought that perhaps she was an easy prey. But, in fact, we saw that . . .

Florina Yes, if you are *exposed*, they come up with a schedule for you, for fucking. . .

Gabriela I think that she was in fact quite vulnerable, perhaps not at her personal and professional best, he gave her a fixed contract – in any case, one is obliged to do so by law – and during her probation, he fucked her mind up . . . unsure of her position, she probably wanted something more certain.

Florina She carried on crying for two months. Nobody cries for two months for no reason. She was depressed.

Gabriela I have no doubt whatsoever about him, he's a skirt-chaser. He accepts what he's being given, and doesn't hold back from actively taking what he isn't offered. But I can't possibly be on her side, either!

Florina Well, you can't be on her side because the two of you didn't quite see eye to eye anyway . . .

Gabriela This has nothing to do with that. Are you saying that you are on her side because you're friends?

Florina No, because she's . . .

Gabriela Come on, let's be objective!

Florina No, I have no intention of doing that!

Gabriela What do you mean?

Florina I would have been on the side of any woman in her place! What's this bullshit about being objective–subjective?

Gabriela Looking at this in an objective way, we haven't solved anything with this scandal. Because nothing will ever change!

Blackout. Long pause. Blacklights on.

Mihaela *steps into the spotlight, takes off her jacket and pulls out an oversized fluorescent human spine from behind her back. She plays with it as if it were a whip.*

Mihaela (*to the audience*) Where there is art, there is civilization, that's a proven fact. Theatre, film, painting, etc. have made me a better and more civilized person.

Painting has shown me that most women have to be in a significant state of undress: from *The Origin of the World* to the bare-breasted *Gypsy Girl* and the *Gypsy Girl with Ox Cart*, *The Flower-Seller* and *The Fortune-Teller*. I learned an awful lot from these nameless figures. My favourite painting is *Head of a Gypsy Girl*. She doesn't have a name, either, but has a fabulous head instead.

I'm disappointed that people no longer go to museums, theatres or even cinemas. Are we about to forget such great directors as Polanski, Woody Allen, or Bertolucci? Where are they? Okay, Polanski may well be in prison still, but I think he has been working from there all along.

Last Tango in Paris. A masterpiece. Sigh, Marlon Brando. Bertolucci, the director. Both men. Both nominated for an Oscar for this film. That anal sex scene, with Marlon Brando rubbing butter into Maria Schneider's bottom instead of lube. A masterpiece. In the Romanian version, Irina Margareta Nistor translated 'Bring the butter' as 'Bring the margarine'.[3] A cultural translation.

Years later, Maria Schneider confessed: 'I felt humiliated, and to be honest, I felt a little raped, both by Marlon and by Bertolucci'. She wasn't told in advance about the margarine scene. She appears naked throughout the film. Brando's character? Never. Brando was paid 250,000 dollars as well as ten per cent of the international takings, which were huge. She got paid 4,000 dollars. Well, thanks, this is where the saying 'both fucked and robbed' really hits home. Maria Schneider died at the age of fifty-eight of cancer, after long suffering. She had been ridiculed all along her career for that one scene with the margarine up her arse. Could trauma possibly influence the appearance of cancer?

So what should we do? Stop watching Bertolucci's films? No, we should separate art from the artist. Are we interested in the fact that Woody Allen has not been found guilty of – or even charged with molesting his adopted daughter when she was only seven?!' No. Because the work of the artist is more important. Seriously, what (would happen) if we banned his films just because he was a paedophile? These impostors with their political correctness want exactly that: for us to set books on fire, to destroy paintings, ban music – let thousands of years of civilization go up in flames! Should the Notre-Dame burn down? No, let Pata-Rât burn instead! Thank you, Cluj City Council for the generous donation.[4]

I've improved myself thanks to culture and civilization! (*Rolls her eyes.*)

Even Mr P, the greatest living Romanian intellectual, has withdrawn from public life as a result of this new form of censorship known as 'political correctness'! Quote:

'Minorities . . . gender . . . these are the latest fashionable ideologies, pondered to be "correct" and validated by propaganda and by the most recent planetary "fads".' Unquote. In short, my civilization and superiority are going to hell!

What would have happened if one of these sad activists had suddenly banned Emil Cioran's work after he wrote: 'there is no present-day politician that I see as more sympathetic and admirable than Hitler'? Who would have been there then to spread our fame abroad? His friend, Mircea Eliade, another racist and legionary, without whom we have to acknowledge that Romanian culture would have been inferior.

Quote from Eliade's novel *Marriage in Heaven*: 'A man who avidly stares at a prostitute's body cannot be accused of indiscretion. Women always invite us to look at them in the way in which they want to be seen. Most of the time, the object shows us how it should be viewed and appraised.' Unquote.

The Universal Values of Romania.

I'm superior. I'm fed up with books, shows and films about sad and illiterate gypsies. There's really nobody out there who'd want to make a film about a happy gypsy woman able to read and write?! *I can play that role.*

Talking of sad gypsies, *researchers* demonstrated that people who have been exposed to pain for a long period of time, through slavery or the Holocaust for instance, can transmit it down the line through their DNA. Transgenerational epigenetic inheritance. I'm superior. This is the name of the science that provides evidence for the survival of pain and its genetic transmission.

Pain and suffering are literally flowing through my veins.

Why would I want to embody on stage the pain and suffering of a white woman, when I'm actually quite pleased with my own darker skin? Moreover, why would the part of a white woman be automatically more important than what we are doing on stage?

It's quite simple: because you have the power to decree that the art of minorities and of women is inferior, while the art of white men is noble and uplifting.

Noble art, my arse! Without lube. The history of white art in which directors with 'a strong personality' slap actresses, and theatre managers do their best to brush it under the carpet. Some claim that director Andriy Zholdak only gave this actress a pat on the shoulder in the interval between two acts, and others that he merely bumped into her.[5] What's certain is that nobody reported anything to the police in the end, but the actress must have surely needed some shaking up so at least the second part came up trumps if she had the temerity to fuck up the first one. After all, this is 'proper' art.

Long pause.

When #MeToo started, I was hoping that justice would be done. That I shall hear the voices of actresses in Romania and that of former female students harassed by their lecherous professors, young and old. Instead, two years have passed and there was more visibility for the campaign #șîeu, a treasure trove of authentic Romanian humour campaigning for motorways. A complete shambles that compares violence against women to the *fucking* business of needing more motorways. Well done, lads, you've managed to rob us yet again. And no thanks, I can no longer *swallow* Bertolucci's films and refuse to read Cioran, because under no circumstances do I want to validate a writer who endorsed Nazism.

Pause.

The entire history of white culture and civilization is a history of rape and abuse.

Burn it all!

Blackout.

The End.

Notes

1. 'Crow' is a derogatory term used by Romanians when referring to Roma people.
2. In Romanian: *Pe o bară / Se căca o cioară / Cra Cra Cra / Fix în gura ta!*
3. At the time the movie was released, butter was very hard to find in Romania.
4. Pata-Rât is the name of a landfill area near the city of Cluj in Northern Romania, where large numbers of Roma families have been forcefully evacuated by the City Council. This is the largest waste-related ghetto in Europe, home to hundreds of people including children. This reference has a strong sarcastic tone, highlighting the hypocrisy of the fact that the authorities simply abandoned a large segment of the local population, while managing to find resources to donate funds for the reconstruction of the Notre-Dame Cathedral in Paris after the arson attack in April 2019.
5. Andriy Zholdak is a Ukrainian theatre director who was accused of maltreating an actress during the rehearsals and premiere of *Rosmersholm* that he directed at the Hungarian Theatre of Cluj in 2017. The incident was widely debated in the press, and although it was largely hushed up in the end, it gave rise to a broader discussion on gender dynamics and the repercussions of seemingly limitless power inherent in director's theatre.

Acknowledgements

Many thanks to Diana Manole for her suggestions in translating the rhyming songs.

Afterword

MELISSA LORRAINE, ARTISTIC DIRECTOR, THEATER Y, CHICAGO

Romania/Romanian theatre has undergone a remarkable refining process in the shifting pressures of the last several decades. Over the years, I have become particularly invested in theatre life in Transylvania and the work of an ethnic Hungarian writer in particular. For many minority communities, the fear of being marginalized insights a deeply subversive voice. The idea that one has little left to lose provides a clarity of perspective and the courage to voice the truth regardless of consequences.

When I first encountered the plays of András Visky, I felt as though I had found a back door to my own soul. The words were mine, but they had been put through a filter of language and history that offered new distance and objectivity with which to explore very personal and delicate existential questions.

There are five elements at play in his dramaturgy that, when combined, provide a new experience for English-speaking audiences:

1. His writing starts with facts rather than fiction – disarming in their rootedness. The events are non-negotiable, so the conclusions are all that remain to debate.
2. He puts these facts into his own life and confesses himself through the stories of others, so that the director, performer, etc. can each, in turn, confess themselves.
3. He writes with a presumptuous meta-narrative – the existence of the divine is a given circumstance. The questions arise out of this given, bypassing the temptation to debate or explain away the unknowable. Visky's theological premise may alienate, but the provocation is both unorthodox and deliberate. It's a subversive gesture that makes transcending worldly and familiar subjectivities possible. It reframes the self as a vertical discourse and exposes belief and doubt to be at the heart of all perception and action, in life as in theatre.
4. He writes in poetry (around the thing, rather than straight into it) leaving space for the performer and ultimately the listener to make personal meanings and associations.
5. He works with translators who do not massage his poetry into native English, so you encounter the thoughts in a new way. You encounter your own language afresh, and discover new thoughts.

Visky's upbringing in a communist prison camp (unfamiliar to most Westerners) adds five new ingredients – also visible in the work of other authors from Romania – that serve as an education for many young English-speakers:

1. The gallows humour: I can't import this gift into my heart as there is no shortcut for the deep humour that many like him have excavated from their pain. Without being excessively optimistic, this is part of the miraculous economy of suffering that gives tragedy its 'bright side' – albeit nothing less than a survival skill.
2. The liberating heresy: His faith makes space for very aggressive and irreverent relationships with the divine, which are refreshing to my heart and ear: a discovery that one earns permission to be bold and brutal when buried in the deep safety of love.

3   The reverse miracle: Visky tells stories of characters with no real power in the world who upend tyrannies by reversing their meanings, thereby stripping the tyrants of their authority. This might require an example: Prisoners in Auschwitz are lined up and told to count off to ten. The guards then shoot each tenth prisoner. Ten is anointed as the word for freedom, and all of the prisoners begin shouting 'TEN!'
4   The profound joy: His plays expose the difference between happiness and joy – happiness as something you obtain for yourself, and joy as something that fills your mouth. His plays become ceremonies wherein you hope to be filled with something far beyond you.
5   The perspective: Far from the hope of entertainment, or worse still, of 'killing time', the theatre of his marginalized generation does not take the right to gather for granted. His theatre was made holy by decades of deprivation. My generation sorely needs a reminder of the value and fragility of our freedom to assemble.

The eager hush of the crowd entering a theatre in Romania and the extended length of the applause following a performance serve as a chilling reminder of the stakes of this 'game' in parts of the world where theatre is, or has ever been, the only place where one can hope to be seen or heard.